The Living
AQUARIUM

The Living
AQUARIUM

Peter Hunnam

Annabel Milne · Peter Stebbing

Photography: Jan-Eric Larsson

CRESCENT BOOKS
New York

This 1989 edition is published by Crescent Books,
distributed by Crown Publishers, Inc.

First published in Sweden by Bonnier Fakta.

Color reproduction by Offset-Kopio,
Helsinki, and Reproman, Gothenburg.
Typeset by Fotocomposición Llovet,
Barcelona.

Printed and bound in Spain
by JOSMAR, S. A.
Artesanía, 17
Polígono Industrial de COSLADA
Madrid

THE LIVING AQUARIUM has been conceived, designed, and produced by Nordbok, Gothenburg, Sweden, in close collaboration with the authors and photographer.

Editor-in-Chief: Turlough Johnston
Graphical design and illustration concepts: Roland Thorbjörnsson
Artwork: Ulf Söderqvist (free line drawings); Lennart Molin (technical drawings); Tommy Berglund (pages 153 and 154); Annabel Milne and Peter Stebbing (pages 61 to 70, with colour by Nordbok); Syed Mumtaz Ahmad (paintings). Photography: Jan-Eric Larsson, except for pages 26, 35, and 39 centre (Lars-Erik Löfgren) and page 39 upper (Roland Thorbjörnsson).

Nordbok would like to express gratitude to the following for their assistance and advice during manuscript and illustration preparation and photography: Rustan Andersson, Argenta, Denmark's Aquarium, Fotokonsult, Herkulesgatan Zoo, Nils-Ove Hilldén, Assar Knutsson, Majornas Zoo, The Gothenburg Maritime Museum, The Museum of Natural History, Stork Zoo, and all those aquarists who allowed their aquaria and fishes to be photographed specially for the book.

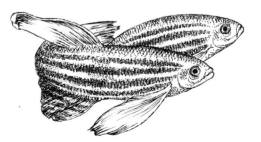

The Authors

Peter Hunnam has written all the chapters except Chapter 3. A marine ecologist and scientific diver, he is an expert on the creation and management of aquaria, and has supervised the establishment of the Qatar National Museum Aquarium. His other work has been concerned with the development of underwater conservation areas, marine parks, and aquaria. In preparing the book, he has been assisted greatly by Valerie Joscelyne, a biologist experienced in the development and equipment of aquarium systems.

Annabel Milne and Peter Stebbing have conceived and written Chapter 3 and have illustrated pages 61 to 70. After training in illustration and zoology, they have worked extensively in publishing, producing illustrations for over forty publications as well as for scientific papers. Their particular interest is fishes and aquatic life.

The Photographer

Jan-Eric Larsson has been photographing aquarium fishes for the past ten years. An experienced aquarist, he is active in several aquarium societies, where his photographic expertise is greatly appreciated.

Contents

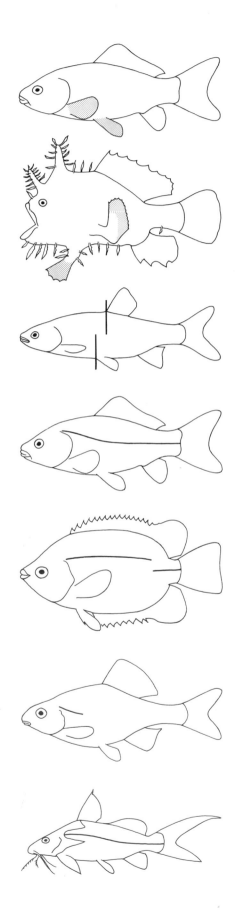

Preface

By most people, the watery places in nature are seen only as surfaces of glittering waves, or as impenetrable mirrors of the sky. The vast expanses of sea, the wonderful diversity of a coral reef community or a tropical river pool, the mysterious depths of cold lakes and mountain streams, the teeming activity of a small pond—these tend to remain beyond human experience. Yet such places cover two-thirds of our planet. The earth is enveloped largely by water which forms its landscapes, regulates the climate, and, above all, is the milieu in which life began and has evolved for millions of years.

The aquarium provides a point of contact between ourselves, as terrestrial animals, and the world of water. It has a volume small enough to handle; it may be set up and maintained in a healthy state far from any natural body of water; it is sufficiently simple and coherent to be understood and appreciated. Yet, it is a living system, whose dynamic complexities reproduce the real workings of a natural aquatic system. Through the window of the aquarium, the lives and requirements of underwater creatures can be observed easily, and their features, habits, and interactions studied and enjoyed.

This book emphasizes the need for aquarists to grasp the basis of what they are doing. Many aquaria are managed poorly, in terms of the conditions under which the inmates are kept, or of the display's visual impact. The designer or user of an aquarium must stand back and think carefully of everything that he or she wishes to accomplish. It is futile to rush ahead, collecting a jumble of ingredients for a "fish tank", mixing them together, and managing the results haphazardly. The stages of planning, equipping, setting up, and management should each be undertaken diligently. An organized approach is crucial for all aquaria, large or small, domestic or public, aesthetic or functional.

The essence of an aquarium is to provide an environment suitable for a specific group of living organisms—and, secondarily, to display this community for an audience. These principles should always be borne in mind, whether the aquarium facility is intended for purposes of education, entertainment, or scientific research. But it is equally important to know the reasons for maintaining certain conditions in an aquarium.

Thus, Chapter 1 reviews the ecology of natural places which are the homes of aquatic plants and animals. Such organisms will be described individually in Chapters 2 and 3. The character of their habitats, and the ways in which their lives are shaped by the ambient conditions, indicate the type of environment that is suitable for each species. The aquarium is fundamentally a reproduction of these natural conditions. Chapter 4 introduces the processes which govern the stability of this artificial environment, and explains the interactions between aquatic organisms and their surroundings. It deals with the main physical influences and chemical elements of the aquarium environment, and with biological factors such as the effect of carbon dioxide upon oxygen availability, of acidity upon ammonia toxicity, and of bicarbonate buffering upon water hardness.

Most organisms, particularly when adult, are able to thrive in a fairly broad range of conditions. This tolerance reflects the variable quality of many natural environments. Hence, many freshwater fishes can adjust to wide changes in salinity or temperature, if these occur gradually. Nevertheless, in the aquarium, full health and longevity are desired rather than only survival, and a stable environment must be maintained. An organism undergoes stress during the periods in which it is adjusting to changes, and such stress may lead to illness and death.

The vital functions of aquatic communities—in nature and in aquaria—and the roles of their diverse members are also discussed in Chapters 1 and 4. In addition to the prominent animal and plant inhabitants, there is an important population consisting primarily of aerobic bacteria feeding on organic detritus or on nitrogenous wastes of metabolism. Many forms of life will grow and reproduce readily in an aquarium, including not only the display specimens but the subsidiary occupants as well: simple algae, micro-organisms, and even fungi are capable of increasing rapidly in abundance if conditions such as nourishment, uncolonized surfaces, light, and temperature are in their favour. To realize the dynamic nature of the aquarium permits one to monitor these changes with time and to accommodate or control them.

Aquarium technology is presented in some detail, introducing the aquarist to the artificial means by which an aquatic habitat can be maintained within definite limits. Besides reviewing the chief items of equipment available, and their principles of operation, Chapter 5 discusses their integration into systems, whose full installation and management will concern Chapters 6 and 7.

The beginner should be encouraged by explanations of the components of an aquarium system and the most suitable choices for practical use. Advantages, drawbacks, and applications of different types of equipment are examined, enabling the reader to combine theoretical information with his or her particular opportunities and requirements. A novice must focus upon the basic principles, and not be daunted by the breadth of activities to which this new interest might lead. Initial projects are best kept simple, minimizing the variety of specimens, the difficulty of maintaining their conditions, and the amount of hardware. Moreover, the tank design and placement, and the interior set, must allow clear viewing of the miniature aquatic scene. For the fascination and enjoyment of an aquarium start with the first glimpse into the water of the display.

Successful aquarium ownership involves aspects of science, technology, and art. Throughout the book, an attempt is made to indicate the wealth of fields which invite further exploration by the advanced aquarist. Among these is the design of aquaria to exhibit biological themes in an advantageous manner. Most of the displays exemplified here, especially in Chapter 4, contain a diverse community of organisms: invertebrates, fishes, and plants are usually found together. In addition to emphasizing the natural-community concept, they show how different types of organisms suit an interior set and appear through the viewing window. The specialist can use this knowledge to illustrate much narrower subjects, such as a single kind of organism. For example, a display of plants with floating leaves, to demonstrate their range of forms and growth patterns, might incorporate viewing of both the top and underside of the water surface, and accommodate numerous rooting systems in its depth and substrates.

A neglected feature of many aquaria is the physical set constructed within the tank. This book constantly notes the relationships between aquatic organisms and their tangible surroundings—the need of attachment to surfaces or sediments, of shelter or shading, of still or moving water, and so on. Such links are often beneficial in nature, ensuring a maximum chance of survival, for example, when a benthic animal chooses a site to settle or spawn upon. However, most species retain some flexibility, so that alternative sites may be used. Awareness of these requirements will enable truly appropriate sets to be created.

While the aquarist has a responsibility to satisfy the biological demands of captive organisms, he or she should otherwise feel free to create any sort of interior. The adaptability of most species is an aid to imaginative style in tank design. The builder can experiment with unusual natural substrates and with visually exciting artificial materials, particularly the transparent plastics. Scale and detail may be very important, as in a display of small bottom-living invertebrates: the size and shape of the tank and the viewing window must be matched to the fineness of the substrate details, as well as to the features of the room housing the aquarium. Because the specimens live in close association with the bottom, it is essential that the interior set and lighting are arranged in proper relation to the window. Holes, ledges, and surfaces should face a window so that their occupants will be in sight. But even burrowing animals or buried rooting systems can be exhibited clearly, with a little forethought. Indeed, there are few limits to the range of aquarium shapes and interior sets, or to the types of aquatic organisms that may be shown ingeniously and informatively.

Aquarium illumination is another underestimated area for the experimenter. Beyond the requirements of plants to photosynthesize, and of many animals which need light to orientate and develop normally, the aquarium may be brightened in all sorts of ways to make visually stunning displays. Light and lighting systems are discussed at length in Chapters 4 and 5. As an odd instance, one might conceive an "upside-down aquarium" in which the fishes respond to light from beneath the glass-bottomed tank by swimming among rocks attached to the tank cover!

All aquaria bring terrestrial mankind closer to the intricacy of

underwater creatures and their lives. It is possible to set up in a cold climate a display of fishes from a sparkling tropical stream, or to maintain, thousands of miles inland from the coast, a community of marine organisms. A particularly valuable type of aquarium presents an aquatic habitat or situation which cannot be viewed in nature. An extreme example would be the exhibition of animals from a subterranean stream—inaccessible except through photographs or pickled specimens, or by a few intrepid pothole-divers. Similarly, the fauna of murky rivers could be shown clearly in an aquarium. In these cases, light control would have to be carefully arranged. But with suitable support systems, many of the features of such habitats are reproducible, allowing the specialized organisms to live almost normally while observed.

As has been emphasized, aquaria are excellent facilities for rendering people more aware of life in water. I feel that, in this respect, the best type of aquarium is one which operates in the most natural manner, with an authentic assemblage of specimens from a familiar habitat. A tremendous opportunity is wasted if the aquarist does not attempt to relate the captive specimens to their wild counterparts, regard them as vital components of the ecological situation in which they evolved, and consider their biological characteristics in this light. It may well be true that many aquarists never think about the origins of creatures that are "bought in the local pet-shop and kept in the front room".

I have tried to correct this imbalance by encouraging the aquarist to make observations in the field, and to use such information or impressions in establishing authentic displays with appropriate specimens, caught by the aquarist personally where feasible. It must be remembered, however, that the aquarist also has a responsibility to the natural environment, as a source of inspiration and livestock. Wild habitats and populations are often vulnerable to damage by man. They may be rare and isolated examples, or particularly fragile and unable to withstand disturbance from pollution, fishing and collecting, or other human effects.

Being a good aquarist entails more than looking after an aquarium adequately. One of the intriguing qualities of aquaria is that they raise many questions about underwater life as well as indicating a few answers. The aquarist is encouraged by indoor observations to go beyond the tank and pet-shop, explore the real world of nature, and penetrate the activities of wild creatures and the ecology of aquatic habitats. Through first-hand field-work, or by study of natural history, the aquarist will be led to investigate the sources of specimens, their natural distribution and rarity, and their habits and relationships with other species. In addition to such ecological enquiries, he or she may proceed to learn more about the evolution of organisms, pondering the whys and wherefores of their form and colouring.

From these ventures, valuable knowledge is gained which makes a better aquarist. But its widest significance is to yield a better human being, more conscious of the natural surroundings over which mankind holds such power, of the dangers in environmental pollution and depletion, and of the requirements that many species have in order to thrive or even survive on the planet. A dedicated aquarist will also rejoice in the beauty of wild creatures. There is staggering diversity, and yet every species of animal or plant is somehow perfect. Each has evolved as a vital unit within its own kind of environment. In endeavouring to recreate a suitable home for a group of aquatic organisms, the aquarist earns priceless insight into the laws and wonders of their watery lives.

1 The Natural Environment

The essential element of the aquarium is water. It is also the substance of greatest importance to life on earth, for all the processes that characterize plant and animal life make use of water. There are roughly 1,500 million cubic kilometres (360 million cubic miles) of water on the planet, in both fresh and salty forms. These have created an endless variety of environments for living communities, which are the basis of the aquarist's knowledge.

Water

Water is a well-understood compound of the inorganic type (containing no carbon). A particle of water is a molecule, consisting of one oxygen atom and two hydrogen atoms, bound together by electric charges. In general, molecules are always in motion, with a speed that is proportional to the temperature; and there are electrical or other forces of attraction between them, becoming weaker as they move faster. Thus, when a substance cools, its particles normally slow down and form clusters, making it increasingly dense, so that it may change in state: from a gas (whose particles rush about with relative freedom) to a liquid, then to a solid (with particles in a firmer structure).

Physical properties

Similarly, water occurs in three states: as a liquid, as solid ice, and as a gaseous vapour or steam. Only the first of these can exist indefinitely, hold salt, or support life, under the conditions—especially of temperature—which are most familiar to us. Even within the liquid state, the variation of water's properties according to the temperature is very important for its nature as a habitat. One extraordinary feature of water, however, is that it expands slightly when freezing, and ice is less dense than the liquid. Water has several other unique qualities, which derive mainly from the shape and components of its molecules.

Water as a medium

Of all known liquids, water has the greatest specific heat (the amount of heat needed to raise its temperature), the greatest latent heat of evaporation (the amount of heat needed to vaporize it), and—with the exception of mercury—the greatest thermal conductivity (the amount of heat that can pass through it). These properties mean that enormous quantities of heat energy from sunlight are stored in the earth's oceans and atmosphere. Their vast volumes of water are warmed and cooled slowly, with little change in temperature between seasons, days, and even hours. For the same reason, the maximum range of temperatures is smaller in the seas (from about 40°C to −2°C, or 104°F to 28°F) than on land (from about 60°C to −70°C, or 140°F to −94°F).

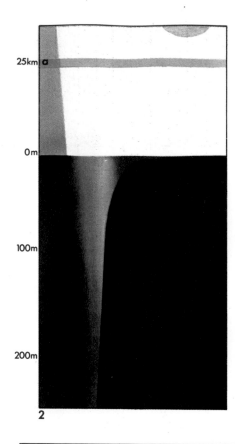

2

1 The energy the sun radiates is indispensable to almost all life and is a prerequisite of photosynthesis. The movement of water around the world is dependent on the sun, for it causes the water to evaporate and the winds to blow, thus bearing the vapour in over land, where it falls as rain or snow. On land, it either evaporates, falls directly on lakes and rivers, runs off the land into streams, or seeps through to join the ground water. Eventually, it finds its way back to the sea.

2 When the sun's rays enter the earth's atmosphere, they are gradually absorbed by the ozone layer (a) and then the atmosphere itself. On striking the sea's surface, the light is absorbed even more, and violet and red, the wavelengths at either end of the spectrum, fade first. Although blue-green wavelengths penetrate further, no photosynthesis takes place below about 100 m (330 ft). It is, therefore, vital that the nutrients in the deep sea are brought up to the surface, where the sunlight reaches the phytoplankton and algae.

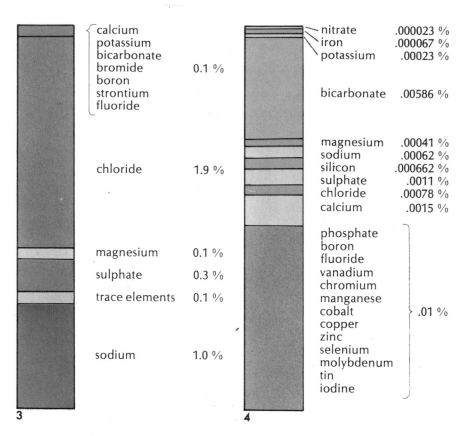

calcium
potassium
bicarbonate
bromide   0.1 %
boron
strontium
fluoride

chloride   1.9 %

magnesium   0.1 %

sulphate   0.3 %

trace elements 0.1 %

sodium   1.0 %

3

nitrate   .000023 %
iron   .000067 %
potassium   .00023 %

bicarbonate   .00586 %

magnesium   .00041 %
sodium   .00062 %
silicon   .000662 %
sulphate   .0011 %
chloride   .00078 %
calcium   .0015 %

phosphate
boron
fluoride
vanadium
chromium
manganese
cobalt   } .01 %
copper
zinc
selenium
molybdenum
tin
iodine

4

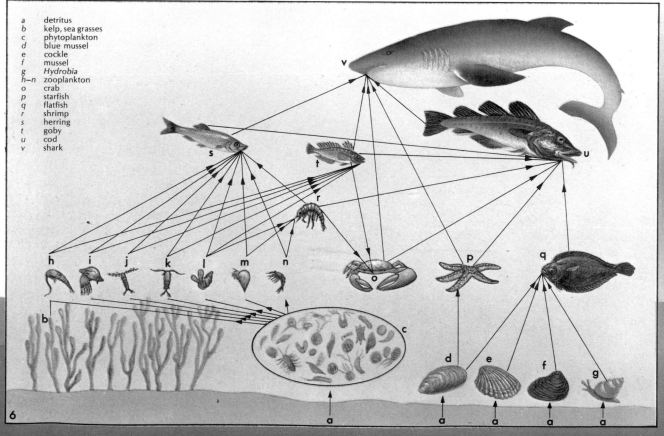

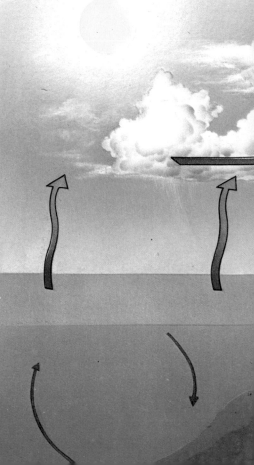

a   detritus
b   kelp, sea grasses
c   phytoplankton
d   blue mussel
e   cockle
f   mussel
g   *Hydrobia*
h–n zooplankton
o   crab
p   starfish
q   flatfish
r   shrimp
s   herring
t   goby
u   cod
v   shark

6

1

3 This cylinder represents the 3.5 per cent of sea water that is not pure water (H₂O). Sodium and chloride, as common salt, make up over 85 per cent of the total substances in sea water.

4 Fresh water is low in inorganic ions but varies in the amount of elements dissolved in it. The cylinder represents the 0.02 per cent of the average of the world's fresh inland waters that is not pure water.

5 A food chain in a temperate freshwater lake. If the lake is small and not much sunlight reaches its surface, then material from the riparian communities can be important.

6 The marine food web depends much more on direct photosynthesis of algae and plants than does the freshwater web.

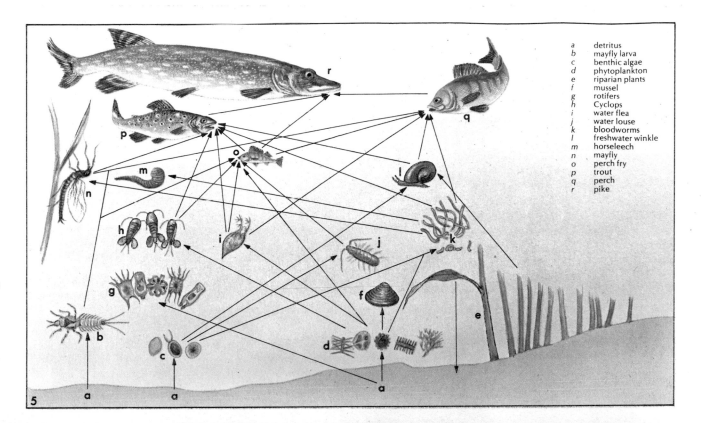

a	detritus
b	mayfly larva
c	benthic algae
d	phytoplankton
e	riparian plants
f	mussel
g	rotifers
h	Cyclops
i	water flea
j	water louse
k	bloodworms
l	freshwater winkle
m	horseleech
n	mayfly
o	perch fry
p	trout
q	perch
r	pike

Water can dissolve almost anything, and dissolved materials tend to remain in solution in water. This is due to another property which is greater for water than for any other substance—its dielectric constant, or insulating capacity. Thus, it separates the charged particles (called ions) of such a material and prevents them from rejoining. The consequences for life on earth are crucial, since all the chemical processes of metabolism in living organisms take place among materials dissolved in water.

As a liquid or a vapour, water is highly mobile. The global transfer of heat by ocean currents, and in the moisture of the atmosphere, is a principal feature of the world's climate. Equally vital is the transportation by water of dissolved materials and suspended particles, and of drifting and swimming organisms. These processes influence the patterns of life throughout the water and land habitats of the biosphere. Plant photosynthesis and transpiration, animal locomotion and feeding, respiration, reproduction, and dispersal of offspring, are all dependent on transport by water.

Light and heat in water

Sunlight passes through the various layers of the atmosphere, and through a cloud cover or plant canopy, to strike the surface of a body of liquid water. The amount of light reaching the surface depends upon the latitude, season, time of day, and weather. At the equator, rays of sunlight pass through less atmosphere and, therefore, are brighter than near the poles. Moreover, reflection from the surface decreases the amount of light penetrating the water. Surface movement by waves and bubbles can reflect up to a third of the incident light.

As light travels through water, it is absorbed and scattered, both by the water molecules and by any dissolved substances or suspended particles. The latter may include sand, silt, and organisms such as algae. This turbidity varies widely between different bodies of water, and with the turbulence and speed of water movement. Rivers in spate, and coastal seas during winter storms, contain extreme quantities of suspended material and are very murky. In addition, some of the colours making up "white" sunlight are decreased more rapidly than others in intensity. Blue-green light penetrates the farthest into water, but it, too, disappears at a depth of more than about 100 m (330 ft), where plant growth becomes impossible.

The rapid absorption of the sun's rays means that heat energy, which is also a form of radiation, cannot penetrate more than a few metres into a body of water. The change in water temperature with depth is an important feature of lakes and ponds. Warmed by the sun, the surface water becomes less dense, and the mixing of water between the surface and the deeper regions is reduced, creating distinct layers of water. This stratification will persist until the surface heating stops, and cold water will then sink down through the layers. Such cyclic events occur in the open ocean as well. At high latitudes, the surface heating is normally inadequate to produce such stratification—but in the tropics, marked layering of the water continues throughout the year.

These processes have a great influence upon life and productivity in aquatic habitats. Temperature layering impedes the vital return of dissolved inorganic nutrients to the sunlit surface waters, where they are required for the production of plant material by photosynthesis.

The earth's water

More than ninety-seven per cent of the water on earth is in the oceans, amounting to some 1,450 million cubic kilometres (348 million cubic miles) of salt water. Eighty-one per cent of the southern hemisphere, compared to about sixty-one of the northern, is underwater. This uneven global distribution has strong effects upon the climate.

Three-quarters of the world's freshwater resources are locked in glaciers and polar caps—around 38 million cubic kilometres (9 million cubic miles) of solid ice. A large proportion of the remainder is deep-ground water, approaching 8 million cubic kilometres (2 million cubic miles). The volume of surface water, in all the freshwater habitats on earth, is estimated at between 250,000 and 400,000 cubic kilometres (60,000 and 96,000 cubic miles). Most of this is contained in the few enormous lakes, with relatively small amounts in the many millions of ponds, streams, and modest rivers.

Fresh and marine waters

Sea water is a dilute solution of virtually all the elements found on earth. Chemically, the sea is a very stable environment, containing 96.5 per cent pure water and 3.5 per cent dissolved salts. The latter consist almost entirely of eleven main substances, over three-quarters being common salt (sodium chloride). These salts occur in constant proportions to one another throughout the world's oceans. But their total concentration, a salinity averaging about 35 parts per thousand, may be as high as 45 in a warm semi-enclosed region such as the Persian Gulf—with more evaporation than rain and river inflow—or as low as 15 in an area like the Baltic Sea, which receives much fresh water from its surroundings.

The minor salts are present in quite low amounts. Among them are phosphates and nitrates, which nourish plants and are often in short supply, as well as elements which are taken up and stored by some living organisms. For example, iodine is accumulated by seaweeds to the extent that a given weight of dried seaweed contains as much iodine as does 100,000 times that weight of sea water.

By contrast, the chemical content of the world's fresh water is extremely variable, both seasonally and between individual streams, rivers, lakes, and ponds. Even rain water is not pure but contains diverse amounts of sodium, magnesium, calcium, chloride and sulphate compounds, and dissolved gases—oxygen, carbon dioxide, and nitrogen. These impurities are picked up in the atmosphere from dust, pollutants, sea spray (which may be carried far inland by winds), and from the air itself.

Most fresh waters show the complex relationships between acidity, carbon dioxide, carbonic acid, carbonates, bicarbonates, and calcium. Because of its high carbon-dioxide content, rain normally has a high acidity. As the acidic rain percolates through the soil, it picks up calcium and magnesium ions. Calcium carbonate is a common constituent of many rocks and is readily dissolved into calcium and bicarbonate ions by a dilute acid. The bicarbonate neutralizes the soil water, opposing an increase of acidity. When carbon dioxide is removed from the water, for example by photosynthesis, the process is reversed, and calcium carbonate is deposited in the soil.

In freshwater habitats under natural conditions, calcium and magnesium compounds are the most important dissolved solids. A shortage of either element may limit biological activity. Shell construction, bone building, and plant precipitation of lime will combine and concentrate the calcium ions, whilst magnesium is a key constituent of chlorophyll in plants. The weight of organisms may be three or four times greater in calcium-rich waters than in calcium-poor ones, and different species will inhabit each kind of water.

Some inland waters have very high concentrations of total salt, produced by rapid evaporation and by the dissolution of surrounding mineral rocks. For instance, the Great Salt Lake, in the United States, is about four hundred times saltier—at 250 parts per thousand—than a normal lake. Its only inhabitants are brine shrimps (of the species *Artemia salina*) and certain insect larvae.

The hydrologic cycle

Consider a shower of rain falling upon vegetation, rocks, and soil. The surfaces are warm, and some of the water evaporates immediately back into the air. Much of the water reaching the ground may penetrate deeply to swell the underground reservoir, or may sleep slowly through the soil to lower-lying land. Water running over the surface will form puddles and replenish pools which are lined with rock or clay or—as miniature natural aquaria—are held by the curl of a plant leaf. Pools in shallow depressions may be filled with plant life, which draws up water and evaporates most of it from the leaves by transpiration, but combines a portion of it with carbon dioxide in the process of photosynthesis.

The shape of the land governs the course of a stream as it rushes downward across a rocky bed. If water flows into a deep lake, it remains for a long time before leaving as vapour or through an outflow. Water may traverse forests, marshes, and grassland, moving faster and cutting deeper when swollen with rain, or drying in stagnant pools during summer droughts. As streams converge and rivers meet, the waters grow and continue until they reach the sea. Here, the load of silt, chemicals, life, and flotsam, carried down by fresh water from the land, joins salt water.

Coastlines suffer constant change under the pressure of moving water. Lagoons are scoured and banked. Sand and silt accumulate, stabilized by marsh and land plants, and are later eroded by storm waters. Waves flow over reefs and pound against cliffs of rock. The coastal sea is dynamic, with endless activity of wind and water, of life and growth, and of man.

In the depths away from the coast, such movement slows. But giant forces of air and current affect the surface. Deep water is dragged upward by great swirls, increasing in light and vitality. Wind blows the spray from crest to trough of the waves, and catches the warm rising vapour, then carries the humid air rapidly across the sea to another land mass.

As it rises, the vapour cools. Reaching another shoreline, the water-laden air is pushed ever higher above the land mass. Eventually, the air temperature decreases so much that the water vapour condenses or freezes, and falls back to the earth as rain or snow. This precipitation exceeds evaporation over the land, while the opposite is true over the oceans. But there is a general balance between the two processes throughout the world, due to the flow of water from land into the sea. About 37,000 cubic kilometres (8,000 cubic miles) of water re-enter the oceans each year as surface run-off, carrying hundreds of millions of tons of minerals.

The ecology of water

Ecology examines how nature works. It is the study of plants and animals, and the relationships which link them to one another, as well as to the physical and chemical environment in which they live. The term "ecology" is derived from the Greek word for "living space" (*oikos*). For every form of life on earth, it sums up a fascinating complexity of resources, requirements, and interactions.

Any organism requires a host of supplies and stimuli: light, food, oxygen, water, heat, and chemical substances. Given living space, the plant or animal may survive to reach maturity and, in groups of the same species, to reproduce. The population may spread or increase in density, if the resources are available and there is no restriction by competing, predatory, or parasitic neighbours.

Over the 3,500 million years since life began on earth, a vast diversity of organisms has evolved, able to use the various combinations of resources in the biosphere of water, land, and air. Some 1,500,000 species—1,200,000 of animals and 300,000 of plants—have now been catalogued. The members of each species have a particular "ecological niche" in which they can survive at a given time. For certain species, this niche is a very narrow range of conditions which they can tolerate, limiting them to tiny populations in only a few localities. Other species occur in huge numbers and are world-wide in distribution. By understanding the many dimensions of such a niche, an awareness is gained of the demands which the species must make on its physical, chemical, and biological surroundings in order to stay alive and healthy, grow, and multiply.

The basic patterns of the ecology of water may be illustrated by examining a fairly small and simple body of water. A woodland pool is a depression in the ground, permanently full of water. Trees surround it, some overhanging and partially shading the water. Little streams flow in and out. Chemicals are washed in from the nearby soil or dissolve from submerged materials. Breezes stir the water surface and mix the contents across the pool.

Living organisms will be found at the pool's surface, in and on the muddy bottom, upon the occasional stone or sunken root or old boot, and around the shore line. Vegetation ranges from microscopic algae to floating, rooted, underwater, or emergent higher plants. The animal inhabitants include many insect larvae, worms, snails, some bivalves, various amphibians and fishes.

Energy flow

A fundamental feature of life on earth is that virtually all biological systems depend upon sunlight for energy. This small ecological unit of a pond is powered by the sunlight penetrating the water surface. Some of the energy is trapped by green plants and used to drive the reaction of photosynthesis. This converts simple chemicals into "energy-rich" organic compounds, whose microscopic molecules can act like charged batteries.

The plants in the pond respire, grow, and produce seed. Animals called herbivores, able to eat and digest the cellular materials of plants, thus obtain food rich in chemical energy. This energy is released by the process of respiration in animals and is made available for the activities of life. Suitable organic substances may be reconstituted as flesh, so that the animal grows and creates reproductive cells.

Carnivorous animals eat their live neighbours and relatives.

Scavengers and detritus-feeders happily consume dead plant debris and animal remains, including material from outside the pond. As in many aquatic habitats, an important source of food is provided by material falling in from the trees or washed in by streams—insects, spiders, leaves, fruit, and pollen.

In these ways, the energy and chemicals making up the organic compounds pass through the pond system. At each level of its use, the energy enables living organisms to work by oxidizing organic material in respiration. Energy is also lost from the system as heat. The complex interactions of many different animals and plants form a multi-linked chain, or "food web", based upon photosynthesis and supporting several levels of life, each feeding on the next. Whilst the flow of energy is in one direction, from sunlight via chemicals to lost heat, the chemical substances are recycled within the system.

Chemical cycles

Plants require some basic nutrients, particularly carbon dioxide, phosphates, and nitrates, with which to build the complex organic molecules. Aquatic plants generally absorb these nutrients from the surrounding water solution, where their concentrations vary greatly.

Bound into organic material, the chemicals pass up the food chain, from plant to herbivore and detritus-feeder, then to carnivore. Dead organic material—fallen leaves, excreta, lifeless bodies—accumulates from each level. The vital link between this material and the inorganic nutrients required by plants are the tiny bacteria and fungi which obtain energy by breaking down the dead material and release its chemicals back into the environment.

A controlling factor in aquatic ecosystems—the watery habitats to be described next—is the restriction of the primary energy source, sunlight, to the surface layers. The production of plants, upon which the entire system depends, is thus restricted to a shallow illuminated zone. So the inorganic nutrients released by decomposer organisms throughout the system must be returned to the surface for use by plants.

Salt-water habitats

From outer space, the earth looks almost blue. Salt water covers more than seventy per cent, or 360 million square kilometres (140 million square miles), of the planet's surface. The inner space of the oceans, governing both global and regional conditions of climate, enables life to exist and determines its many patterns.

The oceans have an average depth of around 3,700 m (12,000 ft), with deep trenches reaching over 10,000 m (33,000 ft). At least seven per cent of the total area of sea bed is under less than 200 m (650 ft) of water. Within this vast realm, salt-water habitats vary in temperature from about 40°C (104°F) to −2°C (28°F), and in salinity from the diluted marginal seas (at less than 29 parts per thousand) to the tropical gulfs and coastal lagoons (reaching 40 to 50 parts per thousand).

Water in the seas is moved by wind, by global trends of heating and cooling, by earthquakes, by the gravitational attraction of the moon and sun, and—on a relatively minor scale—by the activities of living organisms. Life in the sea, as everywhere else, is regulated in turn by the supply of basic needs in suitable form and quantity: energy, space to occupy, and useful chemicals.

The salt content of sea water is so much higher than that of fresh

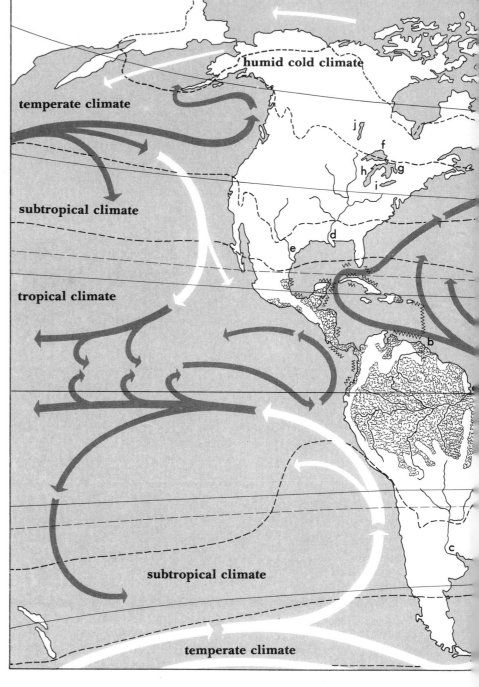

More than ninety-seven per cent of the earth's total water is in the seas; the rest is fresh water, most of which is contained in the few enormous lakes, whilst negligible amounts are to be found in the countless ponds, streams, and small rivers.

The movement of water around the globe is dictated mainly by the prevailing winds and by the difference in temperature that exists between large bodies of water in various parts of the ocean.

On this map of the world, dark arrows indicate the direction of the warm currents, and light arrows that of the cold currents. The ocean currents are vital to marine life, as they help to mix the surface water with the deeper water, thus bringing up nutrients from the depths.

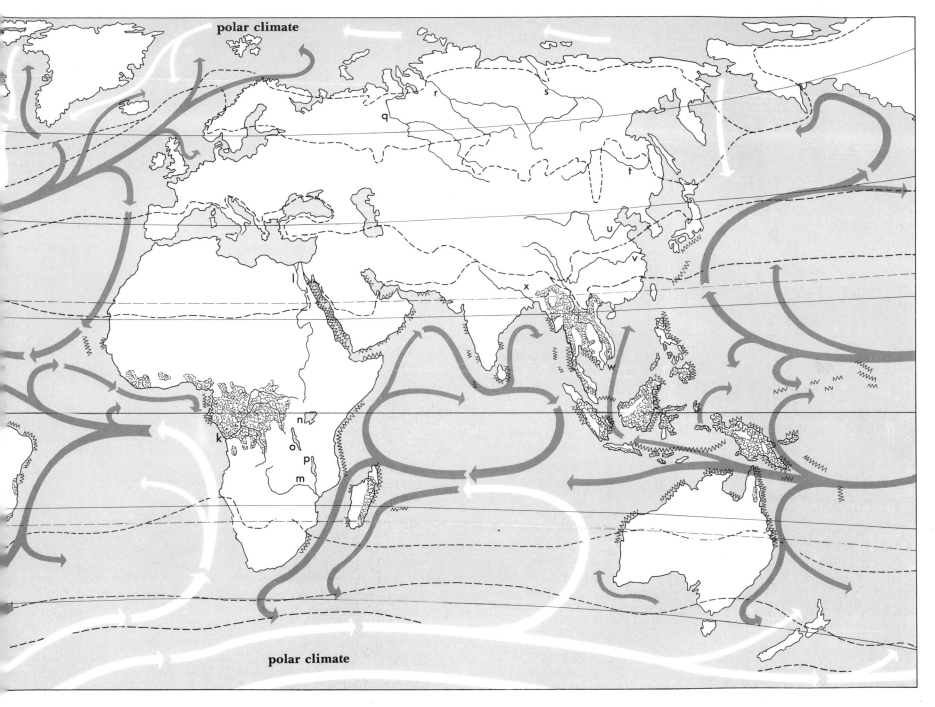

polar climate

polar climate

The most popular freshwater aquarium fishes come from areas of hot rainy climate, where there is constant warmth and humidity: for instance, the Amazon and Zaire basins, and the rivers and streams of parts of southeast Asia. The deep Rift lakes in the tropical savannah regions of Africa are also major sources of freshwater aquarium fishes.

The tropical and sub-tropical seas are the homes of the most colourful of the marine aquarium fishes, and the coral reefs of the world (marked on the map) provide homes for many of these.

The fact that the most popular aquarium fishes come from the tropics does not mean that fishes from temperate waters may not be kept in aquaria. On the contrary, a temperate-water aquarium can be just as fascinating as any tropical aquarium, providing that the choice of fishes, plants, and invertebrates is imaginative.

Some major rivers and lakes of the world are indicated on the map. (a) Amazon. (b) Orinoco. (c) Paraná. (d) Mississippi. (e) Rio Grande. (f) Lake Superior. (g) Lake Huron. (h) Lake Michigan. (i) Lake Erie. (j) Lake Winnipeg. (k) Zaire. (l) Nile. (m) Zambesi. (n) Lake Victoria. (o) Lake Tanganyika. (p) Lake Malawi. (q) Ob. (r) Yenesei. (s) Lena. (t) Amur.

(u) Huang Ho. (v) Yangtse. (w) Mekong. (x) Ganges.

〰️〰️〰️ Tropical rain forests
/\/\/\/\ Coral reefs

waters that very few species can survive in both. Another reason for the striking differences between freshwater and marine organisms is their long separation during the process of independent evolution. The main inhabitants of many marine environments, such as large algae, echinoderms, and coelenterates, are rare or nonexistent in fresh water—whilst higher plants, amphibians, and insects are major elements of freshwater life but are comparatively unimportant in the sea. These differences will be shown below by considering the principal marine regions: the open ocean and its deep bed, the coastal seas, and the shoreland affected by tides.

The open ocean and deep-sea bed

Circulation of water in the sea is caused partly by steady wind-driven waves, and by forces due to the earth's rotation. Surface currents also occur where the warm waters of sunny regions expand and drift towards the poles. An outstanding example is the Gulf Stream. It carries about 50 million cubic metres (1,800 million cubic feet) every second—about forty times the total discharge of the world's rivers—up the North American coast and across the Atlantic.

Major currents in the deeper layers result from masses of water sinking. This happens especially when warm waters, containing relatively much salt, enter the sub-polar seas and are cooled, becoming heavier. Very deep water moves slowly away from the poles to balance this surface inflow. The tides create additional circulation, although it is less extensive in the open sea than along the coasts.

The ocean surface

A variety of specially adapted animals inhabits the ocean–air interface. Siphonophores, molluscs, fishes, birds, and mammals are all present. Two notable examples of siphonophores are the Portuguese man-of-war *(Physalia physalia)*, which inflates a large float above the surface, and the by-the-wind sailor *(Valella valella)*, named for its sail-like projection. These predators trail stinging tentacles up to 10 m (33 ft) long, using venom to catch fishes. The jellyfish is a close relative and also thrives by drifting passively in the ocean currents. Its watery tissues are almost neutrally buoyant, enabling it to stay near the surface with ease.

Among the molluscs are cephalopods, the most highly evolved invertebrate creatures. They include the squids—active and agile predators equipped with excellent vision and a kind of jet propulsion—as well as the chambered nautilus and the argonauts. Another mollusc which rides the interface is a small swimming sea slug *(Glaucus atlanticus)*. It feeds on the deadly man-of-war, whose undischarged stinging cells it even incorporates into its own tissues for defence. Living upside-down against the water surface, it has evolved with a typical reversed pattern of colours. Its dark-blue ventral side is difficult for predators above to see, and its paler dorsal side does not show against the light sky for underwater predators.

Ocean plant productivity

An important zone, called "euphotic", extends from the surface down to the depth at which almost no light remains for photosynthesis. Below this level, plants cannot survive, because insufficient organic material is photosynthesized for their metabolic needs. Such a "compensation point", reached at about 100 m (330 ft) by most plant species even in clear seas, allows only a fraction of the total ocean depth to produce the plants on which all marine life depends.

Erosion by wind and sea has carved a number of different habitats out of this coastline. In the cliffs at the end most exposed to the sea are rocky shores, with tidal pools, and gravel and sand beaches, covered with big boulders. Further down the coast, towards the estuary, it is more sheltered, and we find sandy beaches with the occasional big rock. The estuarine habitat has a specialized flora and fauna, adapted to survive the changing salinity of the water. To the left of the estuary, a salt marsh has been created. Silt carried in the river water has been swept by the ocean current along the shore to form a natural barrier, so that the low-lying land behind it retains much of the tidal waters that pour into it twice a day. An incredibly rich plant and animal life flourishes in the salt marsh, where decaying growth has formed a rich organic mud.

Some of the detritus is trapped by filter-feeding animals, and bacteria break down the rest into dissolved chemicals that fertilize the marsh and, as they are carried out on the ebbing tide, the sea around the marsh.
(*Inset*) Plant life on a typical salt marsh. On the landward side are normally *(a)* rushes (species of *Juncus*).
On the banks of a creek, where the land is reasonably well-drained, are found *(b)* sea aster (*Aster*) and *(c)* sea purslane (*Halimione*). Mid-marsh plants are *(d)* sea spurry (*Spergularia*) and *(e)* sea lavender (*Limonia*). On the seaward side grow *(f)* saltwort (*Salicornia*) and *(g)* sea-cord, or marsh, grass (*Spartina*) whose roots help to stabilize the soft mud. Finally, in the mud and sand flats that stretch towards the water is *(h)* eel grass (*Zostera*).

The main photosynthesizers are tiny diatoms and flagellates, including animals which photosynthesize their own food. There are many species, adapted to slightly different conditions of light, temperature, pressure, and available nutrients. In turn, the phytoplankton plant life is grazed by copepods and foraminiferans, whilst they are eaten by larger zooplankton animals, particularly crustaceans, and these support great populations of small fishes.

Phytoplankton must stay in the well-lit euphotic zone to survive. The organism tends to sink, because its protoplasm and its frequent body-covering are denser than water. But its minute size helps to keep it afloat, with a high ratio of surface area to volume which maximizes friction against water. Flotation is aided in many species by their peculiar shape, having curved or needle-like spines or forming chains or wheels with other cells. Zooplankton may swim or use oil droplets, bladders, or surface projections for buoyancy, and flagellates employ long appendages.

The deep sea

Animals also exist in the cold, dark, plantless region midway between the surface and bottom of the ocean. They depend upon organic material moving down from the euphotic zone, either dead or alive. Among them are strange fish species, generally black and around 15 cm (6 in) long. Some have organs that produce light, or huge gaping mouths to gulp in as much as possible of whatever food is encountered in the water.

Conditions at the bottom are so extreme that less biological activity occurs. But every primary group, or phylum, of marine animals is represented. Holothurians and crinoids are common, besides other invertebrates suited to a crawling, burrowing, or buried life, in or upon the soft sea-bed ooze: starfishes, snails, worms, isopods, and sponges. Various sea squirts and small fishes (species of *Chimaera* and *Harriota*) are to be found as well. The food chains are based on animals filtering or munching the detritus which sinks like a thin rain onto the vast muddy plains.

Life in coastal seas

Around the long coastlines and islands of the earth's land masses, the sea is turbulent, sunlit, and very productive. Tidal currents flow strongly, and wave surges reach the sea bed, mixing the water and sediments, and carrying dissolved and suspended minerals, food particles, and living organisms. Water temperature, turbidity, and nutrient concentrations vary seasonally with the wind and weather.

Here, the plankton is diverse and abundant. Phytoplankton lives throughout the water column, fluctuating in density with the availability of sunlight and minerals. Zooplankton includes seasonal swarms of the eggs and juveniles of the many invertebrates and fishes which live as adults on the sea bed. The nature of the shallow sea bottom—a mixture of rock, gravel, sand, and fine silt—is a main influence upon the types of animals and plants present in that environment.

In the temperate regions, rocky shores descend to reefs and submarine cliffs of bedrock and massive boulders. These substrates occur in places where tidal currents or wave action prevent the settlement of sand or silt. In a sheltered area, these sediments accumulate to form extensive banks and flat plains.

The great variety of life in the open sea is due to the huge supply of food and energy available. Sunlight penetrates in sufficient amounts to about 100 m (330 ft) to allow photosynthesis, and because of this, the greatest range of species lives in the upper layer, which is known as the euphotic zone. In the bathyal zone (sometimes known as the dysphotic zone), there is less variety. The deeper down they live, the more the animals have had to adapt the shape of their body to the water, and in some places it goes down to 6,000 m (20,000 ft). Here, it is shown as ending at this lowest point. Some fishes *(inset)* of the twilight zone use bioluminescence to catch their food, using it either to see or to attract their prey. In the lower bathyal zone, from 2,000 m to the sea bed, there is no light and enormous pressure, and many of the fishes have developed strange shapes. Animals at these depths get their food from organic material sinking from the upper levels. As bacteria decompose the organic material, nutrients are released and brought to the upper layers by upwelling currents or vertical mixing. Below the lower bathyal zone is the hadal zone, which consists of deep fissures in the sea bed. Recent exploration in a specially constructed submarine has discovered ecological systems here which survive without light, apparently through some sort of chemical synthesis triggered by the heat from the earth's crust, which, in these fissures, is comparatively thin.

The illustrated organisms are: *(a)* herring, *(b)* phytoplankton, *(c)* dolphin, *(d)* flying fish, *(e)* baleen whale, *(f)* zooplankton, *(g)* bonito, *(h)* squid, *(i)* marlin, *(j)* seal, *(k)* shark, *(l)* lantern fish, *(m)* sperm whale, *(n)* deep-sea squid, *(o)* octopus, *(p)* abyssal squid, *(q)* Chimaera, *(r)* deep-sea crustacea, *(s)* angler fish, *(t)* gulper, *(u)* sea lily, *(v)* sponge, *(w)* brittle star, *(x)* tripod fish, *(y)* sea pen.

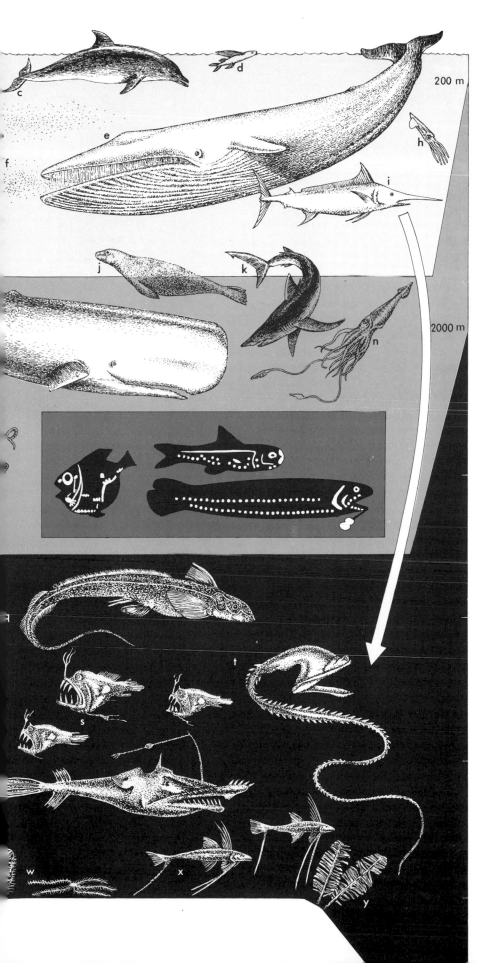

The coral reef

The most diverse and spectacular of shallow marine communities is found on the coral reefs in tropical seas. A coral reef is a rock-like mass of stony corals and other calcium-depositing organisms, whose limestone skeletons have piled layer upon layer for thousands of years. The skeletons of corals and sponges, the protective cases of tube-worms and bivalves, and the cell-wall reinforcement of various red algae, consist of calcium carbonate laid down by the living organisms. Each generation of these settles upon the hard remains of the last, and the reef grows by a few centimetres (or one inch) per year. Huge structures result, and some healthy reefs are now over 1,000 m (3,280 ft) thick. The world's most extensive instance is the Great Barrier Reef, along more than 2,000 km (1,250 miles) of the northeastern coastline of Australia in the Pacific Ocean.

Stony corals are the chief builders of reefs. Related species occur infrequently throughout the seas, but those that build reefs are restricted to tropical waters, with a temperature range of 23.5–25°C (74.3–77°C). The main coral-reef areas today are in the Indo-Pacific and the Caribbean regions.

Only the outer layer of such a reef is alive, with a skin of polyps that are packed together on a rigid framework of calcium-carbonate crystals. The polyp is like a sea anemone, a relative of the corals. It feeds on small animals and particles in the water, catching them with harpoon-bearing tentacles. Asexual reproduction is common, by splitting or budding off new individuals, allowing the colony to grow slowly but steadily.

An important feature of reef-building corals is that microscopic algae, called zooxanthellae, live in the polyp tissue. A close symbiotic relationship exists between the algal cells and their stable protective environment inside the coral animal. The algae are photosynthesizers, removing carbon dioxide, and this helps the polyp to deposit calcium carbonate. The polyp may also benefit from some of the organic products of photosynthesis. These algal partners are what enable the stony corals to thrive in waters where nutrients are scarce and productivity is otherwise low. Some reefs fix 1.3–3.5 kg per square metre (4–12 oz per square foot) of carbon each year, compared to only 20–40 g per square metre (0.07–0.14 oz per square foot) in nearby open waters.

The prominence and beauty of a coral reef are due to the density, variety, shapes, and colours of the animals which live amongst its folds and crevices. The layered mass of limestone provides a rich maze of canyons, holes, tunnels, ledges, cracks, and caves, with millions of surfaces lying at every angle to the light and water movement. While the outer layers are depositing new material, other organisms are busy excavating shelter, eating the live coral, and chemically eroding the reef by growing into it.

The reef's convoluted structure creates a reliable habitat for a fantastic range of animals. Every marine group is represented, often by many species which occur nowhere else. Common reef invertebrates include sponges, polychaetes, anemones, crabs, hermit crabs, lobsters, shrimps, snails, slugs, bivalves, cuttlefishes, starfishes, and sea cucumbers. Coral-reef fishes are unusually colourful, frequently with contrasting patches and stripes of pigment. The shape and behaviour of each species are also finely adapted to its mode of life on the crowded reef. The butterflyfishes (of the family Chaetodontidae) and damsel-

The coral reef is one of the most attractive underwater habitats there is, and it has a most colourful and varied life. There are three types of reef: the coral atoll, formed by corals building on the volcanic crater of a sunken island; the fringing reef, which grows along coasts, quite near to the shore; and the barrier reef (inset above), which also borders a land mass (a), but is separated from it by a lagoon (b) which, at low tide, can form a "lake" with perhaps only one seaward entrance. The reef itself (c) often has a steep incline on the seaward side. The structure of the stony coral is shown at left in the inset. The body of the coral, the polyp, deposits calcium carbonate about itself to form a protective case, or skeleton. Yearly ridges indicate the rate of growth, which can be 2.5 cm (1 in). At right is shown how the stony coral reproduces itself, by budding: a polyp bud develops inside the foot of the first coral and forms a new polyp. Eventually, a whole colony of stony corals is formed.

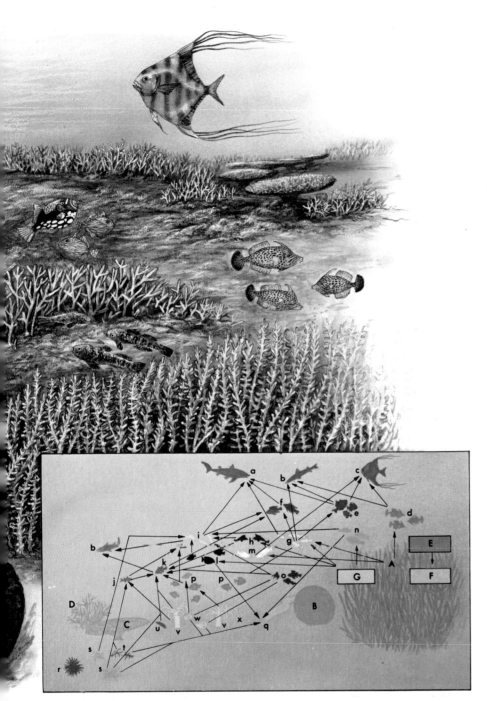

fishes (Pomacentridae) are among the most abundant and characteristic reef-dwellers. Widespread too are the wrasses (Labridae), parrot-fishes (Scaridae), and sweetlips or grunts (Pomadasyidae).

Submarine cliffs

This habitat is common in the turbulent water around coasts and islands, below the lowest tide on the shore, down to depths of several hundred metres (or yards). Increasing depth is accompanied by a fading of the light—which also changes in hue—and of the surge from wind-blown waves.

In shallow water, large brown algal seaweeds flourish on the rocky surface. In cold seas, forests of kelp (species of *Laminaria*) grow densely and provide cover for numerous invertebrates and inshore fish species, including the wrasses (of the family Labridae), sea scorpions (Cottidae), butterfishes (Pholididae), and sea-bream (Sparidae). Red algae can extend into deeper water, being able to make better use of the low light available.

At all depths, the rock may be swept by tidal currents. In strong currents, diverse invertebrates colonize every available fragment of the rock surface, usually settling and growing over one another to form several layers. Most of the animals live by filtering the water as it sweeps past. Food and oxygen are plentiful, and competition for space becomes the major factor limiting populations.

The rock-dweller's way of life consists of growing firmly attached to the piece of substrate which it managed to settle on as a juvenile, crowding out its neighbours if possible, filtering food particles and dissolved oxygen from the water, and casting waste products and offspring or eggs and sperm into the flood. Sponges, hydroids, soft corals, gorgonians, anemones, bryozoans, fan worms, barnacles, and sea squirts, sometimes represented by large numbers of species, all live in this manner on submarine cliffs and rocky reefs.

Other animals are mobile and can graze or prey upon the sessile, attached creatures. Sea urchins (of the family Echinidae) trundle over the rock face on their thousands of hydraulic-tube feet, nibbling at the undergrowth organisms with their large five-jawed mouths. The gastropods are equipped with a broad, gripping foot, and a long toothed tongue. Top-shells (Trochidae) glide over algal fronds, rasping off small pieces. The European cowries (species of *Trivia*) slit open the cells of algae, sponges, and sea squirts, and suck up the contents. Colourful nudibranch sea slugs are specialized predators of the undergrowth organisms and may be found living on particular species. At night, lobsters and crabs move over the rock, scavenging and nibbling at a variety of foods.

The shore and intertidal zones

Where the water meets the land, life is governed by the movements of tides and waves against rock, sand, and mud. This shore habitat experiences a rhythmic rise and fall of tides on the sloping land. Most shores are covered and exposed by sea water twice every twenty-four hours or so, to an extent depending upon time and location. Ceaseless wave activity complicates the process, and a pattern of varying conditions is established up the shore, allowing different kinds of animals and plants to populate each level.

Tides and waves

The main cause of tides is the force of the moon's gravity acting on the

A coral-reef community and its food web: *(a)* shark, *(b)* barracuda, *(c)* threadfish, *(d)* filefish, *(e)* clown triggerfish, *(f)* grouper, *(g)* pufferfish, *(h)* blenny, *(i)* bluestriped snapper and smaller carangids, *(j)* goatfish, *(k)* six-line grouper, *(l)* guinea-hen wrasse, *(m)* parrotfish, *(n)* goby, *(o)* harlequin sweetlips, *(p)* pearl-scale butterflyfish, *(q)* diamond-back moray eel, *(r)* sea urchin, *(s)* starfish, *(t)* prawn, *(u)* sea cucumber, *(v)* anemone, *(w)* sponge crab, *(x)* cowry shell. The corals shown here are: *(A)* finger coral, *(B)* brain coral, *(C)* platform coral, *(D)* staghorn coral. Within the food web, *(E)* phytoplankton, *(F)* zooplankton, and *(G)* benthic algae, play a vital rôle.

earth. It affects the liquid sea much more than the solid land, producing a bulge of waters on the earth's side towards the moon, with a balancing bulge on the opposite side. About every day, the earth turns once beneath the moon, and a given place on earth passes through both bulges. At each bulge, the local water level rises and falls, generating a high (flood) tide and a low (ebb) tide. The total duration of these two cycles is slightly longer than a day, since the moon is rotating around the earth in the same direction, and its local effects are repeated only if the earth has made more than a complete turn.

The sun exerts a similar but weaker force on the earth. This adds to the moon's influences when all three bodies are in line with each other, at the times of the new and the full moon, resulting in the largest (spring) tides. Yet at mid-phases of the moon, the two forces act along different lines, yielding the smallest (neap) tides. Thus, as the moon rotates around the earth once every month, a cyclical change occurs in the size of the daily tides. There are some further, related although less important, contributions to the rhythm of tides, varying in the course of the month and year.

This basic regularity is distorted by the uneven character of the oceans. The heights and timing of tides depend greatly on the shapes and orientations of the coastline and sea bed. In a nearly enclosed region like the Mediterranean, the basins are such that very little vertical tidal movement occurs. By contrast, the Bay of Fundy in Canada has a funnelling combination of shores and shallow bottom, producing a daily change in water level of over 14 m (46 ft). The tidal range elsewhere is normally 5–10 m (15–35 ft).

Waves are more variable, and usually more powerful, than tides. Their frequency, speed, and size are determined by the wind conditions, the distance over which they can build up, and the shape of the nearest shore or sea bed. Consistent weather patterns mean that a coast is subjected routinely to a particular kind of wave action. And shores may be classified according to degrees of exposure or shelter. The most wave-exposed shores consist of bare cliffs, rocky slopes, or surf-swept sand. With increasing shelter, there is an accumulation of small stones, sandy pockets, silt, and organic detritus.

The rocky shore

A shore of rock and boulders is inhabited by numerous plants and animals which attach themselves permanently, to be covered periodically by the tides and struck in turn by the waves, sun, and rain. Their firm grip is essential, as death awaits those that lose it. Species vary in susceptibility to damage from the sea and from materials carried shoreward. Many organisms have developed structures or behaviour patterns for survival in extreme shore conditions. Seaweeds, barnacles, limpets, winkles, and fishes all have specially adapted representatives which make optimum use of this demanding environment. There are also marked differences between communities on exposed and on sheltered shores.

A zoned distribution of organisms is most apparent on steeply sloping shores. Above the reach of the tides, the land is swept by storm waves and salt spray, or is open to desiccation. This "splash zone" is one of the hardest to colonize, and its characteristic occupants are limited to lichens, isopod crustaceans, and a few salt-tolerant land plants.

Just below the highest tide level, the shore is inundated by daily tides—but only during two parts of the month, around the spring tides. In this "upper shore zone", residents are subjected alternately to long dry intervals and to considerable immersion in salt water. Black lichens, some species of winkles, and barnacles are particularly content with such a régime.

The "middle shore zone", between high- and low-water levels during the neap tides, is covered and uncovered twice each day in most regions. When the tide recedes, many organisms become inactive. Barnacles, abundant here, clamp their valve plates together when exposed, to retain some of the water in which they lie. Small winkles have a hinged plate which can be sealed to prevent water loss. The thick skin of certain brown seaweeds (such as *Pelvetia canaliculata*) slows down evaporation and reduces penetration by harmful components of sunlight. As the tide falls, other organisms follow it down or move into rock pools. At high water, they return to join the more permanent inhabitants, sharing the rewards of life in this environment: plentiful food, light, and oxygen, as well as a restricted number of species competing for space.

Beneath the lowest neap tides is the "lower shore zone", exposed daily during only the spring-tide parts of the month. Its conditions resemble those of the shallow sea, and many species can move thus far onto the land. Large brown and red algae, the familiar seaweeds, form a dense cover on the least wave-swept rocks and influence the abundance of various animals. At low water, delicate creatures of the sea bed are often accessible, including sea squirts, anemones, crabs, and polychaete worms.

Life in a tidal pool

As the tide drains away from the rocky shore's uneven surface, pools of salt water remain, isolated from the sea until the tide rises to their zone again. This period ranges from minutes to hours in the middle zone, and to several days in the upper zone, whilst splash-zone pools may be isolated for weeks without receiving replenishment by waves, spray, or rain.

By living in a shore pool, organisms avoid desiccation at low water, a major problem of habitation between the tide levels. But other risks arise, since the pool is affected by conditions of climate during its exposure to the air. On tropical shores, high air temperature and intense radiation from the sun prevent the development of the rich and colourful pool communities which make temperate-coast pools so fascinating. Even in temperate pools, there are wide fluctuations of the water's warmth, oxygen, carbon dioxide, acidity, and salinity during the tidal cycle.

The smaller a pool is, and the higher it lies on the shore, the more variable are its conditions. It may even evaporate to salt crystals or be full of rain water for days. It will be colonized sporadically by diverse algae and invertebrates—such as the green filamentous alga (species of *Enteromorpha*) and small crustaceans—which can benefit from the brief wet periods. Lower shore pools are occupied by distinct species, unable to tolerate much if any emersion from water. Fine red seaweeds, and delicate anemones such as *Anemonia sulcata* in Europe, have no means of reducing water loss or of supporting their own mass, if taken out of water. The largest and deepest of these pools will, indeed, contain many animals and plants that normally inhabit the subtidal zone.

The vertical zonation of the organisms on a cliff face stretches from above the splash zone of the highest tides, where the hardy land lichens live, down to the low-water level, where barnacles and dahlia anemones are found. Beneath the low-water level, different seaweeds and invertebrates find their niche. As the tide floods, food is carried in to the animals on the cliff face, and desiccated organisms can replace moisture that they have lost. Predators can now get at food on the cliff face that was previously out of reach.

(Inset) Diatomic phytoplankton (a); benthic plankton: (b) crab, and (c) starfish, larvae; pelagic plankton: (d) species of *Calanus*.

The organisms shown in the main illustration are: (a) land lichen, (b) periwinkle, (c) sea lichen, (d) limpet, (e) barnacle, (f) seaweed (species of *Fucus*), (g) shore crab, (h) sea squirt, (i) blue mussel, (j) dahlia anemone, (k) oarweed, (l) sea cucumber, (m) edible crab, (n) painted top snail, (o) plumose anemone, (p) sea urchin, (q) horn coral, (r) starfish, (s) finger coral, (t) wrasse, (u) shanny, (v) mullet, (w) bass, (x) jellyfish.

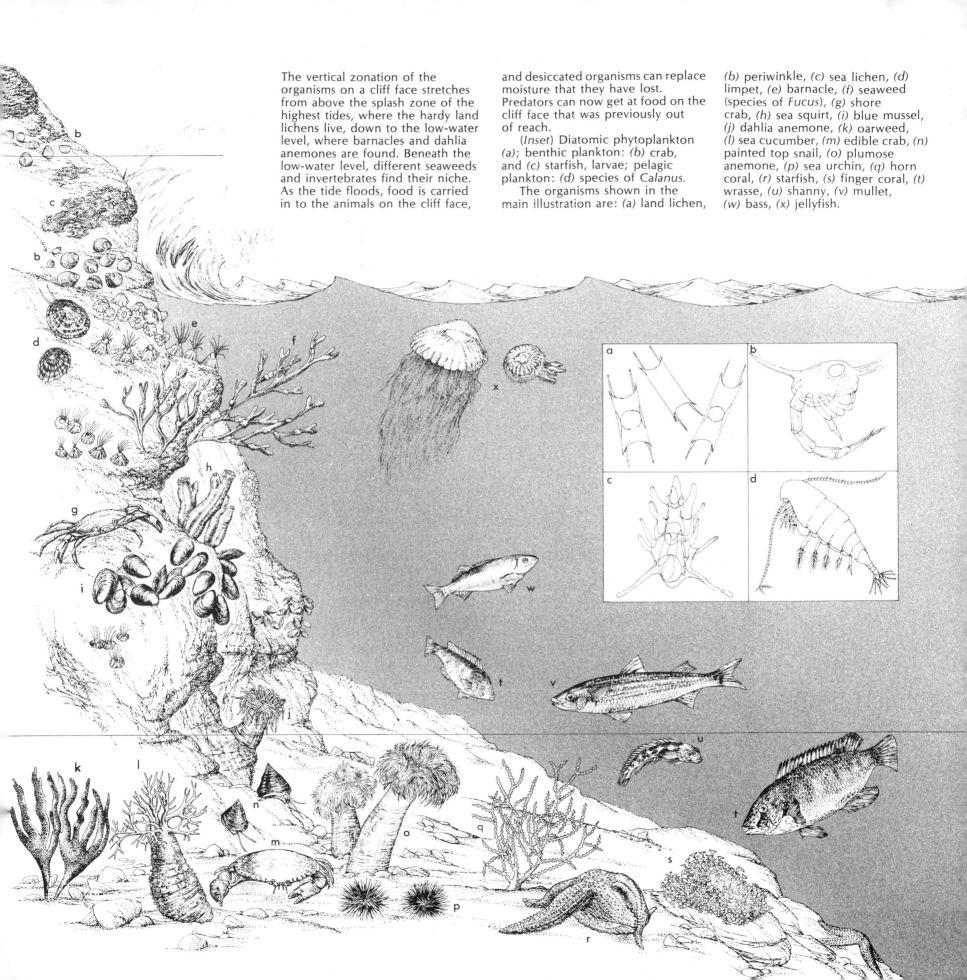

The permanent rock pool at left is flooded twice daily and holds many organisms (visible are green algae). At right is a permanent pool at ebb, with *(a)* kelp, *(b)* barnacle, *(c)* top shell, *(d)* limpet, *(e)* green algae, *(f)* Jaera, *(g)* prawn, *(h)* parasitic anemone on hermit crab, *(i)* goby, *(j)* blenny, *(k)* anemone, *(l)* seaweed, *(m)* mussel. The pool is the first shown on the inset. Organisms in the upper pools must be progressively hardier to survive desiccation and extreme conditions. The graph shows how conditions vary in a permanent pool during a full day. The light background indicates that the pool is isolated; the dark, flooded. The colours represent: temperature in °C (blue), oxygen in mg/litre (yellow), pH (red), carbon dioxide in mg/litre (solid black). Salinity (broken black) varies little, as the water is refilled twice daily. The horizontal axis shows the time, and the periods of light and darkness.

Life in sand and mud

Rocks on a shore are continuously eroded by the impact of the sea. Offshore, where the water churns less violently, sand and silt accumulate, and particles fall out of suspension to form a sediment. The area covered by underwater rock is small in comparison to that of sand, silt, and sediment on the continental shelves and the deep-sea bed.

On the shore itself, wherever drowned valleys, bays, and other coastal configurations provide shelter from the waves, particles are deposited, and their size is proportional to that of the water movement. The gradation from storm surf to gentle backwater produces a range of sediments, from coarse clean sand of great mobility on a steep and rapidly draining beach, through muddy sands, to the sloppy black ooze of an almost isolated mud flat.

Unlike the rock-dwellers firmly attached to stone, organisms in sand and mud burrow beneath the surface, seeking protection from predators and—for intertidal animals—from the extremes of desiccation and inundation. Surf-swept sand supports little life, because of the constant movement and abrasion by its coarse particles. But, apart from the most exposed beaches, a few specialists manage to thrive in sand, chiefly on the lower shore with slow drainage. As the sand is cleaned of organic debris by the waves, food must be collected from the overlying water. Here, one finds many burrowing bivalve molluscs, tellins (of the family Tellinidae), and wedge shells (Donacidae). Their delicate shells are shaped with keel-like anterior edges for traction

through sand. Razor shells (Solenidae) burrow so rapidly when alarmed that a jet of water is squirted back into the air. These bivalves feed by extending long siphon tubes up to the sand surface, drawing in water to filter large volumes for nutrients and oxygen.

On more sheltered beaches, the sand is finer and fairly stable, with organic detritus. Heart urchins and sand dollars thrive, pushing through the upper sand and leaving a ploughed wake, while eating any detritus. Other echinoderms, the starfishes, churn quickly on tubular feet and spines, preying on live amphipods, snails, and bivalves. The necklace shell (species of *Natica*) also feeds voraciously on buried bivalves, drilling a circular hole in the victim's shell and cutting out its flesh with a long toothed tongue.

Underwater meadows of sea grass (species of *Zostera*, *Posidinia*, and others) occur in the shallows of sand and mud. In sheltered waters, organic material settles onto the bottom along with fine silt and clay. Also contributing to this layer are rotting seaweed, dead animals, marsh plants, and overhanging trees. Over five per cent of the mud's weight may be detritus, a rich source of food for the local fauna.

Enormous populations of bacteria live in the mud and digest these materials. Their respiration reduces oxygen levels in the sediment and the slow water above it. So they live anaerobically, producing hydrogen sulphide, which converts ferric oxide in the mud to black ferric sulphide.

The great mass of organisms supported by a mud flat includes algae, worms, bivalves, snails, shrimps, and tunicates. They must over-

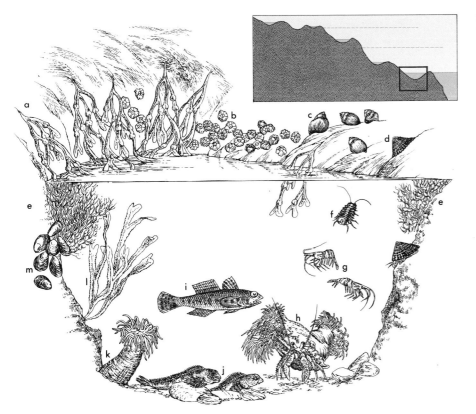

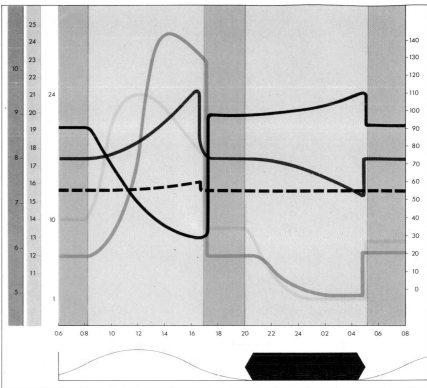

come shortage of oxygen, clogging by particles, fluctuations of temperature and salinity, and pressures from predation. At low water, the muddy shores are visited by birds and land mammals, such as gulls, waders, and fishermen for cockles. When the tide floods again over the flat, dogfishes, skate, rays, flatfishes, mullet, crabs, and shrimps move from below the shore to feed on the productive invertebrate occupants.

Estuary survival

Where freshwater streams and rivers flow from the land into the sea, a region of mingling and change is formed. This estuary is a habitat characterized by muddy channels, sand banks, bleak marshes, and wooded borders, with frequent variations of warmth and salt in the water. Salinity ranges from 1 to 35 parts per thousand, between the inflowing streams and the full sea water. The salinity pattern is complicated throughout the estuary, due to differences in the strength of river flow, in the heights of tides, and in the retention of water by sediments.

Most estuarine animals have evolved from the sea rather than from freshwater habitats, and have needed to overcome the problems of reduced and varying salinity. Some can tolerate extremes of salt concentration by raising or decreasing the salinity of their body fluids with that of the surrounding water. Others control their exposure to water of low salinity: for example, mussels and barnacles close their shells and valves tightly, and pump water through only when flooded by tides of high salinity. Certain marine worms and bivalves live far

upstream in an estuary, burrowing into the mud where the water remains salty during low tides, partly because the sea water flows beneath the less dense stream water.

Extremes of temperature are also encountered in the estuary. A mud flat in winter may cool the incoming tidal water almost to freezing, whilst in summer, the dark mud absorbs maximum sunlight and becomes dangerously hot. Patterns of siltation and sediment composition, too, are produced by the mixing of river and tidal currents with dissimilar contents.

Abundant food enters such environments in the rivers and tides, to be deposited as detritus in the mud at sheltered places. Species able to live in the estuary are, therefore, often present in large numbers. A small bivalve mollusc (Scrobicularia plana) may occur in densities of 3,000 per square metre (280 per square foot), and a tiny snail (Hydrobia ulvae) may be seven times as common in those places. Thus, the vast quantities of dead organic material which accumulate are converted by humble invertebrates into mollusc, crustacean, or polychaete flesh. This is eaten in turn by thousands of mullet, flounder, dogfishes, crabs, shrimps, and other animals, which swim into the estuary with the rising tide, followed by flocks of birds that paddle and sift at the edge of outgoing waters.

The salt marsh and swamp

Rich sediments are deposited where the shore is sheltered from wave action and tidal currents, making the land grow slowly seawards. Specially adapted plants are among the first colonizers of this new wet

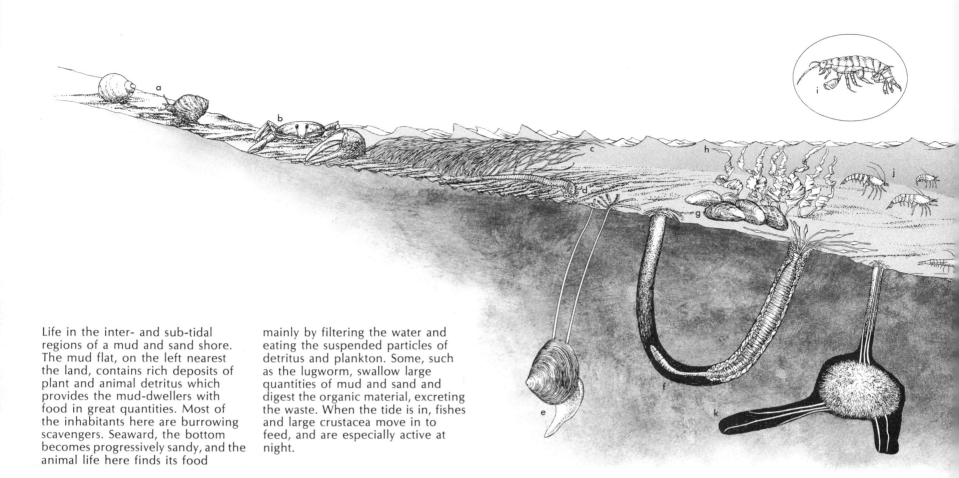

Life in the inter- and sub-tidal regions of a mud and sand shore. The mud flat, on the left nearest the land, contains rich deposits of plant and animal detritus which provides the mud-dwellers with food in great quantities. Most of the inhabitants here are burrowing scavengers. Seaward, the bottom becomes progressively sandy, and the animal life here finds its food mainly by filtering the water and eating the suspended particles of detritus and plankton. Some, such as the lugworm, swallow large quantities of mud and sand and digest the organic material, excreting the waste. When the tide is in, fishes and large crustacea move in to feed, and are especially active at night.

terrain. Typical examples are the salt-marsh growths along temperate coastlines, and mangrove trees on calm tropical shores. Such dense stands of rooted vegetation stabilize the deposited mud, trapping further sediment and organic debris. Marsh and swamp animals are provided with food and ideal moist cover.

Thriving in the undergrowth are fiddler, hermit, marsh, and mangrove crabs, as well as marsh snails and ghost shrimps. Many of these creatures can live out of water for much of the time, obtaining oxygen from the air through gills which are modified as primitive lung-like structures. The mangrove tree offers its leaves as food for crabs, and its branches as a home for the planktonic larvae of oysters, mussels, barnacles, and sea squirts, which are carried in on the tide and are preyed upon by various crabs and snails. This rich ecosystem nourishes other predators such as fishes, birds, reptiles, and land animals.

Freshwater habitats

Bodies and courses of fresh water occupy a meagre fraction of the world's land area and contain few of its total water resources. But they are of sufficient influence, utility, and grandeur to be major features of most types of landscape. As habitats, they differ widely on a global scale, due in particular to the climatic variations of temperature and rainfall. These factors govern the quantity and nature of the surface's fresh water. Within each mass of water, the temperature changes seasonally at a specific rate, between certain maximum and minimum values. This range is tolerated by distinctive kinds of living organism, and such adaptation largely determines the distribution of plants and animals.

The tropical regions, lying between the Tropic of Cancer (latitude 23°N) and that of Capricorn (23°S), are characterized all year round by relatively high temperatures and constant numbers of daylight hours. These stable, warm conditions promote biological growth and development, with a notable diversity of fauna and flora. About eight thousand species of freshwater fishes are known, and over thirteen hundred of them occur in the hot Amazon river system alone, compared to less than two hundred in the whole of Europe.

The amount of rainfall varies greatly in the tropics. It is highest within the equatorial belts of the main land regions. Over 150 cm (60 in) may fall, more or less continually, throughout the year. The abundant water, sunlight, and warmth encourage a luxuriant cover of jungle. Huge permanent rivers traverse the equatorial rain forests, whose overhanging canopy is mirrored by dark pools. The multi-layered vegetation is very important in regulating the flow of water off the land, and in creating aquatic habitats.

Away from the equator, rainfall decreases and the steamy forest is replaced by woodland and grasslands. Rainy and dry seasons occur: torrential downpours lead to flooding and erosion, followed by long droughts that evaporate swamps and stifle rivers. Seasonal variations in climate increase with the latitude, because of the sun's apparent movement across the equator twice each year, bringing cold winters and

A typical community in a mud and sand habitat would consist of: (a) *Hydrobia* snail, (b) fiddler crab, (c) green algae, (d) ragworm, (e) peppery furrow shell, (f) lugworm, (g) mussel, (h) oarweed, (i) sand hopper, (j) sand shrimp,

(k) sea potato, (l) cockle, (m) pod razor, or razor clam, (n) ghost shrimp, (o) flounder, (p) *Fucus* seaweed, (q) tellin bivalve, (r) starfish, (s) hermit crab with parasitic anemone, (t) sand dollar, (u) dog-fish.

warm or hot summers to the temperate zones. Coastal regions are always more uniform in climate than are central continental regions, since the ocean is warmed and cooled more slowly than the air or land.

Animal and plant life in the fresh water of temperate zones is adjusted to such seasonal patterns in many ways. Reproductive cycles, growth of offspring, and feeding habits have evolved to take advantage of the abundant food in spring and summer. The winter cold is survived by hibernating, overwintering as seed or eggs, or contracting the whole life cycle into the warm months of the year.

Life in rivers and streams

Differences between running waters may result from latitude, climate, altitude, sources of supply, local geology, degrees of shading and of shelter from wind, riparian vegetation, and the influences of animals—among them man. Conditions also change along the length of a river or stream. From source to mouth, the decrease in altitude and in the slope of the stream bed causes progressive trends in water temperature, speed of flow, levels of dissolved oxygen and inorganic salts, and in the composition of bottom substrates. This gradient produces a succession of diverse plants and animals from the upland stream to the lowland river.

A temperate river

At its source on a hill or mountainside where rainfall is high, a river's tributary streams pour turbulently down a narrow rocky bed. The water is clear and cold, generally below 10°C (50°F) even in summer, and dissolved oxygen is always plentiful. Acidity and mineral content depend upon the local climate and geology.

To survive in these rushing headwaters, an organism must avoid being swept away. Plant life is limited to mosses, liverworts, and algae which attach firmly and closely to the bedrock. They are well adapted in structure, with strong stems and holdfasts. Equally capable animals are the broad-footed limpets (of the family Ancylidae) and flatworms such as *Crenobia alpina*. Mayfly nymphs also have flattened bodies, and the cases of caddis worms (species of *Tremona*) in this habitat are limpet-shaped. Some free-living caddis worms, and the larval black flies (of the family Simuliidae), use hooks for attachment. Certain fly larvae even produce silk from large salivary glands. The larva hooks itself to a tangled mat which is fixed on a current-swept stone. Then it ties a silken safety-line to the mat and, if dislodged, can climb back along the thread, as fallen spiders do.

Fishes in these swift streams are the trout, salmon parr, and bullheads. The first two have streamlined oval bodies tapering towards the tails. They are typical cold-water fishes, able to feed and remain active, with a high basal metabolism, even in icy water. They need large amounts of oxygen throughout life, from egg development in a well-aerated gravel "nest" to busy adulthood. Much energy is spent in fighting the current, and trout are observed largely among the eddies behind boulders or under the banks. The bullhead (*Cottus gobio*) looks like a sluggish fish but has its own technique for coping with fast water. It can wriggle under stones or flatten against the bottom, and it gets food by darting briefly out of shelter.

The middle reaches

As the small streams descend to join in wider and deeper courses, the water flows rapidly over boulders and loose stones, with little backwaters having patches of gravel and coarse sand. The water is slightly warmer now, although rarely above 15°C (59°F), and is still rich in oxygen. Algae and mosses continue to be the main plants, but occasionally higher plants occur in the backwaters—such as the milfoil (species of *Myriophyllum*), starwort (*Callitriche*), and river crowfoot (*Ranunculus fluitans*). The latter have tough, flexible stems, finely divided leaves, and many adventitious roots binding the loose gravel.

To avoid the current, fishes and invertebrates make use of boundary layers and patches of dead water against rocks. Small stones and sand are employed by caddis worms to construct well-ballasted cases. The zebra mussel (*Dreissena polymorpha*) thrives in slower backwaters in this region of the river, unlike other freshwater bivalves, probably because it retains its attachment threads (byssus) into adult life. Taking food which the running water carries past is an efficient method of saving energy and has been adopted by various species through evolution.

The fishes characterizing this zone in northern Europe are the grayling (*Thymallus thymallus*), minnow (*Phoxinus phoxinus*), dace (*Leuciscus leuciscus*), and stone loach (*Noemacheilus barbatulus*). The loach's flattened head and cylindrical trunk reflect its life-style, keeping near the bottom and darting between stones. The other fishes are all active and muscular species, able to stay in position by swimming against the current.

When the river comes down from the hills, its slope becomes slighter and its current decreases. Gravel and sand are deposited, fairly stable and covering much of the bed. Water turbidity from suspended organic detritus and fine minerals is lowered. Here, the water temperatures are higher, usually above 15°C (59°F) in summer. During this season, concentrations of dissolved oxygen may fall, for the first time in the course of the river. This is due to the reduced turbulence and aeration, the lower solubility of the gas in warm water, and the increase in bacteria decomposing detritus while they respire.

With the slower currents, and finer sediments into which roots can grow, higher plants begin to dominate the vegetation. They spread across the river bed and provide the community with food, oxygen, and stable silt. Species vary between the acid non-calcareous rivers, where European examples include *Potamogeton polygonifolius*, *P. natans*, and *P. alpinus*, and the calcium-rich rivers which contain *Sparganium simplex*, *Potamogeton perfoliatus*, *Sagittaria sagittifolia*, and *Hippurus vulgaris*.

Thriving on the rich plant growth are diverse bottom-living invertebrates, such as oligochaetes (worms), isopods, amphipods, insect larvae, hydra, and snails on the leaves and stems. Fishes in this part of the river are deep-bodied and use broad flexible fins to move leisurely through the vegetation. Barbel (*Barbus barbus*) and chub (*Leuciscus cephalus*) are the main species. Roach (*Rutilus rutilus*), rudd (*Scardinius erythrophthalmus*), and the predatory perch (*Perca fluviatilis*), pike (*Esox lucius*), and eel (*Anguilla anguilla*) may be common.

The lowland river

Along the last section of the river, it flows sluggishly over a muddy bottom rich in organic debris. The water may be murky with a heavy load of fine silt and detritus, reducing light penetration. Here, the channel is wider, meandering through deep pools and shallow shoals. In summer, the water may become very warm, usually over 20°C (68°F), and oxygen concentration then diminishes markedly towards the bottom.

Now the plentiful phytoplankton makes an important contribution to photosynthetic production. Microscopic diatoms (single-celled algae) may be the chief plants, particularly in larger rivers, and show great fluctuations in quantity as the light, turbidity, temperature, discharge, and water chemicals change during the year. Rooted higher plants grow densely in this zone, although restricted by turbidity and depth to the shallower margins and shoals. Common emergent species include *Phragmites communis*, *Glyceria* varieties, and *Scirpus lacustris*.

Invertebrates are populous in the fine sands, silt, and mud mixtures. Among the abundant insect larvae can be found burrowing mayflies (species of *Ephemera*), dragonfly larvae (*Aeshna*), and chironomid midge larvae in self-made tubes. Tubifex worms and small bivalves (*Sphaerium*) may be frequent in the finer, de-oxygenated muds. Fish species which are able to tolerate the low levels of dissolved oxygen feed upon the invertebrates as well as detritus. Bream (*Abramis brama*) and carp (*Cyprinus carpio*) are main instances, with chub, dace, eel, tench (*Tinca tinca*), and others.

Waters of the equatorial rain forest

For many months of the year, the equatorial belts of the principal land masses are inundated by rain. In the Amazon basin, for example, over 300 cm (120 in) of rain fall annually. The wettest period is between May and July to the north of the equator, and between November and January to its south. Thus, the large rivers draining the central tropics experience a double peak of flooding. Rivers spread over huge areas of the rain-forest territory at such times. The Amazon rises by 15 m (50 ft) in some places, whilst the Zaire overflows its normal course in a belt of forest and woodland 75 km (50 miles) wide.

The Amazon and the Zaire are the world's largest river systems, draining the South American and the African tropics respectively. The Amazon and its tributaries drain 6.5 million square kilometres (2.5 million square miles) from the Guyanan highlands in the north to the Matto Grosso in the south, extending 6,000 km (nearly 4,000 miles) from the Andes in the west to the Atlantic in the east. The Zaire catchment area stretches for 1,500 km (1,000 miles), draining over 3.5 million square kilometres (1.4 million square miles), with tributaries into Angola, Zimbabwe, Cameroun, and Central Africa.

These systems are integrated with the dense jungle which covers much of the river basins—eighty per cent in the Amazon and thirty-four per cent in the Zaire. The resulting environments, among the most spectacular and productive on earth, fulfill a large part of the planet's oxygen requirements, and are major elements of its hydrologic cycle which regulates the movement of fresh water. They create suitable conditions for an incredible variety of wildlife. The forest canopy tends to prevent the energy of sunlight and wind from reaching the river water, but also provides fallen plant debris, pollen, flowers, fruit, leaves, insects, and spiders, which serve as food and alter the water chemistry, playing a basic role in the life of the river.

Some of the teeming wildlife in a southeast Asian mangrove swamp: (a) Indian kingfisher, (b) crocodile, (c) mangrove snake, (d) archerfish, (e) tigerfish, (f) Asian pufferfish, (g) scatfish, (h) mudskipper, (i) moonfish. Buried in the mud are countless bivalves, while snails and crabs live in great number around the roots of the tree. The root system of the red mangrove is shown on the right. The red mangrove's seeds germinate on the branch, before falling into the mud, where they quickly become established.

The mangrove swamps of the world are found in muddy estuarine flats of the tropics and subtropics. The water there is brackish, and the aquatic life is adapted to survive fluctuations in salinity. The swamps are dominated by different species of mangrove trees, whose roots provide shelter for the aquatic life at the same time as they trap detritus, sand, and mud in a land-building process that gradually extends the land area into the sea.

(Inset) A section through a southeast Asian mangrove swamp (a) shows the zonation of the species of mangrove tree. Pioneer mangroves (species of Sonneratia) occupy the outside, seaward, zone to the right. Behind them grow stands of red mangrove (Rhizophora). Sonneratia have numerous aerial roots by which they breathe and from which lateral roots form (c). Nearest dry land are found Brugueira mangrove trees, with their roots buried in the mud, leaving only "knees" visible above the water (b).

The central river

The open water of the main river and of its large tributaries is a remarkably stable habitat. Temperature in the main Amazon varies only between 28° and 30°C (82° and 86°F) throughout the year. A pelagic (upper-layer) community of plant and animal plankton is present, with great shoals of planktivorous fishes such as the Zaire's small clupeids (species of *Microthrissa* and others), characoids *(Clupetersius),* and cyprinids *(Barbus).* There are also predatory fish-eaters, such as *Hydrocynus vittatus,* and the big shoaling characoids and cyprinids, which feed on stranded aerial insects.

The river water is deep and turbid, and the bottom is composed of mud, sand, and—depending on the current—some rock, often with masses of waterlogged branches and tree stumps. But no light reaches the bottom to allow plant production. The community consists of burrowing and crawling insect larvae that feed upon detritus and are eaten in turn by bottom-living fishes, many of which have nocturnal habits and dwell in holes or amongst tree debris. Examples from the river Zaire include mormyrids, siluroids, citharinids (such as species of *Distichodus* and *Citharinia*), cyprinids (such as *Labes*), and cichlids (such as *Tylochromis*).

The river margins

Shores, side-creeks, oxbows, pools, and sandbanks, forming the margins of the major channels, are the richest areas of these vast rainforest river systems. In their shallow waters, the most diverse and active community is encountered. The current is slight, and water temperatures remain high, between 25° and 35°C (77° and 95°F). Stretches open to the sun and wind alternate with forested banks and islands which provide dense shade. Usually the water is just a few metres (or yards) deep, with a few pools and channels reaching 10 m (33 ft).

The water is clear enough for submerged plants (such as species of *Echinodorus*) to grow on the bottom, offering shelter and food. Fish and invertebrate populations are abundantly nourished by bottom-living insects, snails, and worms, as well as by plant material and organic detritus. The uneven physical environment ensures protection from the main current and from predatory fishes, birds, and land animals.

Both permanent and transitory fishes are plentiful here. Many of the species found in other equatorial-forest waters spend some time in these marginal habitats. Common varieties are the tetras (of the family Characidae), pencilfishes (Hemiodontidae), armoured catfishes (Callichthyidae), and cichlids such as the discus and freshwater angelfish.

Rain-forest pools

Within the rain forest, away from the river bank, large swampy pools remain when the floods subside. They provide an extreme type of habitat for animals able to tolerate the conditions. Sunlight and wind are effectively shut out by the dense vegetation. The water is normally only a few metres (or yards) deep, and is choked with quantities of fallen, decomposing plant debris.

This water is stained dark brown by organic acids from the rotting plant material (acidity ranges around 4–5 in pH). The oxygen content tends to be very low, depending upon how much water is mixed by breezes. The temperature in a pool may rise above 30°C (86°F). There is little plankton and virtually no aquatic vegetation. But the pool bottom

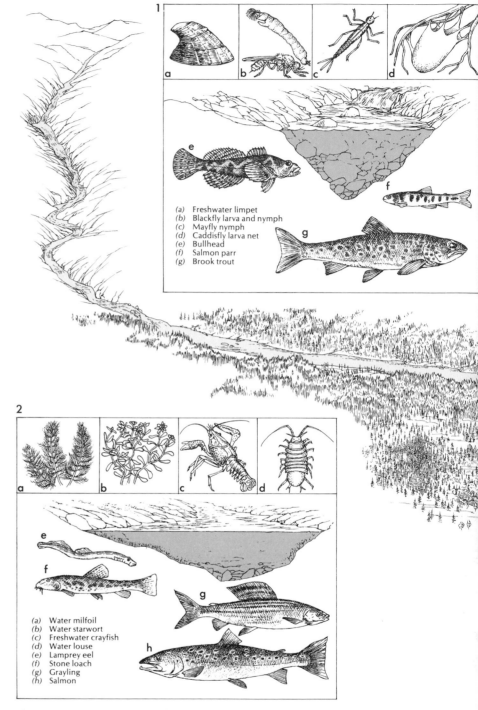

(a) Freshwater limpet
(b) Blackfly larva and nymph
(c) Mayfly nymph
(d) Caddisfly larva net
(e) Bullhead
(f) Salmon parr
(g) Brook trout

(a) Water milfoil
(b) Water starwort
(c) Freshwater crayfish
(d) Water louse
(e) Lamprey eel
(f) Stone loach
(g) Grayling
(h) Salmon

The temperate river typically begins high in the mountains and ends its course in the estuary, where its fresh water meets with the salt water of the ocean.

1 The upland stream is a cascading, oxygen-rich, and cold body of water. It tumbles downhill over an irregular, rocky bottom. The organisms that live here are adapted to the conditions, either being strong swimmers, like the trout and the bullhead, or being equipped with suckers or grippers to attach themselves to the rocks.

2 The upper middle reaches are deeper, and the flow is not so fast. The water is still well oxygenated, the bottom is a mixture of stones and rocks with patches of sand and gravel, and life is more varied.

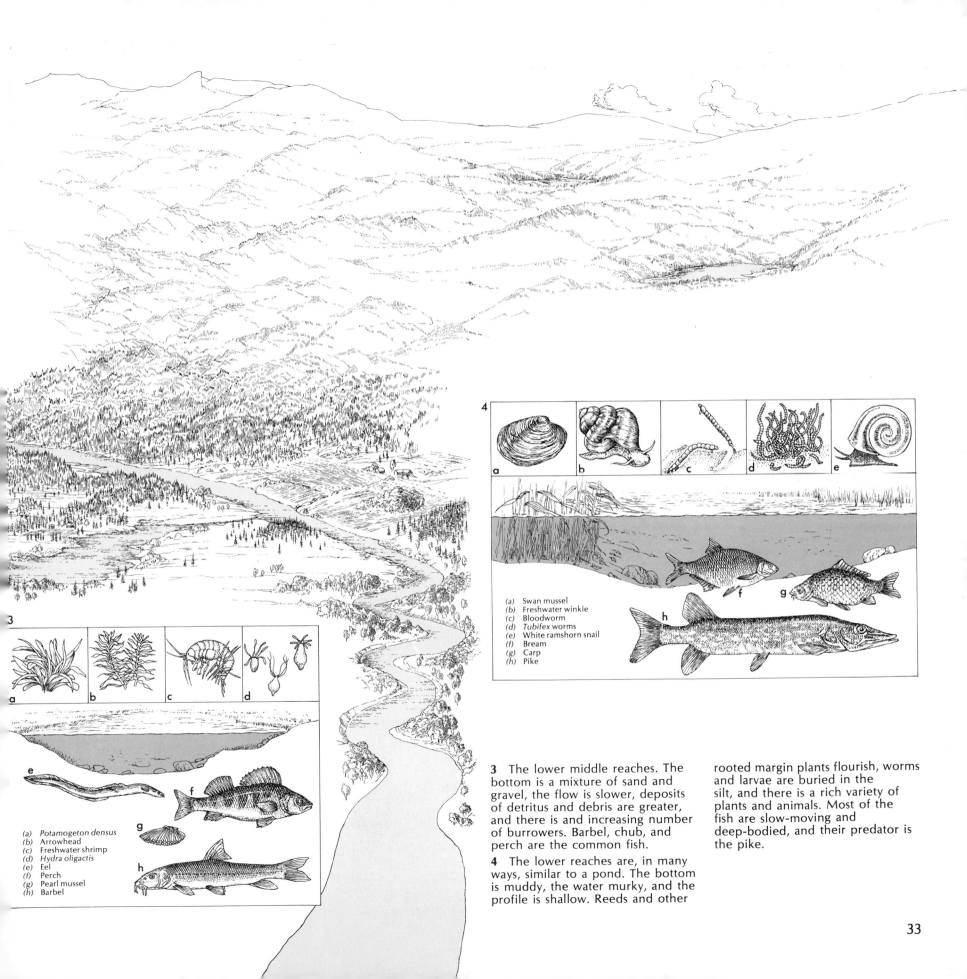

4
(a) Swan mussel
(b) Freshwater winkle
(c) Bloodworm
(d) *Tubifex* worms
(e) White ramshorn snail
(f) Bream
(g) Carp
(h) Pike

3
(a) *Potamogeton densus*
(b) Arrowhead
(c) Freshwater shrimp
(d) *Hydra oligactis*
(e) Eel
(f) Perch
(g) Pearl mussel
(h) Barbel

3 The lower middle reaches. The bottom is a mixture of sand and gravel, the flow is slower, deposits of detritus and debris are greater, and there is and increasing number of burrowers. Barbel, chub, and perch are the common fish.

4 The lower reaches are, in many ways, similar to a pond. The bottom is muddy, the water murky, and the profile is shallow. Reeds and other rooted margin plants flourish, worms and larvae are buried in the silt, and there is a rich variety of plants and animals. Most of the fish are slow-moving and deep-bodied, and their predator is the pike.

33

The river Amazon's drainage area, on
the map, is the largest in the world,
and the river discharges more water
than any other river. It has some two
hundred tributaries, examples from
the north (where the water is
clear and acidic) being the Napo,
Icá, Japurá, and Negro, and from the
south (where the water is filled with
silt) the Huallaga, Javari, Purús,
Madiera, Tapajós, and Xingu. At right
is a typical stream hurtling over a
fall in the rain forest.

The extraordinary lushness of the
rain forest results in a steady
supply of nutrients to the river.
Silt and sand easily gather to form
shoals behind which the fishes can
shelter, and the roots of trees and
bushes also give protection.
Illustrated at left are: *(a)* giant water
lily, *(b)* banded leporinus, *(c)* water
lettuce, *(d)* marbled hatchetfish,
(e) lemon tetra, *(f)* black-line tetra,
(g) angelfish, *(h)* mud plantain, *(i)*
fanwort, *(j)* Amazon sword plant, *(k)*
dwarf sword plant, *(l)* velvet cichlid,
(m) black Amazon sword plant, *(n)*
discus cichlid. The invertebrate life,
especially the crab life, is very rich
in the Amazon drainage area.

is organically rich, consisting of anoxic black mud and covered by leaf and tree fragments.

Food substances, plant litter, and particularly insects, fall in from the forest canopy or are brought in by small streams. The animals in this habitat must be adapted to using low levels of dissolved oxygen. Many of the fishes have accessory organs for respiration. Invertebrates also often benefit from the greater availability of oxygen above the air—water interface.

Tropical hill streams

Running through the densely forested hills of southeast Asia, and similar country in Africa and South America, are streams and small rivers which provide a distinct and dynamic habitat. In these tropical uplands, rainfall is very heavy and localized. Stream levels rise and fall rapidly as storms pass over the watershed. The water gushes down steep slopes to the gentler foothills or the low river plain.

Light and temperature are governed by the amount of forest on the stream banks. Generally the temperature varies little, from 24° to 28°C (75° to 82°F), although it may reach 33°C (91°F) in unshaded water where trees have been cleared. In a densely shaded area, aquatic plants are represented by species of *Cryptocoryne* in Asia, able to tolerate faint light, with healthy stands spreading over deposits of sand and gravel.

The stream community is largely dependent upon materials from the surrounding forest, including many insects and spiders. Variations in current have an important effect. Fast-flowing stretches with bare sand and rock alternate with backwaters and small pools where organic detritus settles on the bottom. Leaves and fallen debris, as well as tree roots and tumbled stones, accumulate to become food or shelter.

The pattern of feeding habits is comparable to that of other streams and rivers. Fish species in the upper rapid waters are nourished mainly by stranded aerial insects. Downstream, in slower currents and amongst increasing deposits of sediment and detritus, bottom-dwelling fishes feed on aquatic invertebrates and plant debris. Barbs, danios, minnows (family Cyprinidae), and loaches (Cobitidae) are common.

Seasonal rivers and tropical swamps

Outside the equatorial zone, although the rainfall becomes increasingly seasonal, it can inundate enormous areas of flat grassland. During the spring and summer, as days lengthen and temperatures soar, the water rises in river beds, backing up empty creeks and marginal channels, then spreading across the plains. This annual flood connects many pools and swamps with the main river. Their water is rich in mineral nutrients from organic matter, such as vegetation and animal droppings, which has been broken down during the low-water season.

Plentiful light and warmth create an explosive growth of plankton, algae, and bacteria, followed by ever greater numbers of insects and aquatic invertebrates—snails, crustaceans, and worms. Both rooted and floating species of aquatic plants are adapted to these conditions. They grow, flower, and produce seed during the season of high water, then die down as the flood subsides and the plain dries up.

When the water rises, many fishes swim up the river, to join others which are released from the permanent pools and swamps. Eggs are spawned, and ripen and hatch very quickly. The young fishes are pro-vided with optimal conditions of food and plant cover, resulting in rapid development. Once the water recedes, the pools and swamps are isolated. Some fishes escape to the main river channels, but the rest are stranded on the plain. Here the water stagnates, and only fishes able to risk deoxygenation or desiccation can survive through the dry season.

The African lungfish (species of *Protopterus*) can encapsulate itself in mucus beneath the mud, and is also able to wriggle overland between pools through the damp vegetation. Other fishes survive only as eggs, which are resistant to drought. In South America, many species, especially of catfishes (of the family Auchenipteridae), find damp shelter in cracks of tree stumps or in mud, when the savannah pools dry up. Some fishes have evolved additional respiratory methods using parts of the alimentary canal or the swim-bladder, to cope with the stagnant conditions. Avoiding predation is equally important for the fishes trapped in shrinking pools, and several species have developed stout spines, armoured skin, or subtle camouflage.

In the tropics, vast areas of swamps and pools persist throughout the year. They cover hundreds of thousands of square kilometres (or square miles) in Africa alone, with major consequences for ecology and human life. The swamp is a shallow habitat of still water dominated by dense aquatic vegetation. Its abundant moisture, sunlight, and warmth cause extremely rapid plant growth and decomposition all the year round.

Many swamps are fringed with plants standing above the water surface, blocking much of the sunlight and air movement. Papyrus (*Cyperus papyrus*) is the characteristic swamp plant of central and eastern tropical Africa, growing in mud which is continuously waterlogged, and propagating by large branched underground stems or "rhizomes". The rhizome network traps decomposing organic matter and silt, enabling the papyrus to extend out from lake shores on its own mat, floating above the bottom. Such islands of papyrus are common and, for instance in the Nile's Sudd swamp, grow large and stable enough to support fishermen and their huts.

The upper parts of the densely packed papyrus plants are kept growing by photosynthesis. When they die and become waterlogged, masses of submerged debris result, decomposing anaerobically in the warm oxygen-deficient water. Inside the papyrus stand, light is dim and there are few submerged algae or higher plants, so that production of oxygen remains very low. Instead, the water has high carbon-dioxide levels and some organic acids (causing an acidity of 6.0 to 6.5 in pH).

Even in these difficult conditions, the animal life may consist of ciliate protozoans, nematode and oligochaete worms, molluscs, insects, and crustaceans. Common fish species in African swamps include *Protopterus aethiopicus*, *Polypterus bichir*, *Clarias lazera*, and *Ctenopoma muriei*.

Away from the shore and papyrus swamps, distinct zones of vegetation may occupy the varying depths of water: submerged plants such as species of *Ceratophyllum*, *Potamogeton*, and *Utricularia*, and rooted plants with floating leaves, such as the water-lily and water-chestnut (species of *Nymphaea* and *Trapa*). Sunlight still penetrates the water in these zones, and they produce abundant oxygen by photosynthesis. Temperatures are high, around 26°C (80°F), and the acidity changes to about 8.5 in pH. The aquatic plants support a wealth of invertebrate fauna, and shelter large populations of young fishes from the predators in both air and water.

Life in lakes and ponds

Enclosed bodies of fresh water are formed in various natural ways—by geological faulting, glacial scouring, dissolution of limestone rocks, damming by landslides or wind-blown material, long-shore drift, plant growth, the activity of beavers, and so on—in addition to those made by man. Such lakes and ponds, due to their isolation and their range of sizes and types, tend to be relatively brief habitats on the scale of evolution, often with peculiar conditions and living communities.

At one extreme is the small shallow pond, with little water flowing through it. The bottom may be covered with rooted plants, or choked by fallen plant debris and filamentous algae, so that photosynthesis creates wide differences in the amounts of dissolved oxygen and nutrients. At the other extreme are large deep lakes, usually occurring in the V-shaped valleys of mountainous country. These lakes have steep sides and narrow marginal shallows, with more rock than sediment, thus discouraging rooted plants. The water is low in dissolved and suspended materials, so that transparency is high.

Despite such diversity, most bodies of standing water consist of three main regions, each occupied by typical animal and plant species: the open water, the littoral zone, and the bottom.

The open water

A lake usually includes a broad expanse of deep open water away from the shore. The surface waters are brightly lit and support phytoplankton, as well as a community of zooplankton which feed on this and on each other. The phytoplankton of ponds and lakes is exemplified by diatoms, blue-green and green algae, and photosynthesizing flagellates (the single-called organisms with whiplike appendages for locomotion or sensation). Seasonal "blooms", or "explosions", occur in many lakes, when the diatoms or the blue-green algae may reach 10–20 million cells per litre (1.8 pints).

These blooms result from changes in light, temperature, and nutrients, which interact with seasonal changes in the physiology of the different species. Similarly, zooplankton show bursts in population growth at different times of the year. They consist chiefly of rotifers (such as species of *Karatella*) and microscopic crustaceans (such as *Bosmina* and *Daphnia*).

The littoral zone

In the shallow, well-lit areas of lakes and ponds, higher plants—submerged, rooted, or floating—can flourish. These may extend over the entire bottom of a uniformly shallow lake. From the lake shore into deeper water, a succession of plant and animal species can be observed. This is also varied by fluctuations in water level, and by wave action near shores and shoals.

Along a typical lake fringe is emergent vegetation, dominated by rushes, sedges, and grasses. They remove mineral nutrients and water from the lake bottom through their long leaves and stems, while photosynthesizing and respiring with carbon dioxide and oxygen taken from the air. Their contribution of dead plant material to the lake detritus is important. Beyond this fringe, rooted plants with floating leaves often occur, such as water-lilies (species of *Nymphaea* and *Nuphar*) and pondweed (*Potamogeton*), in addition to free-floating plants such as the duckweed (*Lemna*) and water fern (*Azolla*). The surface leaves form a canopy, screening out sunlight, leading to reduced photosynthesis and to depletion of oxygen underwater.

The lower surfaces of leaves and roots support an interesting mini-community (sometimes known as an "Aufwuchs") of animals and algae. This includes a variety of snails (species of *Planorbis* and *Physa*), beetles (*Donacia* and *Gyrinus*), and other insects that attach their eggs to the leaves. Breeding and nest-building fishes, for example the sunfishes (family Centrarchidae) in North America, are present too.

Farther from the shore, in a zone of submerged vegetation, the plants have long flexuous leaves, or are bushy with fine branched leaves. Pondweed (species of *Potamogeton*), hornwort (*Ceratophyllum*), *Najas*, milfoil (*Myriophyllum*), waterweed (*Anarcus*), and some kinds of arrowhead (*Sagittaria*), are common and widespread in this habitat, together with the large green stonewort (*Chara*) where the water is hard.

Many sources of food exist in the littoral zone—plants, plankton, detritus, and animals. For those invertebrates, amphibians, and fishes able to thrive in still water, the zone provides good cover and varied living space, and the community is similar to that found in the lower reaches of rivers.

The lake bottom

As elsewhere in a lake, the life at its bottom is governed by water conditions of temperature, transparency, dissolved oxygen and chemicals, and currents. These vary with the shape and nature of the lake basin and its inflowing streams, as well as with the local climate and biological factors such as food, shelter, competition, and predation. Depth is of major significance, as distinct communities succeed one another from the littoral zone of submerged vegetation to the lowest parts of the basin.

Deep areas are characterized by lack of light, low oxygen, and high carbon dioxide. They have soft fine sediments, rich in organic detritus. Although green plants are absent, the top layers of mud enable fungi, bacteria, and certain protozoans to flourish. Oligochaete worms (such as species of *Tubifex*), bivalve molluscs (of the family Sphaeridae), some gastropods, and dipteran insect larvae (for example, species of *Chironomus* and *Chaoborus*) are the most abundant of larger organisms burrowing or buried in the mud.

Life in a tropical lake

Particularly impressive in the tropics are the great lakes of the African continent. Except for Lake Chad, they lie among the catchment basins and drainage channels of eastern and central Africa. The two Great Rift Valleys, and the enormous Lake Victoria basin, were formed by extensive movements of the earth's crust some fifteen million years ago. Such large and isolated bodies of water, in a region previously having only smooth hills, plateaux, and rivers, offered a new variety and volume of fresh habitats to the ancient aquatic flora and fauna.

In this situation, unprecedented genetic changes and environmental adaptations led to distinctive species. Each of the Rift Valleys has a very high degree of endemism—the occurrence of a species only in one place. This is especially true of the fishes, which are much less able to move between isolated waters than are invertebrates. In each of the lakes, over ninety per cent of the cichlids are endemic.

The Rift Valley lakes are quite long and deep, with precipitous

At left, a tropical savannah lake in Africa. In the dry season and times of drought, the tributaries and the lake itself dry up completely, so the aquatic animals that live here must be able to adapt to the very low oxygen content of the scarce water or to breathing air. Below right is a section of a savannah river showing (a) papyrus, (b) matelite reed, (c) water lily, (d) snail, (e) catfish, (f) bichir (juvenile), (g) lungfish, (h) worms. Below is shown how the lungfish burrows into the bottom vigorously by blowing water at the substrate and then wriggling into the cavity thus created. As the water level sinks, it envelops itself in a moist mucus cocoon, which later dries into a protective case. Air filters in from the top, and the fish lives during its period of dormancy on its reserves of fat.

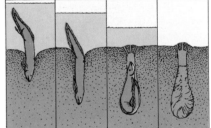

Opposite are shown three other freshwater environments that can usefully serve as models for aquarium environments.

1 A temperate lake in northern Europe. The shallower parts of the lake resemble a pond in many ways, and on pages 132–133 is illustrated an aquarium environment for a temperate freshwater pond.

2 A river in the Gir area of Gujarat, India. The monsoon climate of the Indian sub-continent brings torrential rains which widen the river banks. This photograph shows the river in the dry season.

3 A fast-flowing river in Kenya. At left in the foreground are papyrus reeds, while at right is travo grass.

coastlines and narrow littoral zones. Lake Tanganyika, the largest, is 650 km (400 miles) long and about 50 km (30 miles) wide, with a maximum depth of 1,500 m (5,000 ft). The inflowing streams are short, seasonal torrents that drain the surrounding ridges, whilst most loss of water is by evaporation. The salinity is fairly high (over 0.5 parts per thousand), with a peculiar composition for a freshwater body: high ratios of chloride to sulphate, and of magnesium to calcium.

The tropical conditions produce persistent stratification and deoxygenation in deep water. Temperatures fluctuate only in the upper 200 m (650 ft), remaining constant at 23.3°C (73.9°F) below this. The enormous volume of permanently deoxygenated water beneath the upper zone, loaded with hydrogen sulphide, is a striking feature of the ecology of such lakes. Three-quarters of the lake's total mass may not contain sufficient oxygen to support life.

The open water

The vast expanse of open water in the Rift Valley lakes is similar in ecology to that of the ocean. Strong winds stir the surface and the shallow zone, periodically increasing the levels of nutrient at the surface, and leading to rises in phytoplankton production. The depth of the euphotic (light-receiving) zone varies but, in very clear water, is probably around 30 m (100 ft). Thus, the volumes of revitalized water and its contents are high.

The pelagic community includes small herrings and sardines (of the family Clupeidae), which feed on zooplankton copepods, cladocerans, and rotifers. In Lake Malawi, the second largest Rift Valley lake, some sixteen endemic species of *Haplochromis* cichlids have evolved, shoaling in open water and feeding on zooplankton. Fish-eating predators are exemplified by catfishes (species of *Bagrus* and *Ramphochromis*). There are also swimming prawns and occasional swarms of the freshwater medusoid jellyfish *(Limnocnida).*

The littoral zone

In the tropical lakes of eastern Africa, the inshore water is so clear that enough light penetrates to allow plant life on the bottom, down to about 20 m (65 ft). The littoral zone in Lakes Tanganyika and Malawi consists largely of cliffs of bedrock and tumbled boulders, resembling coral atolls and the submarine cliffs of coastal seas. These rock surfaces are covered by small brown and green algae, with an undergrowth fauna of crustaceans, rotifers, and insect larvae. In Lake Tanganyika is a unique community of prosobranch mollusc species, including several of *Paramelania* and *Spekia,* which are strong-shelled grazers of the algae.

Prawns, crabs, and many fishes—six or more per square metre (or yard)—find shelter among the massive boulders, often hiding in holes by day. The fish species are commonly endemic to a particular lake and confined to the rocky areas. Small, brightly coloured cichlids scrape and suck up the attached algae (species of *Limnotilapia* and *Petrochromis* in Lake Tanganyika). Other cichlids, with protruding teeth, nip tiny crustaceans and insect larvae from the undergrowth, and still others prey upon crabs and other fishes. Some species, for instance *Genyochromis mento* in Lake Malawi, have become adept at biting scales and bits of fin from other fishes.

Alternating with the rocky shores and underwater cliffs are the shallows of sand and mud, a quite different habitat. Rooted plants (such as species of *Vallisneria* and *Ceratophyllum*) form submerged forests, sheltering and feeding a rich fauna of crabs, copepods, ostracods, prawns, insect larvae (of caddis, chironomid, and dragon-flies), gastropods, and bivalves. Many cichlids are adapted to living here, and their range of feeding habits is well illustrated in Lake Malawi: *Haplochromis mola* eats molluscs, *H. similis* and *Tilapia mela-nopleura* nibble at plants, *T. saka* is nourished by sunken detritus and phytoplankton, and species of *Lethrinops* grub for buried insect larvae.

The lake bottom
Life below 200 m (650 ft) consists almost entirely of anaerobic micro-organisms. In shallower areas, much of the sediment is very soft, organic ooze, on which chironomid midge larvae, copepod and ostracod crustaceans, and molluscs thrive. Bivalves and prosobranchs, for example in Lake Tanganyika, may be adapted in body form to the consistency of the mud, sometimes with projecting shell spines that are proportional in length to the sediment softness. Organic detritus fall-ing from above is the food source for most animals in deep waters.

There are many kinds of bottom-living fishes, particularly endemic cichlids. Notable instances from Lake Tanganyika are the species of *Trematocara, Hemibates, Haplochromis,* and *Synodontis,* as well as several mormyrids.

2 Botany for the Aquarist

Plants are the only living organisms able to absorb the radiant energy of sunlight and store it in molecules of organic chemicals. This process of photosynthesis keeps an amount of energy on the earth which is equivalent to the output of over two thousand million large power stations. Without it, there would be no life on the planet, because such molecules are food for both plants and animals. Plants require food in order to survive periods when energy from photosynthesis is inadequate; the organic material they produce can be stored in their stems and roots. Animals must eat organic materials, dead or alive, from plants or other animals, in order to obtain energy for all activities.

Equally important to life on earth is oxygen, a by-product of photosynthesis. Free oxygen is essential to living organisms for respiration. Plants release it when light energy splits their water molecules into atoms of hydrogen and oxygen. The process also uses carbon dioxide in building organic molecules, and thus helps to remove excessive quantities of this gas from the environment.

Aquatic plants

Plants growing underwater have several advantages over those that dwell on land. For example, the latter must grow erect towards the sunlight in a non-supporting medium of air. Submerged plants can do without strengthening tissue in their stems and leaves, since they are buoyed up by the dense medium of water. Many are fine and flexible plants which offer little resistance to moving water but which would collapse if taken out of water.

Aquatic plants face no danger of desiccation, and therefore, many have lost the waterproof cuticle which protects land plants from drying out. Moreover, their thin epidermis enables inorganic nutrients, organic secretions, dissolved gases, and water to pass through the whole submerged surface of the plant. Whilst terrestrial plants must absorb inorganic nutrients from the soil, aquatic plants usually do so through their leaf or frond surfaces. They are bathed by a solution of inorganic as well as organic chemicals.

Oxygen is scarce underwater, compared to its abundance in air. It may be quite absent from the bottom silt in still bodies of water. This is a problem for the roots of aquatic plants, in satisfying their need of oxygen for respiration. Many such plants contain air spaces which extend throughout the plant, so that oxygen can diffuse down to the roots. Similarly, the carbon dioxide (CO_2) required by photosynthesis can exist freely only in water which is acidic. In alkaline conditions, the gas forms bicarbonate ions (HCO_3^-) that can be used only by certain kinds of plants.

Hygrophila polysperma   *Vesicularia dubyana* (Java Moss)   *Microsorium pteropus* (Java Fern)   *Cabomba* species

Vallisneria americana

Limnobium stolonlferum

Pistia stratiotes (Water Cabbage)

Echinodorus tenellus (Amazon Sword Plant)

43

The need of light

The most serious difficulty of aquatic plants is in obtaining sufficient light. Light reaching a submerged plant has been reduced—often considerably—by shading, reflection, and absorption.

Freshwater habitats are naturally surrounded or lined by trees and shrubs, which may overhang the water and reduce the entering light by over ninety per cent. In densely shaded streams, there may not be enough light for any higher forms of plant life to survive at all.

Penetration of light into and through water is greatly restricted by surface reflection, and by absorption into suspended particles or dissolved chemicals. Up to fifty per cent of light reaching the surface may be reflected. The remaining light, when passing through the water, decreases in intensity at an ever larger rate (logarithmically). Thus, the intensity may be reduced by fifty per cent in the first metre (3 feet) of depth. In very turbid water, less than two per cent of the incident light may reach a depth of 2 m (6 ft).

As a result of these combined losses, inadequate light is almost always the major limiting factor to underwater plant growth. Many lowland rivers are devoid of submerged flowering plants for this reason. Even in clear waters of the open ocean, the maximum depth at which plants may survive is about 100 metres (330 feet). Thus, an average sea depth of 3,500 metres (11,500 feet) is left to be occupied only by animals, all dependent upon plant production near the surface.

Chlorophyll, a pigment contained by plants, is their most important light-absorbing substance. It is activated by some wavelengths of light more than by others. Unfortunately, in this main "action spectrum", the colours of maximum value to the chlorophyll are violet and red, which have relatively little energy in sunlight. Underwater, the situation is complicated further by selective absorption. The light which best penetrates through water is of blue-green wavelengths, and these are least useful to chlorophyll.

Some of the plants known as algae can overcome these difficulties to an extent. They possess additional photosynthetic pigments, which absorb wavelengths other than those preferred by chlorophyll. In brown algae, the pigment fucoxanthin absorbs green light. In red algae, phycoerythrin and other pigments absorb green, yellow, and blue light. Such pigments enable these algae to use the underwater light more fully than in plants containing only chlorophyll. On the rocky slopes of a submarine reef, whose substrate is suitable for algae, there is a general zonation of algal types—with green algae restricted to the shallows, brown algae dominating the middle zone, and reds extending into deeper water.

The benefit of shelter

Plants have another important function in all communities, including aquatic ones, where enough light exists for them to flourish. They provide the community with a variety of spaces and surfaces, giving shelter and shade, as vital structural elements of the surroundings.

Higher types of plants, rooted in the shallow zones of lakes and rivers, form a layered canopy rising towards the water surface. The volume of water is divided up by the three-dimensionality of a plant. Fishes can hide and rest among its branches. The stems, leaves, and roots provide large areas away from the bottom mud, for settlement by small algae and invertebrates, and for the attachment of eggs by fishes, snails, crustaceans, and other creatures. The roots and buried stems of a plant can bind fine silt and detritus, encouraging a rich population of burrowing animals. In swiftly flowing streams, the rock smoothed by water is carpeted with moss, whose dense growth creates refuges and attachment for many small invertebrates.

Likewise, in the marine environment, on rocky ledges and slopes of shores exposed to waves and of reefs swept by currents, the larger algae provide additional niches. One example is the familiar kelp (species of *Laminaria*): mats of bryozoans live on its broad flat frond; a zoned community of red algae, hydroids, barnacles, snails, sponges, and tunicates can occupy its long, tough stipe and surfaces; within the branching structure, detritus and fragments of shell and sand accumulate, as a habitat for burrowing worms and crabs. Up on the shore, the large fucoid seaweeds or wracks form a dense cover, which lies draped against the rocks as the tide recedes. Beneath this tangle of fronds, animals and smaller algae are protected from desiccation, extreme air temperatures, and predators.

In the following sections, the main divisions of the plant world are introduced with the aquarist in mind, and their principal features and representatives are described. The scientific names of such divisions are worth remembering, in their order of decreasing generality: the phylum, class, family, genus, and species. For many of the species, an indication is given of suitable conditions for their maintenance in an aquarium: water temperature, light intensity, and the kind of water needed. Light intensity is specified on a four-point scale, using the units of lux (defined in Chapter 5) to measure the light reaching the plant. The value 1 will mean 500–1,000 lux; 2 means 1,000–2,000 lux; 3 means 2,000–5,000 lux; and 4 means 5,000–10,000 lux.

The plant kingdom is divided into Thallophyta (algae and fungi), Bryophyta (mosses and liverworts), Pteridophyta (ferns and fern allies), and Spermatophyta (flowering plants). The last is divided into two classes: Gymnospermae and Angiospermae, the former containing no aquarium plants. Angiospermae are divided into monocotyledons and dicotyledons. Shown here is the aquarium-plant kingdom, as described in the following pages, with an example from each family. (1) Chlorophyta (Enteromorpha). (2) Chrysophyta (Biddulphia sinensis). (3) Phaeophyta (Fucus vesiculosus). (4) Rhodophyta (Rhodymenia palmata). (5) Nitellaceae (Nitella capillaris). (6) Ricciaceae (Riccia fluitans). (7) Fontinalaceae (Fontinalis antipyretica). (8) Hypnaceae (Vesicularia dubyana). (9) Polypodiaceae (Microsorium pteropus). (10) Isoetaceae (Isoetes lacustris). (11) Azollaceae (Azolla filiculoides). (12) Marsileaceae (Marsilea hirsuta). (13) Acanthaceae (Hygrophila polysperma). (14) Alismataceae (Echinodorus paniculatus). (15) Aponogetonaceae (Aponogeton crispus). (16) Araceae (Pistia stratiotes). (17) Cabombaceae (Cabomba aquatica). (18) Callitrichaceae (Callitriche palustris). (19) Ceratophyllaceae (Ceratophyllum demersum). (20) Cyperaceae (Eleocharis acicularis). (21) Elatinaceae (Elatine macropoda). (22) Haloragaceae (Myriophyllum spicatum). (23) Hippuridaceae (Hippuris vulgaris). (24) Hydrocharitaceae (Elodea canadensis). (25) Lemnaceae (Lemna minor). (26) Lentibulariaceae (Utricularia exoleta). (27) Menyanthaceae (Nymphoides peltata). (28) Najadaceae (Najas marina). (29) Nymphaeaceae (Nuphar advena). (30) Onagraceae (Ludwigia arcuata). (31) Plantaginaceae (Litorella uniflora). (32) Polygonaceae (Polygonum amphibium). (33) Pontederiaceae (Eichhornia crassipes). (34) Potamogetonaceae (Potamogeton gayii). (35) Primulaceae (Hottonia palustris). (36) Ranunculaceae (Ranunculus fluitans). (37) Scrophulariaceae (Bacopa amplexicaulis).

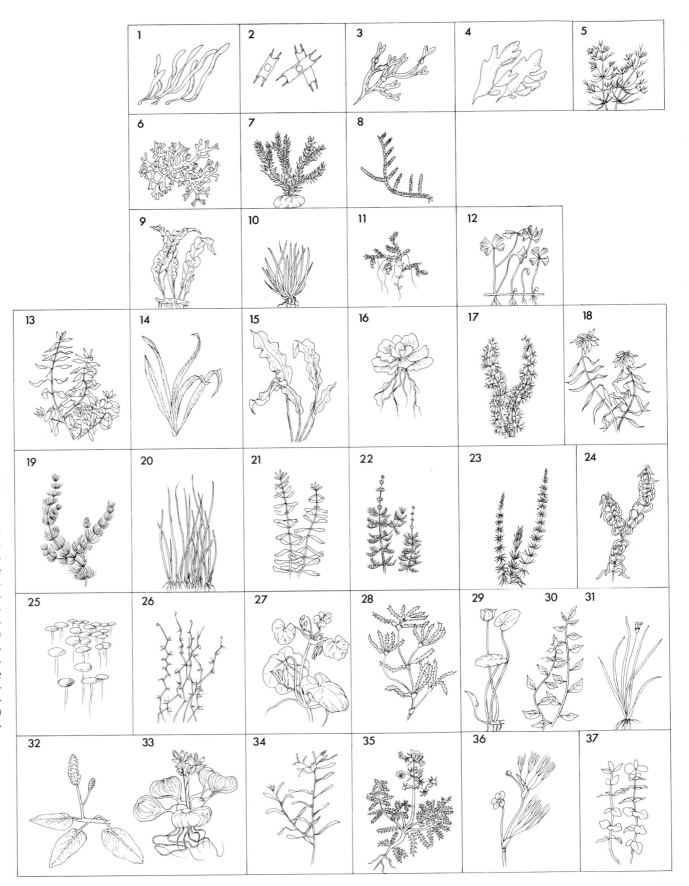

The algae

Algae are considered to be the most primitive of plants. They are mostly simple in structure, not differentiated into root, stem, and leaves. But many of the large species have a recognizable frond, an anchor structure or "holdfast", and possibly a stalk or stipe. All have photosynthetic pigments, and they are classified primarily according to these—into green, brown, red, and other divisions.

Most algae are aquatic, and they are amongst the most important components of shallow marine and freshwater communities. They range widely in form and size, from microscopic diatoms to the familiar wracks on rocky shores, and giant kelps. Many of the tiny forms are planktonic: there are probably around 1,500 species of algae in the phytoplankton. These are the photosynthesizers of large bodies of water. The production and survival of life in the oceans and lakes is dependent upon the organic materials fixed by the many millions of these simple, minute plants.

Most of the macroscopic species of algae are found on particular firm surfaces of rock, wood, or other plants. In some habitats, including hot springs, steep-sided rocky rivers and canals, and shallow submarine cliffs, they are the only photosynthetic organisms present.

Algae were the first forms of life to evolve sexual reproduction, and modern algae show a complex range of developments upon this basic theme. Distinct male and female cells are produced, fusing together to create a zygote, from which the new plant grows. The zygote is often resistant to adverse conditions and may thus enable the species to survive a period of drought or low oxygen.

Chlorophyta—the Green Algae

Almost all members of the phylum Chlorophyta contain two types of chlorophyll (a and b) which colour the plants green, together with lesser amounts of carotene and xanthophyll pigments. Ninety per cent are freshwater species, but there are several important ones in shallow marine waters.

Many species are unicellular and tiny, including phytoplankton members such as *Chlamydomonas* and *Chlorella*. The latter is also able to live symbiotically within the body of some protozoan and coelenterate animals, including species of *Hydra* and most shallow-water stony corals (Scleractinians). Other chlorophytes form long filamentous growths (such as species of *Cladophora* and *Spirogyra*) or hollow spheres (*Volvox*). Thin sheet-like growths are formed by *Ulva* and *Enteromorpha,* prominent genera in marine and brackish waters.

The range of species, and their characteristically rapid growth and reproduction, mean that the green algae are familiar sights in most shallow-water bodies. Many are "opportunist" species, occurring in low numbers until the right conditions coincide, then "blooming" into a dense population.

Enteromorpha occur all over the world in coastal and estuary waters. The plants grow up to 30 cm

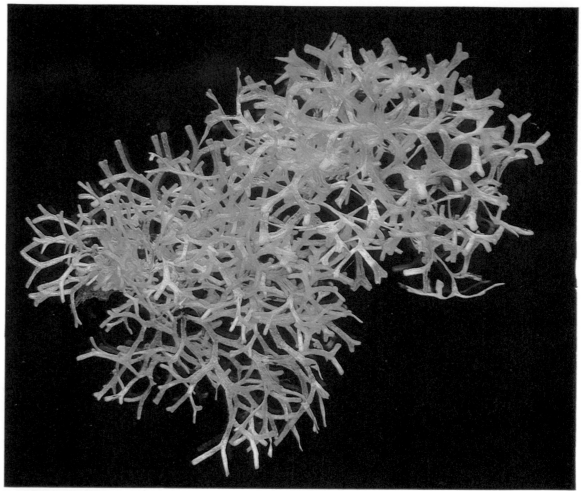

Riccia fluitans (Liverwort)

Cladophora rupestris (Blanketweed)

Cryptocoryne nevillii

(1 ft) long and attach to stones, shells, wood, other algae or, in very sheltered habitats, the mud surface. They are typical of sites where grazing invertebrates, particularly gastropods, are absent, because of low salinity, seasonal sand abrasion, or pollution.

TEMP: 8–20°C (46–68°F)   LIGHT: 3–4   WATER: saline (5–35 parts per thousand)

Ulva are commonly known as sea lettuce or green laver. The thin flat frond, usually around 10 cm (4 in) long, may reach 50 cm (20 in). This is a marine alga and grows on stones or rock in sheltered shallows and intertidal areas. The plant attaches to the substrate by means of a mat of microscopic sticky threads. But it can live as a floating frond if detached, until it is carried into deep water or cast up on the shore.

TEMP: 8–20°C (46–68°F)   LIGHT: 3   WATER: full sea

Caulerpa prolifera is an unusual marine alga, being found attached by root-like threads to a sandy substrate. It has a colourless stem which grows across the bottom and gives rise to leaf-like green lobes. Extensive underwater meadows of this plant occur in the warmer areas of the Mediterranean. Its reproduction by vegetative growth of broken fragments is common.

TEMP: 18–21°C (64–70°F)   LIGHT: 2–3   WATER: sea

Acetabularia acetabulum is another Mediterranean species. It grows as clusters of stalked, light-green leaves on shallow stones, shells, and wood. The leaves are wedge-shaped and arranged around the stalk, giving the appearance of a small delicate umbrella, 3–8 cm (1–3 in) tall. The plant is stiff in texture with a surface deposit of calcium carbonate from the water.

TEMP: 18–21°C (64–70°F)   LIGHT: 2–3   WATER: sea

Cladophora, known as blanketweed, are common in habitats of both fresh and marine water. They are branching, filamentous algae which grow as dense masses, usually attached to the bottom stone, sand, or mud, or to other plants, although some species are free-floating. The dark-green threads may reach 400 cm (13 ft) in length but are normally about 20 cm (8 in) long. They can tolerate rapid water flow by streaming downstream with the current. Marine species include C. *rupestris*, C. *sericea*, and C. *mediterranea*, whilst C. *glomerata* colonizes streams and lakes as well as thriving in polluted rivers.

Chrysophyta—the Yellow-Green Algae

Within this phylum are the microscopic algae called diatoms, containing chlorophyll, which abound in marine and fresh waters in the plankton and the benthic community. They are so common in the open sea as to be the main photosynthesizers. In stony streams, they form a slimy carpet over submerged surfaces and are a major element of the flora. Many aquatic food webs are based upon populations of diatoms.

The unique characteristic of diatoms is their

construction: each is unicellular but is enclosed by two "shells" made of silica. These form a glassy "pill-box", which may be adorned with spines or a surface pattern. In some species, colonies are composed of diatoms stuck together into long filaments or wheel shapes.

Phaeophyta–the Brown Algae

Most of the Phaeophyta, a division of over a thousand species, are seaweeds on shores and sub-tidal reefs, where rock and stone are available for attachment. They occur mainly in temperate and polar seas. Some species (such as *Fucus ceranoides*) inhabit the brackish waters of estuaries, and there are also a handful of freshwater species. The Phaeophyta contain chlorophyll, but its colour is masked by fucoxanthin and other pigments, which give the characteristic olive-green or brown colour. They are usually large, multicellular plants and consist of distinct fronds, stems, and holdfasts.

The genus *Macrocystis* or giant kelp is one of the largest and most rapidly growing plants in the world, reaching over 80 m (262 ft) in height. Dense forests are formed by it in the cold Pacific coastal waters, becoming a dominant feature of the environment.

One species of the genus *Sargassum* is unusual in that it does not attach to a surface but floats freely on the open seas by means of gas-bladders. Among its tangle of fronds and branches lives a unique community of crabs, prawns, and juvenile fishes, hundreds of miles from the shore and thousands of metres above the sea bed.

The large brown algae are generally difficult to maintain in a closed aquarium system. Large quantities of organic mucus are secreted by the plants, partly to excrete the calcium carbonate deposited during photosynthesis. Rapid circulation and filtration of the water are essential. But some of the smaller species might be kept in an aquarium. One example is the *Padina*, or peacock tail. It grows in a fan shape, 4–10 cm (1.5–4 in) in height, on bedrock and stones in the shallow coastal waters of temperate and subtropical seas.

Rhodophyta–the Red Algae

The Rhodophyta are multicellular, relatively complex algae, which exhibit a great variety of forms and colours. They contain the red pigment phycoerythrin, together with both types of chlorophyll and with xanthophyll, carotene, and phycocyanin. They are represented by over 3,000 species throughout the world's seas. Most are seaweeds, attached to rock and stones from the shore down to a depth of over 100 m (330 ft) in clear seas. A few species live in fresh waters, mainly in streams. Many species are epiphytic—living attached to other plants—and some show remarkable specificity for particular hosts. In most cases, the exact nature of this close relationship is unknown. The subtidal and shore species often have a basically similar form of growth, attached to the hard substrate by a holdfast, frequently of root-like threads.

Rhodymenia palmata is a common example, found on sheltered lower shore rocks. The plants have flattened purple or violet-red fronds, 15–35 cm (6–14 in) in length, and sometimes with a fringe of small lobes.

TEMP: 8–20°C (46–68°F) LIGHT: 2 WATER: sea

Polysiphonia is a diverse genus of thin, filamentous, branched plants, growing on other algae, or on rocky shores, and into deeper water.

TEMP: 8–20°C (46–68°F) LIGHT: 1–2 WATER: sea

Corallinaceae is a family characterized by heavy calcium-carbonate encrustation, or calcification. The *Lithothamnion* and its relatives form lumpy rock-like growths. Members of the other side of the family, such as *Corallina officinalis*, form erect plants with jointed limbs. These red algae are of great importance in tropical reef systems, where they are responsible—with the stony corals—for laying down the massive outcrops of calcium carbonate over the centuries. In mid-shore tidal rock pools, the substrate is often completely covered with the pink-cream or pink-grey algal growth.

TEMP: 8–20°C (46–68°F) LIGHT: 2–3 WATER: sea

Charophyta–the Stoneworts

Stoneworts are algae consisting of a jointed main stem, with whorls of fine, forked side-shoots. They are up to 30 cm (1 ft) long, being delicate freshwater plants, remarkably similar in appearance to aquatic higher plants. As important members of lake communities, they form extensive meadows in well-lit shallows and are often the dominant plants in deeper zones. Since they are algae, they have no proper roots, but anchor in the mud with a holdfast of threads.

There are two main genera, *Chara* and *Nitella*. Some species are brittle and stony in texture due to deposited calcium carbonate on the plant's surface. Stoneworts are usually found in hard, calcium-rich waters, but some *Nitella* can tolerate softer water, where they lose the stony deposit.

TEMP: 8–20°C (46–68°F) LIGHT: 1–2 WATER: fresh, hard to very hard

Bryophyta

Leaving the algae, we come to the Bryophytes, fairly small photosynthesizing plants which do not have flowers or the xylem and phloem characteristic of the ferns and angiosperms. This division includes the *Hepaticae*, or liverworts, and the *Musci*, or mosses. All are species of moist terrestrial or freshwater habitats, and there are no marine species.

Bryophytes can reproduce and spread by means of spores released from capsules on the stem, or by vegetative growth in which small fragments break off and drift downstream. Most of the liverworts have a flattened thallus, or simple body structure, which spreads over areas of wet stones and boulders. In general, the liverworts are species on the damp margins of fast-running streams. They prefer cold, soft, or acid waters.

Riccia fluitans is a cosmopolitan species, with a slender branched thallus, which floats beneath the surface of still pools and ditches, or may become tangled round rooted plants.

TEMP: 10–20°C (50–68°F) LIGHT: 1–2 WATER: fresh

The mosses occur in streams and small rivers all over the world and are represented by a large number of genera and species. Unlike most higher plants, mosses do not use dissolved bicarbonate as a source of carbon dioxide for photosynthesis and are, therefore, restricted to habitats such as acid streams where free carbon dioxide is present in solution. In calcareous waters, mosses generally occur only where shallow-water turbulence increases the level of dissolved carbon dioxide from the atmosphere.

Fontinalis is a genus comprising the true water mosses. These are floating and rooted plants that live in both still and running waters. *F. antipyretica* is a common species in many types of water, including those with organic pollution. The plants, with stems up to 70 cm (28 in) or more in length, form large waving or floating tufts. They attach to stable boulders, bedrock, and tree trunks—and, in still waters, are also found loosely attached to stones and sand deposits. The willow moss, as it is called, is an important member of deeper freshwater meadows, both as a producer of oxygen and organic material, and for the good shelter it offers to a busy community of small invertebrates.

TEMP: 10–20°C (50–68°F) LIGHT: 1–2 WATER: fresh, neutral to slightly acidic

Vesicularia are amphibious mosses of tropical and subtropical Africa and Asia. They can grow rapidly and spread over wet rock and tree surfaces.

TEMP: 20–28°C (68–82°F) LIGHT: 1–2 WATER: fresh, slightly acidic

Pteridophyta

Differing from all the above plants are the Pteridophytes, or ferns. These are non-flowering vascular plants: they have specialized xylem and phloem vessels, as do the flowering plants, but ferns produce spores rather than flowers. Their life cycle is complex, involving alternate generations of a spore-producing stage (the characteristic fern) and a sexual gamete-producing stage (which is a tiny specialized structure).

Unlike the Bryophytes, most ferns have a well-developed root system, and a stem and leaves. There are many species, particularly in tropical habitats such as the rain forest, and in damp places all over the world. Several families contain fully aquatic representatives, all in fresh waters.

Microsorium pteropus is an amphibious member of the Polypodiaceae, the largest family of ferns. It is a native of southeast Asia, commonly known as the Java fern. Underwater, it lives rooted to stony or gravel substrates among fallen tree branches and roots. The creeping rhizome gives rise to clusters of broad, tapering green leaves, around 20 cm (8 in) long.

Cryptocoryne wendtii

Anubias nana

Isoetes lacustris, commonly known as the quill-wort, is another amphibious species, able to live submerged in clear, still, fresh waters. It is a native of Europe and North America. It has a short rhizome base, with roots anchored in silt and gravel substrates. The erect leaves are cylindrical and rush-like, forming a rosette 10 cm (4 in) or more in height.

TEMP: 8–20°C (46–68°F) LIGHT: 1–2 WATER: fresh, neutral, soft

Azolla are small, floating ferns, sometimes known as fairy moss, in tropical and temperate latitudes. *A. filiculoides* is a North American species which has become established in Europe, following its introduction as an aquarium and ornamental plant. It grows to only 1.5 cm (0.6 in) in diameter and has thick overlapping fronds, green or red in colour, each consisting of a floating lobe and a submerged lobe on a short branching stem. Small fine roots hang into the water. The plants grow and reproduce vegetatively at a great rate and can cover the water surface of pools completely in a short time. This leads to excessive shading of the water below, and to depletion of dissolved oxygen.

TEMP: 20–25°C (68–77°F) LIGHT: 2–3 WATER: fresh

Marsilea are known in North America by the names of water shamrock and pepperwort. They are found in still fresh waters in areas of the tropic, subtropic, and temperate zones. Underwater, they usually root into gravel and sand substrates, with a buried rhizome which gives rise to a long stalk, terminating in leaves subdivided into four lobes. The plant also occurs as a free-floating form.

Flowering plants

The higher plants produce flowers and seeds, and possess specialized xylem and phloem vessels for conducting water and food materials through the plant. They are adapted primarily to life on land—aquatic vascular plants are a small minority within the very large and diverse group. The two main classes are the Gymnospermae, including the conifers, and terrestrial in virtually all species, and the Angiospermae, which are the major group of flowering, seed-producing plants.

There are around 200,000 known species of angiosperms, but relatively few are adapted to living under or in water. Of these aquatics, there are only about fifty species which live in sea water. The angiosperms are divided into two subclasses, on the basis of the number of embryonic leaves, or cotyledons: the Monocotyledons and the Dicotyledons. Monocotyledons, in which the mature plant has parallel-veined leaves with a sheathed base, include eighteen exclusively aquatic families, as well as several aquatic representatives of primarily terrestrial families. The few marine angiosperms are all monocotyledons, with most species belonging to one of two widely adapted families (the Najadaceae and the Hydrocharitaceae). Dicotyledons, the larger subclass, usually have net-veined leaves, and contain some ten families which are mainly or exclusively of aquatic species.

The angiosperms evolved as land plants, and problems have had to be overcome by species attempting to colonize aquatic habitats. For example, pollination of flowers is difficult underwater, and many aquatic angiosperms spread mainly by vegetative means. Most aquatics raise their flowers above the water surface, and the pollen is transferred by insects or wind, or floats downstream. However, some species do have underwater flowers, including the sea grasses and the hornworts (species of *Ceratophyllum*). Floating seeds are produced by many species and are able to drift away from the parent plant.

The majority of aquatic angiosperms is distributed in relation to particular grades of sediment, which in turn depend upon the speed of water flow. The root must be able to anchor the plant firmly if the species is to survive in running waters. Many angiosperms develop extensive rooting systems with rhizomes or runners and adventitious roots, forming a mat which binds the sediment together.

Even within a species, the effects of current upon the form of growth of various higher plants may be seen. In general, with increasing current, the leaves are smaller, and leaf stalks as well as the distances between leaves are shorter. In some species, such as *Myriophyllum spicatum* or *Nuphar lutea,* the plant is altogether smaller. On the other hand, the whole plant may grow much longer: this may be seen in *Potamogeton densus* or *Ranunculus calcareus.*

Most aquatic angiosperms are able to use bicarbonate ions as their source of carbon dioxide in alkaline waters. Some species, such as *Potamogeton lucens* and *Myriophyllum spicatum,* photosynthesize better on bicarbonate than on carbon dioxide, and thus are usually associated with alkaline waters. Others cannot use bicarbonate and are found only in acid waters: for example, some species of *Potamogeton,* and *Myriophyllum alterniflorum.* Certain species which are rooted in anoxic mud can absorb carbon dioxide through their roots and pass it up to the photosynthesizing leaves through the air spaces in the stem.

Features and representatives of the main twenty-five families of aquatic angiosperms are introduced below in alphabetical order.

Acanthaceae

The Acanthaceae are a family of dicotyledons, comprising some 250 genera and over 2,500 species of shrubs and herbs, which include only two genera of aquatic plants: *Hygrophila* and *Justicia.*

In *Hygrophila* are about eighty species of aquatic and marsh plants, mostly occurring in the tropics and subtropics of Africa and Asia. Many species are able to live either submerged or emerged, and tend to develop different forms of leaf below and above the water surface. Minute purple or white flowers are borne above water in the leaf axils. The plants may spread vegetatively by means of stem fragments.

H. augustifolia is a native of southeast Asia and Australia, where it inhabits the still waters of canals, dykes, and ponds, as well as marshland. The plant roots in a variety of sediments and can grow underwater to 50 cm (20 in) in height. Straight narrow leaves, up to 15 cm (6 in) long, grow in opposite pairs along the stout stem.

TEMP: 20–28°C (68–82°F) LIGHT: 3 WATER: fresh

H. difformis, known as the water wisteria, is another Eastern water plant, found from Indonesia to India. The rooted plant has a fairly thick, tough stem, which may grow to 60 cm (24 in) high. A dense array of deeply cut, bright-green leaves grows towards the water surface.

TEMP: 20–28°C (68–82°F) LIGHT: 2–3 WATER: fresh

H. polysperma is a native of the Indian subcontinent. The fairly small plant lives in still, clear, freshwater ditches and pools, but is mainly a marshland variety. The slender stem grows across the substrate, carrying long feather-shaped leaves which are light-green with dark veins.

TEMP: 15–25°C (59–77°F) LIGHT: 2–3 WATER: fresh

Alismataceae

This family contains monocotyledons, called the water plantains and sword plants. Its species number over 100 and are distributed between cold, temperate, subtropical, and tropical freshwater habitats. Many of the species are emergent marsh plants—colonizers especially of areas which are periodically flooded. Others live permanently underwater, in slow-moving or still pool margins, ditches, canals, and ponds. The family is characterized by a buried rhizome, from which leaf stalks (petioles) rise and support leaves that are shaped like an arrowhead, or are ovate or rounded. The grown plants range between 7–250 cm (3 in–8 ft) in height. *Alisma* is a genus represented by different species throughout the world. *A. plantago-aquatica,* the common water plantain, is widespread in Europe. More often found, living completely submerged, is the species *A. graminuum,* also a native of Europe. Both species have a rhizome thickened into a tuber and root well in muddy sediments in shallow still bays, ponds, and ditches, or in flowing streams where the sediment is fine sand. Ribbon-shaped leaves form underwater, and a pyramidal flower-spike bearing reddish-white flowers may grow above the surface.

TEMP: 10–20°C (50–68°F) LIGHT: 1–2 WATER: fresh

Echinodorus is a major genus containing many American species, particularly from the Amazon region. The majority inhabit shallow water and marshy sites, where little or no water flows and fine silt is deposited. *E. teneilus* is a species of very small plants, usually around 3–8 cm (1.2–3 in) tall. These propagate vegetatively by root runners from the rhizome, spreading across and through the substrate to cover areas of the bottom. Their narrow ribbon-shaped leaves rise in clumps, producing tiny white flowers, which are borne above the water surface on a small stalk. This is a tropical and subtropical species of Central America and the southern United States, requiring bright light and constant, moderately high water temperature.

TEMP: 16–28°C (61–82°F) LIGHT: 3 WATER: fresh, neutral, soft to medium hard

Many species of *Echinodorus,* known as sword plants, inhabit shallow, still, marginal pools of the Amazon and other river catchments. Typical of the larger species is *E. amazonicus,* which grows as an erect rosette of leaves to 20 cm (8 in) or more in height. *E. bleheri* has broader leaves about 5 cm (2 in) wide, again in a dense clump, around 20 cm (8 in) tall. *E. quadricostatus* has similar leaves, but without leaf stalks (petioles), and smaller—10 cm (4 in) long and 1–2 cm (0.4–0.8 in) broad. Long root runners form readily, so that an area of the bottom is soon covered with a bright-green carpet. Many species in this genus form small buds which enable the plants to reproduce vegetatively. Young plants also form at intervals along root runners and are easily separated from the parent plant.

TEMP: 15–30°C (59–86°F) LIGHT: 2–3 WATER: fresh, soft to medium hard

Aponogetonaceae

These monocotyledons are mostly tropical and subtropical species of Africa, southern Europe, Asia and Australia. Some species live in marshes or swamps, but the majority are permanently submerged. The single genus *Aponogeton* contains over fifty species. The plants characteristically have robust stalks and long spear-shaped leaves with thin fronds. A long spike of a flower stalk grows above the water surface and develops many tiny yellow, white, or pink flowers. Seeds set readily and germinate easily to form new plants. Several species normally die down in the winter. Some species will grow from a split rhizome.

A. crispus is a native of Sri Lanka, where it is common in both running streams and still ponds. The plant has a long, horizontal, buried rhizome, from which ribbon-like leaves grow up to 30 cm (1 ft) in length. The floral spike may reach to 80 cm (31 in) long.

TEMP: 15–23°C (59–73°F) LIGHT: 3–4 WATER: fresh
MEDIUM: plug of soil

A. fenestralis is characterized by its leaves, which are not entire, but form a delicate lattice when older. They grow up to 20 cm (8 in) long, on a slightly shorter stalk, from the buried rhizome. This is one of possibly several species native to Madagascar and known as lace plants.

TEMP: 15–25°C (59–77°F) LIGHT: 3 WATER: fresh
MEDIUM: plug of soil

A. ulvaceus is another species native to Madagascar. It has delicate green leaves up to about 30 cm (1 ft) long and 6 cm (2.4 in) wide, with wavy edges and, sometimes, coiling tips. It lives in clear streams and shallow ponds, and produces a forked flower-spike above the water surface. The many tiny yellow flowers are pollinated by insects.

TEMP: 12–18°C (54–64°F) LIGHT: 3 WATER: fresh

Araceae

This is a very large family of monocotyledons, containing over 100 genera and nearly 200 species. These show a wide variety of botanical forms, from tiny herbs to tree-sized shrubs. Most are inhabitants of the tropics and subtropics, particularly in southeast Asia and in Africa. The flowering structure of such plants is distinctive, with very small flowers arranged on a fleshy finger-like growth (a spadix), which is wrapped round by a large modified leaf (the spathe). The plants often spread rapidly across an area of substrate, by vegetative budding from the main root stock. Extensive underwater meadows of single species can be formed. Flowers are produced only on emergent plants. *Cryptocoryne* is the principal genus of aquatic representatives. All of its species live in southern Asia, from Ceylon and India to Indonesia and the Philippines. They grow as marsh plants or submerged in still pools and ditches, as well as in streams flowing fast or moderately. Probably about 100 such species exist. *C. balansae* lives in swift-flowing streams, too, and roots in the stony or sandy bed. This plant has stalked leaves with wavy margins and a thickened mid-rib. The leaves may reach 30 cm (1 ft) in length, and are about 3 cm (1.2 in) wide. *C. bullosa* is an Indonesian species, in shallow still waterways. Its green and brown-red leaves are carried on long rising stalks and are elliptical in shape, with a raised crinkly surface.

TEMP: 20–30°C (68–86°F) LIGHT: 1–2 WATER: fresh

Pistia stratiotes, the water cabbage, belongs to the same family. It occurs throughout the tropical zones of the world. It forms a cabbage-like rosette, about 15 cm (6 in) in diameter, of large, rounded, light-green leaves. New plants grow on runners floating out from the stock, and extensive floating masses can be formed. Dense roots hang down.

TEMP: 15–25°C (59–77°F) LIGHT: 2–3 WATER: fresh

Cabombaceae

These dicotyledons, called fanworts, include two genera of aquatic plants, *Cabomba* and *Brasenia,* which are represented throughout the tropical and subtropical areas of the American continents. *Cabomba* are all soft-leaved plants, which live permanently underwater and cannot survive for long in air. They grow from a rhizome which creeps across the sediment and is attached by fine roots. Stems, up to 2 m (6.6 ft) long in some species, grow up from the rhizome towards the water surface and carry very fine forked leaves in fan-shaped whorls. If the plant reaches the surface, floating leaves are produced, which are less divided and more entire. In most species, the stem and leaves are delicate and rather easily broken or bruised. Small white, yellow, or red flowers are produced on short stalks at the water surface.

C. aquatica is typical of the South American species. It inhabits pools and moderately flowing shallows in the central Amazon region.

TEMP: 25–30°C (77–86°F) LIGHT: 2–3 WATER: fresh, soft and slightly acidic

C. piauhyensis is another South American species, living in waters similar to those of the preceding species, but extending into Central America.

TEMP: 25–30°C (77–86°F) LIGHT: 3–4 WATER: fresh, soft neutral

C. caroliniana is a common North American and Central American species. It inhabits shallow silty pools and streams, throughout the subtropical climate zone. Surface-floating leaves are shaped like an arrow barb, whilst the underwater leaves are fine, forked, and arranged in a fan shape.

TEMP: 15–25°C (59–77°F) LIGHT: 2–3 WATER: fresh, soft neutral

Callitrichaceae

This family of dicotyledons, known as water starworts, occurs in temperate fresh waters. It can colonize the beds of swift and moderately flowing streams and shallow rivers, as well as still lakes, pools, and ditches. Different leaf forms are produced by several species. The species themselves are difficult to differentiate, but ten or more are native to Europe.

Callitriche stagnalis, C. platycarpa, C. hamulata, and *C. palustris* are very common and widespread species. They are small plants of similar appearance. *C. stagnalis* has rounded leaves, whilst the other three produce both elongate, submerged leaves and broader, floating leaves. Male and female aerial flowers occur together on a single plant, and small flattened, winged fruits form. The plant has an elongate, straggling stem, which attaches by adventitious roots at intervals to the bottom soil.

TEMP: 10–20°C (50–68°F) LIGHT: 2 WATER: fresh

Ceratophyllaceae

This family consists of only two species: *Ceratophyllum demersum,* the rigid hornwort, and *C. submersum,* the soft hornwort. They are dicotyledons and cosmopolitan in distribution, the first being most common. The second is the more sensitive to water flow, shading, drought, and pollution. Both species inhabit pools, dykes, and canals, but *C. demersum* alone is able to extend into slow-flowing and even slightly brackish waters. It normally grows in depths of 1–2 m (3–7 ft) but is occasionally found down to 8 m (26 ft) or more.

The hornwort is a submerged plant with a branching stem, which reaches to 50–100 cm (20–40 in) long. Large floating masses can form, and the plant may be anchored to the mud by a colourless portion of the stem. There are no true roots. Whorls of many leaves line the stem. In *C. demersum,* the leaves are rigid and brittle, with bristly spines, whilst in *C. submersum,* they are spineless and delicate.

Vegetative spread is by means of stem fragments breaking off and floating away. Sexual reproduction is apparently rare: minute flowers form underwater, in the leaf axils, and the stamens detach, rise to the surface, split and release the pollen, which sinks down onto the underwater female flower. Special starch-rich buds are also formed in the winter. These are thorny and become detached from the plant to form new, small plants in the spring.

TEMP: 12–20°C (54–68°F)   LIGHT: 1–2   WATER: fresh

Cyperaceae

This is a large family of monocotyledons, containing some sixty genera and over 3,500 species. The great majority are terrestrial plants, although many species inhabit wetlands. The large African swamp plant known as papyrus *(Cyperus papyrus),* and the bulrushes *(Schoenoplectus),* are in this family. *Eleocharis acicularis,* the hair grass, or slender spike rush, is a species which can live healthily underwater. It is widely distributed between temperate and tropical latitudes, and colonizes the sandy shores of lakes, as well as slow or moderately flowing streams and river shallows. It has slender rooted runners, which creep across the bottom, giving rise to tufts of fine, soft, hair-like leaves up to 20 cm (8 in) long. Densely carpeted areas can be formed. A tall thin spike carries the simple flowers above the water surface.

TEMP: 12–20°C (54–68°F)   LIGHT: 3   WATER: fresh

Elatinaceae

These so-called waterworts comprise the genus *Elatine,* which has about ten species of dicotyledonous plants. They live submerged in shallow water or are creeping marsh plants. *E. hydropiper, E. macropoda,* and *E. hexandra* are natives of central and southern Europe. The plants have stems which grow across the substrate, with short roots anchoring the plant, and side shoots carrying small rounded leaves vertically. They inhabit both ponds and lake margins, down to about 50 cm (20 in) in depth, often in otherwise unvegetated areas exposed to waves, where they form compact stands about 10 cm (4 in) tall. Flowers are produced underwater in leaf axils. In nature, as water temperatures fall in the autumn, the waterworts die down, and they survive the winter as seeds. With constant conditions, the plants can live for several years.

TEMP: 12–22°C (54–72°F)   LIGHT: 2   WATER: fresh

Haloragaceae

Within this large family of dicotyledons are about forty species of water-milfoils, the genus *Myriophyllum.* They are characterized by a central stem, which may or may not be rooted in the sediment, and by whorls of from three to six fine, delicate, feather-like leaves at intervals along the stem. Most of the milfoils are fragile, soft-leaved plants which live completely submerged, apart from the emergent flower stalk, although there are some amphibious species dwelling in marshes. Different species occur all over the world, in various temperature zones between the tropics and temperate

Myriophyllum species (Water Milfoil)

Ludwigia repens   Anubias nana   Aponogeton madagascariensis   Eleocharis acicularis (Hair Grass, or Slender Spike Grass)   Echinodorus magdalena

Nymphoides aquatica

Aponogeton madagascariensis   Nymphoides aquatica (Underwater Banana)

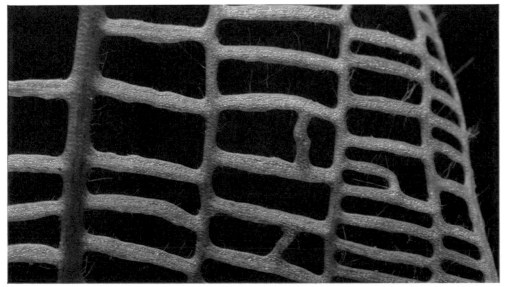

regions. In the latter, some species survive cold winters by means of semi-dormant buds, made up of many small, densely packed leaves.

M. spicatum occurs throughout Europe, North Africa, and North America. It is found in both still and running waters, including swift streams, and especially in limestone districts where the water is hard and alkaline. In clear lakes, it lives in up to 2 m (6.6 ft) of water. The fine leaves are 2–3 cm (0.8–1.2 in) long, being feathery and arranged in whorls of four.

TEMP: 10–22°C (50–72°F) LIGHT: 2 WATER: fresh, prefers hard alkaline

M. aquaticum is a native of the southern United States, and Central and South America. It forms mainly underwater leaves which are light-green, feathery, and soft, arranged in fives. The plant may also grow up above the water surface, and its aerial leaves are more rigid, thicker, and darker green.

TEMP: 18–30°C (64–86°F) LIGHT: 2–3 WATER: fresh, soft, neutral to slightly alkaline

Hippuridaceae

These dicotyledonous perennial plants, called mare's tails, are related to the water-milfoils. In Europe, they are plants of marshlands and shallow waters—pools, dykes, and streams.
Hippuris vulgaris is the widespread European mare's tail. The plant has short, narrow, dark-green leaves, which are soft in texture and arranged in dense whorls along the length of the erect stem. This may reach to 1–1.5 m (3–5 ft) and has a creeping rhizome rooted into the bottom sediment. The mare's tail can live completely submerged and is found in depths of up to 4 m (13 ft) where the water is clear. But typically, it lives emerged partly or halfway, with aerial leaves and flowers borne above the water surface. The flowers are very small and form in the leaf axils.

TEMP: 10–20°C (50–68°F) LIGHT: 2–3 WATER: fresh, hard alkaline

Hydrocharitaceae

This so-called frogbit family contains monocotyledonous species from both freshwater and marine habitats. They vary greatly in the form of leaves, growth, and type of flower. Floating as well as submerged species are represented. Important freshwater genera include, in northern temperate regions, *Stratiotes, Limnobium,* and *Hydrocharis;* in subtropical and tropical zones, *Lagarosiphon, Vallisneria, Egeria,* and *Hydrilla.*
Stratiotes aloides is the widespread European water soldier. It is an unusual plant, consisting of a dense rosette or cluster of spiny, saw-edged leaves, and lives completely submerged or floats half-submerged. The leaves are up to 35 cm (14 in) long, and 4 cm (1.6 in) broad. Long unbranched roots hang down through the water. Buds form in the leaf axils and grow into long offshoots, forming new small plants. In this way, floating masses of plants are produced, and the species spreads vegetatively. Conspicuous flowers, white with green,

are borne above the water in summer, and in the winter, the whole plant sinks to the bottom.

TEMP: 8–20°C (46–68°F) LIGHT: 2–3 WATER: fresh, medium hard, slightly alkaline

Elodea canadensis is the abundant and well-known Canadian pondweed, also called water thyme. It is a native of cool, temperate, fresh waters in North America but was introduced by man into Europe during the nineteenth century, and is now widespread. It occurs in virtually all bodies of still water and tolerates moderate currents as well. Its rapid growth and reproduction has made it an occasional nuisance in waterways. Reproduction is almost entirely vegetative from small fragments. *Elodea* has a long branching stem, which roots and binds the bottom sediments of fine silt and sand. The stem is completely submerged and carries dense whorls of narrow leaves. Another such pondweed is *E. nutallii,* a smaller plant up to 10–15 cm (4–6 in) long, with narrow and finely serrated leaves up to 1 cm (0.4 in) long.

TEMP: 5–24°C (41–75°F) LIGHT: 2–3 WATER: fresh

Egeria densa is a species of the temperate and subtropical zones in South America. It is similar in appearance to *Elodea* and has also been introduced to other parts of the world. It has a long unbranching stem which lives permanently submerged, with groups of adventitious roots anchoring the plant to the bottom, and dense whorls of small bright-green leaves along its length. The species inhabits still waters and is common in some areas within shallow pools, canals, and permanent ditches.

TEMP: 8–25°C (46–77°F) LIGHT: 3–4 WATER: fresh, medium hard, slightly alkaline

Hydrocharis morsus-ranae is the frogbit. It occurs throughout temperate Europe in still or slow-flowing ditches, canals, and pools. This plant floats unattached, close to the water surface, with unbranched roots hanging down through the water. A rosette of round leaves like that of water-lilies is produced, and white flowers with three petals grow clear of the water on short stalks. The plant reproduces vegetatively by stolons which grow out from the leaf axils: an extensive floating carpet can thus be formed. In the autumn, when water temperatures fall, "winter buds" develop on the stolons. Each is egg-shaped, 1–1.5 cm (0.4–0.6 in) long, and contains an embryo plant with a starch food store. The buds detach and sink to the bottom for the winter. In the spring, they develop gas spaces and, having used up the food, float to the surface as young plants.

TEMP: 10–18°C (50–64°F) LIGHT: 3 WATER: fresh, hard, alkaline

Lagarosiphon major is a native of South Africa and, like many of its relatives, has been introduced to various parts of Europe. It resembles a luxuriant and robust form of *Elodea*: a long, stout, and fairly stiff stem carries dense spirals of thick, dark-green, translucent leaves. The leaves are about 2 cm (0.8 in) long and coiled up. Adventitious roots attach the stem to the substrate, and the plant

lives permanently submerged, in still bodies of water. Small whitish flowers are produced which float free on reaching the water surface.

TEMP: 15–23°C (59–73°F) LIGHT: 3–4 WATER: fresh, medium hard, slightly alkaline

Vallisneria is a genus represented by a dozen species in tropical, subtropical, and temperate fresh waters throughout the world. They are known as the freshwater eel grasses, wild celeries, or vals. The plants are dense growths of long, strap-like or ribbon-like leaves, which twist along their length. Mature stands will form tangled, coiled masses at the water surface. The plants produce both floating female flowers, and male flowers which form underwater, float up when ripe, and open on the surface. Reproduction is vegetative, by runners from the buried rhizome, and can yield dense stands.
V. americana is a native of the southern United States, where it inhabits streams and pool margins. The plant will grow to about 30 cm (1 ft) in height.

TEMP: 15–28°C (59–82°F) LIGHT: 1–2 WATER: fresh, soft to medium hard, neutral to slightly acidic

V. spiralis is a widespread species of the same genus, in southern Europe and throughout the world's subtropics. It is also recorded in England, in the warmed effluent waters of industrial mills. It inhabits moderately flowing waters, and roots in various types of sediment. Leaves are commonly over 1 m (3.3 ft) in length, and about 1 cm (0.4 in) wide. *V. asiatica* is the Eastern representative of the genus, inhabiting running streams and other clear freshwater bodies in Indonesia, China, and Japan. It grows less vigorously than the last two species and forms thinner clumps of narrower bright-green leaves, which float rather stiffly towards the surface.

TEMP: 15–28°C (59–82°F) LIGHT: 2–4 WATER: fresh

Lemnaceae

These are the smallest monocotyledons, known as duckweeds. They are tiny free-floating plants, consisting of very simple flat leaves (thalli), with single or clumped rootlets hanging down through the water. The family contains several genera—*Lemna, Spirodela, Wolffia,* and *Wolfiella*—with representatives distributed from the tropics to temperate fresh waters. Temperate species overwinter by sinking to the bottom and hibernating. *Wolffia arrhiza,* the least duckweed, is the smallest flowering plant known, with a diameter of only 1–1.5 mm (0.04–0.06 in). It has no roots and grows in extensive floating rafts, usually with other duckweeds. It can extend even into slightly brackish waters such as coastal dykes.
Lemna species are common in still or slow-flowing ponds, ditches, and canals, particularly where the water is enriched by mineral or organic nutrients. The plants are capable of rapid vegetative reproduction, as the simple leaves form buds which grow rootlets and break away. Large rafts can spread over the water surface in this way. *L. minor* is the most cosmopolitan species and is common throughout Europe. The egg-shaped thalli are mostly 2–3 mm (0.08–0.12 in) in diameter. *L. trisulca,* the ivy-leaved

duckweed, is also found all over the world. The plants consist of elongate leaves, about 8 mm (0.32 in) long, which are often joined by narrow stalks into groups, and they float completely submerged, just below the water surface. Both of these species have single rootlets from the thallus underside. *L. polyrrhiza* grows in a form similar to *L. minor* but is slightly larger, about 5–8 mm (0.2–0.32 in) in diameter, and has a bundle of rootlets growing from the reddish underside of each thallus.

TEMP: 10–25°C (50–77°F) LIGHT: 2–3 WATER: any fresh, but fairly enriched

Lentibulariaceae

This family of dicotyledons includes wetland and terrestrial species as well as true aquatic plants, the bladderworts. The main genus is *Utricularia*, containing several hundred species represented in the tropics, subtropics, and temperate zones of the world. They are characterized by an ability to catch and "digest" insects. This carnivorous habit enables the plant to live in waters such as peat-bog pools, which are very poor in nutrients.

In most species, no roots are formed, and the plants float freely underwater. In other species, some of the leaves serve as roots, and anchor the plants loosely to the bottom sediment or to other vegetation. The leaves of the bladderworts are extremely fine and divided—and, in most species, carry many tiny sacs or bladders which can trap small aquatic animals. The prey decomposes within the bladder, and the nutrient soup is absorbed into the plant.

Bladderworts spread primarily by vegetative reproduction but also form flowers and set seed. The flowers are remarkably large and highly coloured, and are held above the water surface on a long stalk. Temperate species are annuals in the wild, overwintering as seeds, whilst many of the tropical species are perennial.

Utricularia exoleta is a native of Africa, Asia, and Australia. It inhabits the tropical and subtropical regions in still, shallow pools and ditches, where its fine stems and leaves form dense tangles of growth underwater. White flowers are carried on an emergent stalk which may be 10 cm (4 in) long.

TEMP: 15–30°C (59–86°F) LIGHT: 2 WATER: fresh, soft, neutral to slightly acidic

U. vulgaris is the greater bladderwort of calm ditches, pools, and slow river reaches throughout Europe. Found in up to 1 m (3.3 ft) of water, it has golden-yellow flowers on aerial stalks and overwinters by forming compact buds.

TEMP: 10–20°C (50–68°F) LIGHT: 2 WATER: fresh

Menyanthaceae

The dicotyledonous buckbeans and bogbeans are floating and marsh plants, common in tropical and subtropical areas. Among the important genera are *Menyanthes* and *Nymphoides*. The latter plants have a stiff swollen rhizome, which grows across and through the bottom sediment attached by roots. Long, thin leaf stalks grow from the rhizome

and carry the flat, round, fairly large leaves away from the bottom. The leaves are submerged or float on the water surface.

N. aquatica is a native of North America. It is known as the underwater banana, because it produces a bunch of bulbous tubers, 2–4 cm (0.8–1.6 in) long, at its base. Inhabiting pools, canals, and slow stream margins, it occurs in up to 50 cm (20 in) of water. Submerged, flattened leaves are produced at first, and older plants have long-stalked leaves which float on the water surface. These are bright-green on their upper sides, and fleshy and purple-green underneath. White bell-shaped flowers form at the water surface.

TEMP: 15–22°C (59–72°F) LIGHT: 1–2 WATER: fresh

N. peltata is a small European species, known as the fringed water-lily. Circular floating leaves grow up to 12 cm (5 in) in diameter, on long thin stalks which arise from the tips of a thin, branched rhizome. Flower stalks grow up above the water surface and carry yellow funnel-shaped flowers, about 3 cm (1.2 in) wide, with fringed edges.

TEMP: 10–25°C (50–77°F) LIGHT: 1–2 WATER: fresh, neutral to slightly acidic

Najadaceae

Within this diverse monocotyledonous family are a dozen or more genera, containing around sixty species of submerged aquatic plants. Distributed from tropical to cool temperate latitudes, they include freshwater and brackish representatives in still lakes or pools, and fully marine specimens known as sea-, turtle-, or eel-grasses. They are completely adapted to aquatic life, and even pollination occurs underwater: inconspicuous flowers, having a single stamen or pistil, form at the leaf axils. The plants spread vegetatively as well, by means of stem fragments and stolons. Among the sea-grasses are the genera *Zostera*, *Posidinia*, *Thalassia*, and *Halodule*. These exist throughout the world, forming dense meadows in shallow bays and estuaries. Where the light and sediments are suitable, they grow to cover extensive areas. A rich animal community, of both temporary and permanent inhabitants, is provided with food, shelter, and spawning and nursery grounds within the dense stands.

Najas indica is a species of tropical southeast Asia, in still and slow-moving waters. It forms submerged tufts of growth, with firm unbranching stems, anchored by adventitious roots to the sediment, and growing up through the water. The leaves are well under 1 cm (0.4 in) wide but grow in a hooked shape up to 4 cm (1.6 in) long. They are bright green with fine toothed edges.

TEMP: 18–28°C (64–82°F) LIGHT: 3–4 WATER: fresh, neutral, soft to medium hard

N. graminae is a subtropical species of southern Europe, Africa, southern Asia, and Australia. Its long, branching stems are rooted at intervals and grow upwards. They are easily broken, and fragments readily form tufty new plants. The leaves are narrow, around 2 cm (0.8 in) long, with fine teeth

along the edges, and form dense, bright-green clusters.

TEMP: 15–25°C (59–77°F) LIGHT: 3 WATER: fresh, soft, neutral to slightly acidic

N. marina, the holly-leaved naiad, and *N. flexilis*, the slender naiad, are cool temperate-zone species, although very rare in some regions. They inhabit still pools in northern Europe, and *N. marina* can tolerate slightly brackish waters.

Zostera marina is a widely distributed species in temperate coastal seas of the northern hemisphere. It grows up to 15–20 cm (6–8 in) high and spreads by means of stolons.

TEMP: 8–18°C (46–64°F) LIGHT: 2 WATER: sea

Posidinia oceanica occupies extensive areas of the Mediterranean, in depths between 2–3 m (6–10 ft) and 35 m (115 ft).

TEMP: 10–25°C (50–77°F) LIGHT: 3–4 WATER: sea

Nymphaeaceae

About seventy species of these water-lilies have been described from the world's tropical, subtropical, and temperate regions. They are dicotyledons, and the majority develop submerged leaves when the plant is young, later producing the well-known large, flat, floating leaves. The leaf stalks arise from the plant's stout rhizome, which grows across the sediment attached by adventitious roots. The plants grow in up to 2 m (6.6 ft) of water and are found in still or slow-flowing waters sheltered from the wind. The broad floating leaves of the larger, more vigorous species can cover the water surface completely. This reduces considerably the light reaching the water and any submerged plants, as well as reducing the effect of surface winds upon water movement and aeration, so that dissolved oxygen may fall to low levels.

Nymphaea is a genus containing about forty species. They form attractive flowers above the water surface. *N. alba*, a widespread species in the northern temperate zone, has a large plant with a rhizome 1 m (3.3 ft) or more long, and white-petalled flowers about 10 cm (4 in) in diameter.

TEMP: 10–20°C (50–68°F) LIGHT: 1–2 WATER: fresh

Nuphar, a genus occurring throughout temperate latitudes, has plants which often live completely submerged for several years, before they develop floating leaves and flowers. *N. lutea* is the most common European species, extending into North Africa and temperate Asia.

TEMP: 15–25°C (59–77°F) LIGHT: 1–2 WATER: fresh

Barclaya species are smaller water-lilies. A typical representative is *B. longifolia*, a native of southeast Asia. The plant forms a cluster of thin, delicate, submerged leaves from the rooted rhizome. The leaves are green to brown-red, up to 30 cm (1 ft) long and 5 cm (2 in) broad.

TEMP: 22–28°C (72–82°F) LIGHT: 2 WATER: fresh, soft, neutral SOIL: fairly rich

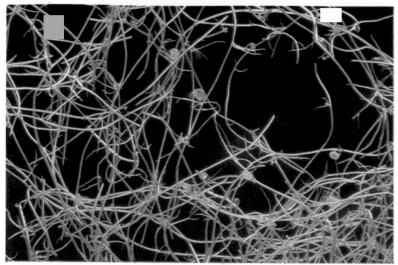

Utricularia exoleta (Dwarf Bladderwort)

Subularia aquatica (Awlwort)

Aglaonema simplex

Onagraceae

This dicotyledonous family of the willow herbs, evening primroses, and fuchsias contains many wetland species—but only one genus, *Ludwigia*, of true aquatic plants. These have low or creeping stems, with fairly long and narrow submerged leaves.

L. arcuata is a native of the southern United States, where it lives in pools, ditches, and dykes with still or slow-moving water. The stem is branching and grows to 40 cm (16 in) long. The leaves, green and red, are up to 2 cm (0.8 in) long, but less than 0.5 cm (0.2 in) wide. *L. repens* is another species in the same region and in still water. It has a creeping stem and dark, glossy leaves which are red or purple underneath.

TEMP: 15–28°C (59–82°F) LIGHT: 2–3 WATER: fresh

L. palustris is a European species, whose branching stem forms roots and oval leaves at intervals. Small flowers without petals form at the leaf bases.

TEMP: 15–20°C (59–68°F) LIGHT: 2 WATER: fresh

Plantaginaceae

The dicotyledonous plantains are a family of small plants which occur worldwide, in a great range of habitats. *Litorella* is the only genus containing aquatic and amphibious species. *L. uniflora*, known as the shoreweed, grows on the gravel bottoms of pools, lakes, and reservoirs, in up to about 4 m (13 ft) of water. It is common throughout central and northern Europe. The plant is a rosette or cluster of leaves rooted to the sediment. The leaves are up to 5 cm (2 in) long, pointed and curled in cross-section. Slender stolons grow from the base, giving rise to new plants, so that a dense carpet can spread across the bottom. *L. australis* and *L. americana* are similar species, native to temperate South and North America respectively.

TEMP: 10–20°C (50–68°F) LIGHT: 1–2 WATER: fresh, slightly hard and alkaline

Polygonaceae

These so-called bistorts, or persicarias, are dicotyledons and include the widespread European species *Polygonum amphibium*. It is amphibious, occurring in diverse places—lakes, reservoirs, ditches, canals, and streams—where the water is still or moved by waves. It can live in up to 2 m (6.6 ft) of water, as well as out of water on banks. The plant has a rhizome rooted to the soil and a slender stem bearing long leaf stalks and glossy, elliptical, dark-green leaves. A head of small pink flowers, about 10 cm (4 in) long, grows clear of the water.

TEMP: 10–25°C (50–77°F) LIGHT: 1–2 WATER: fresh

Pontederiaceae

This diverse dicotyledonous family contains some ten genera, with about thirty species of tropical and subtropical marsh and aquatic plants. It includes the floating water hyacinths, and the submerged mud plantains and pickerel-weeds.
Eichhornia crassipes is the water hyacinth of tro-

pical African rivers, canals, and pools. It roots in shallow water or floats freely on the surface, with its tangle of roots hanging down through the water. The plant forms a rosette of broad oval leaves, about 5 cm (2 in) long. The beautiful orchid-like flower forms above the water surface, in the centre of the rosette.

TEMP: 15–28°C (59–82°F) LIGHT: 20–3 WATER: fresh, soft, neutral to slightly acidic

Heteranthera zosterifolia is a submerged plant native to the Amazon basin. The plant's stem, about 30 cm (1 ft) long, is slender and soft. It straggles across the bottom sediment, rooting at intervals. Floating side-shoots arise, bearing small, oblong, green or red-green leaves.

TEMP: 22–30°C (72–86°F) LIGHT: 2–3 WATER: fresh, soft, slightly acidic

Zosterella dubia is an inhabitant of the subtropical southern areas of North America. The plant has many long ribbon-like leaves, which are slightly coiled and float vertically from a slim branching stem. It is rooted in the bottom sediment and may grow to 1 m (3.3 ft) high.

TEMP: 15–28°C (59–82°F) LIGHT: 2 WATER: fresh

Potamogetonaceae

These monocotyledons, called pondweeds, comprise a very large number of species of rooted freshwater plants, occurring throughout tropical and temperate latitudes. They are medium-sized plants, growing from branching rhizomes which creep through and over the substrate and, in some species, form an interwoven mat that binds the silt together. Three different leaf forms are produced: broad, submerged, and soft-tissued; finely divided, submerged, and grass-like; elongate, ovate, floating, and tough-tissued. In nature, most of the temperate species lose their leaves in the autumn and overwinter on the rhizome food store.

The pondweeds produce a cylindrical flower-spike above the water surface. It bears inconspicuous brownish-green flowers, which are pollinated by insects. The plants also spread vegetatively, by means of stem or rhizome fragments, and some species rapidly cover a bottom area with runners from the rhizomes. Vegetative winter buds are also created by various temperate species.
Potamogeton coloratus, the fen pondweed, is a native of central and western Europe, inhabiting the still shallows of calcareous fen pools. Its stalked leaves grow up to the water surface and are beautifully thin, net-veined, and elliptical in shape. *P. compressus*, the grass-wrack pondweed, is less common although widespread in Europe. This plant lives in small pools and slow-flowing streams of calcareous water, with a creeping rhizome that produces a stem which may reach 2 m (6.6 ft) in length. Along the stem grow long ribbon-like leaves in pairs, up to 20 by 0.5 cm (8 by 0.2 in) in dimensions. *Groenlandia densa*, the opposite-leaved pondweed, is also widespread in Europe, colonizing clear water in streams and dykes with a slow to moderate flow. The plants are small and

compact, with pairs of elliptical leaves opposed along the densely covered stem.

TEMP: 12–20°C (54–68°F) LIGHT: 2 WATER: fresh, hard, alkaline

P. perfoliatus, another common European species, lives in still and running waters and can colonize clear pools and canals up to 2 m (6.6 ft) deep. Elongate shoots are formed in running water. The rhizome creeps extensively and gives rise to a branching stem with oval leaves, about 2 by 2 cm (0.8 by 0.8 in) in size, which clasp the stem. *P. crispus* is the familiar European curly pondweed, inhabiting both still and moderately fast waters, on all types of sediment. Its rhizome grows long and thin, branching frequently with roots along the length. The stem, and the wavy-edged, toothed, oblong leaves, are often reddish-green. *P. pectinatus* is called the fennel, or sago, pondweed, because its extremely slender, pointed leaves are formed as two thread-like tubes. Its habitats resemble those of the last species but can extend into brackish waters (up to a salinity of 5 parts per thousand). The stem is very branched, and dense stands are usually formed in shallow water. It grows in clear waters up to 2.5 m (8 ft) deep.

TEMP: 12–20°C (54–68°F) LIGHT: 2 WATER: fresh

P. gayii is a widely distributed South American species. It grows from a long rhizome which covers the bottom, roots adventitiously, and gives rise at intervals to slender floating stems. The leaves are green-red, long and narrow, up to about 10 by 0.8 cm (4 by 0.3 in). *P. malaianus*, widespread in the American and Asian tropics and subtropics, inhabits both still and flowing waters. The buried rhizome produces a rising stem, which carries the delicate, semi-transparent, long, narrow leaves.

TEMP: 15–28°C (59–82°F) LIGHT: 2 WATER: fresh

Primulaceae

This large dicotyledonous family contains over thirty genera and 800 species of small flowering plants, throughout the northern temperate zone. There are a few aquatic representatives.
Hottonia palustris, the water-violet, is common in Europe and Asia, inhabiting shallow and still ponds, pools, and ditches where the substrate is sandy. The plant has a thin rooted rhizome, which straggles across the bottom and produces a more erect, slender stem. The leaves are submerged, delicate, and feather-like, 4–5 cm (1.6–2.0 in) long. The stem grows into a spike above the water surface, with pale-violet flowers. In the wild, winter buds are produced at the tips of shoots.

TEMP: 8–20°C (46–68°F) LIGHT: 2 WATER: fresh

Ranunculaceae

These are the dicotyledonous water crowfoots, characterized by finely divided, forked, underwater leaves which trail out from the main stem, and by lobed floating leaves. There are also intermediate leaf forms. Many such species occur throughout the temperate regions of the world in ponds,

Limnophila sessiliflora

Bacopa amplexicaulis

shallow bays, canals, dykes, and running waters. The crowfoots produce single flowers on stems above the water surface. Most of these have white petals and sepals, with a yellow centre.

Ranunculus fluitans, the European river crowfoot, is one of the few species of higher plants which are able to live in fast-flowing streams, in currents up to 70 cm (28 in) per second. It has a stout stem rooted to the substrate in up to 2 m (6.6 ft) of water. Long roots push down through the coarse gravel and stones of its natural habitat. Only submerged leaves are produced, fine, soft, and brush-like, 5–25 cm (2–10 in) long.

TEMP: 5–15°C (41–59°F)   LIGHT: 1   WATER: fresh, neutral, medium hard

R. aquatilis is another European species, one of several which occur in still and slow-moving waters, producing both submerged and floating leaves. The latter are robust and rounded, but deeply cut and variable, whilst the submerged leaves are soft and finely forked.

TEMP: 10–20°C (50–68°F)   LIGHT: 1–2   WATER: fresh

Scrophulariaceae

This is a large family of dicotyledonous plants, containing several thousand species in over 200 genera. About seventeen genera include aquatic species. Figworts, speedwells, and eyebrights belong to the family.

Veronica anagallis-aquatica is the blue water speedwell, and *V. catenata* is the pink variety. Both are widespread and occasionally common in Europe. They inhabit diverse waters, from shallow pool margins and ditches to moderately flowing streams, and are often found as early colonizers after the bottom soil has been cleared or disturbed. They grow to a height of 30–50 cm (12–20 in), with pairs of pointed leaves, about 5 cm (2 in) long and 2 cm (0.8 in) broad, clasping the erect stem. The small pale flowers are carried on stalks from the bases of emergent leaves.

TEMP: 10–20°C (50–68°F)   LIGHT: 1–2   WATER: fresh

The brooklime, *V. beccabunga,* is another European species.

Bacopa amplexicaulis, known as the water hyssop, is an amphibious species of the southern United States. Underwater, a long central stem, rooted at intervals, grows across the bottom of shallow pools and ditches. Soft smooth leaves, 2–3 cm (0.8–1.2 in) long, with dark veins, grow mainly on rising, floating shoots up to 20 cm (8 in) above the bottom. Flowers form only on emergent stems and are dark-blue.

TEMP: 15–28°C (59–82°F)   LIGHT: 1–2   WATER: fresh, soft, slightly acidic

Limnophila (or *Ambulia*) is a genus containing over thirty species of wetland and aquatic plants distributed through Asia, Australia, and Africa. *L. aquatica* is native to India and Ceylon, where it inhabits ditches, ponds, and drainage canals. The plant has a round stem which grows over the bottom and attaches by roots. The rising, growing tip of the stem carries delicate, finely divided leaves in bushy whorls about 5 cm (2 in) across. If the stem reaches the water surface, it produces leaves that are smaller and elliptical. Clusters of lilac flowers form at the stem tips.

TEMP: 18–28°C (64–82°F)   LIGHT: 2   WATER: fresh

Heteranthera zosterifolia

3 Zoology for the Aquarist

Annabel Milne
Peter Stebbing

Introduction

The illustration at left shows shrimpfishes swimming amongst the spines of the hat-pin sea urchin. Such colloquial names of living organisms are often ambiguous. Therefore, as the preceding chapters exemplify, biologists have given every organism a scientific name with two words. For the fishes shown, this is *Aeoliscus strigatus* (Gunther, 1860). The second word is the species name of the organism, and the first word names the larger group, or genus, to which the species belongs. These words are latinized and usually derived from Latin or Greek. In strictly conventional usage, the species name is followed by that of the author of the first published description with its date. If the latter terms are bracketed, the generic name has been changed from that in the original description.

A species is a group of organisms which can interbreed. Taxonomists compare species and classify them into a hierarchy of more inclusive groups expressing the evolutionary relationships between organisms. Thus, *Aeoliscus strigatus* belongs to the family Centriscidae, in the order Syngnathiformes, in the class Osteichthyes (bony fishes), in the phylum Chordata (including vertebrates), in the kingdom Animalia. The table below shows how the phyla discussed in this chap-

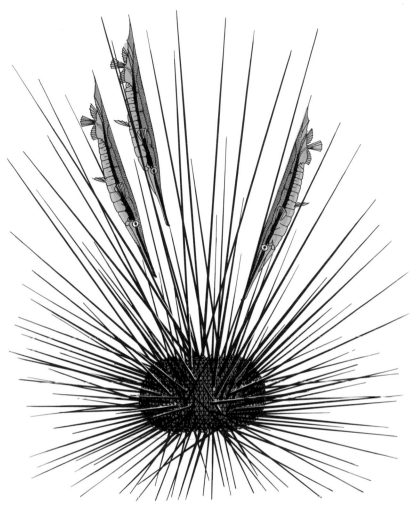

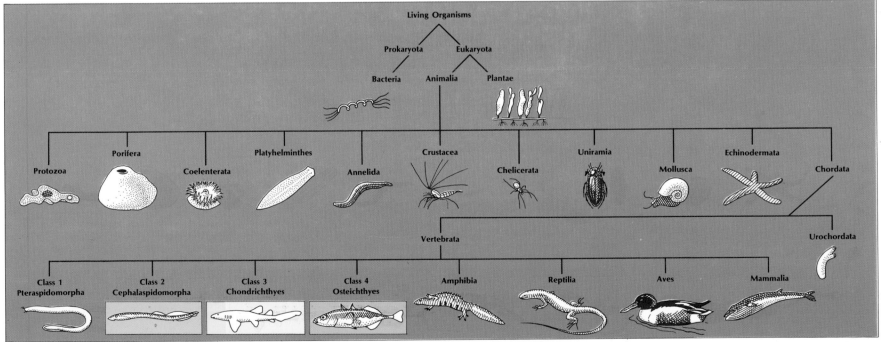

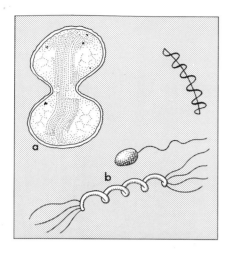

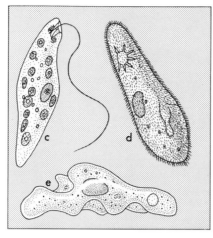

(a) Dividing cell of *Nitrosococcus* (x 11,000), one of the nitrifying bacteria in water. (b) Unicellular bacterial forms. (c) A flagellate, *Euglena viridis*. (d) A ciliate,

Paramecium caudatum. (e) Amoeba proteus, which moves by extruding its protoplasm. (c-e) are examples of true protozoan animals.

ter and some other familiar groups are classified. The following summary of phyla will concentrate on the aquatic groups, especially fishes, emphasizing their characteristics.

A feature of aquatic life is the plankton, that drifting assemblage composed mostly of small and microscopic organisms, as well as including the eggs and larvae of numerous larger species. Bacteria are amongst the smallest planktonic organisms; they also occur in all other environments, breed rapidly, and are essential for the re-cycling of waste products. Bacteria are classified in a group termed Prokaryota, as their cells do not have distinct structures, unlike those of plants and animals, the Eukaryota.

The animal kingdom

The phylum Protozoa consists of microscopic unicellular animals. Some well-known groups are flagellates (with a whip-like flagellum), ciliates (covered in hair-like cilia), and amoebas.

The phylum Porifera contains sponges. Except for one freshwater family, these are marine animals. They have no nervous system and constitute a subkingdom called Parazoa. All are multicellular, sessile filter-feeders, with a simple body structure having several types of cells and spicules, which surround a cavity with an exhalant opening. The spicules vary between species and are important for the identification and classification of sponges.

In the phylum Coelenterata are jellyfishes, hydroids, corals, and anemones. They have stinging cells, termed cnidoblasts, used for predation and defence. They exist in two main forms, free-swimming and polyp. Those of the class Hydrozoa (hydroids) pass through both forms during their life. Scyphozoa (jellyfishes) live mostly in the free-swimming form and are rarely kept in a home aquarium. Anthozoa (corals, anemones) never develop beyond the polyp stage.

In the phylum Platyhelminthes are flatworms—parasitic flukes, tapeworms, and many free-living species such as planarians and marine polyclads. The last are usually less than 1.25 cm (0.5 in) long. Larger tropical species are brightly coloured and of interest to the aquarist. Flatworms have three layers of cells, and the middle one, or

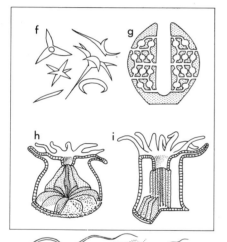

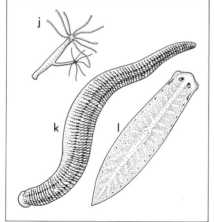

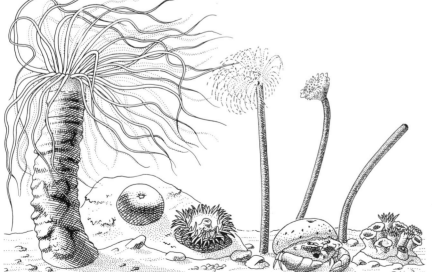

At left is a Mediterranean scene. From left to right: the anthozoans *Cerianthus membranaceus* (crowned by over 200 tentacles, growing up to 30 cm (12 in), with solidified sheath of mucus and particles) and *Actinia equina* (beadlet anemone, shown with tentacles retracted and extended); the polychaete worm *Spirographis spallanzanii*, whose tentacles (patterned yellow, brown, and white) retract when disturbed, and are used for respiration and collecting food; the crab *Dromia personata*, carrying the poriferan *Suberites*; and a colony of the stony coral *Astroides calycularis*.

(f) Diverse spicules from sponges. (g) Cross-section of a sponge: flagellated chambers pump water through tubular canals. (h) Stony coral polyp, with cup forming. (i) Sea anemone, with gastrovascular cavity and tentacles bearing cnidoblasts. (j) Freshwater hydra of class Hydrozoa. (k) The horse leech, clitellatan *Haemopis sanguisuga*, and (l) the triclad *Dugesia lugubris*, are temperate freshwater species. Crustacea: (m) brine shrimp (*Artemia salina*) and (n) water flea (*Daphnia pulex*) are primitive examples of the class Branchiopoda. (o) Mantis shrimp (*Squilla mantis*), a predatory stomatopod. (p) *Gammarus pulex*, mesoderm, forms muscle and other tissue which permits more complex animal activity.

The phylum Annelida consists of worms with soft segmented bodies containing a cavity, or coelom. Its two main groups are the Clitellata (hermaphroditic earthworms and leeches) and the Polychaeta (unisexual bristleworms, chiefly marine, in over 8,000 species).

The "arthropods"

The three following phyla were once classified in the larger phylum Arthropoda (meaning jointed-limb animals). This is now obsolete, as research shows that they evolved from different ancestors.

In the phylum Crustacea are water-fleas, shrimps, lobsters, and other species. Mostly marine, they have two paired antennae and, usually, two-branched limbs and two or three pairs of mouth-parts. The classes Ostracoda and Copepoda (containing planktonic forms) and Cirripedia (including barnacles) are rarely kept in an aquarium. The largest class, economically important to man, is the Malacostraca, comprising orders such as the Stomatopoda (primitive forms), Isopoda, and Amphipoda. Isopods tend to be flattened dorso-ventrally, and amphipods laterally. The order Decapoda displays ten thoracic limbs.

The phylum Chelicerata contains king-crabs, sea-spiders, spiders, and mites. The last two make up its largest class, the Arachnida, whilst most aquatic species are of the classes Merostomata (king-crabs) and Pycnogonida (sea-spiders). All lack antennae but have two distinct body regions, normally four or more pairs of legs on the anterior portion, and a pair of chelate (pincer-like) appendages in front of the mouth. Species of interest to the aquarist are the king-crabs, whose larvae pass through a "trilobite" stage indicating the archaic ancestry of these strange animals. They occur along the northwest Atlantic and western Pacific coasts. Also of interest is the freshwater spider (class Arachnida) which builds a silken diving-bell and is widespread in Europe and Asia.

The phylum Uniramia includes a subphylum, Hexapoda (insects), containing aquatic species. Insects have six legs, usually two pairs of wings, and a body divided—sometimes by clear constrictions—into a

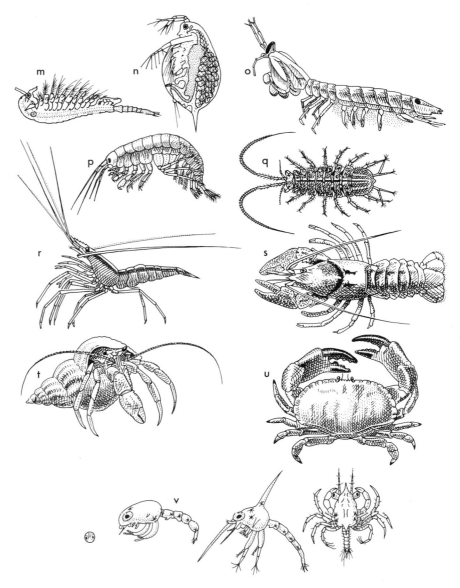

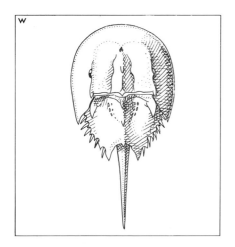

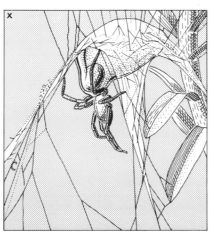

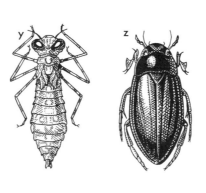

an amphipod in temperate fresh waters. (q) Freshwater louse (*Asellus aquaticus*), an isopod. Of order Decapoda are (r) a tropical fish-cleaning shrimp (*Hippolysmata grabhami*), (s) freshwater crayfish (*Astacus pallipes*), (t) hermit crab (*Pagurus bernhardus*), inhabiting shells of gastropods; (u) edible crab (*Cancer pagurus*) with (v) development stages. Chelicerata: (w) king-crab (*Limulus polyphemus*) of class Merostomata, from North American east coast, (x) water-spider (*Argyroneta aquatica*) in diving-bell. Uniramia: (y) dragonfly nymph (*Aeshna* species), (z) great silver water-beetle (*Hydrophilus piceus*).

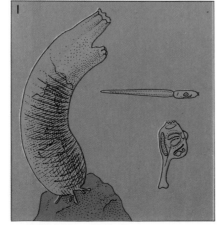

Mollusca, showing foot and shell in colour: *(a)* chiton *(Tonicella lineata),* a polyplacophoran; the gastropods *(b) Patella aspera,* limpet, *(c) Phyllidia bourguini,* sea slug, and *(d) Planorbis corneus,* freshwater snail; *(e)* scallop, *Pecten maximus,* bivalve; *(f)* cuttlefish, *Sepia officinalis,* cephalopod. Echinodermata and their tube-feet: *(g) Antedon bifida,* crinoid; *(h) Linckia laevigata,* asteroid; *(i) Ophiothrix fragilis,* ophiuroid; *(j) Echinus esculentus,* echinoid; *(k) Holothuria forskali,* holothuroid. Urochordata: *(l)* sea squirt, *Ciona intestinalis,* with juvenile forms.

head, thorax, and abdomen. Since insects cannot tolerate the high salinity of sea water, none live in it, although some inhabit its surface, such as the ocean striders (family Gerridae). But there are freshwater examples in nearly half of the insect orders: Odonata (dragonflies) exemplify the many which only develop in water, leaving on maturity, whilst some Coleoptera (beetles) have a truly aquatic life.

The molluscs

The phylum Mollusca is very diverse and difficult to define, often being discussed in terms of an hypothetical ancestor from which its present forms may have evolved. They possess a muscular foot, and their shell may be external, internal, or absent. The shell is secreted by a tissue layer, the mantle, which normally encloses the gills. Some of the principal groups are as follows.

The class Polyplacophora (chitons) is easily distinguished by eight slightly overlapping plates along the back of a flattened body. Chitons are mainly intertidal browsers and feed on encrusting algae. They roll up for protection when removed from the substrate. The class Gastropoda (slugs and snails) occurs in marine, freshwater, and land habitats. They have a muscular foot, and many possess a shell containing the viscera, which twists during the larval process that is known as torsion.

The class Bivalvia (clams, oysters) is characterized by a single shell with two valves, joined dorsally by a ligament. Its members, all aquatic, are mostly marine filter-feeders, living in or attached to a substrate, although a few species can swim. In the class Cephalopoda (cuttlefishes, squids, octopi), the shell is usually either internal or absent. The head has well-developed eyes and eight, ten, or more prehensile tentacles. Cephalopods include the fastest and most intelligent invertebrates.

The echinoderms

The phylum Echinodermata (named from Greek words meaning a spiny skin) exhibits a five-sided body plan, and a hydrovascular system sustaining many tubular feet which are adapted for movement and food collection. These animals are distributed worldwide in five main groups.

The class Crinoidea (sea lilies and feather stars) is identified by five arms, usually branched, which arise from the body disc and are used to catch, for example, plankton. Sea lilies have a single stalk in contact with the substrate, whilst the mobile feather stars have a number of cirri, or small branches, for temporary attachment. The subclass Asteroidea (starfishes) possess up to fifty arms, projecting laterally and, because of their thickness, not always clearly demarcated from the body. Along each arm is a ventral groove bearing rows of tube feet, which may have suckers (except in most of the burrowing forms). The subclass Ophiuroidea (brittlestars, basketstars) have small distinct bodies, with long arms which break easily and, in the genera of basketstars, are branched. The tube feet are used as tentacles for feeding and arise between plates covering the ventral arm-groove. Some species are predatory, but most feed on organic matter in suspension or upon the substrate.

The class Echinoidea (sea urchins) exhibits a rigid shell, or test, carrying many spines of various sizes, which articulate in a ball-and-socket manner. Radially symmetrical forms live on the substrate, and bilaterally symmetrical ones are adapted to burrowing into it. The class

Identification of a fish requires some knowledge of its anatomy, which is introduced in the next illustrations. A koi is shown below, with basic terms which apply to most fishes: (a) mouth, (b) lip, (c) nostril, (d) barbel, (e) preoperculum, (f) operculum, (g) anus or vent, (h) lateral line, (i) caudal peduncle; the fin (j) origin, (k) base, and (l) termination; (m) dorsal, (n) pectoral, (o) pelvic, (p) anal, and (q) tail or caudal, fins.

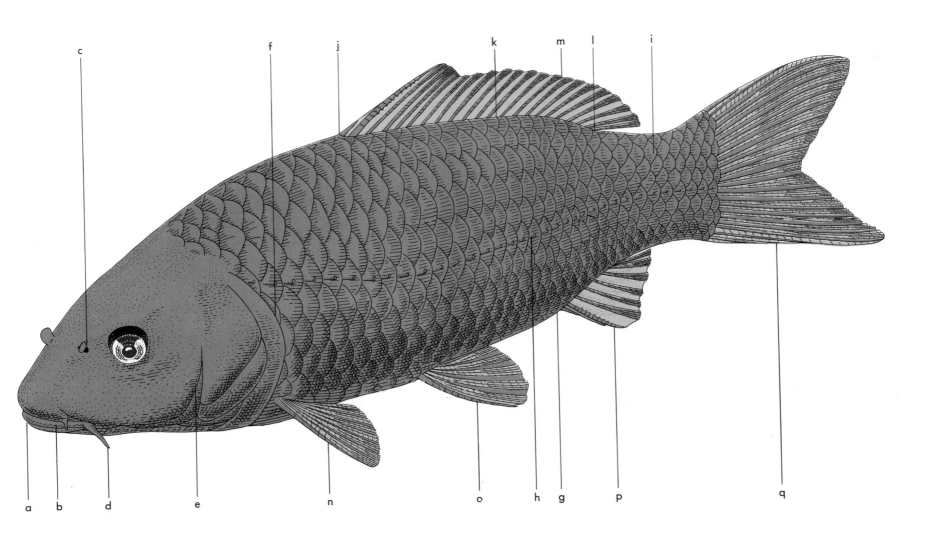

A shark, ray, bony fish, and bony flatfish (below, from left to right) demonstrate fins of comparable origin and structure.

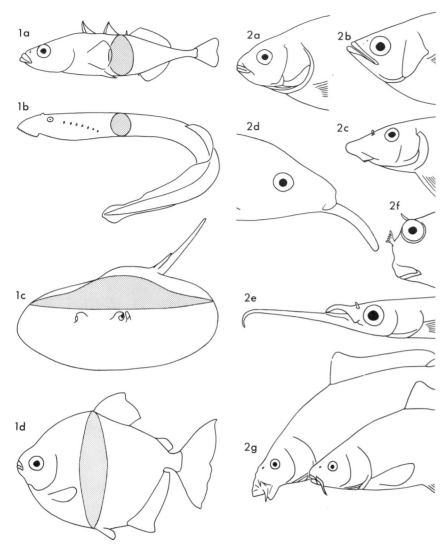

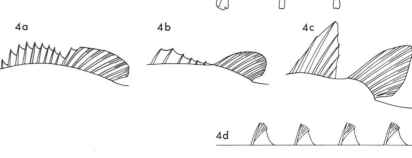

The fins consist of supporting structures called spines and rays. *(3a)* Spines are usually very stiff, pointed at the tip, and not divided or segmented. Where both spines and rays occur, the spines normally precede the rays. *(3b)* Rays are softer, usually segmented and also branched *(3c)*.

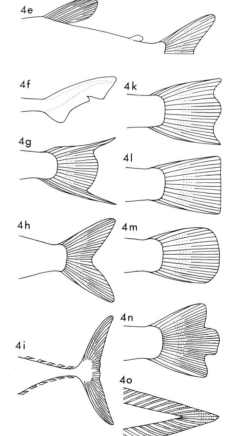

Median or unpaired fins are located along the mid-dorsal and mid-ventral plane. They include the dorsal fin(s) which may be *(4a)* continuous, *(4b)* contiguous, or *(4c)* two separate fins. *(4d)* Separate finlets occur in some species, dorsally and/or ventrally. *(4e)* The adipose fin occurs in certain fish groups, and may have a supporting spine. The caudal fin or tail exhibits various forms: *(4f)* heterocercal, *(4g)* lyretail, *(4h)* forked, *(4i)* lunate, *(4j)* indented or emarginate, *(4k)* double indented, *(4l)* truncate, *(4m)* rounded, *(4n)* with elongate middle rays, *(4o)* pointed or confluent (dorsal, caudal, and anal), *(4p)* naked. The anal fin is located ventrally behind the anus. Many species have *(4q)* sexually dimorphic fins so that mature adults, normally the males, possess extended rays in one or more fins. In certain species, some rays of the anal fin of males are modified into a copulatory organ.

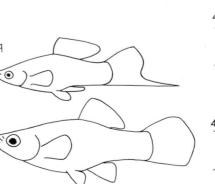

All fishes may be regarded as having a variation of the hydrodynamic fusiform shape, which will be used in this chapter as the basis for describing the body form.

Body forms, with silhouetted cross-sections: *(1a)* fusiform shape, shown by *Gasterosteus aculeatus,* stickleback; *(1b)* elongate, *Lampetra planeri,* brook lamprey; *(1c)* depressed, *Potamotrygon motoro,* river stingray; *(1d)* compressed, *Metynnis hypsauchen,* silver dollar.

The head usually varies between species, due to their different diets and feeding habits, although they may have similar bodies. The mouth can be *(2a)* terminal, if both jaws are equal, as in the roach (*Rutilus*

rutilus); *(2b)* superior, if the lower jaw is prominent, as in the archerfish (*Toxotes jaculator*); *(2c)* inferior, if the upper jaw—or also the snout—is prominent, as in the sucker loach (*Gyrinocheilus aymonieri*). Peculiarly adapted species are *(2d)* *Gnathonemus petersi,* the Ubangi mormyrid, with a flexible appendage on the chin, and *(2e)* *Dermogenys pogonognathus,* the red halfbeak, with a developed lower jaw. Appendages on the head include the barbels (illustrated on page 65) and, in some species, the cirri, which are small fleshy flaps around the eyes or nostrils. *(2f)* is *Ophioblennius atlanticus,* the redlip blenny. *(2g)* A protractile or protrusible mouth, in many species, is extended to eat.

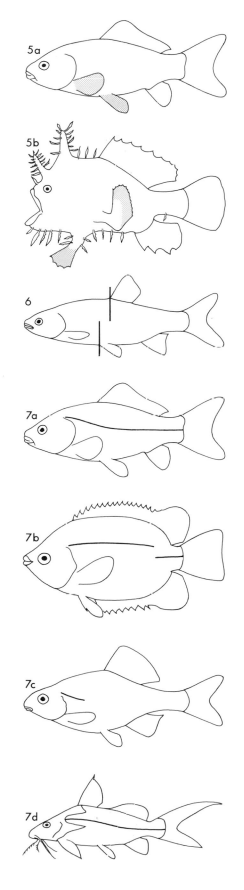

Paired fins are shown by the tone in (5a). The pectoral fins are usually located behind the head from mid-flank to ventrally. The pelvic fins may be variously located along the ventral surface, even in front of the pectoral fins as in (5b) the sargassum fish (*Histrio histrio*). The pelvic fins or both paired fins may be absent in some species.

The relative position of fins may be noted in describing a fish, as when (6) the dorsal fin origin is said to be behind the pelvic fin origin (on a perpendicular line through each).

The lateral line is an important sense organ in fishes, used for locating pressure waves in the water. The main types are (7a) complete, (7b) divided or interrupted, (7c) incomplete, (7d) complete in a scaleless catfish. The scales of the lateral line are described as pierced, having small holes connected to the line canal.

The scales of fishes are of several types, mainly (8a) cycloid resembling a disc, and (8b) ctenoid bearing a comb-like structure. Other types are (8c) placoid and (8d) ganoid or rhombic. The shaded area here shows the embedded part of the scale. A species may have more than one type, or be entirely naked of scales.

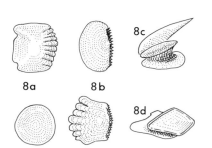

The markings of the body are referred to by regions: *(a)* head, *(b)* humeral region or shoulder, *(c)* flank, *(d)* caudal peduncle, *(e)* abdomen.

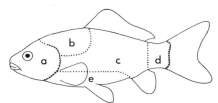

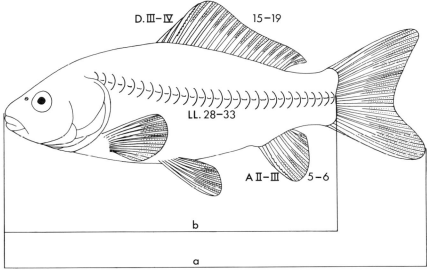

The fin-and-scale formula (meristics) is used to express the numbers of spines, rays, and scales, as an aid in identifying fishes. This formula employs a conventional order of terms as follows. D = dorsal fin; if more than one dorsal fin is present, they are indicated 1D and 2D. A = anal fin. Pect. = pectoral fin. Pel. = pelvic fin. LL = lateral line. The fins are noted with roman numerals for the spines and/or unbranched rays, and arabic numerals for branched rays. Strictly, roman numerals should refer only to spines, but they are difficult to distinguish from unbranched rays on a live fish, and are sometimes counted together with these, as is done here. For example, the meristic formula of a goldfish is D.III–IV,15–19, A.II–III,5–6, LL.28–33. Therefore, it has three or four spines or spine-like rays, and fifteen to nineteen branched rays, in the dorsal fin (and similarly for the other fin(s) listed), and has twenty-eight to thirty-three scales in the lateral line. (The last ray of D. and A. may be branched at the base and counts as one ray.) The length of a fish, stated as the size, refers to the total length *(a)*. Sometimes reference is made to the body length *(b)*, also known as the standard length.

Holothuroidea (sea cucumbers) have elongated bodies with five sides, the mouth and anus being at opposite ends. The tube feet on three sides are more numerous, providing support and movement. The feet around the mouth are adapted for feeding and, in some species, are the only ones present.

The chordates

The phylum Chordata includes, firstly, a subphylum called Urochordata (sea squirts). Their ancestors are thought to be an evolutionary link between the invertebrates and vertebrates, because they have a larval stage with a notochord, the precursor of the vertebral column. Adults are covered by a gelatinous test, and filter water for food and oxygen. Some species are sessile, and others pelagic—either solitary or colonial—but all are marine.

The subphylum of vertebrates is composed of four classes of fishes and the amphibians, reptiles, birds, and mammals. The illustrations show representatives of some of the fish families to be discussed and may serve as a visual aid to identifying fishes. They are grouped into orders, and the numbers shown refer to the families described.

The fish classes are, firstly, Pteraspidomorpha (hagfishes), and—class two as illustrated here—Cephalaspidomorpha (lampreys). Both of these flourished during the Silurian and Devonian periods, from 435

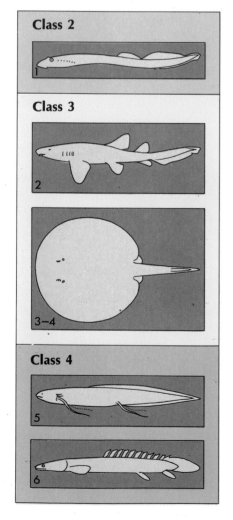

Class 2

1

Class 3

2

3–4

Class 4

5

6

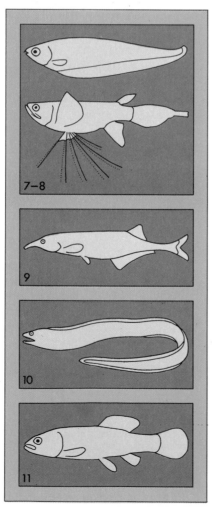

7–8

9

10

11

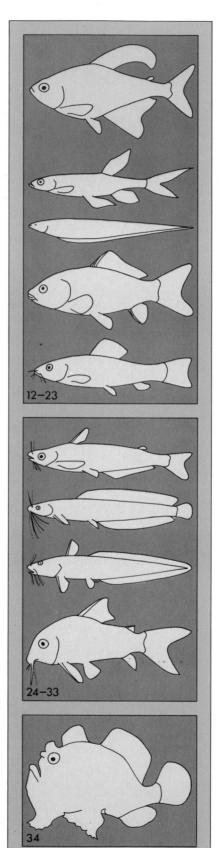

12–23

24–33

34

35–43

44–45

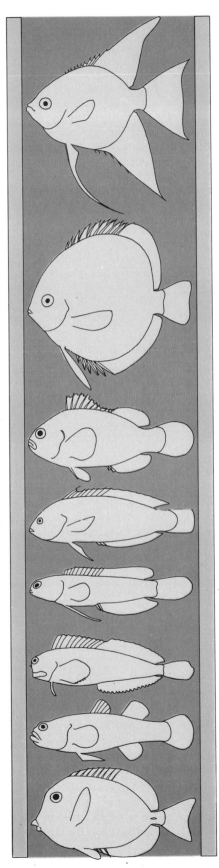

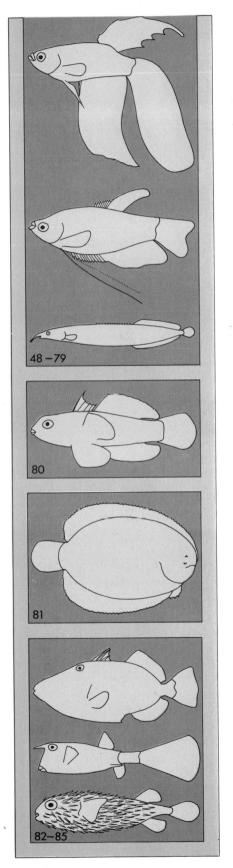

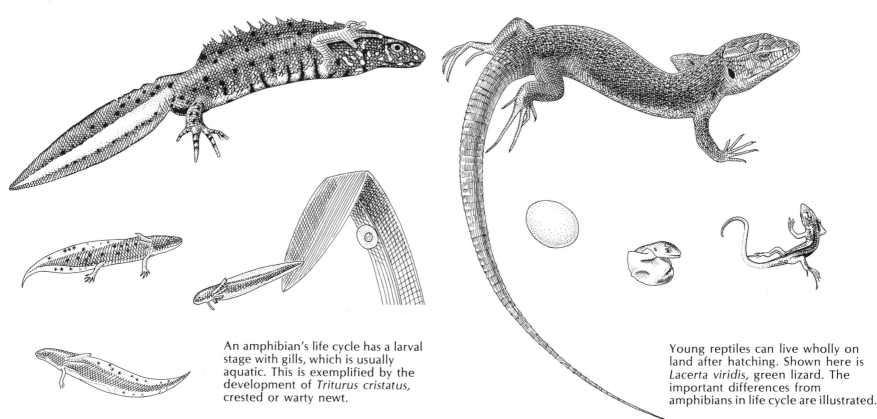

An amphibian's life cycle has a larval stage with gills, which is usually aquatic. This is exemplified by the development of *Triturus cristatus*, crested or warty newt.

Young reptiles can live wholly on land after hatching. Shown here is *Lacerta viridis*, green lizard. The important differences from amphibians in life cycle are illustrated.

to 345 million years ago, and are now extinct except for about thirty species in each. Of a third class, Chondrichthyes (sharks and rays), with over six hundred species, most are unavailable to the aquarist or impossible to keep because of the size to which they grow. The fourth class, Osteichthyes, comprises about 19,000 species of bony fishes. In this chapter, the first fish class is omitted because hagfishes are not normally kept in aquaria; the last class includes the majority of aquarium species.

Amphibians

The class Amphibia was established by the end of the Devonian period. It is thought to have evolved from the rhipidistians, a group of lobefin fishes related to the coelacanth. Amphibia depend on water or moist conditions, primarily because they respire through their skin, whose glands secrete mucus to help in keeping it moist. A feature of their life cycle is the production of shell-less eggs which develop into larvae with gills, the larvae then metamorphosing into adults. Of the three amphibian orders, one—Caecilia, resembling earthworms—is not normally kept in aquaria and will be omitted below.

In the order Urodela are salamanders and newts, sometimes termed Caudata, a reference to their tail. Usually four-legged, they feed on various small aquatic and land animals, and range from fully aquatic species to completely terrestrial and ovoviviparous ones. For example, the hellbender (*Cryptobranchus alleganlensis*) has adapted entirely to water, but the crested or warty newt (*Triturus cristatus*) lives aquatically only during its breeding season, whilst the European salamander (*Salamandra salamandra*) usually lives on land and reproduces ovoviviparously (the young develop in eggs inside the mother until they hatch, and then they are expelled).

The largest order of amphibians is Anura, with frogs and toads, also very diverse in life-style. They have a short body, no tail, and well-developed hind legs which, in many species, are adapted for jumping. The South African aquatic clawed toad (*Xenopus laevis*) burrows into the mud when its habitat dries up and, until this is replenished by water, becomes dormant. The family Hyalidae (tree-frogs) have suckers on their feet and can climb easily, living in trees. The family Rhacophoridae (flying frogs) glide between trees by using their interdigital webs as aerofoils. The families Ranidae (frogs) and Bufonidae (toads) live aquatically only during the breeding season.

Reptiles

The ancestors of the class Reptilia evolved from amphibians during the Carboniferous period, 345 to 280 million years ago. Reptiles evolved into many species which once dominated all the main habitats. They have a scaly dry skin, lay shelled eggs containing a self-sufficient environment for the developing young, and are primarily terrestrial, but with many aquatic species. Three of the four reptilian orders are of interest for a keeper.

The order Chelonia includes terrestrial tortoises, aquatic turtles, and semi-aquatic terrapins. They have a body encased in a bony shell, and some turn their head aside for protection, whilst others retract it. In the order Squamata are two groups: Sauria (lizards, geckos, iguanas) with four limbs, movable eyelids, and external ear openings, and Serpentes or Ophidia (snakes) with no limbs or external ear openings. The order Crocodilia (alligators, caimans, gavials), related to the extinct dinosaurs, is semi-aquatic and mostly freshwater, and has a compressed tail for swimming and an extended snout with many teeth.

Fishes

The fishes constitute about fifty per cent of all vertebrate species. Fishes can be defined as aquatic vertebrates with gills and fins, although the latter are sometimes absent—and their body temperature vares with that of the surrounding water, so that they are "poikilothermic". The tunnies and some sharks are the exceptions to the last condition, as these maintain a temperature above the ambient. Fishes are amazingly diverse in form, colour, behaviour, and habitat, as the accompanying photographs indicate. The following text will describe many fish species and discuss important features of their close relatives.

A systematic order, or natural classification, is to be employed. It is based upon the structural similarities between organisms and the ways in which they develop. It places the most primitive or lower organisms (such as protozoa) at the beginning, and higher forms (such as mankind) at the end. The classification now widely accepted for bony fishes (Greenwood, Rosen, Weitzman, and Myers, 1966) is used below, with certain modifications (Nelson, 1976), as the ordering of families. The species are in alphabetical order of their scientific names, within families.

The diagnoses of families and species include details of the readily visible characteristic features. Meristics are given only where they provide the simplest means of identifying fishes. Sometimes a partial statement of them is sufficient: for example, "A.III, and rays" means that the anal fin has characteristically three spines and a non-characteristic number of rays, whilst "A.III plus, and rays" means that the fin has three or more spines as well as its rays.

Many fish species are subject to changes of colouring and markings, during different stages of development and during distinct patterns of behaviour such as mating, brood care, and territorial activity. Dietary deficiencies can also result in faded colours. These variations should be taken into consideration when identifying fishes.

At the end of each species entry, further information is given as an aid both to identification and to correct maintenance of the fish. The "size" refers to the total length of an adult fish, as was illustrated above. The "distribution" gives the fish's region(s) of natural occurrence, unless otherwise stated. The "temperament" is an indication of the fish's most probable behaviour in the aquarium, depending upon conditions inside the tank.

The "water" suitable for a fish is described as fresh, brackish, or marine (sea). Its temperature shows the range at which the fish should be kept. Its quality includes additional details in the case of freshwater species. In measurable terms, soft water will be equivalent to 0–10 degrees of hardness on the German scale (DH), medium hard water to 11–18° DH, and hard water to 19–30° DH. The water's pH value is stated as acid (below pH 6.0), slightly acid (pH 6.0–6.5) neutral (about pH 7), slightly alkaline (pH 7.5–8.0), or alkaline (above pH 8.0). These factors will be discussed in the following chapters.

1 Petromyzonidae (Lamprey family)

Diagnosis: These fishes have teeth on the oral disc and tongue, no jaws, and well-developed eyes. The naked body is eel-like. There are seven pairs of external, lateral gill openings, and no paired fins or fin rays.
Distribution: Temperate zones. Unknown between latitudes 30°N and 34°S.

The twenty-four species of lamprey are amongst the most primitive vertebrates. Their respiration and gills differ from those of bony fishes. A bag with seven gill pouches connected to either side extends from the front of the intestine. Each pouch leads to one gill opening, so that when the mouth is clamped on prey or rocks, water can be pumped in and out of the openings. Some species are parasitic: adults feed by rasping into the flesh of their hosts with their sucker mouths, around which they have numerous teeth.

The river lamprey (lampern), *Lampetra fluviatilis*, starts life as a small egg which, after twenty-one days, hatches into a larva known as an ammocoete. Its eyes and mouth do not develop until after metamorphosis, and it feeds by filtering water taken in through the mouth. After about four years of living in the river mud in this state, it commences its metamorphosis. The eyes, dorsal and tail fins, and mouth develop, and the belly becomes silvery white. Emerging from the mud, it swims to sea, where it parasitizes herring, shad, and salmon. After a year, it ceases feeding and returns to a river or stream, where it mates in April or May, the eggs sinking into the mud. Shortly afterwards, the adults die.

Lampetra planeri (Brook Lamprey)
Diagnosis: The first and second dorsal fin are contiguous, the teeth are blunt, and the eyes are large and silvery. There is no parasitic stage.

The brook lamprey's back is olive-brown or blue-grey, with a silver under-belly. Non-migratory, it lives in the river's upper reaches. The larval stage is a filter-feeder, indistinguishable from that of the river lamprey. After metamorphosis, the brook lamprey does not go through an adult feeding stage but reproduces in the following spring. It chooses a shaded stream with a gravel or sandy bottom and makes a nest by removing pebbles to form a shallow depression, where the eggs are laid. It does not feed from the time of its metamorphosis until it dies.
Size: 20 cm (7.9 in), and larva 12 cm (4.8 in).
Distribution: Europe, western North America, Asia.
Temperament: peaceful. *Water:* fresh, 10–15°C (50–59°F), slightly acid.

2 Orectolobidae (Carpet, or Nurse, Shark family)

Diagnosis: This family does not have the typical shark form. Both dorsal fins are well developed, and the origin of the first is either above or behind the origin of the pelvic fin. Both nostrils have barbels on their anterior edge and are joined to the mouth by a groove. The fourth and fifth gill openings are behind the origin of the pectoral fin.
Distribution: In all oceans, but only one species (*Ginglymostoma cirratum*) occurs in the Atlantic.

The family has about twenty-five species, the largest attaining a length of over 4 m (13 ft). Some species lay eggs, whilst others are ovoviviparous. The Indo-Pacific species are attractively marked and mottled, blending in with the rocky coral reefs that they inhabit. The Australian species are called wobbegongs, or carpet sharks, and may grow to 3.2 m (10.5 ft). These nocturnal foragers have feelers in front of the mouth to detect prey in the dark. The males can be distinguished by their claspers, intromittent appendages on the pelvic fins, which have longitudinal grooves. During mating, the claspers are held together inside the female's aperture, allowing the transfer of seminal fluid. Pelvic claspers are a feature of the entire class Chondrichthyes, or cartilaginous fishes, including the sharks, skates, and rays.

Ginglymostoma cirratum (Atlantic Nurse Shark)
Diagnosis: The caudal fin has no lower lobe. Colouring is an even greyish brown and the juveniles have black spots.

Although the nurse shark shares its common name with the dangerous *Carcharinus* species in Australian waters, it is a quite different species. But only young specimens can be kept: at birth, they already measure about 28 cm (11 in) long, and a specimen of 2.6 m (8.5 ft) weighs some 160 kg (350 lb). Juveniles are more attractively marked than adults; as they mature, the spots disappear and the ground colour becomes more even.

Unlike most sharks, this species does not actively seek prey but lives on the bottom in food-rich littoral waters of coral and rocky reefs, waiting for prey to come within range. This shallow habitat provides a varied diet including small and juvenile fishes, crustaceans, molluscs, and echinoderms. The same environment is enjoyed by humans, and, whilst not aggressive, the nurse shark has been known to attack in defence when provoked, biting with great tenacity, although no mortalities have occurred. It is ovoviviparous and up to twenty-eight of the young "pups" have been recorded at a single birth.
Size: 4.3 m (14 ft). *Distribution:* west African coast up to Cape Verde, west Atlantic from Florida Keys to Brazil, east Pacific from California to Ecuador. *Temperament:* peaceful. *Water:* marine, 20–26°C (68–79°F).

3 Dasyatidae (Stingray family)

Diagnosis: These cartilaginous fishes have a very depressed body shape. Well-developed pectoral fins extend along the sides and are joined in front so that the head is indistinct. The head, body, and paired fins (pectoral and pelvic), when viewed from above, resemble a distorted disc. The dorsal fins are absent in most species, and usually one or more serrated dorsal spines point backwards on a very flexible tail.
Distribution: Atlantic and Indo-Pacific.

6 *Polypterus* species (Bichir)

7 *Xenomystus nigri* (African Knifefish)

72

9 *Gnathonemus petersi* (Ubangi Mormyrid)   10 *Echidna* species (Moray Eel)

8 *Pantodon buchholzi* (Butterflyfish)

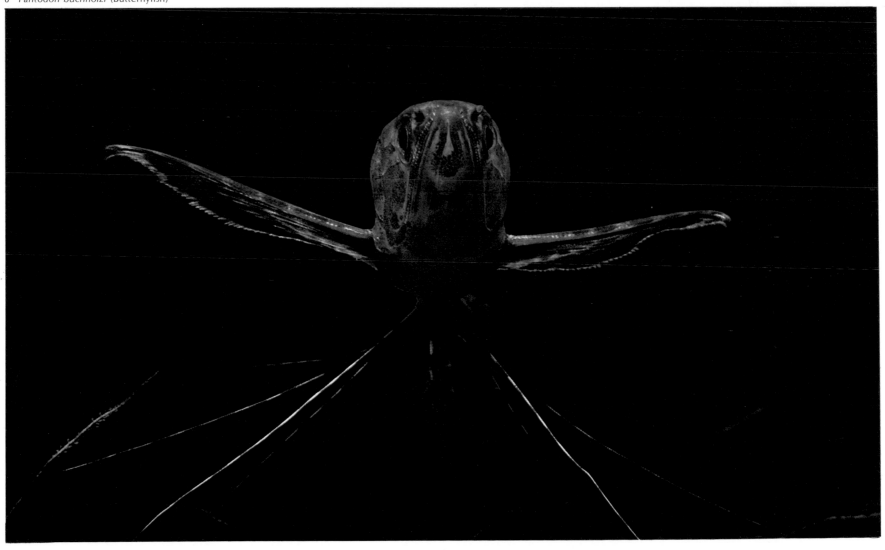

Most species are marine, but a few can be found in brackish and fresh waters. There are three subfamilies, the largest being Dasyatinae, the stingrays, with about thirty-five species (including *Dasyatis kuhlii* described below): they have a tail longer than the disc breadth, and no caudal fin. The second subfamily, Gymnurinae, are the butterfly rays, not usually kept in aquaria—they lack a caudal fin and have a disc broader than the body length. Finally, the Urolophinae, round stingrays, are identified by a caudal fin on the tail and include several species which can be kept in aquaria. One of these is the yellow spotted stingray from the Caribbean, *Urolophus jamaicensis*. It reaches sexual maturity when the disc breadth is 31 cm (12.2 in), and it gives birth to fully formed young which are a quarter of its own size. Adults attain 73 cm (2.5 ft) in length.

The group Dasyatinae contains some of the largest stingrays, up to 4.3 m (14 ft) long with discs 2 m (6.5 ft) broad. Great care should be taken when keeping stingrays, as their venom has proved fatal to people stung in the body. Stings require immediate medical treatment. The toxin is broken down by heat, and the wounded area should be immersed in almost intolerably hot water for between thirty and ninety minutes. Stingrays often attack because they are trodden on by people wading in shallow waters. Difficult to see when half-buried in the sandy or muddy substrate, the disturbed ray flicks up its tail to sting the offender, sometimes with enough force to penetrate the planks of a small boat. Stingrays come inshore to feed on molluscs, which they expose in the substrate by undulating their pelvic fins. They also eat various invertebrates and fishes, which they grind with their teeth, which resemble paving-stones. When not actively seeking food, they may remain buried in the sand, with only their eyes and spiracles visible. (A spiracle is a respiratory opening behind the eye.) Most species of stingrays are ovoviviparous.

Dasyatis kuhlii (Blue Spotted Stingray)

Diagnosis: The disc is broader than its length, and the tail is about as long as the disc. The body and disc have blue spots. This species should not be confused with the blue spotted lagoon ray *(Taeniura lymma)*, which has a rounded disc with blue spots and a tail that is distally compressed, with two blue lines along its length.

The juveniles are distinctively marked on their dorsal surface with many small black spots, which are replaced in the adult by fewer bright blue ocelli ("eyespots"). These stingrays are small compared to other tropical kinds, which attain disc widths of over 1 m (3.3 ft). But like other rays, this species buries itself in the sand as a disguise, sometimes leaving only its eyes and spiracles above the surface. It lives amongst coral reefs, waiting for prey to approach, or excavating food from the sand. Its varied diet includes fishes, bivalves, and crustaceans; as with many other bottom-feeding cartilaginous fishes, it has teeth well adapted for eating shelly food. Because it reproduces ovo-viviparously, there is no egg case or "mermaid's

purse", characteristic of many species of rays. It occurs down to a depth of 36 m (120 ft).
Size: disc width 35 cm (13.8 in). *Distribution:* Red Sea to western Pacific and Australia. *Temperament:* peaceful, but very dangerous when provoked. *Water:* marine, 24–26° (75–79°F).

4 Potamotrygonidae (Freshwater River Stingray family)

Diagnosis: Body and pectoral fins are as in the preceding family, except for a difference in the skeleton. This family, too, has one or more venomous spines on the tail. These rays are unique in being an entirely freshwater family.
Distribution: Central and South America, Africa, southeast Asia.

This family consists mainly of the genus *Potamotrygon* and is best represented in South America, where eighteen species are recorded. They lie half-buried in the sand or mud of shallow river beds, camouflaged also by their colouring. Their sting is greatly feared and comes from a serrated spine within tissue containing venom cells. Many rays lose their spine-sheaths, which are replaced by new growth. River stingrays feed on snails and fishes, and on plant debris. They are ovoviviparous. The so-called stupid ray *(Potamotrygon brachyrus)* is reported to be relatively gigantic, with specimens weighing over 120 kg (265 lb) and 1.7 m (5.6 ft) long.

Potamotrygon motoro (South American Freshwater Stingray)

Diagnosis: The disc, formed almost entirely by the pectoral fins, is circular and boldly marked by dark ocelli with orange centres, which become smaller towards the disc edge and line its circumference. The round eyespots distinguish this species from the similar *P. brachyrus,* which has hexagonal markings. The tail has a central row of short spines (or bucklers), pointing backwards, in front of the defensive spine.

This species eats diverse invertebrates as well as molluscs and fishes. It is described as one of the most dangerous species and occurs in numerous rivers in South America.
Size: 60 cm (23.6 in). *Distribution:* Amazon, Paraná, and Paraguay Rivers, and rivers south of Rio de Janeiro. *Temperament:* active and solitary. *Water:* fresh, 23–25°C (73.5–77°F); soft, slightly acid, with added peat.

5 Protopteridae (African Lungfish family)

Diagnosis: The caudal fin is confluent with the dorsal and anal fins. The paired fins are slender and whip-like. The eyes and scales are small, and the teeth are fused into numerous sharp, ridged, bony plates.
Distribution: Tropical Africa.

This family has four species, closely resembling their fossilized ancestors from the Devonian and Triassic periods. Lungfishes are anatomically peculiar in having a pair of primitive lungs and

reduced gills. The lungs are very important during the dry season when the fish buries itself in the mud, curls into a ball, and secretes a cocoon of mucus around its body. This prevents dehydration and enables the fish to survive by breathing through a hole in the cocoon. Such inactivity during the summer is known as aestivation. The fish can exist in this state for over a year and, when the rains come, it emerges to resume an aquatic existence. Its unusual ability to breathe air allows the lungfish to live in poorly oxygenated waters or where the waters dry up annually.

Protopterus annectens (African Lungfish, or Mudfish)

Diagnosis: There are 41–55 scales in a series from the gill opening to the pelvic fin origin. The body is elongate, with whip-like paired fins, a pale yellowish underside, and no spots under the head. This species is very similar to *P. amphibius,* but the latter's head has a white underside with dark spots.

This fish lives in marshy, marginal regions, often with insufficient water for it to swim freely, yet inhabitable because it breathes air. Before aestivating, it feeds on small reptiles and amphibians to build up a reserve of fat, which makes it a popular food fish for the local natives. The lungfish is renowned as an aggressive predator that can kill other fishes and even members of its own species.
Size: 20–70 cm (7.9–27.5 in). *Distribution:* Senegal, Niger, Lake Chad, Zambesi River. *Temperament:* aggressive, solitary. *Water:* fresh, 16--32°C (61–90°F), soft, acid.

6 Polypteridae (Bichir and Reedfish family)

Diagnosis: The dorsal fin consists of 5–18 finlets, each having one spine and one or more soft rays. The pectorals are stalked and fan-shaped. The body is elongate or eel-like, with tubular nostrils and with a skin covered in rhombic, ganoid scales.
Distribution: Tropical Africa.

The eleven species of this family closely resemble fossil records of primitive fishes. Their swim-bladder, divided into two uneven sections and connected with the oesophagus, is very like a primitive lung. The fish breathes by rising to the surface, gulping air, and returning to rest on the bottom. There are two genera, *Calamoichthys* (reedfishes), with no pelvic fins, and *Polypterus* (bichirs), with pelvic fins. The latter name refers to "many fins", specifically the finlets of the unusual dorsal fin. The fish lays these back when swimming, to streamline the body, but raises them when alerted. Polypteridae are nocturnal, resting on the bottom by day and feeding at night on worms, crustaceans, and small fishes that are eaten whole. Their courtship is spectacular: they leap from the water and pursue one another, the male nudging and pressing the female. Little is known of their mating but, during August and September, gravid females and fry can be seen in the overgrown margins and flood-zones of their river habitat. The young resemble newt larvae, with tree-like external gills. In the aquarium, good access to air is essential for these fishes.

Polypterus ornatipinnis (Bichir)
Diagnosis: The body is elongate and compressed, with 10–11 dorsal spines (finlets) and with pelvic fins. The snout slightly overhangs the lower jaw, and the pectoral fins end before the first dorsal spine. (The photograph shows an unidentified species of *Polypterus*.)

This beautiful species is covered on the back and flanks by a dramatic marbled pattern of black on white or grey. The belly is yellow, and each dorsal finlet bears a black spot on white. The paired fins, used like paddles for support and swimming, have black transverse bars.
Size: 37 cm (14.6 in). *Distribution:* Zaire. *Temperament:* peaceful, solitary. *Water:* fresh, 22–28°C (71.5–82.5°F), soft.

7 Notopteridae (Featherback and Knifefish family)

Diagnosis: The body is large, elongate, and slightly compressed, with an anus situated far forward. The pectorals are well developed, the scales are small, and the lateral line is complete.
Distribution: Africa to southeast Asia.

Like some of the preceding families, these fishes rise to the surface to gulp air, as they too have a swim-bladder adapted as an accessory breathing organ. They are nocturnal bottom-feeders which, during the day, rest near the bottom in an oblique head-down position. They live in quiet, weedy backwaters, and little is known about their reproductive behaviour. The long confluent anal and caudal fins are used for swimming: rhythmic waves, passing either backwards or forwards along the fins, effect movement in the opposite direction.

Xenomystus nigri (African Knifefish)
Diagnosis: This species is easily identified, as it has no dorsal fin.

This is one of the smaller members of the family and is very hardy, with no clear external sex differences. It is thought to change colour during the breeding season, becoming reddish purple with an olive-green fin, although it is usually a mousy grey or brown.
Size: 20 cm (7.9 in). *Distribution:* upper tributaries of Nile River, to the west coast of tropical Africa. *Temperament:* secretive, shoaling when young and territorial when mature. *Water:* fresh, 24–28°C (75–82.5°F), soft, slightly acid, filtered through peat.

8 Pantodontidae (Butterflyfish family)

This family has only one species.

Pantodon buchholzi (Butterflyfish)
Diagnosis: The pectoral fins are large and wing-like. Viewed laterally, the fish is boat-shaped, with a large superior mouth and tube-like nostrils.

This fish is nocturnal and lives in weedy, stagnant, tropical waters. It rests under floating leaves, hiding from predators and waiting for small insects to fall onto the water surface where they can be eaten. It may also catch prey in flight by leaping from the water and gliding, sometimes as far as 2 m (6.5 ft), with the aid of its pectorals. These probably explain the origin of its name. Males can be distinguished from females by their concave anal fin. The reproductive behaviour is dramatic, and the fish has been bred successfully in captivity.
Size: 15 cm (6 in). *Distribution:* tropical west Africa. *Temperament:* peaceful, solitary. *Water:* fresh, 23–30°C (73–86°F), soft, slightly acid, filtered through peat.

9 Mormyridae (Elephantfish family)

Diagnosis: These fishes look peculiar and are very variable in shape. Most have small eyes covered in skin, small cycloid scales, and forked tails with a narrow caudal peduncle. The bottom-feeders have a snout or mental appendage (as in *Gnathonemus elephas*, *G. petersi*, and *Mormyrops boulengeri*), which is absent in mid-water species.
Distribution: Nile and Zaire deltas.

All have exceptionally large brains containing a cerebellum proportionately larger than that of any other fish. This may be correlated with the development of the modified muscle tissue in the caudal peduncle, which forms an electric organ. The organ can generate microvoltages to create a sensory field that is believed to act like radar detection. This is used to locate food and other objects in the natural habitat of river deltas with turbid waters and low visibility. These are the most intelligent of fishes, with great "playfulness" and capacity for learning. Little is known of their breeding behaviour, but some species are thought to build bubble nests on the surface.

Gnathonemus petersi (Ubangi Mormyrid)
Diagnosis: The chin is prolonged into a tapering mental appendage, unlike the cylindrical snout of the similar species G. elephas.

This is a crepuscular and territorial fish, living in very shady and marshy conditions, where the bottom consists of soft mud and the plants are profuse. Its "snout" is used to forage through the bottom for food, which includes small insects and crustaceans. It has no known sex differences.
Size: 24 cm (9.4 in). *Distribution:* from Nigeria to Zaire. *Temperament:* shy, solitary. *Water:* fresh, 20–30°C (68–86°F), not critical in quality.

10 Muraenidae (Moray Eel family)

Diagnosis: There are no paired fins or scales, and no pores except on the lateral line. The head has high posterior nostrils, usually above the front of the eye.
Distribution: Tropical and temperate seas.

This is a large family of colourful marine eels. They tend to be nocturnal and often live in holes in rock and coral, awaiting prey, which they consume fiercely. The bigger species are very dangerous and will attack humans with no apparent provocation. Their tough scaleless skin also covers the confluent dorsal, anal, and caudal fins. The mouth has a wide gape and powerful jaws, with very sharp teeth whose arrangement varies between species and is used for identification.

Lycodontis tessalata (Black Spotted, or Leopard, Moray)
Diagnosis: The pattern is characteristic of both young and mature specimens. Large depressed canine teeth are in the front of the jaws, and the vent is about midway along the body.

This species has a reputation for aggressiveness and typifies its family in being amongst the most dangerous of marine creatures. It occurs in shallow waters, especially around the edges of reefs and old wrecks, where it may threaten the passing diver.
Size: 75 cm (29.5 in). *Distribution:* eastern and southern Africa, Indo-Pacific. *Temperament:* very aggressive, hardy. *Water:* marine, 24–26°C (75–79°F).

11 Umbridae (Mudminnow, or Houndfish, family)

Diagnosis: D.10–17, A.7–16, LL.30–100. These fishes have a short head, a rounded snout, posteriorly positioned dorsal and anal fins, and a faint or absent lateral line.
Distribution: Western Alaska, the Great Lakes, and eastern North America, and parts of Europe.

This freshwater family, due to its extreme variation in chromosome numbers, has caused many problems of classification. Its three genera include five species, all hardy and able to survive under conditions of extreme cold or low dissolved oxygen. One species, the Alaska blackfish (*Dallia pectoralis*), can live frozen in ice, the body fluids remaining unfrozen at temperatures slightly below 0°C (32°F).

Umbra krameri (Mudminnow, or Houndfish)
Diagnosis: D.15–16, A.7–8. This fish has a high dorsal profile with the dorsal fin set well back over the origin of the pectoral fins. The main colouring is brown with dark brown spots on the head and sides.

This is a benthic (bottom-living) fish, found chiefly over the muddy substrates of streams and lakes, especially near the banks amongst weed growth. It feeds primarily on insect larvae, water beetles, and other insects, as well as on freshwater molluscs. It spawns in spring, usually in March or April. The female, larger than the male, lays about 150 eggs in a hole, and guards them until they hatch. The fish has evolved a method of gulping air and holding it as a bubble in the gill chamber, to be adsorbed through the gill membrane. The swim-bladder is also reportedly used as a supplementary respiratory organ.
Size: 12 cm (4.8 in). *Distribution:* Danube and other rivers draining into the northeast Black Sea. *Temperament:* peaceful. *Water:* fresh, 4–20°C (39–68°F), neutral.

12 Characidae (Characin family)

Diagnosis: A.less than 45, Pel.5–12. An adipose fin is usually present, and the anal opening lies well

12 *Astyanax mexicanus* (Blind Cavefish)

12 *Cheirodon axelrodi* (Cardinal Tetra)

12 *Micralestes occidentalis*

12 *Gymnocorymbus ternetzi* (Black Tetra)

12 *Hyphessobrycon pulchripinnus* (Lemon Tetra)

behind the head. The mouth is not protractile and the teeth are highly developed.

Distribution: Africa, South and Central America, southwestern North America.

Initially, these fishes were classified within one family (Characinidae) of over 1,000 species, but this was divided into sixteen families in a superfamily (Characoidae), eight being of particular interest to the aquarist (families 12–19 here). In common with other ostariophysans (a larger group including also the cyprinids, electric eels and other gymnotids, and catfishes), many of the characoids exhibit an "alarm reaction" (*Schreckreaktion*). This occurs when an individual is injured, for example by a predator: specialized skin cells release a substance (*Schreckstoff*) that is detected by other members of the shoal, which then take flight.

The distribution of families such as the characins in both Africa and America was initially important to theories of continental drift. But the splitting of South America from Africa does not seem to explain satisfactorily these regions' fauna,

which are much less closely related to each other than are African and Asian fauna. Experts now propose that the ancestral characins and catfishes spread across Asia, into North America by the Alaskan land-bridge, and through Central to South America.

The species selected below are mostly from the major groups of Characidae. They include the African tetras, with examples in the genera *Arnoldichthys, Brycinus, Micralestes,* and *Phenacogrammus,* all being small shoaling fishes. This family does not contain only small aquarium species: some of the African tigerfishes (species of *Hydrocynus*) grow to over 1 m (3.3 ft) long and have large canine teeth used to kill other fishes. Amongst the American characins are the piranha fishes, including infamous carnivores such as *Serrasalmus,* lesser-known herbivores such as *Metynnis,* and the fish parasite *Catoprion.* The other major group of South American characins, including tetras, has genera such as *Aphyocharax, Cheirodon, Hemigrammus, Hyphessobrycon,*

Nematobrycon, and *Thayeria.* Most of these are brightly coloured, insect-eating, shallow-water fishes. Some of the exceptions with unusual habits are the Mexican blind cavefish *Astyanax* and the scale-eating fish parasite *Exodon.*

Characins are a freshwater family, living predominantly in warm shallow habitats overgrown by terrestrial vegetation. The latter is rich in invertebrate life and, because of its nearness to the water, contributes significantly to the diet of many characins. Numerous characin species are sexually dimorphic, with the males possessing elongate fins and brighter colours than the females. Spawning is very energetic, occurring amongst thick vegetation and culminating as the partners press against each other's sides. The female quivers briefly and then expels the eggs into the water, where they are fertilized by the male's milt. The eggs fall to the substrate or, if they have an adhesive exterior, may stick to the vegetation. After one or more days, according to the species, the fry hatch and soon begin to feed on microscopic organisms.

12 *Brycinus longipinnis* (Longfinned Characin)

12 *Hyphessobrycon ornatus* (Ornate Tetra)

12 *Hemigrammus erythrozonus* (Glowlight Tetra)

Aphyocharax anisitsi (Bloodfin)

Diagnosis: A.18–23. All the fins except the pectoral and the adipose are bright red.

This is an omnivore, feeding mainly on small invertebrates in the upper water layers. Oddly, the female is the larger sex, and the male has tiny sexual hooks on the ends of the anal fin rays. Breeding behaviour contrasts with the fishes' normal peacefulness: during courtship, they swim about vigorously and sometimes leap out of the water before the female expels the eggs. The fish has long been known as *A. rubripinnis,* a name given in 1921, but that of *A. anisitsi* accompanied the first description in 1903 and takes precedence by rules of scientific nomenclature.

Size: 6 cm (2.4 in). *Distribution:* Argentina. *Temperament:* peaceful, shoaling. *Water:* fresh, 17–28°C (62.5–82.5°F), soft to medium hard.

Arnoldichthys spilopterus (Red-Eyed Characin)

Diagnosis: This species is the only one of its genus. It has a dorsal fin with a large black spot, a distinctly forked caudal fin, and an adipose fin. The scales are small on the lower half of the body and enlarged on the upper half.

This is an attractive fish with iridescent scales and a dark bar extending from the eye to the rear edge of the caudal fin. The male has a convex anal fin, usually marked with horizontal black stripes or a tricolour, whilst the female has a straight-edged anal fin and a black spot on the last rays. The fish is active and lives in large shoals near the surface, feeding on various aquatic insects and larvae as well as on terrestrial insects trapped by the water's surface tension. Breeding has occurred in captivity, but the behaviour is not yet recorded.

Size: 7 cm (2.8 in). *Distribution:* tropical west Africa. *Temperament:* peaceful, shoaling. *Water:* fresh, 24–28°C (75–82.5°F), soft, slightly acid, with peat.

Astyanax mexicanus (Blind Cavefish)

Diagnosis: This is a blind characin with vestigial eyes overgrown by skin. The body is pale pink, with silvery scales.

The fish is a natural variety of the Mexican tetra, with which it has reportedly hybridized, and this has happened naturally in at least one cave where the two varieties occur together. The blind cavefish was once regarded as a distinct species and named *Anoptichthys jordani.* Its young have small eyes, which become vestigial as the fish grows and are replaced by highly developed senses of smell and "touch". These are lively fishes, and it is thought that the pressure waves caused by their activity are used to perceive their surroundings by detecting the echoes. The caves in which they live are usually inhabited by bats, and they feed on partially undigested insects in the bats' faeces. Cavefishes mate by pressing their bodies together at the water surface, where the eggs and milt are expelled together.

Size: 8 cm (3.2 in). *Distribution:* Central America. *Temperament:* Peaceful, active, and shoaling. *Water:* fresh, 18–23°C (64.5–73.5°F), medium hard, slightly alkaline.

Brycinus longipinnis (Longfinned Characin)

Diagnosis: LL.26–27. A black bar on the lower half of the caudal peduncle extends from before the end of the anal fin onto the caudal fin. Males have very elongate dorsal fin rays. This species is quite similar to another from west Africa, *B. chaperi* (Chaper's characin), but the latter has 28–30 lateral line scales.

This fish, like Chaper's characin, is well known to the aquarist. Its habitats are varied but tend to be the upper and middle regions of large and swiftly moving waters. It feeds on insects such as mosquito larvae and other small invertebrates, and it has good visual acuity in order to catch them. This perceptiveness makes it a shy fish to keep, and little is known about its breeding behaviour.

Size: 16 cm (6.3 in). *Distribution:* tropical west to central Africa. *Temperament:* peaceful, active, and shoaling. *Water:* fresh, 23–25°C (73.5–77°F), soft, slightly acid, with added peat.

Catoprion mento (Wimple Piranha)

Diagnosis: The lower jaw is much more prominent than in any of the other piranhas and has outwardly pointing teeth. The first rays of the dorsal fin are extended and reach back at least level with the adipose fin. The operculum bears an orange or red spot. The body is silvery, the caudal fin is black, and the anal fin is red.

This fish is also known as the scale-eater, revealing its parasitic habits. It lives in shoals in the lower and middle water levels, and attacks its hosts by striking upwards at their flanks, removing scales with its outwardly pointing teeth. Experts suggest that this species and its method of feeding evolved from a previously carnivorous form. Two related species (*Metynnis hypsauchen* and *Serrasalmus nattereri*) will be described below.

Size: 15 cm (6 in). *Distribution:* lower Amazon. *Temperament:* aggressive and shoaling. *Water:* fresh, 23–25°C (73.5–77°F), soft, slightly acid, with added peat.

Cheirodon axelrodi (Cardinal Tetra)

Diagnosis: A brilliant red band extends from the caudal fin origin, level with the pupil, to the operculum. Sometimes, the red extends onto the throat. Above the band is an iridescent blue-green stripe which extends from the adipose fin onto the eye.

This beautiful tetra was described relatively recently. It lives in the dimly lit middle and lower layers of forest pools, where its bright iridescent colouring—due to aligned guanine crystals—is believed to be an aid to species recognition when shoaling. Although in captivity it lives longer than a year, it may be an annual fish in the natural habitat, which is thought to lack sufficient food to sustain the adults for a second season after they have bred. Breeding is similar to that of the neon tetra and occurs amongst vegetation. Here, the eggs are laid, the fry hatch after one to one and a half days, and they remain hanging on plants. Once they have started to move, they feed on plankton and grow quickly during the first weeks.

Size: 4 cm (1.6 in). *Distribution:* upper and middle River Negro. *Temperament:* peaceful, active, and shoaling. *Water:* fresh, 23–25°C (73.5–77°F), soft, slightly acid, with added peat.

Crenuchus spilurus (Sailfin Characin)

Diagnosis: D.17–18, A.11, LL.29–32. The body is elongate and compressed, with a small adipose fin and a distinctly forked caudal fin. On the male, during its second and third years, the mandible and maxilla of the mouth become larger, giving the fish a vaguely salmoniform appearance, whilst the dorsal and anal fins are enlarged and have brown and orange-red patterns. The body is reddish brown with a yellow-white abdomen, and the scales have dark edges, particularly on the back of the fish. There is a large black spot on the lower half of the caudal peduncle at the tail base. A dark horizontal stripe runs from the operculum to the tail base and has a yellow upper edge.

This fish, like some other characins, inhabits weedy waters shaded by dense vegetation along the banks. It feeds on various small invertebrates and fishes. Spawning is reported to resemble that of cichlids: the bright red eggs are attached to flat surfaces such as stones or large leaves, near the bottom, and are cared for and fanned by the male. The fish has recently been observed to possess an organ similar to one which occurs in some catfishes, halfbeaks, and other species. This is an unusual organ on the top of the head, indicated by an unpigmented spot, and thought to allow the perception of light by a pineal body, or "third eye".

Size: 6 cm (2.4 in). *Distribution:* Guyana and the middle Amazon basin. *Temperament:* secretive, peaceful. *Water:* fresh, 23–25°C (73.5–77°F), soft, slightly acid, filtered through peat.

Exodon paradoxus

Diagnosis: There are two intensely black round spots, one covering the caudal peduncle, the other on the upper side of the flank and in front of the dorsal fin. An adipose fin is present.

On this exceptionally beautiful characin, the body and caudal fin are yellow and the other fins have bright red anterior margins. The fish reportedly lives over sandy bottoms in the rivers of savannah regions. It feeds on scales which are removed from fishes—with an efficiency of about fifty per cent—by stabbing towards their free edges in a rapid circular movement, using specially adapted teeth. It spawns by forceful swimming amongst vegetation.

Size: 15 cm (6 in). *Distribution:* northeastern South America. *Temperament:* active, aggressive, and shoaling. *Water:* fresh, 23–28°C (73.5–82.5°F), soft, slightly acid, with added peat.

Gymnocorymbus ternetzi (Black Tetra)

Diagnosis: A.40–42. The anal fin margin is convex and the small scales cover the fin base. The fish has two dark vertical humeral bars. The rear half of the body, and the dorsal, anal, and adipose fins, are black on the juveniles but become grey with age.

These fishes occur in diverse habitats with slow-moving water shaded by vegetation. They prefer to feed on insects which fall onto the water surface from plants along the banks. They are very

prolific. When spawning, the male and female press vigorously together, depositing the eggs amongst weeds.
Size: 6 cm (2.4 in). *Distribution:* Brazil, Paraguay, Bolivia. *Temperament:* peaceful, shoaling. *Water:* fresh, 23–25°C (73.5–77°F), soft, medium hard.

Hemigrammus erythrozonus (Glowlight Tetra)
Diagnosis: The "glowlight" is a red iridescent lateral stripe, with a golden line, visible in good light, along its top. The anterior margin of the dorsal fin bears a red patch.

This fish ranges in habitat from small jungle streams to bogs, feeding omnivorously. The sexes are difficult to distinguish, the males being slightly slimmer. The breeding behaviour is not typical of the characins. The two partners embrace each other with their fins and roll over, then the female sheds her eggs and these are fertilized by the male. The eggs stick to vegetation, as they have an adhesive surface, and the fry hatch after about a day.
Size: 5 cm (2 in). *Distribution:* northeastern South America. *Temperament:* peaceful, active, shoaling. *Water:* fresh, 23–28°C (73.5–82.5°F), soft, slightly acid, with added peat.

Hyphessobrycon ornatus (Ornate Tetra)
Diagnosis: The fish has no humeral patch, usually not more than thirty-three scales in the longitudinal series, and an irregular dark blotch on the dorsal fin. In males, this fin has a white anterior border on the foremost rays, and the dorsal and anal fins are elongate.

There is some confusion over the naming of this species, because of its similarities with some of the other tetras. About six species are closely related in the genus *Hyphessobrycon* and have been called the "blood characins". The ornate tetra lives mostly in the lower layers of slow-flowing streams and jungle swamps, amongst dense vegetation. It feeds on small aquatic invertebrates and plants, spawning in the way typical of characins. The eggs are red or brown and are laid in clusters amongst thick vegetation.
Size: 6 cm (2.4 in). *Distribution:* Guyana and lower Amazon. *Temperament:* peaceful, shoaling. *Water:* fresh, 23–26°C (73.5–79°F), soft, slightly acid.

Hyphessobrycon pulchripinnis (Lemon Tetra)
Diagnosis: The upper half of the iris is brilliant red. On the anal fin, the first rays are yellow, and the margin is black in the male.

This omnivorous species is similar in life-style to the preceding one. When breeding, the male and female squeeze amongst the vegetation, shedding the eggs in the typical manner.
Size: 5 cm (2 in). *Distribution:* Amazon basin. *Temperament:* peaceful, active, shoaling. *Water:* fresh, 23–25°C (73.5–77°F), very soft, slightly acid, with added peat.

Megalamphodus megalopterus (Black Phantom)
Diagnosis: There is a large dark humeral bar. The dorsal and anal fins are dark and, in the adults, well developed.

This is a shoaling fish and prefers to live in the shady regions amongst thick vegetation. It is carnivorous and readily takes insects from the surface as well as eating other small invertebrates. Unusually for the characins, the female is more brightly coloured than the male, with the anal, pelvic, and sometimes adipose fins red. The males sometimes threaten each other by spreading their fins. Breeding occurs between older males and young females. The fry, which hatch after a day, feed on small rotifers and crustaceans.
Size: 4 cm (1.6 in). *Distribution:* Argentina. *Temperament:* active, shoaling. *Water:* fresh, 23–26°C (73.5–79°F), soft, slightly acid, with added peat.

Metynnis hypsauchen (one of the Silver Dollars)
Diagnosis: This genus is distinguished by the extent of the adipose fin base, which equals one and a half times the distance between the dorsal fin termination and the adipose fin origin. The body is almost as deep as it is long. There are usually no spots, but possibly one or even two humeral blotches, and older fish may have some spots or stripes in vertical rows.

This species has the alternative name *M. schreitmuelleri* but no common species names. All members of the genus are known as silver dollars, because of their colouration and compressed, deep body form. The fish occurs in waters with prolific plant growth, as it needs much vegetable food, although it also eats the small invertebrates living amongst the plants. Its breeding behaviour is typical of characins. The female lays about 2,000 eggs, and the fry hatch after three days.
Size: 18 cm (7 in). *Distribution:* Guyana, the Amazon and Paraguay basins. *Temperament:* active, peaceful, shoaling. *Water:* fresh, 24–27°C (75–80.5°F), soft, slightly acid, with added peat.

Micralestes acutidens
Diagnosis: A.14–16, LL.26–29. An indistinct dark band extends along the entire body and caudal fin. The dorsal fin has a black tip, and the anal fin is larger on the male than on the female.

This species lives in the middle and upper layers of the typical characin habitat. It is mainly carnivorous, eating various aquatic insects. When it breeds, the eggs fall to the substrate, as they are not sticky. The fry begin to swim freely six days after they hatch.
Size: 6.5 cm (2.6 in). *Distribution:* tropical central Africa. *Temperament:* peaceful, shoaling. *Water:* fresh, 22–28°C (71.5–82.5°F), soft, slightly acid.

Nematobrycon palmeri (Emperor Tetra)
Diagnosis: The caudal fin has two lobes and a central spike which can extend beyond the lobes and is most pronounced on the male. A dark band extends the full length of the body and onto the spike. The adipose fin is absent and the lateral line is complete.

This typical characin inhabits the lower water layers, preying on various small invertebrates such as crustaceans, insects, and larvae. During breeding, the male vigorously pursues the female, enticing her into the vegetation with his quivering fins and lateral body movements. About seventy-five eggs are laid and the fry hatch after two days.
Size: 6 cm (2.4 in). *Distribution:* Colombia. *Temperament:* peaceful, shoaling. *Water:* fresh, 25–26°C (77–79°F), soft, slightly acid.

Paracheirodon innesi (Neon Tetra)
Diagnosis: This species is similar to the cardinal tetra except in the extent of the red band. Here, the band runs from the caudal fin origin to halfway along the body, usually ending between the dorsal and pelvic fin origins. Above the band, and extending from the adipose fin onto the eye, is a brilliant blue-green iridescent stripe.

The fish occurs in small streams, pools, and swamps in the tropical rain forests. It is omnivorous, preying on diverse small animals, including insects, larvae, crustaceans, and rotifers. Breeding takes place amongst vegetation and resembles that of the cardinal tetra.
Size: 4 cm (1.6 in). *Distribution:* Amazon headwaters. *Temperament:* peaceful, shoaling. *Water:* fresh, 21–23°C (70–73.5°F), soft to medium hard, slightly acid, filtered through peat.

Phenacogrammus interruptus (Congo Tetra)
Diagnosis: A.15–21. The dorsal and caudal fins of the male have long filamentous rays. The lateral line is incomplete, and there is an indistinct darker band along the side.

This omnivorous fish lives in large shoals in the surface layers, continually searching for prey and quickly consuming any insects that fall onto the water. Breeding occurs on sunny days and begins with a very active courting behaviour. The female then lays about 300 eggs, which sink to the bottom, where the young hatch after about six days.
Size: 12 cm (4.8 in). *Distribution:* Zaire (Congo) basin. *Temperament:* peaceful, active, shoaling. *Water:* fresh, 23–26°C (73.5–79°F), soft, slightly acid, with added peat.

Pristella maxillaris (X-ray Fish)
Diagnosis: This species has a humeral spot, a red caudal fin, and distinctively tricoloured anterior portions on the dorsal and anal fins. These are coloured lemon-yellow, black, and white, proceeding distally.

This fish was once placed in the genus *Hemigrammus* but was renamed because the teeth are arranged differently. It is omnivorous and breeds like a typical characin. The eggs are shed randomly and fall to the substrate. After hatching, the fry hang near the surface for several days. The species has long been known by its synonym *P. riddlei*, but the above name is older and has precedence.
Size: 5.5 cm (2.2 in). *Distribution:* the Amazon, Venezuela, and Guyana. *Temperament:* active, shoaling. *Water:* fresh, 20–26°C (68–79°F), soft, slightly acid, filtered through peat.

Serrasalmus nattereri (Red Piranha)
Diagnosis: The teeth of both jaws are very sharp and fit closely together like two interlocking saw blades. The anal fin and the belly are red, and the

12 *Paracheirodon innesi* (Neon Tetra)

12 *Pristella maxillaris* (X-ray Fish)

juvenile has dark spots on its body. The adipose fin is not tufted as in *S. piraya*.

Piranhas have a spectacular reputation, and there is much controversy about their ferocity. They are usually described as preying on other fishes and even on their own species. The shoaling Amazonian piranha *(S. piraya)* unaccountably attacks large mammals which may try to swim across rivers. But in some areas, the natives are known to swim regularly in waters infested by piranhas without being harmed, whilst elsewhere the inhabitants have suffered minor mutilation. Apparently, it is when people or animals enter the water with openly bleeding wounds that danger arises. Why piranhas should be so excited by blood is still not clearly understood, although this aspect of behaviour is probably advantageous, just as their teeth are specially adapted for their mode of feeding. Piranhas, like sharks, may associate the "smell" of blood in the water with a ready source of food. Little is known about their breeding, but the males are thought to brood the eggs, and a disturbance of these by an intruding mammal could explain a localized and seemingly irrational attack. The piranha subfamily, Serrasalminae, includes two other species described here (*Catoprion mento* and *Metynnis hypsauchen*), with different feeding habits.
Size: 30 cm (11.8 in). *Distribution:* the entire Amazon basin. *Temperament:* shoaling, aggressive. *Water:* fresh, 24–27°C (75–80.5°F), soft, slightly acid, with added peat.

Thayeria boehlkei (Black-Line Penguin Fish)
Diagnosis: A black band extends from the upper gill cover and along the entire body onto the lower lobe of the caudal fin. The lower lobe may be up to one quarter longer than the upper lobe. Similar in form and life-style is the penguin fish (*T. obliqua*), whose band extends from below the adipose fin onto the lower caudal lobe, which may be up to one-third longer than the upper lobe.

The black-line penguin fish is thought to be the commonest within its genus. It prefers to live amongst the dense vegetation of jungle streams and river margins shaded by plant growth on the banks. Here, its bold stripe may enable it to be camouflaged by merging into the shadows. This colouring may also be important in the shoaling behaviour of such fishes, as they tend to orientate themselves in the same direction, enhancing the inanimate effect of their stripes. The fish can maintain a head-up position in the water, obliquely at thirty degrees, due to its specially shaped swim-bladder. It feeds on insects and other small invertebrates, and is prolific enough to hatch as many as 1,000 fry from only one spawning.
Size: 8 cm (3.2 in). *Distribution:* basin of the River Maranon, Peru. *Temperament:* active, peaceful, shoaling. *Water:* fresh, 23–28°C (73.5–82.5°F), soft, slightly acid.

13 Lebiasinidae
Diagnosis: A.8–14. There are eighteen to thirty large scales in the longitudinal series. The mouth is small and usually does not reach the eye. An adipose fin may be present, and the dorsal fin is always in front of the anal fin.
Distribution: South America.

This family is divided into two subfamilies, as follows. The Lebiasininae includes a species *Lebiasina bimaculata*, the two-spotted lebiasina, which is of interest because it has a swim-bladder adapted for breathing air. The Pyrrhulininae includes the three species described below. Breeding behaviour has been studied in many species and is varied and fascinating.

Copella arnoldi (Spraying Characin, or Splashing Tetra)
Diagnosis: Adults have an S-shaped maxilla, an elongate body, filamentous fins, and no adipose fin. The colouring is characteristic, especially the black stripe extending from the mouth to the eye, and on the male's dorsal fin. The maxilla and fins are more pronounced in the male.

These beautiful fishes live in the upper water layers, feeding on small insects and larvae from the surface. Their good jumping ability is utilized when spawning, on broad leaves above the surface. The male periodically swims to the surface below the egg mass and, by bending his body away from it, can flick his tail to splash water over the eggs, keeping them moist. This activity ceases during rain and in generally humid conditions. The young hatch after thirty-six hours.
Size: 8 cm (3.2 in). *Distribution:* lower Amazon, River Para. *Temperament:* shy; the males are territorial. *Water:* fresh, 26–28°C (79–82.5°F), soft, slightly acid, filtered through peat.

Nannobrycon eques (Tube-Mouthed Pencilfish)
Diagnosis: The body is torpedo-shaped, with a distinctly larger lower caudal lobe and sometimes no adipose fin. There are twenty-four to twenty-five scales in the longitudinal series. The colouring can serve for identification; it fades at night.

This species, like all others in its genus, swims at an oblique angle with the head up. Sometimes, it is seen to be vertical, especially when close to the surface and feeding. It lives in shallow water with overgrown banks. The male is brighter in colour and less rounded than the female and has blue spots on the pelvic fins. When breeding, the two fishes press together and lay up to three eggs on broad leaves; they may mate several times, producing as many as eighty eggs. The eggs may be eaten

12 *Metynnis* species (Silver Dollar)

12 *Phenacogrammus interruptus* (Congo Tetra)

by hungry adults but usually hatch within twenty-four hours. In less than a week, the young are feeding and have a ribbon-like adipose fin.
Size: 5 cm (2 in). *Distribution:* Guyana and the middle Amazon. *Temperament:* peaceful, shoaling. *Water:* fresh, 22–28°C (71.5–82.5°F), very soft, acid, with added peat.

Pyrrhulina vittata (Striped Pyrrhulina)
Diagnosis: LL.20–22. The characteristic colouring includes spots on the body. The female has colourless fins and is larger than the male, which sometimes has an elongate upper lobe on the caudal fin.

All members of this genus are charming dwarf fishes which swim at the surface and are good jumpers. They live in still, sluggish water, particularly with dense plant growth near the banks. Spawning occurs on large submerged leaves, which are first cleaned meticulously by the male. He drives and prods the female until she lays the eggs on a leaf. Then he fans the eggs with his tail, and most fall to the bottom where they hatch within twenty-four hours.
Size: 7 cm (2.8 in). *Distribution:* Amazon and the River Tapajoz. *Temperament:* peaceful, active. *Water:* fresh, 24–26°C (75–79°F), medium hard, slightly acid.

14 Gasteropelecidae (Hatchetfish family)

Diagnosis: A deep and very compressed body and head form the hatchet shape. An adipose fin may be present. These are the only fishes known to fly in the air by using their own propulsive force.
Distribution: South America from Panama to the River Plata.

These "flying" fishes, in the true sense of the word, have pectoral fins with powerful muscles attached to an enlarged girdle. This enables the fish to flap its fins vigorously and propel itself through the air after leaping from the water. The purpose is believed to be evasion of predators.

Carnegiella marthae (Black-Winged Hatchetfish)
Diagnosis: This is one of the smaller members of the family, with no adipose fin. The colouring includes a dark stripe running from the gill covers to the caudal peduncle, and a dark line edging the entire ventral keel.

The fish lives in shoals in slow-flowing shady streams with much humus. There are no sexual differences, but the swollen female can be recognized when in a gravid condition. Spawning occurs amongst the roots of plants. The male performs a butterfly-like courtship dance, and clusters of two to three strongly adhesive eggs are extruded just below the water surface. The eggs hatch in less than three days and the fry soon begin to feed on micro-organisms. They start to resemble the adult form within about twenty days.
Size: 3.5 cm (1.4 in). *Distribution:* Venezuela, Peru, Amazon basin, River Negro. *Temperament:* shy, shoaling. *Water:* fresh, 23–30°C (73.5–86°F), soft, slightly acid, with added peat.

15 Prochilodontidae

Diagnosis: The body is elongate and strongly compressed, with a long caudal peduncle and a deeply forked caudal fin. The narrow mouth is turned back as a sucking-disc and covered with small papillae.
Distribution: South America.

This is a family of large freshwater fishes, superficially resembling the genus *Labeo*. Many are brightly coloured when young, developing dramatic markings on the tail as they mature. The suctorial disc on the mouth is used to graze algae from the bottom. But these fish are omnivorous and also consume small insects and other vertebrates.

Prochilodus insignis (Flag-Tailed Prochilodus)
Diagnosis: LL.about 45. The young are beautifully coloured, having a silver body with a blue-green tinge, dark streaks on the flanks, a yellow ground on all the fins, blue markings on the dorsal, anal, and caudal fins, and a red sheen on the belly and paired fins. Adults have only the anal fin markings and dark diagonal stripes on the tail.

This fish is a good jumper, particularly lively when in shoals. It prefers plant food. There seem to be no discernible sexual differences, and little is known of the breeding behaviour.
Size: 35 cm (13.8 in). *Distribution:* Guyana and the Amazon basin. *Temperament:* active, shoaling. *Water:* fresh, 22–26°C (71.5–79°F), soft, slightly acid, with peat.

16 Anostomidae (Headstander family)

Diagnosis: The main trait of almost the entire family is a small, narrow, non-protractile mouth surrounded by folded lips. The lateral line is straight, usually with more than thirty-four scales.
Distribution: South and Central America and the West Indies.

All species in the family are omnivorous, feeding from the bottom and on algae that grow upon water-plants. They are adept at swimming obliquely or even upside-down to obtain food. They can also swim very fast horizontally to evade predators. Attractively patterned and coloured, they live in sluggish weedy waters. Most species are small and of interest to the aquarist, but some of

14 *Carnegiella marthae* (Black-Winged Hatchetfish)

16 *Abramites microcephalus* (Marbled Headstander)

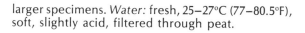

16 *Leporinus arcus*

the largest are valued as food by the local inhabitants. Two subfamilies exist as follows. Leporellinae contains only the genus *Leporellus*, whose many species are rare but widely distributed throughout all the South American basins. Anostominae contains several genera of which three are represented below.

Abramites microcephalus (Marbled Headstander)
Diagnosis: The body is compressed and elongate, with a small head and an acute snout. The colouring is variable.

Although this species is rare and little is known of its reproductive behaviour, it is believed to spawn amongst thick weeds in a manner similar to that of many other characoids. The sexes differ little, but the female has a more rounded body and less intense markings.
Size: 13 cm (5.1 in). *Distribution:* lower Amazon. *Temperament:* shy, with aggressiveness between

larger specimens. *Water:* fresh, 25–27°C (77–80.5°F), soft, slightly acid, filtered through peat.

Anostomus anostomus (Striped Anostomus)
Diagnosis: The colouring is striking, especially three dark longitudinal stripes and the red-tinged caudal and dorsal fins. The head has a flat top, and the mouth is superior.

The superior mouth of fishes in this genus was once thought to show that they are surface-feeders, but this is not true. Like other members of the family, they tend to swim at an oblique angle when feeding from the bottom and must sometimes swim upside-down because of the superior mouth. The streamlined body permits rapid swimming through the dense vegetation to escape predators. The sexes are very similar in external appearance, but the male is smaller and more strongly coloured. Little is known of the breeding behaviour.
Size: 15 cm (6 in). *Distribution:* Guyana and the

Amazon south of Manaus. *Temperament:* active, shoaling. *Water:* fresh, 24–27°C (75–80.5°F), soft, slightly acid, filtered through peat.

Leporinus arcus
Diagnosis: There are four longitudinal stripes along the sides, a black spot on the pectoral fin base, a slightly convex profile over the eyes, and a slightly inferior mouth. Another species, *L. striatus*, looks very similar but is somewhat smaller.

This species is a member of the largest genus in the family. All such members favour a habitat with a gravelly or sandy bottom, and like to hide amongst the roots of trees. They are herbivores and good jumpers, requiring adequate cover for an aquarium tank.
Size: 40 cm (15.7 in). *Distribution:* Venezuela and the upper Amazon. *Temperament:* active, peaceful. *Water:* fresh, 24–27°C (75–80.5°F), soft, slightly acid, filtered through peat.

13 *Nannobrycon eques* (Tube-Mouthed Pencilfish)

13 *Copella arnoldi* (Spraying Characin)

16 *Anostomus anostomus* (Striped Anostomus)

18 *Chilodus punctatus* (Spotted Headstander)

17 Hemiodontidae

Diagnosis: Pect.18–23, LL.50–125. The body is usually fusiform and compressed. The dorsal fin is small, an adipose fin is present, and the caudal fin is deeply forked. The scales on the back are smaller than those on the abdomen.
Distribution: Northern South America.

This family consists of three subfamilies, two having only about six species. The other species belong to the single genus (*Hemiodopsis*, previously known as *Hemiodus*) of the subfamily Hemiodontinae. The family name means "half-toothed ones" and refers to the usual lack of teeth on the lower jaw. This is the main trait distinguishing these fishes from the characins.

Hemiodopsis microlepis
Diagnosis: LL.100 plus. The mouth is small, and the caudal fin is large, with its lobes set at a wide angle.

The lower lobe has a dark stripe and is red like the pelvic fins. The flank bears a round dark spot.

This species belongs to the largest genus of the family. It swims rapidly and is a voracious feeder, eating various small invertebrates but mainly plant material.
Size: 15 cm (6 in). *Distribution:* Amazon and the Rivers Negro and Guapore. *Temperament:* peaceful. *Water:* fresh, 23–25°C (73.5–77°F), soft, slightly acid.

18 Chilodontidae (Headstander family)

Diagnosis: Pect.13–16, LL.25–31. This family should not be confused with the Anostomidae, although the two have many features in common.
Distribution: South America.

This family contains two genera, *Caenotropus*, with some of the many headstanders, and *Chilodus*, which probably has only the species described below. As the latter is known to be very variable, certain authorities consider it synonymous with a species of similar appearance named *C. zunevei*. All members of the family live in a habitat like that of the Anostomidae and swim in the typical head-down position.

Chilodus punctatus (Spotted Headstander)
Diagnosis: LL.25–27. A black longitudinal band extends from the mouth to the eye. The dorsal fin is spotted, and a brown spot occurs at the base of the large scales on the back and flanks.

This fish periodically makes a loud clicking noise, usually when feeding or before mating. It also changes in its colouring before mating: the longitudinal stripe and dorsal markings become softer, and two blotches appear behind each gill cover, while the anal and adipose fins become darker. The female grows more robust during

spawning, when the eggs are laid on water-plants and hatch after about four days. The fry begin to swim freely after about two or three days, and soon adopt the head-down position when seeking food on the bottom.
Size: 9 cm (3.5 in). Distribution: northeastern South America. Temperament: active, and peaceful although it may attack members of its own species. Water: fresh, 25–27°C (77–80.5°F), very soft, slightly acid, filtered through peat.

19 Citharinidae

Diagnosis: The lateral line is straight, and the ctenoid scales sometimes cover the large adipose fin.
Distribution: Africa.

This family is found in various habitats, but it abounds in swampy regions, spawning during the flood season. The smaller species are suitable for the home aquarium, whilst the larger ones are important as food for the local inhabitants. Some of the larger species have very deep flattened bodies and are colloquially known as "moonfishes".

Nannaethiops unitaeniatus (One-Striped Characin)
Diagnosis: LL.35–38. The body is moderately compressed and elongate, with a deeply forked tail.

In this species, the male is more colourful and slimmer than the female. During spawning, the anterior of the dorsal fin and the upper lobe of the caudal fin are bright red. The partners apparently enjoy sunlight and are stimulated to spawn by it, over the sandy bottom of their river habitat, where the eggs are scattered and fall amongst the sand grains. The eggs hatch within about twenty-four hours, and the fry swim freely after five days.
Size: 50 cm (19.7 in). Distribution: equatorial Africa, from the White Nile to the west coast. Temperament: peaceful, shy. Water: fresh, 22–27°C (71.5–80.5°F), soft, slightly acid, filtered through peat.

20 Gymnotidae (Knife Eel, or Naked-Back Fish, family)

Diagnosis: These fishes are elongate, eel-like, almost circular in section anteriorly, and compressed posteriorly. They have small scales, no dorsal or caudal fins, and can produce a weak electric charge.
Distribution: Central and South America.

This family belongs to a superfamily whose members also include the families Electrophoridae (electric eels), Apteronotidae (black ghosts, or sternarchids), and the Rhamphichthyidae (knifefishes). They all have elongate eel-like bodies and are nocturnal. This family has only one genus with three species, two occurring in Central America alone, and the following species being the most widespread.

Gymnotus carapo (Banded Knife Eel)
Diagnosis: A.200–260, Pect.I,14–15. The dorsal, caudal, and pelvic fins are absent, the anal opening is under the head, and the superior, oblique mouth is broad. The colouring may be uniform and flesh-like or may have dark vertical stripes.

This fish's anal fin provides its only means of propulsion and is used in much the same way as the confluent anal and caudal fins of the Notopteridae. Its small electric organ can produce several types of electrical signal. A threat signal, used when fighting, consists of sharp increases in frequency followed by decreases. Ceasing to discharge for a second or so indicates a desire to flee, and ceasing for a longer time is a sign of appeasement.
Size: 60 cm (23.6 in). Distribution: from the River Plata west to the Andes and north to Guatemala. Temperament: solitary, aggressive. Water: fresh, 22–28°C (71.5–82.5°F), soft.

21 Cyprinidae (Carp and Minnow family)

Diagnosis: These fishes have no adipose fin, no scales on the head, and no teeth in the mouth, but possess a dorsal fin usually with one to three spiny rays. Species are sometimes identified by the shape and arrangement of their pharyngeal teeth in the throat.
Distribution: North America, Africa, and Eurasia.

This is the most plentiful kind of fish in the majority of areas within its distribution. It is the largest of all fish families, with about 1,600 species in 275 genera. In North America, the dominant genus is Notropis, including the well-known emerald shiner (N. atherinoides) and red shiner (N. lutrensis), which occur in large shoals and are widely distributed. In Eurasia, the genera Barbus and Rasbora are dominant. The family is chiefly freshwater, although some species, such as the roach (Rutilus rutilus), can adapt to living partly in brackish or even marine waters. The habitats and feeding methods are diverse, as is indicated by the differing shapes of the pharyngeal teeth. Generally, the herbivorous species have teeth like grinding molars, whilst the carnivorous species have pointed or hooked teeth. The teeth are arranged in three rows on the curved pharyngeal bone underlying the gill covers, or operculum. These teeth cannot be seen properly without dissection of the dead fish, so they are not described here as an aid to identification.

The classification of fishes in this family has been much debated. For example, many species have two pairs of barbels, especially those which inhabit the lower water layers. But the barbels alone do not help in classifying species, because they may be either present or absent in closely related species. Thus, species have been given various generic names over the years. Some belonging to the genus Barbus have been placed in genera such as Systomus, Puntius, Barbodes, and Capoëta, whilst certain authors regard the latter names as synonymous. These points should be kept in mind when consulting the literature.

Barbus conchonius (Red Barb, or Rosy Barb)
Diagnosis: LL.24–28. The body shape is typical of the genus, and the mouth has no barbels. The characteristic colouring includes a dark spot situated centrally above the anal-fin termination. The male fish has dark tips on the anal and dorsal fins.

Almost all members of the genus Barbus live over a soft peaty bottom and like to scavenge through the substrate for food. They are omnivorous and live in large shoals. This species inhabits both still and flowing water and is common throughout its distribution. As with many barbs, it has beautiful markings. It becomes rosy red during spawning, which the female initiates. The partners rub vigorously together as the eggs are expelled and fertilized. The eggs, which are slightly sticky, hang from plants and soon begin to swell considerably. They hatch after thirty-six hours, and the fry grow quickly, becoming sexually mature in about one year.
Size: 14 cm (5.5 in). Distribution: northern India, Bengal, and Assam. Temperament: active, shoaling. Water: fresh, 17–25°C (62.5–77°F), soft, slightly acid.

Barbus schwanenfeldii (Tinfoil Barb, or Schwanenfeld's Barb)
Diagnosis: LL.35–36 and complete. The body is deep and strongly compressed, and in older fishes the nape becomes raised. There are two pairs of barbels around the mouth. The dorsal and caudal fins are brilliant red with black markings. The other fins are orange-yellow.

This is one of the largest barbs, and a voracious, omnivorous feeder. Although gregarious when mature, it becomes aggressive to members of its own species when fully grown. Breeding is similar to that of the red barb, except that this species scatters its eggs, sometimes as many as 500, onto the river bottom where they hatch after about twenty-four hours.
Size: 35 cm (13.8 in). Distribution: Sumatra, Borneo, Malacca, Thailand, and Indonesia. Temperament: active, shoaling. Water: fresh, 20–25°C (68–77°F), soft, slightly acid.

Barbus tetrazona tetrazona (Sumatra Barb, Tiger Barb, or Banded Barb)
Diagnosis: The markings are characteristic: four broad vertical stripes cross the head and body. A similar subspecies (B. tetrazona partipentazona) has an extra half-stripe from the dorsal-fin base to midway down the flank. Both subspecies have a terminal mouth.

These two subspecies live in very similar habitats and have the same breeding behaviour as B. conchonius. Both exhibit some sexual dimorphism. The females are more rounded, and less colourful on the anal and dorsal fins, than the males. When driving the females, the males become slightly paler. This is a prolific species, laying from 600 to 1,000 eggs which hatch after about a day. The fry begin to swim freely after six days.
Size: 7 cm (2.8 in). Distribution: Borneo, Sumatra, Singapore, and southeast Thailand. Temperament: peaceful, shoaling. Water: fresh, 20–27°C (68–80.5°F), not critical in quality.

19 Nannaethiops unitaeniatus (One-Striped Characin)

21 Barbus schwanenfeldii (Tinfoil Barb)

Brachydanio rerio (Zebra Danio)

Diagnosis: LL.26–28 and incomplete. The body is elongate and slightly compressed, with two pairs of barbels around the mouth.

The genus to which this species belongs is found all over India. These are all shoaling fishes and prefer to spawn over a gravelly bottom. This usually occurs during the early morning sunshine, and the eggs fall amongst weed growth. The fry hatch after about twenty-four hours and hang from leaves until the yolk sac is adsorbed. Adult females are "loyal" to their mates and often spawn repeatedly with them. Males are distinguishable from females by having slimmer bodies and brighter colours.

Size: 4.5 cm (1.8 in). *Distribution:* eastern India. *Temperament:* active, shoaling. *Water:* fresh, 18–24°C (64.5–75°F), not critical in quality.

Carassius auratus (Goldfish, or Asiatic Golden Carp)

Diagnosis: D.III–IV,15–19, A.II–III,5–6. There are deeply and posteriorly serrated, unbranched, bony rays on the dorsal and anal fins. In the wild forms, the body colour is olive-green on the back and gold on the flanks. Those in captivity range from gold, yellow, red, and silver, to mixtures of these and other colours on the body.

The golden carp was kept as a food fish until about 1,000 AD, when the Chinese probably started to keep it as a pet. It was brought to Europe by the seventeenth century, and soon introduced to the Prussian Court, being kept in Prince Potemkin's winter garden, which made it very fashionable. Its natural habitat is a slow-flowing, muddy-bottomed river and, like its close European relative the crucian carp (*C. carassius*), it can live in water with a low oxygen content. It feeds on invertebrates and algae; it also sorts through mouthfuls of mud before spitting out the debris. When breeding, the sexes become distinguished: the female grows more rounded and the male develops white tubercles, known as pearl organs, on the pectoral fins and head. The male follows the female around, fertilizing the eggs as they are shed by her. She lays between 500 and 1,000 eggs, which usually stick to the water-plants and hatch within about seven days. The larvae remain holding onto the plants for two days or so, until their fins have developed. Then, they begin to swim freely and feed on microscopic organisms.

Size: 18 cm (7 in). *Distribution:* China to eastern Europe. *Temperament:* active, shoaling. *Water:* fresh, 4–24°C (39–75°F), not critical in quality.

Carassius auratus: the varieties

Hundreds of varieties of goldfishes have been produced by the selective breeding of specific variations and mutants over many years. The varieties originated in China but have become popular in Europe and America. Each variety can be bred with different types of colour and scale. All the colours in a goldfish are derived from only three pigments—orange, yellow, and black—other colours being due to combinations of these or to light refraction in the body scales. A "metallic-

85

scaled" or "scaled" fish has a bright mirror-like sheen, caused by deposits of guanine in the scales. Secondly, a "matt" or "scaleless" fish has no guanine in the scales. Thirdly, "nacreous" scales are semi-matt and enable the colours of the fish to show through. Such varieties are more delicate than the common goldfish and need higher temperatures which do not go below 15°C (59°F).

The fantail goldfish is a variety with a short egg-shaped body and long flowing fins. Its caudal is divided into two fins side by side, showing the forked shape of the normal goldfish when viewed laterally. Many other varieties have the fantail characteristics, for example the pearl-scale, with raised or domed scales. The veiltail is a distinct kind, possessing a short body like that of the fantail, but also an extremely long caudal fin extending below the body. This tail recurs on many varieties, such as the veiltail moor. The bubble-eye is a goldfish with bulbous sacs filled by fluid under the eyes, and no dorsal fin. It has several varieties with distorted eyes, including the celestial (whose eyes turn upwards as the fish matures) and the fantailed moor (a completely black fish with protruding eyes). The lionhead is characterized by a rounded body, a fantail caudal fin, no dorsal fin, and a head with a swollen wart-like growth to which the name refers. A similar variety is the oranda, with a dorsal fin.

Carassius auratus gibelio X Carassius carassius (Nishikoi, Koi, or Japanese Coloured Carp)

Diagnosis: These fishes have elongate carp-like bodies, with two barbels on each side of the mouth. Their main trait is a wide range of colour variations.

The keeping of ornamental carp has been popular in the Orient for over 1,000 years. Written records of coloured varieties begin around 300 AD when black, blue, red, yellow, and white ones were being bred. But the major koi varieties did not arise until the late eighteenth century. These fishes, like *C. auratus,* can occur in diverse colours and degrees of scalation. The three scale groups are leather (with very few visible scales), mirror (with a single row of large scales along each side), and armoured (with large scales irregularly distributed over the body). There are four types of pigment cells: melanophores (black), elisophores (red), xanophores (yellow), and guanophores (white), which combine to yield all the hundreds of colour varieties. The latter have acquired different names and fascinating pedigrees, as might be expected with a fish so long bred and admired. The varieties cannot be fully discussed here but are divisible into three main groups.

The group of single-colour koi includes many varieties of each pigmentation, such as the rare silver "Nezu-Ohgon", the golden-orange "Orenji-Ohgon", and the cardinal-red "Hi-aka". Amongst the two-colour koi is the popular red-on-white "Kohaku". Finally, the multi-colour koi may combine from three to five colours. All these koi are hardy, omnivorous fishes and—like other carp—favour a muddy substrate in which they can forage for food. The female has a fuller body than the male. They spawn prolifically and usually produce

21 *Brachydanio rerio* (Zebra Danio)

21 *Labeo bicolor* (Red-Tailed Black Shark)

about 10,000 eggs, which are scattered at the roots of aquatic plants.

Size: 60 cm (23.6 in). *Distribution:* eastern Asia. *Temperament:* peaceful, shoaling. *Water:* fresh, 18–21°C (64.5–70°F), not critical in quality.

Chela dadiburjori (Dadio)

Diagnosis: This species has an elongate and compressed body. The dorsal and anal fins are set well back, and the long pectoral fins extend beyond the origin of the pelvic fins. A dark-blue stripe runs horizontally from the head to the caudal-fin origin.

This fish was reportedly discovered by, and is named after, Shri Sam J. Dadyburjor of Bombay. It is lively and swims in small shoals, feeding omnivorously on small animals and algae. When spawning, it is thought to attach the eggs to the undersides of large leaves. Less than 100 eggs are laid, hatching within twenty-four hours. The fry swim and feed after six days and mature within three months.

Size: 3 cm (1.2 in). *Distribution:* Bombay (India). *Temperament:* active, shoaling. *Water:* fresh, 22–25°C (71.5–77°F), soft, medium hard.

Gobio gobio (Gudgeon)

Diagnosis: LL.38–44. The body is elongate, round in section anteriorly, and compressed posteriorly. The mouth is inferior and has one short barbel at each corner. The anal and dorsal fins have short bases. The colouring is grey-green on the back, merging to yellow on the sides, and silver on the belly. Along the flanks is a row of dark spots from the head to the tail. The dorsal and caudal fins are heavily spotted, the other fins having a red tinge.

This fish occurs in diverse habitats, from fast-flowing upstream rivers to sluggish lowland rivers, as well as the brackish waters of the northern Baltic Sea. It needs a relatively high oxygen content and feeds benthically on insect larvae, small molluscs, crustaceans, and sometimes fish eggs, sucking the food into its protractile mouth. The sexes are difficult to distinguish except during the spawning season, when the male—which is slightly larger than the female—develops a rash of white tubercles, or pearl organs, on the head. The spawning occurs in shallow water between April and July. From 1,000 to 3,000 eggs are laid at intervals over several days, usually at night. The eggs are slightly sticky and adhere to stones or plants, normally hatching within ten days unless the water is cool, when they take up to thirty days. The fry live in shoals near the spawning area, feeding on plankton, and are mature by the third year, preferring to overwinter in deeper waters. Anglers occasionally fish for gudgeon to be used as bait, but in France, it is regarded as an exceptional food fish despite its small size.

Size: 15 cm (6 in). *Distribution:* temperate Europe and Asia. *Temperament:* active, shoaling. *Water:* fresh and brackish, 4–20°C (39–68°F), well-aerated.

Labeo bicolor (Red-Tailed Black Shark)

Diagnosis: LL.30–35. All species of the genus *Labeo* have strongly developed inferior mouths, which are used as effective sucker organs. This species has two pairs of barbels. Its body is elongate and slightly compressed, with a flag-like dorsal fin which originates just in front of the pelvic fins. It has a black body, orange-red tail, and crimson fins.

This handsome fish tends to be very aggressive to others of its species. It lives in flowing waters with good plant growth and grazes on algae by using its sucker mouth, but it also eats worms and other small invertebrates. The sexes are very similar, the female being somewhat more robust than the male, especially during the spawning period. She lays between thirty and sixty eggs, which are carefully placed so that they can easily be defended, usually by the male, until they hatch after about three days. The larvae swim freely after another three days or so, when they have adsorbed their egg sacs. After eight weeks, the juveniles are still rather grey but begin to develop the adult colouring, although they retain the white tip on the dorsal fin for a while. Unfortunately, these fishes are said to be difficult to breed in aquaria.

Size: 20 cm (7.9 in). *Distribution:* Thailand and the Malay peninsula. *Temperament:* active, territorial. *Water:* fresh, 22–27°C (71.5–80.5°F), soft, slightly acid, with added peat.

Leuciscus idus (Ide, or Silver Orfe, and Golden Orfe)

Diagnosis: LL.55–61, A.III,9–10. The ide has a slight hump behind the head. The mouth is terminal and oblique, with no barbels. The adult colouring is grey-black on the back, fading to silver on the belly. The pectoral, pelvic, and anal fins are orange-red, and the eye is yellow. The golden variety is yellow to orange on the back and sometimes has dark blotches.

This is a hardy fish which lives in large shoals. It prefers deeper waters, especially the brackish regions of rivers and occasionally lakes, where it spends the winter. But in March or April, it starts to migrate upstream, seeking a suitable place to spawn. The males become more brightly coloured and reach the spawning area a few days before the females, which are slightly larger. For spawning, ides favour shallow water with a sandy or stony substrate and some weed growth. The spawning occurs from April to May and is accompanied by much activity and leaping out of the water. Be-

21 *Carassius auratus* (Goldfish)

21 *Barbus tetrazona* (Sumatra Barb) 21 *Barbus conchonius* (Red Barb, or Rosy Barb)

21 *Chela dadiburjori* (Dadio)

21 *Carassius auratus* (Goldfish, Bubble-eye)

21 *Carassius auratus* (Goldfish, Bubble-eye)

tween 40,000 and 100,000 eggs are shed and fertilized, adhering to plants or rocks. After about fifteen days, they hatch and the larvae begin to feed on planktonic animals. The males mature within five or six years, and the females take some eight years. Soon after spawning, the parents start to return downstream in shoals, in order to overwinter in deeper waters where they feed on insects and benthic invertebrates. The fish is relatively popular with anglers, and in certain areas, it is fished commercially, as its flesh has a good flavour. The golden variety makes an attractive aquarium fish when young but is more suitable for ponds when mature. *Size:* 50 cm (19.7 in). *Distribution:* northwestern and central Europe. *Temperament:* peaceful, shoaling. *Water:* fresh and brackish, 4–20°C (39–68°F), not critical in quality.

Phoxinus phoxinus (European Minnow)

Diagnosis: The body is elongate and compressed posteriorly. The mouth is small with no barbels. The scales are small and the lateral line, which is incomplete and broken, terminates below the rear edge of the dorsal fin. The colouring is dark olive-green on the back and creamy white on the belly. A longitudinal gold stripe extends from behind the eye to the tail and bears several dark blotches, the largest being at the tail base.

This fish inhabits the upper layers of clean flowing water and feeds on surface insects, algae, and diatoms. Although it often feeds and swims with young trout, it is preyed upon by adult trout as well as pike, perch, and chubb. When one member of a shoal is attacked, the others exhibit the "alarm reaction" (already described for the Characidae), which was first discussed and named by von Frisch after he observed it in this species. From May to July, these fishes prepare to spawn and gather in large shoals in shallow waters. The male, slightly slimmer than the female, changes colour: his belly, pectoral and pelvic fins turn red, and his back becomes darker. Males also develop prominent tubercles, on the head and pectoral fins. The females, depending on their maturity, lay between 200 and 1,000 eggs. After being fertilized, the eggs drop onto the gravelly bottom or are attached to stones. The fry hatch within five days, stay among the stones for some thirteen days while adsorbing the egg sacs, and are mature within a year. Easy to obtain and relatively hardy, these fishes have been used widely as laboratory animals. They have excellent senses of smell and hearing, particularly in discriminating between differences in sound pitch.

Size: 14 cm (5.5 in). *Distribution:* temperate Europe and Asia. *Temperament:* peaceful, shoaling. *Water:* fresh, 4–20°C (39–68°F), neutral, well-aerated.

Rasbora heteromorpha (Harlequin Fish, or Red Rasbora)

Diagnosis: D.II–III,7, A.III,5, LL.26–27, incomplete and curved with only six to nine scales pierced. The mouth is superior, and a wedge-shaped blue-black mark appears on the flanks and caudal peduncle.

This is one of the most popular of freshwater tropical fishes in its genus. As reported by staff at the Raffles Museum in Singapore, it inhabits acid waters, both flowing and still, and small streams where it keeps to the upper layers. It feeds on small crustaceans and insect larvae. Although it is gregarious, males may become aggressive to each other, especially when spawning. The female is larger, and her black mark does not reach so far forward. Spawning occurs after she is vigorously driven, and the eggs are laid on plant tufts or leaf undersides, hatching in about twenty-four hours. The larvae hang on water-plants and swim freely after four days or so, then grow rapidly. The parents are notorious for robbing spawn and need careful attention in the aquarium.

Size: 4.5 cm (1.8 in). *Distribution:* Malay peninsula, Thailand, eastern Sumatra. *Temperament:* peaceful, shoaling. *Water:* fresh, 22–26°C (71.5–79°F), soft, slightly acid, filtered through peat.

Rhodeus sericeus (Bitterling)

Diagnosis: D.III,9–10. The body is small and laterally compressed, with an incomplete lateral line which pierces only five to six scales. The mouth is small and inferior. A blue-green stripe extends laterally from the centre of the tail base and fades under the dorsal fin.

This is probably the most attractive and

interesting of European freshwater fishes. It is well known for its symbiotic relationship with the freshwater swan mussel *(Unio)*, whereby the two aid each other in reproduction. Spawning occurs between April and June, when the bitterling sexes develop special colouring. The male becomes olive and emerald-green on the back, iridescent with many colours on the flanks, orange-red on the throat and belly, bright red on the dorsal and anal fins, and green on the caudal fin, while large white tubercles develop about the upper lip and eye. The female becomes more yellow-green and grows a fleshy egg-laying tube 6 cm (2.4 in) long. The male finds a suitable mussel, claims it as the centre of his territory, and tries to court the females that pass by. He leads a willing female to his mussel, holding his tail to one side as a signal.

When the female is ready to spawn, she maintains an oblique head-down position over the mussel, and touches its exhalant siphon with the erect proximal part of her egg-laying tube. Then she inserts the stiffened tube into the siphon and releases the eggs, usually one to four, into the mussel's gill chamber. Once she has withdrawn her tube, the male releases his milt over the mussel's inhalant siphon, so that it is drawn through the mussel and fertilizes the eggs. This sequence is repeated several times until the female has laid from 40 to 100 eggs. These are protected by the mussel and hatch after two to three weeks, the young leaving two days or so later when the yolk sacs are adsorbed. Frequently, the mussel's glochidia larvae leave the parent by attaching themselves to the young bitterling and remain in this parasitic state until developing into small mussels and dropping to the substrate. The bitterling is named for the very bitter taste attributed to its flesh.

Size: 9 cm (3.5 in). *Distribution:* central and eastern Europe, Asia Minor. *Temperament:* active, peaceful. *Water:* fresh, 4–22°C (39–71.5°F), not critical in quality.

Rutilus rutilus (Roach)

Diagnosis: D.III,9–11, LL.42–45 and complete. The dorsal fin is directly above the pelvic fin termination. The body is deep with large scales, having a terminal mouth with no barbels. The colouring is olive-green on the back and silver on the flanks. The belly is white. The paired fins and the anal fin are yellow to red, and the eye is red.

This is one of the most abundant fishes in the lakes and slow-flowing rivers within its distribution. The smaller specimens live in shoals at medium depths, and the larger ones tend to stay in deeper waters. They feed mainly on small invertebrates, including caddis fly larvae, freshwater shrimp *(Gammarus)*, and pond snails, and on some vegetable matter. Although the species is predominantly freshwater, localized populations have adapted well to brackish waters such as the Baltic estuaries and the Black Sea. Here, they migrate in shoals to overwinter or spawn, but in some areas like Lake Aral they may spawn in salt water. Spawning occurs from April to June, depending on the water temperature, which

21 *Carassius auratus* (Goldfish)

21 *Carassius auratus* (Goldfish, Fantail)

21 *Tanichthys albonubes* (White Cloud Mountain Minnow)

22 *Gyrinocheilus aymonieri* (Sucker Loach)

should be 14–15°C (57–59°F). Males arrive in the spawning area some days before the females and develop a rash of tubercles on the head and back.

When the somewhat more robust females arrive, the fishes proceed to mate in a manner similar to *Leuciscus idus,* producing 5,000 to 20,000 eggs per female. These hatch in nine to twelve days, the larvae attaching to vegetation while adsorbing the yolk sacs. Maturation varies with the temperature and food supply but generally takes two or three years for the males, and three or four for the females. Due to its profusion and its resistance to pollution, the fish is popular amongst anglers and great skill is required to land large specimens. In central Europe and especially the Baltic region, it is caught commercially as a food fish and sometimes eaten smoked or salted.
Size: 25 cm (9.8 in). *Distribution:* northern and middle Europe, including Russia but not Scotland or Norway. *Temperament:* peaceful, shoaling. *Water:* fresh and brackish, 4–20°C (39–68°F), not critical in quality.

Tanichthys albonubes (White Cloud Mountain Minnow)
Diagnosis: D.II,7, A.III,8, LL.about 30. The mouth is very oblique and terminal. The back is coloured olive-green or yellow-brown, the belly is white, and a brilliant stripe runs from the eye to the caudal-fin base. A more bright and iridescent stripe enhances the colouring of the young.

This beautiful fish was probably first described by the Chinese zoologist Lin in 1932 from a specimen found near Canton. Initial publications caused confusion about its relationship to another species, *Aphyocypris pooni,* but the two are now thought to be synonymous. The fish is omnivorous and favours dense vegetation of river margins, where it is believed to spawn. The eggs should hatch in about two days. In captivity, it has been seen eating the eggs. When mature, the sexes are distinguishable, as the male is smaller and slimmer.
Size: 5 cm (2 in). *Distribution:* the White Cloud Mountain (China). *Temperament:* peaceful, shoaling. *Water:* fresh, 16–22°C (61–71.5°F), not critical in quality.

22 Gyrinocheilidae (Sucker Loach family)

Diagnosis: D.III,9. The mouth is adapted into a ventral sucking organ. There are no barbels. Above the operculum is an inhalant opening. *Distribution:* Southeast Asia.

This small family of freshwater fishes consists of three species in one genus. Their method of breathing is quite unusual, having become adapted to living in fast-flowing hill streams. The inferior mouth has lips evolved into an efficient sucking organ and thus cannot take in water for respiration. But water is inhaled into the gill chamber through the opening above the operculum and leaves by the lower opercular openings when it is expelled from the chamber. The method of feeding is also modified: the folds or lips forming the sucker have special rasps to scrape algae off rocks. Sucker loaches have very small swim-bladders, which are useless in providing buoyancy, and so they maintain control with their fins. Breeding has been reported for the following species.

Gyrinocheilus aymonieri (Sucker Loach, Indian or Chinese Algae-Eater, or Suckerbelly Loach)
Diagnosis: Well-marked specimens have a zigzag pattern of blotches along a slightly darker lateral band.

This fish lives in well-aerated hill streams. Its feeding, typical of the family, is not very efficient, as much indigestible material is consumed. As a result, the alimentary canal has become very extended, measuring fourteen times the fish's body length. The male has more tubercles on its snout than the female, which tends to be more robust. Eggs are reportedly laid in a depression excavated by the parents, which care for the brood by guarding and cleaning the eggs and, later, the fry.
Size: 25 cm (9.8 in). *Distribution:* Thailand. *Temperament:* peaceful when juvenile, becoming aggressive. *Water:* fresh, 21–30°C (70–86°F), not critical in quality.

23 Cobitidae (Spiny Loach family)

Diagnosis: There are three to six pairs of barbels. Many species have erectile spines near the eye, either singly or doubly pointed. Some species have an adipose fin, and the lateral line may be absent or incomplete.
Distribution: Europe, Asia, and parts of Africa.

These fishes are so named as many have a defensive spine near the eye. Birds and other fishes have been found dead with spiny loaches caught in their throats. Three subfamilies exist: the Botiinae, Cobitinae, and Noemacheilinae, the last being largest with about 110 species. Loaches live in varied environments, from oxygen-rich mountain streams to low-oxygen swampy waters where other species cannot survive. As well as using the gills for respiration, some species swallow air and adsorb the oxygen through the lining of the intestine. The weather fish (*Misgurnus*) uses a further method, respiring through the skin to obtain over sixty per cent of its oxygen, while excreting over ninety per cent of its waste carbon dioxide. It can also increase its oxygen consumption through the skin to over eighty per cent, if the gills become very deprived. It is even able to survive a temporary drought by burrowing into the mud and slowing its metabolic activity for short periods. Some species burrow into the substrate for protection or feeding. They are well adapted to a benthic life-style, with barbels around their mouths which are highly sensitive to touch and taste. These are used in detecting worms, insect larvae, and plant food which may be buried under the substrate.

Another adaptation is the small swim-bladder. This allows the fish to retain a negative buoyancy and stay on the substrate, avoiding the strong currents of its river habitat. The swim-bladder has a very small posterior portion, and the rest is encased in a bony capsule. This is thought to be the organ which perceives the changes in barometric pressure, to which some species are sensitive. The latter ability is acute in *Misgurnus fossilis,* which exhibits nervous behaviour during these changes and, when in captivity, swims excitedly about the aquarium. As a result, it has reportedly been kept as a weather forecaster and been named the weather fish. Some species of loach use the swim-bladder during courtship, releasing air from a duct to produce a high-pitched sound. The breeding behaviour of some loaches has been observed and begins with the male wrapping his smaller body around the female. The eggs are shed and fertilized during and after the pair's swim to the surface. Consequently, the eggs are scattered randomly over the vegetation or substrate, where they may even become buried due to the parents' activity.

Acanthophthalmus myersi
Diagnosis: The body bears ten to fourteen dark-brown, broad, vertical stripes which merge dorsally. The base colour varies from pink to yellow. There are three pairs of barbels around the mouth, and a spine beneath the eye.

This species lives on the shallow sandy beds of hill streams and slow-flowing rivers, feeding on the typical loach diet of small benthic creatures. It is nocturnal and prefers to shelter from the light during the day. Its small eyes are protected by a transparent membrane, so that they are not damaged when the fish searches for food in the substrate. The male has more developed pectoral fins than the female, which is more lightly coloured on the abdomen. Little is known about the breeding behaviour of the species in this genus.
Size: 8 cm (3.2 in). *Distribution:* Thailand. *Temperament:* shoaling. *Water:* fresh, 24–30°C (75–86°F), soft, slightly acid.

Botia macracantha (Clown Loach)
Diagnosis: D.11–12. Four of the eight barbels originate from a common base on the upper lip. The spine below the eye has two points. The colouring is dramatic, with an orange-red body having three broad vertical stripes, one across the head and two across the body.

Some species of the genus *Botia* are active at dusk, whilst others are nocturnal. But the clown loach is active by day and, when threatened, makes knocking sounds and hides. It feeds on algae as well as worms and small invertebrates. Little is known of its eating or breeding habits and, although it has bred in captivity, its secretive behaviour has prevented observation of mating. The sexes seem not to differ externally.
Size: 30 cm (11.8 in). *Distribution:* Sumatra, Borneo. *Temperament:* active, peaceful, shoaling. *Water:* fresh, 24–30°C (75–86°F), soft to medium hard, slightly acid.

Noemacheilus botia
Diagnosis: D.II,10–12, A.II,5. There are three pairs of comparatively long barbels, but no spine beneath the eye. The caudal fin is slightly emarginate. The body is coloured grey-brown or grey-green with irregular darker stripes.

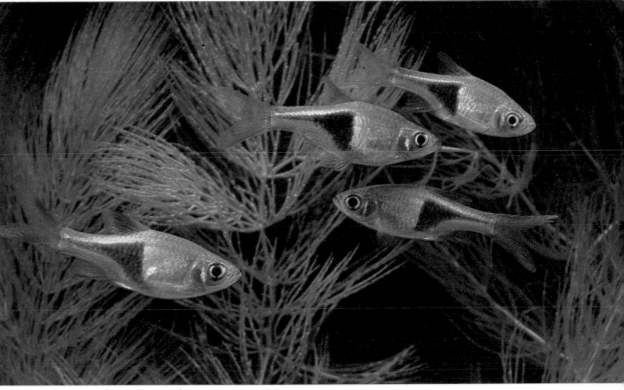

21 *Rasbora heteromorpha* (Harlequin Fish)

21 *Rhodeus sericeus* (Bitterling)

23 *Botia macracantha* (Clown Loach)

23 *Acanthophthalmus myersi*

This nocturnal loach lives on stony and sandy substrates. It is herbivorous, feeding on the algal films growing upon rocks and stones. No external sexual differences are known.
Size: 12 cm (4.8 in). *Distribution:* northwest to northeast India. *Temperament:* territorial. *Water:* fresh, about 24°C (75°F), soft to medium hard.

24 Bagridae (Naked Catfish family)

Diagnosis: D.I and rays. There are three to four pairs of barbels and, often, a large adipose fin is present.
Distribution: Africa, Asia Minor, and southeast Asia.

This family of catfishes includes some species with extraordinary features. They are mostly nocturnal and live in fresh waters but can emerge on land, as their swim-bladders enable them to "breathe" air. Their barbels are organs of taste and touch, helping to identify food at night. Predominantly carnivorous, they feed on various small invertebrates, chiefly worms, insects and larvae. Some species excavate nests in the substrate when they breed and defend the eggs from predators by making noises—using their fins to make scraping sounds and their swim-bladders to make croaking or grunting noises. One species (*Bagrichthys hypselopterus*), from the rivers of Sumatra and Borneo, is remarkable for its elongate

dorsal fin, nearly 6 cm (2.4 in) long in one of the first specimens described, which had a total length of 10 cm (4 in). Its body is dark brown and the lateral line bears a thin white stripe. It can grow up to 40 cm (16 in), but why such a long spine on the dorsal fin evolved is a mystery.

Leiocassis poecilopterus
Diagnosis: D.I,7, A.15–16. The adipose fin is present, and the barbel on the upper jaw does not extend beyond the head. The colouring is dramatic and variable, with distinct, irregular, light-brown blotches on a much darker body. Two notable blotches are those in front of the dorsal–and adipose-fin origins.

This species lives amongst the aquatic vegetation of rivers and streams. It has a peculiar preference for resting vertically against plant stems. At this angle, and with its bold, well-adapted markings, which are not significantly paler on the underside of the body, the fish is disguised in the dappled light of its natural habitat. Another species of the genus, the bumblebee catfish (*L. siamensis*), is similarly marked and has a renowned vocal ability to make croaking noises in or out of the water. Breeding behaviour is not recorded, and any sexual differences are unknown.
Size: 18 cm (7 in). *Distribution:* Java, Sumatra, Borneo, Thailand. *Temperament:* peaceful. *Water:* fresh, 22–25°C (71.5–77°F), soft, slightly acid.

25 Siluridae (Eurasian Catfish family)

Diagnosis: D.absent or with less than seven fin rays, and no spine. The anal-fin base is very long and may have up to ninety fin rays. The adipose fin is absent, and the pelvic fins are either small or completely absent. There are two or three pairs of barbels.
Distribution: Europe and Asia.

This is a large freshwater family divided into two subfamilies, the Silurinae and the Kryptopterinae. In the first, one of the biggest species is the European wels (*Silurus glanis*), recorded in specimens over 4 m (13 ft) long and weighing 295 kg (650 lbs). The wels is a nocturnal predator, feeding mainly on fishes and other animals, even birds (which it is reported to drag underwater from the surface by catching their feet with its mouth). During the day, it hides in holes or under immersed tree stumps. It builds nests from weeds and lays up to 100,000 eggs, which are thought to be guarded by the male. The second subfamily contains the fishes that are popular amongst aquarists. These belong to the genus *Kryptopterus*, including some of the most transparent fishes. One of the latter, a glass catfish (*Ompok bimaculatus*), grows up to 45 cm (17.7 in) long, and is a food fish. Its juvenile stage is transparent, but it loses this quality with age and develops the grey-green or brownish colour of

24 *Leiocassis poecilopterus*

25 *Kryptopterus bicirrhus* (Glass Catfish)

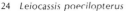

the adult. The lack of pigment cells resulting in transparency is a characteristic of the young of many fish species and is retained by the adult in some of the glass catfishes, providing camouflage and explaining their name.

Kryptopterus bicirrhus (Glass Catfish)

Diagnosis: D.I, A.53–70. The body is compressed and transparent. The anal fin is not contiguous with the caudal. The caudal fin is deeply forked, and its lower lobe is usually larger than the upper lobe. There is only one pair of barbels, the others being vestigial or absent.

This small fish is so transparent that most of its internal anatomy may be directly observed. It is carnivorous, feeding on various small invertebrates. It lives amongst vegetation, which enhances its camouflage since the plants are clearly visible through its body. A mid-water species, it maintains an oblique head-up position by undulating its anal fin. During the day, small shoals stay in the shadows of leaves or other plants. Similar in appearance and habits is the species *K. macrocephalus*, but its adult is less transparent and looks mottled. There seem to be no external sexual differences, and little is known about the breeding behaviour.
Size: 10 cm (4 in). *Distribution:* southeast Asia. *Temperament:* active, shoaling. *Water:* fresh, 20–26°C (68–79°F), soft to medium hard, slightly alkaline.

26 Schilbeidae (Schilbeid Catfish family)

Diagnosis: The dorsal fin, which is usually present, has a strong spine, and the anal-fin base is very long. The adipose fin may be absent, and two to four pairs of barbels are present.
Distribution: Southeast Asia, and Africa south and east of the Sahara.

This family contains about forty species in many genera. Two species are *Physailia pellucida*, the African glass catfish, which has no dorsal fin, and *Parailia longifilis* which, in bright light, lies rigidly on the substrate as though dead, but soon becomes active in darkness. Some species previously classified in this family are now in the family Pangasiidae, which includes the large herbivore *Pangasianodon gigas,* the Mekong catfish, a popular food fish, growing up to 2.3 m (7.5 ft) and weighing 114 kg (250 lbs).

Etropiella debauwi (Three-Striped Glass Catfish)

Diagnosis: D.I,5, A.III–IV,35–43. There are three pairs of short barbels, an adipose fin, and a forked caudal fin. Three distinctive horizontal stripes run along the body, the central one passing through the eye and being usually the most clearly marked.

This little fish feeds on small crustaceans and worms. It is very active and swims restlessly about

10–15 cm (4–6 in) above the substrate in an oblique head-up position. The females are more lightly marked and more rounded than males. Breeding behaviour is scarcely known.
Size: 8 cm (3.2 in). *Distribution:* Stanley Pool and other localities in Africa. *Temperament:* active, peaceful, shoaling. *Water:* fresh, 24–27°C (75–80.5°F), soft, slightly acid.

Schilbe mystus (Butterfish)

Diagnosis: D.I,6, A.III–IV,55–56. The fish has a short base to the dorsal fin, no adipose fin, and four pairs of barbels. The dorsal edge of the caudal peduncle has a narrow fin flange. There is a large black spot after the operculum across the lateral line.

This species is nocturnal, preferring to hide by day amongst roots and vegetation. It feeds on small fishes and invertebrates. External sexual differences and reproductive behaviour are apparently unknown, except that spawning occurs during the rainy season.
Size: 35 cm (13.7 in). *Distribution:* Nile, Zaire, and Zambesi basins, and African lakes. *Temperament:* active, shoaling. *Water:* fresh, 22–26°C (71.5–79°F), soft, slightly acid.

27 Clariidae (Air-Breathing Catfish family)

Diagnosis: D.usually 30 plus. The dorsal and anal

fins have very long bases and only soft rays, and some species possess an adipose fin. There are four pairs of barbels around the mouth, and accessory breathing (labyrinthic) organs allow some species to emerge onto dry land.

Distribution: Africa, Syria, and southern Asia from India to the Philippines.

This family is noted for its air-breathing and terrestrial habits, exemplified by the walking catfish (*Clarias batrachus*). Some of the African genera (such as *Channallabes* and *Gymnallabes*) have very slim eel-like bodies with small or absent paired fins, and are adapted for burrowing. They can survive summer droughts by burrowing into the mud, where they remain until the rains return to replenish the swampy lakes. Other genera, two of them including only blind species, inhabit rivers and lakes. Many species are voracious feeders and eat until their stomachs become roundly distended. They feed mostly on invertebrates, small fishes, and some vegetable matter. The breeding behaviour of many species has not been recorded.

Clarias batrachus (Walking, Air-Breathing, or Albino Catfish)

Diagnosis: D.62–76, A.45–58. Males have a dark spot on the posterior portion of the caudal fin. The dorsal, anal, and caudal fins usually have a dark edge.

This fish originated in southeast Asia but has unfortunately been introduced in Florida. Attempts to eliminate it by poisoning the waters have failed, as it could move to neighbouring waters and the native fishes were killed instead. The region contains the Everglades, a unique nature preserve, and the future effects on the ecosystem are unpredictable. Such artificial introductions may result in the decline and extinction of native species, because these may be preyed upon or faced with competition for food by the introduced species. Thus, several American states have prohibited the possession or importation of walking catfishes, and similar laws exist against piranhas.

Electron microscope studies of this fish confirm that the gill structures at the rear of the gill chamber have become modified into arborescent, or labyrinthic, organs. These are richly supplied with blood-vessels and are used to breathe air. The walking catfish is so well adapted to this ability that it cannot obtain sufficient oxygen from the water by its gills and must come to the surface for air. It is crepuscular and often leaves the water at dusk to seek food, sometimes travelling up to half a kilometre (a third of a mile). A voracious feeder, it uses its barbels to find food, mainly small fishes, worms, other invertebrates, and some plants. It walks by "elbowing" on the stiff spines of the pectoral fins, which are covered in a venomous mucus secreted by glands near the spine base. It is also known as the albino catfish, since this species has a high occurrence of albinos. The normal colouring is brownish to green-blue; the ventral side is pale. Breeding has not been recorded.

Size: 55 cm (21.7 in). *Distribution:* Sri Lanka and eastern India to the Malay archipelago; introduced into Florida, Guam, and Hawaii. *Temperament:*

active. *Water:* fresh, brackish, 20–25°C (68–77°F), not critical in quality.

28 Mochokidae (Upside-Down Catfish family)

Diagnosis: A.less than 10. The long-based anal fin has ossified rays. The dorsal and pectoral fins have short, smooth, serrated spines. The upper jaw bears one long pair of barbels, and the lower jaw two shorter pairs which may be feathered—bearing a number of finer barbels.

Distribution: Africa, south and east of the Sahara.

This freshwater family, deriving its name from the curious habit of a few of its members, contains about ten genera and 150 species. These are nocturnal and crepuscular fishes, inhabiting lakes, backwaters, and slow-flowing rivers. They hide during the day, and some like to rest vertically against plant stems or other surfaces. In certain parts of Africa, they are known as "squeakers" because they make strange noises, which are thought to emanate from joints of the dorsal- and pectoral-fin spines when these are rotated, and which may have a social function amongst the fish's large nocturnal shoals. Feeding is omnivorous, using the barbels to find food. Usually, the females can be recognized by their rounder bodies and, although little appears to be generally known about their breeding behaviour, that of the spotted upside-down catfish (*Synodontis angelicus*) has been observed. During courtship, the two fishes swim determinedly at each other and collide head-on, doing so a number of times at intervals of about half a minute. How they conclude this peculiar activity is not recorded.

Synodontis nigriventris (Upside-Down Catfish)

Diagnosis: D.I,7, A.IV,4–9. The anterior surface of the dorsal-fin spine is smooth. The barbels on the lower jaw are feathered with smaller tentacles. The belly is black, giving rise to the species name (from *nigri,* meaning black, and *ventris,* meaning belly), and the fish bears a number of dark brown spots.

This nocturnal fish consistently swims upside-down, a habit which may have evolved from its preference for feeding on algae and small invertebrates that live on the undersides of aquatic plant leaves. It also eats small animals near the water surface and, without its swimming habit, its mouth would be inconveniently situated for such prey. Its colouring is adapted to the habit as well, because the counter-shading on its body is reversed. At night, it continually probes the surroundings with its barbels, which are sensitive to touch and taste. By day, it shelters upside-down in hiding places. The species has been bred in captivity, but this behaviour, occurring under shelter, is little known. The female seems to have a more rounded body.

Size: 9 cm (3.5 in). *Distribution:* Zaire. *Temperament:* peaceful, shoaling. *Water:* fresh, 22–27°C (71.5–80.5°F), soft, slightly acid.

29 Aspredinidae (Banjo Catfish family)

Diagnosis: The body is depressed anteriorly, lacks

an adipose fin, and bears many large tubercles but is otherwise naked. Two subfamilies are distinguished by their anal fin counts: A.50 or more in the Aspredininae, and A.12 or less in the Bunocephalinae.

Distribution: Western Amazon basin and tropical South America.

This family contains some of the most curious-looking catfishes. In the subfamily Aspredininae are species from fresh and brackish waters, the latter occurring in the Guyana mangrove province. One species, like some of the others in the family, has an unusual method of brooding its eggs: the female carries them around attached by spongy tentacles on the abdomen. In the second subfamily are about twenty-one freshwater species, including those of interest to the aquarist. Their ugly appearance serves as camouflage, enabling them to hide amongst decaying leaves by day, and they emerge after dusk to scavenge for food.

Bunocephalus coracoides (Banjo Catfish)

Diagnosis: D.I,4–5, A.II,5. Three pairs of barbels are around the mouth, one long pair originating above it and two shorter pairs on the lower jaw. The first pair of chin, or mental, barbels is shortest and does not reach the base of the second pair behind.

This is a nocturnal scavenger, hiding under leaves or even burying itself in the substrate by day. Females are fuller in body than males. Before breeding, the parents excavate a shallow hole beneath a rock or plant by fanning their fins. After spawning, the eggs are guarded by the parents, who rest over them until they hatch. Other species in the genus reportedly breed in a similar way and are apparently prolific, the young numbering several thousands.

Size: 12 cm (4.8 in). *Distribution:* South America, in the Uruguay River and the Amazon basin. *Temperament:* peaceful. *Water:* fresh, 20–27°C (68–80.5°F), not critical in quality.

30 Plotosidae (Catfish Eel family)

Diagnosis: The body is naked, elongate or eel-like. The second dorsal fin and the anal fin are confluent with the caudal fin, which is pointed or bluntly rounded. The first dorsal fin is located well forward, and many species have an external dendritic organ with branching processes behind the anus.

Distribution: Indian Ocean and eastern Pacific regions from Japan to Australia.

This family contains over twenty species in marine, fresh, and brackish waters, although only a few are marine. The freshwater species make nests with gravel and stones on stream beds, where they spawn and then guard the eggs until these hatch. Usually, the sexes are not distinguishable.

Plotosus lineatus (Striped Catfish Eel, Saltwater Catfish, or Poison-Spined Catfish)

Diagnosis: 1D.I,4–5, 2D.80–100, A.70–77. The second dorsal-fin origin is behind the pectoral-fin origin. A post-anal dendritic organ is present.

This fish is feared because of its spines on the dorsal and pectoral fins, which have venom glands

along their sides and can cause a painful wound at the slightest touch. The juveniles form dense shoals and inhabit inshore waters, endangering people who frequent such areas. When threatened, the shoal becomes a compact mass with the fishes' heads orientated outwards—resembling a large moving object which predators are known to avoid attacking, supposedly because it may seem to be a big animal. The mouth of this species has four pairs of tentacles, which are used to seek food such as worms, shrimps, and other small crustaceans. The post-anal dendritic organ is connected by tissue to a vertebra but, as with the other species in which it occurs, its function is seemingly unknown. The sexes are not externally distinctive, and little is known of their breeding behaviour, except that spawning occurs from July to August, the eggs being laid in shallow water in rock crevices.
Size: 91.5 cm (3 ft). *Distribution:* tropical Indo-Pacific. *Temperament:* shoaling. *Water:* fresh, brackish, and marine, 24–26°C (75–79°F), hard, alkaline.

31 Pimelodidae (Fat, or Long-Whiskered, Catfish family)

Diagnosis: The body is naked and has an adipose fin. Around the mouth are three pairs of barbels, one pair being usually very long. The dorsal fin is located anteriorly and normally has a stout spine. *Distribution:* South and Central America to southern Mexico.

This is a freshwater family of fifty-six genera with nearly 300 species, all crepuscular and nocturnal. By day, they hide amongst roots and vegetation, becoming active feeders at dusk. Food is located in the dark by means of their barbels, which possess an acute sense of smell. One species of the family is blind and occurs only in a cave at São Paulo, Brazil. Little is known of the breeding behaviour. Several species are kept in aquaria, and some of the popular ones are from the genera *Pimelodella, Pimelodus, Microglanis, Pseudoplatystoma,* and *Sorubim.*

Sorubim lima (Shovel-Nose Catfish)
Diagnosis: D.I,7, A.III,18. The head is very compressed, and the snout is spatulate with an inferior mouth. The caudal fin is deeply forked. The body is marked with a horizontal black bar passing through the eye and onto the caudal fin.

This species rests against vertical plant stems with its head towards either the surface or the substrate, or it may stay close to the bottom amongst the vegetation. It feeds on benthic life such as worms and crustaceans as well as small fishes.
Size: 60 cm (23.6 in). *Distribution:* South America, the Amazon and its tributaries, the Rivers Plata and Magdalena. *Temperament:* peaceful. *Water:* fresh, 20–26°C (68–79°F), soft, slightly acid.

32 Callichthyidae (Armoured Catfish family)

Diagnosis: The body is enclosed by rows of bony

27   *Clarias batrachus* (Walking Catfish)

28   *Synodontis nigriventris* (Upside-Down Catfish)
26   *Etropiella debauwi* (Three-Striped Glass Catfish)

29   *Bunocephalus coracoides* (Banjo Catfish)
26   *Schilbe* species

plates, each flank bearing two rows of overlapping plates. The adipose fin is supported by an anterior spine. The mouth has two pairs of tentacles on the upper jaw.
Distribution: South America and Panama.

This freshwater family includes eight genera with about 130 species, all in fresh waters. Some of the genera are *Hoplosternum*, *Callichthys*, and *Aspidorus*. The largest genus, *Corydoras*, with about 100 species, is the only one with fishes active by day, the others being nocturnal. Armoured catfishes inhabit slow-flowing streams, living in shoals and feeding on worms, small invertebrates, and any other edible matter, even emerging from the water to seek food on the banks. They have been seen to move many metres (or yards) over the ground looking for new waters, due to the arid climate drying up their old habitat. They are sustained on land by swallowing air and adsorbing the oxygen through the lining of the stomach and intestine. Their armour protects them from both predators and dehydration during these vulnerable excursions. The females have fuller abdomens than the males and are usually larger. Some members of the family are peculiar amongst the catfishes since they use bubbles from the intestine to buoy up their nesting structures. This is done by a species of *Hoplosternum* which makes a nest of grass and vegetation, and by a species of *Callichthys* which lays its eggs under a leaf. The latter may lay up to 120 eggs at one spawning. The nest is guarded by the male, who makes loud grunting sounds at this time.

Corydoras metae (Masked Corydoras)
Diagnosis: This species is distinguished by its colouring. A dark vertical stripe through the eye continues along the dorsal surface of the body and descends across the tail base. The proximal half of the dorsal fin and the leading soft rays are also a dark smoky black.

This is a relatively uncommon representative of a genus which has become very popular amongst aquarists. It lives benthically in shallow muddy rivers and ponds. It tolerates waters of poor quality with low oxygen, supplementing its oxygen requirement by occasionally swimming up to the surface and swallowing some air, which is adsorbed through the stomach lining. It lives in small shoals, feeding on the organic matter in the substrate. Suitable food is identified with its barbels, which may become shortened by wear in old individuals. The females have rounder bodies than do males. Breeding behaviour is apparently typical of the genus, although reports of the details may conflict. After some preliminary excitement, the female lays a few eggs which are retained in a basket formed by her pelvic fins. How the eggs are fertilized is controversial: the female is sometimes said to extract the sperm with her mouth, but this has been denied. It seems likely that the sperms are directed towards the eggs by currents due to respiratory action and/or to fin movements. The female then places the eggs on the prepared site or sites, and one observer states that they are deposited individually. A spawning period may continue for several

days with the female laying up to 250 eggs during this time.
Size: 5 cm (2 in). *Distribution:* Guyana. *Temperament:* active, shoaling. *Water:* fresh, 22–26°C (71.5–79°F), soft, slightly acid.

Dianema longibarbus (Porthole Catfish)
Diagnosis: The head is depressed, and less steep in profile than that of *Corydoras*. Two pairs of long barbels originate over the mouth. There is an irregular line of usually distinct spots along the flank where the two rows of bony plates meet. The forked caudal fin is unpatterned, but a similar species, the stripe-tailed flagfish (*D. urostriata*), has about five bold horizontal stripes on this fin.

This is a hardy bottom-living fish which feeds on worms and other small invertebrates. The sexes appear indistinguishable and little, if anything, is known of the breeding habits.
Size: 9 cm (3.5 in). *Distribution:* South America, the Amazon and Ambyiacu Rivers. *Temperament:* active. *Water:* fresh, 25–28°C (77–82.5°F), not critical in quality.

33 Loricariidae (Armoured Catfish family)

Diagnosis: The body is rarely naked and is usually armoured with three or four series of lateral bony scutes. There may be an adipose fin with a supporting spine at the anterior edge. The mouth is ventral with small barbels around it, and the ventral lip bears several small papillae.
Distribution: Northern and central South America.

This family comprises about fifty genera with over 400 crepuscular species. Most of these live in small mountain streams, but a few inhabit mildly brackish rivers. They are benthic and use their sucker mouths to cling on rocks. Their streamlined bodies have evolved to minimize water resistance and, although some are only weak swimmers with elongated tails, many are so shaped that the current deflects them down towards the substrate. A number of species feed upon algae growing on the rocks. In contrast to teleost fishes, which have a fixed pupil and cannot control the amount of light entering the eye, armoured catfishes have an iris lobe that descends over the pupil to control the light entering the eye, as in rays. Breeding behaviour is unknown in many species. Some are sexually dimorphic, the males having larger barbels which bristle from their heads.

Loricaria parva (Whiptailed Catfish, or Vieja)
Diagnosis: D.I,7, A.I,5. The upper and lower rays of the caudal fin are very extended and nearly equal. There are twenty-nine scutes in the lateral series, and between the series are three or four rows of ventral scutes.

This benthic fish has a mottled colouring which allows its body to merge with the gravelly bottoms of streams. It feeds mainly on algae supplemented by worms and other small invertebrates. Its lips are typically adapted for attaching itself onto rocks. The breeding is thought to resemble that of another species (*L. filamentosa*) which has been observed in

detail. The male cleans a site, the female lays her eggs on it, and the pair then lie side by side to perform a variety of movements during which the eggs are fertilized. The eggs number between 100 and 200, and the young hatch after nine to twelve days. But the whiptailed catfish prefers to breed in a dark shelter, and aquarists have found that the breeding can be greatly encouraged if the fishes are fed with a high proportion of plant matter.
Size: 11 cm (4.3 in). *Distribution:* Paraguay, region of River Plata. *Temperament:* peaceful. *Water:* fresh, 21–25°C (70–77°F), soft to medium hard.

34 Antennariidae (Frogfish family)

Diagnosis: The body is flabby, misshapen, slightly compressed, and oval, with a large superior mouth. The skin is either smooth or covered with small prickles. The first one or two dorsal spines form moderately well-developed lures, or illicia. The colouring is cryptic and beautiful.
Distribution: All tropical and subtropical seas.

This marine family has about sixty species, divided into two subfamilies: the Tetrabrachiinae with one species, and the Antennariinae with all the other species. Their paired fins are used for crawling and supporting their bodies on the coral and rocks of the reefs they inhabit. The one or, in some species, two lure-like dorsal spines attract prey, such as small fishes, within the striking range of the frogfish's gaping mouth. It resembles parts of the reef due to its camouflage, and can even slowly change its colour to match the substrate. Breeding behaviour has been observed in the sargassum fish (*Histrio histrio*) and involves the male crawling closely behind the female. At the moment of spawning, the pair rushes to the surface, where the eggs are ejected. These form a raft or veil, over 2.7 m (9 ft) long and 16 cm (6.3 in) wide in some species, and resembling a balloon in another species. Several rafts may be spawned in a short time, but it is not clear exactly when the fertilization by the male occurs.

Antennarius phymatodes (Wartskin Frogfish)
Diagnosis: The caudal peduncle is distinct, and the dorsal and anal fins terminate at some distance from the caudal-fin base. The head and body have conspicuous warts. A band of pale yellow, pink, or brown, contrasting with the base colour, extends obliquely forwards and downwards from the origin of the second dorsal fin and broadens on the cheek, from where it ascends obliquely to the eye.

This fish lives in tidal pools and on reefs, crawling with its jointed pectoral fins while supported by its pelvic and anal fins. The pelvic fins are positioned ventrally in front of the pectoral fins. Like other frogfishes, it is sessile, but prey attracted by the lure is taken very quickly. It feeds on small fishes and crustaceans.
Size: 13 cm (5.1 in). *Distribution:* Indo-Australian archipelago, Indian Ocean, and the Philippines. *Temperament:* territorial. *Water:* marine, 24–26°C (75–79°F).

35 Exocoetidae (Flying Fish and Halfbeak family)

Diagnosis: D.8–16, A.8–16, LL.usually 38–60. These fishes have elongate bodies, small teeth, large scales, and no isolated finlets. There are two sub-families: the Exocoetinae, well-known marine flying fishes, with long pectoral and—in some of the species—large pelvic fins, and the Hemirhamphinae, or halfbeaks, whose lower jaw is much longer than the upper jaw.

Distribution: Atlantic Ocean and Indo-Pacific region.

The Hemirhamphinae include about eleven genera and sixty species in fresh, brackish, and marine waters. Their strange adaptation, the "halfbeak", is used by the marine species to direct plankton into the mouth. The freshwater species feed on aquatic insects, their larvae, and insects that fall onto the water surface. It is thought that the mouth may also help to steer and stabilize the front of the fish in the water. The males of one genus *(Dermogenys)* are renowned for their pugnacity and fight or "wrestle", using their beaks. This ends quickly in the wild, but in Thailand, such fishes have been bred for fighting contests, as is the Siamese fighting fish *(Betta splendens)*. Thus, *Dermogenys* was named the "wrestling fish" by Dr. H. M. Smith after he observed its behaviour in Thailand in 1923. Specimens are bred for their prowess and, unlike wild ones, can "wrestle" sometimes for over an hour. The two contestants are awarded points according to the holds which they can sustain on each other. Usually, one of them loses by being unable to continue, but it is apparently rare that a fish becomes seriously wounded or dies from exhaustion. The favoured species is *Dermogenys pusillus,* the wrestling halfbeak. Species of the same genus, as well as some of the other freshwater genera, are viviparous—giving birth to live young.

Dermogenys pogonognathus (Red Halfbeak)

Diagnosis: The pelvic fins are located anterior to the dorsal-fin origin. The body has a delicate red tint, to which the popular species name refers. Whilst the males are the larger sex, the opposite is true in the two other species, *D. pusillus* (the wrestling halfbeak) and *D. sumatranus* (the Sumatran halfbeak).

This fish lives on the surface and uses its lower jaw to direct dead insects and larvae into its mouth. Its peculiar jaw restricts it from taking food off the bottom. Much of its time is spent in resting just below the surface. Adult males are mutually aggressive and fight in the typical manner.

Courtship is initiated by the male, which swims underneath the female and touches her abdomen with the point of his lower jaw. If she is receptive, he presses his flanks against hers. The anterior rays of his anal fin are modified into an intromittent organ, used for passing sperm to the female and fertilizing the eggs internally. The gestation period lasts up to eight weeks, and the mother may produce as many as twenty live young which are about 1 cm (0.4 in) long.

Size: 9 cm (3.5 in) for males, 6 cm (2.4 in) for females. *Distribution:* Malay peninsula and the Indonesian archipelago. *Temperament:* secretive. *Water:* fresh and brackish, 25–30°C (77–86°F), neutral in hardness.

36 Belonidae (Needlefish family)

Diagnosis: LL.130–350. The body is very elongate, with a complete and low lateral line. The jaws bear many teeth and are extended so that the mouth resembles a bird's beak. The dorsal and anal fins are opposite each other and near the tail. There are no isolated finlets.

Distribution: All oceans, and fresh waters in South America and southeast Asia.

This family has only about ten genera, whose species are marine and brackish, although some species live permanently in fresh water. Their extraordinary shape is advantageous, as it allows them to hide from predators amongst the reflection of surface ripples. Usually, they feed on shoals of small fishes with their toothed "beaks". At times, they avoid predation by sculling along the water surface, using their tails, with their bodies out of the water in an almost vertical position. They are also very fast swimmers and can even evade predators or boats by leaping from the water. They may, indeed, be attracted at night by the lights on fishing boats, and this has resulted in injuries to fishermen who are pierced by the leaping fishes. Little is known about their breeding habits, but the breeding of the garpike *(Belone belone)* has been studied. This species lays its eggs in May or June in estuaries. Each egg bears about fifty to sixty entangling threads which act as holdfasts and may measure up to 18 mm (0.7 in) long. The eggs rest near the bottom, attached to seaweed.

Xenetodon cancila (Silver Needlefish)

Diagnosis: D.15–18, A.16–18, LL.250 plus. The dorsal and anal fins are deeply concave and the caudal fin is truncated. Dorsally the body is dark grey-green with small black spots, the flanks are silver-green, and the ventral area is white. A horizontal stripe runs from snout to tail and is edged with a fine dark line.

This fish is one of the exceptions in a family of mostly marine species. But it typically inhabits the surface waters, preying on small fishes, invertebrates, and amphibians. Females differ from males in having dark edges on their dorsal and anal fins. Care should be taken not to frighten such a fish, as it is a powerful jumper and can damage itself seriously when agitated.

Size: 30 cm (11.8 in). *Distribution:* southeast Asia. *Temperament:* peaceful. *Water:* fresh, brackish, 20–26°C (68–79°F), not critical in quality.

37 Cyprinodontidae (Egg-Laying Toothcarp, or Oviparous Killifish, family)

Diagnosis: The body is usually scaled with a flattened head. The mouth has no barbels, is terminal

30 *Plotosus lineatus* (Striped Catfish Eel)

31 *Sorubim lima* (Shovel-Nose Catfish)
32 *Corydoras metae* (Masked Corydoras)

32 *Dianema longibarbus* (Porthole Catfish)

34 *Antennarius* species (Frogfish)

37 *Aplocheilus lineatus* (Sparkling Panchax)

33 *Loricaria parva* (Whiptailed Catfish)

37 *Aplocheilichthys johnstoni* (Johnston's Topminnow)

or superior, and bears small teeth on the jaws. There is no adipose fin or lateral line, and the males lack a gonopodium, or copulatory organ.
Distribution: Southeast Canada to South America, Africa and Madagascar, southern Eurasia.

The family term "killifish" is derived from two Dutch words meaning fish and small waterways. Most broadly, the term refers to all families in the superfamily Cyprinodontoidae: the others are Goodeidae (the goodeids), Anablepidae (four-eyed fishes), Jenynsiidae (jenynsiids), and the popular Poeciliidae (live-bearers), each containing well-known aquarium species. In the present family, all species exhibit some sexual dimorphism, usually very pronounced, with the female being smaller than the male. All species are oviparous (laying eggs from which the young hatch), and some have a life cycle in which the egg stage is adapted to undergo a resting period out of water. This dormant period of aestivation, in hot climates, ensures the survival of the fish population in pools which dry up each year between the rainy seasons. Most of the egg-laying toothcarps are small, less than 20 cm (8 in) long, but they have been of great benefit to mankind through their use in medical research and biology. This family contains about fifty genera and 300 species. In addition to the following examples, some of the genera are *Aphanius*, *Fundulus*, *Lucania*, *Oryzias*, *Pachypanchax*, *Rivulus,* and *Roloffia*, all containing species which are suitable for the aquarium.

Aphyosemion australe (Lyretail)
Diagnosis: D.9–11, A.14–16, LL.29–32. Wavy red lines colour the lower jaw and operculum, extending brokenly above the pectoral fins. The caudal fin has a horizontal red stripe on each lobe, dividing the outer lobes from the bluish ground colour in the centre of the fin. Outside the red stripes, the tail is edged with yellow anteriorly and white posteriorly onto the extended rays.

Little has been recorded about the natural habitat of this species. Probably, it comes from brackish swamps, ditches, and pools, where it swims in the middle and lower waters. It feeds mainly on mosquito larvae and other small invertebrates. It is known as an egg-hanger, meaning that the adhesive eggs are deposited on plants. Usually, each mating results in one egg, but the breeding period may last for several weeks, during which the fishes spawn daily. At first, the number of eggs laid daily may reach thirty, but this decreases over the period. The eggs are large and glassy. Some species of this genus bury their eggs by flicking them into the substrate with their tails. The present species survives annually through its eggs, which remain in the dry beds of pools and streams until the next rainy season.
Size: 6.5 cm (2.6 in). *Distribution:* Africa, in Cameroun and Gabon. *Temperament:* secretive. *Water:* fresh and brackish, 20–24°C (68–75°F), slightly acid, filtered through peat.

Aplocheilichthys johnstoni (Johnston's Topminnow)
Diagnosis: LL.27–32. The perforated scales of the lateral line continue onto the posterior part of the

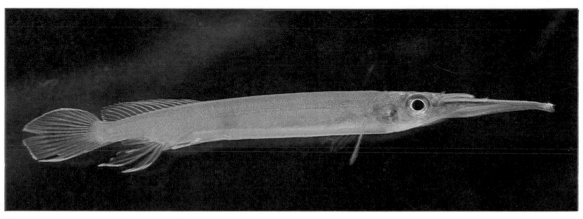

37 *Cynolebias nigripinnis* (Pearlfish)   35 *Dermogenys pogognathus* (Red Halfbeak)

head.. The mouth is superior, and the dorsal-fin origin is above the middle of the anal-fin base.

This species is a plankton feeder, preying on small crustaceans, insect larvae, and other invertebrates. It lives in small shoals in the upper and middle water layers. The female has a less colourful, more rounded body than the male. Little is known about the breeding.
Size: 5 cm (2 in). *Distribution:* west Africa and Lake Kariba. *Temperament:* shoaling. *Water:* fresh, 23–26°C (73.5–79°F), soft, slightly acid, with added peat.

Aplocheilus lineatus (Sparkling Panchax)
Diagnosis: In this genus, the dorsal-fin origin is usually almost over the termination of the anal-fin base. In this species, the leading ray of the pelvic fin is extended so that the fin resembles a spike. There are normally six to eight dark vertical stripes on the flanks, and they are particularly prominent on the female.

This fish occurs in the still and slow-moving waters of rice fields, canals, and estuaries. It feeds on mosquito larvae and, in some parts of Asia, its value as an eradicator of those pests is recognized, and certain species in this genus are protected by law. The diet also includes small fishes and invertebrates. Spawning adults lie beside each other with their ventral surfaces in contact. The tough, shelled eggs are about 2 mm (0.08 in) in diameter.
Size: 12 cm (4.8 in). *Distribution:* India (Kerala and Madras) and Sri Lanka. *Temperament:* aggressive to its own species and to similarly shaped fishes. *Water:* fresh, brackish, 20–25°C (68–77°F), not hard, otherwise not critical in quality.

Cynolebias nigripinnis (Pearlfish)
Diagnosis: Male, D.26, A.25; female, D.20–21, A.18–21, LL.28. The uniformly coloured body, velvety black to dark blue-black, is flecked with pale spots in the males. The dorsal and anal fins have a bluish-green border.

This small killifish complete its life cycle in only about eight months. At the beginning of the rainy season, when water fills the dried-up pool beds, the young hatch from eggs in the mud. The resulting populations of pearlfishes feed on crustaceans and

insect larvae. As the fishes quickly grow larger, the weaker ones are eaten by the healthier ones. Maturation is rapid, and courtship involves burrowing into the mud where the eggs are deposited. The adults are quite tired after weeks of vigorous spawning, and die as their pool dries up. The eggs left in the mud are very resilient to drought and reportedly can remain viable for up to three years submerged in the anaerobic soil of a pool bottom.
Size: 6 cm (2.4 in). *Distribution:* South America, the Plata basin. *Temperament:* aggressive. *Water:* fresh, 17–25°C (62.5–77°F), soft, slightly acid.

Epiplatys dageti (Firemouth Epiplatys)
Diagnosis: D.8–11, A.14–17. Two subspecies are distinguished by their colouring. *E. dageti dageti* usually has six dark vertical stripes along its flanks on a bronze ground, and the throat is anteriorly white, grey, or pink. *E. dageti monroviae* has an orange-red throat and normally five vertical stripes on a greenish-blue ground.

This is another annual fish which has contributed to the control of mosquitoes. It lives in shallow forest pools and streams that dry up each year, leaving its eggs to survive. The eggs are hard-shelled and resistant to pressure, and are stimulated by the next rain to hatch. The emerging fry feed on aquatic insects and their larvae, and on other small invertebrates. They become adult in eight to twelve weeks and start to breed. Courtship involves the male "riding" on the female's back and directing her towards the substrate, where he embraces her and mating occurs. The adults lay and fertilize only one egg at each mating and deposit it in the substrate. Mating continues over a period of several weeks, and the adults die as the waters dry up.
Size: 6.5 cm (2.6 in). *Distribution:* Sierra Leone. *Temperament:* peaceful. *Water:* fresh, 20–25°C (68–77°F), soft, slightly acid.

Jordanella floridae (American Flagfish)
Diagnosis: D.I,15–16, A.11–13, LL.25–26. The body is quite deep and rather compressed. The dorsal fin is marked with rows of red-brown spots or bands, and usually has a vague blotch under its origin.

This fish, although variably coloured, often bears some resemblance to the striped half of the national flag of the United States. It lives in ponds, swamps, and marshes, feeding omnivorously on algae and diverse invertebrates, remaining shyly amongst vegetation. When breeding, the male exhibits very vivid colours. Courtship occurs amongst the plants over a site where the male may have found, or prepared, a depression in the substrate for eggs. The pair embrace, and the female may lay about five to seven eggs. The male drives the female away, to prevent her from eating the eggs, and then he fans them into the depression. Sometimes, they become scattered, but usually, he manages to trace them all and ensure that they are safely hidden. Breeding continues for several days, and the male guards the eggs for up to a week after they are laid. The fry hatch within a week and begin to feed on algae.
Size: 6 cm (2.4 in). *Distribution:* northern Central America, Yucatán, and Florida. *Temperament:* aggressive. *Water:* fresh and brackish, 19–22°C (66–71.5°F), not critical in quality.

Nothobranchius rachovii (Rachow's Egg-Laying Toothcarp)
Diagnosis: D.15, A.15–16, LL.25–26. The dorsal and anal fins are turquoise, with irregular, dark carmine spots and stripes. The caudal fin is turquoise with several vertical carmine stripes, and parallel with its rounded edge are two coloured stripes: a black distal one along the fin edge, and an orange-red inside stripe.

Most of the males of the species in this genus are exceedingly colourful. The present fish also has the usual habitat of a pool or stream that dries up annually. Its eggs survive desiccation for between six weeks and six months, until the rains return. The young fishes eat the same food as *Aphyosemion australe* and become mature within six to eight weeks after hatching. Breeding continues for about two weeks and is initiated when the male swims above the female to force her down on the substrate. There, he holds her in position by clasping his dorsal and anal fins over and under her respectively. Several eggs are ejected and fertilized, accompanied by trembling of the adults. In some

species, the male is reported to flick the eggs into the substrate with his tail. The number of eggs laid varies, but one species is stated to lay up to 2,000 eggs.
Size: 5 cm (2 in). *Distribution:* Mozambique. *Temperament:* peaceful. *Water:* fresh and brackish, 20–26°C (68–79°F), soft, slightly acid, with added peat.

Terranatus dolichopterus (Sabre Fin)
Diagnosis: The dorsal- and anal-fin bases are almost opposite each other, with the dorsal-fin origin slightly in front of the anal-fin origin. The anterior rays of both fins are very elongate and, when the fins are extended, the distance between their tips is almost equal to the fish's length.

This rare species inhabits muddy pools which dry up between December and May. But the eggs survive in the typical manner, hatching in about seven days when the rains fill the pools. The young feed mainly on mosquito larvae and mature in ten weeks or so. Females do not have the spectacular fins possessed by mature males.
Size: 4 cm (1.6 in). *Distribution:* Venezuela. *Temperament:* aggressive to its own species, solitary. *Water:* fresh and brackish, 20–25°C (68–77°F), soft, slightly acid, with added peat.

38 Anablepidae (Four-Eyed Fish family)

Diagnosis: The eyes are prominent, dorsally set, and horizontally bisected. The body is elongate and anteriorly depressed, with a broad terminal mouth. The dorsal outline is nearly straight from behind the eye to the origin of the dorsal fin, which is set far back. The caudal fin is rounded, and the anal fin is modified in the male as an intromittent sexual organ.
Distribution: Southern Mexico to northern South America.

When these fishes float just underneath the water surface, their unusual eyes can be clearly seen on it like small spheres. The eyes are bisected and have pear-shaped lenses to permit vision above and below the surface simultaneously. Due to this facility for aerial vision, they are commonly thought to be insectivorous fishes, although this feeding behaviour has probably not been observed. But they have been seen to lie on estuarine mud and filter detritus from the receding waters. Such waters are also the feeding grounds for birds, including terns and herons, which eat fishes and invertebrates. It is likely that the anablepid's eyes detect these predators and allow the fish to escape. The sexes in this species are easily distinguished because of the prominent intromittent organ on the male. However, not every male can mate with every female, since the female's aperture is covered by a small scale which restricts the opening to either the left or right, whilst the males can only move their gonopodium to either the left or right. Thus, the population is divided into two mating groups: for example, a female with a right-opening aperture can only copulate with a male having a left-moving gonopodium. The mothers give birth to between one and five young, which measure up to 6 cm (2.4 in) long. The family contains only one genus.

Anableps anableps (Four-Eyed Fish)
Diagnosis: LL.50–55. The fish is olive-green with a darker back and has four or five horizontal grey stripes along its flanks. The latter colouring distinguishes it from the other two species in this genus, as do their lateral line counts: *A. dovii,* LL.64–70; *A. microlepis,* LL.81–90.

This species lives in the intertidal coastal waters with shifting muddy bottoms, in brackish lagoons, and even in inland freshwater lakes. It can be found upriver during the dry season when the brackish waters may extend 80 km (50 miles) inland. The turbidity of its habitat is due to sediment deposited by rivers or stirred up by the sea. It feeds on animals in the mud, possibly including polychaete worms and small crustaceans, as well as taking food below the water surface. It appears to have difficulty in swimming towards the substrate but will descend from the surface to evade predatory birds or may even jump violently out of the water.
Size: 30 cm (11.8 in). *Distribution:* tropical Central America and northernmost South America. *Temperament:* peaceful, shoaling. *Water:* fresh, brackish, and marine, 24–28°C (75–82.5°F), not critical in quality.

39 Poeciliidae (Live-Bearing Toothcarp family)

Diagnosis: The male has a gonopodium, or intromittent organ—usually composed of the third, fourth, and fifth rays of the anal fin—for internal fertilization. He is normally smaller than the female and, in most species, the sexes have dimorphic fins.
Distribution: Eastern North America to northeast Argentina.

This family is divided into three subfamilies, two having one species each. The third, Poeciliinae, contains about twenty genera and 136 species, including many popular aquarium fishes. Their fertilization is usually internal, and the young are born alive. Some species are very beneficial to mankind in being used for the biological control of mosquitoes and for genetic and behavioural research.

Belonesox belizanus (Pike Live-Bearer)
Diagnosis: D.8–10, A.10, LL.52–65. The body is slightly compressed, the eyes are large, and the dorsal fin is near the tail. The snout is extended and the mouth is deeply cleft, resembling a bird's beak with pointed teeth, which are larger on the inside of the jaw. The fish is olive-grey dorsally, with olive-green to grey-yellow flanks, colourless or slightly yellowish fins, and a distinct black spot on the caudal fin base. The male is smaller and has a gonopodium.

This species is exceptional in being a predator in a family of omnivorous fishes. It lives near the surface and feeds on smaller fishes, insect larvae, tadpoles, and other invertebrates, lying in wait for its prey. The female attains twice the length of the male, and can be quite prolific, with four broods between May and September, averaging 136 eggs per brood. The young are distinctively marked with a broad, black, horizontal stripe. Their behaviour is adapted to the avoidance of predation by the parents: the young descend from the surface waters to seek food when the adults are absent but remain stationary at the surface when adults are present.
Size: 20 cm (7.9 in). *Distribution:* eastern Central America, from southern Mexico to Nicaragua. *Temperament:* secretive. *Water:* fresh and brackish, 25–30°C (77–86°F), not critical in quality.

Gambusia affinis (Mosquito Fish)
Diagnosis: D.6–7, A.8–10, LL.29–30. This species is readily distinguished from the guppy by its spotted caudal fin.

This small fish, although not very popular amongst aquarists due to its belligerence, is famous for its preferred diet of mosquito larvae. In parts of North America, its distribution is organized by authorities responsible for mosquito control. It is slightly larger than the guppy and eats its own weight of larvae daily. As a biological control, it has been quite successful because of its voracity and its tolerance of a wide range of conditions from fresh water to brackish swamps varying between 10° and 30°C (50° and 86°F). It reproduces from April to October. Pregnant females bear a black blotch on the abdomen, and produce up to eighty juveniles. There are two subspecies, *G. affinis affinis* (the spotted gambusia, or western mosquito fish) and *G. affinis holbrookei* (the eastern mosquito fish). Its success in the Panama region has enabled humans to inhabit the area, and further introductions have been made in Japan, China, Australia, and countries bordering the Mediterranean.
Size: 6.5 cm (2.6 in). *Distribution:* river systems of San·Antonio and Guadalupe in Texas. *Temperament:* aggressive. *Water:* fresh and brackish, 18–24°C (64.5–75°F), not critical in quality.

Heterandria formosa (Mosquito Fish)
Diagnosis: D.7–8, Pect.11–12. A horizontal broad black stripe runs along the flanks from the snout to the tail and is crossed by less distinct vertical stripes.

This is one of the world's smallest vertebrates and is reported to be amongst the smallest live-bearing vertebrates. It inhabits the middle and lower water layers of small streams, living near vegetation and feeding omnivorously on algae, small crustaceans, and insect larvae. Sexual dimorphism is not marked, but the male is smaller, growing to only 2 cm (0.8 in), and has a long gonopodium. Small broods are produced and up to eight young have been recorded at a single birth. The eggs are fertilized in the same order in which they are formed, so that a female may carry embryos at up to six different stages of development. The time taken for the development of an individual egg varies according to the number and stage reached by the embryos she may already be developing. An average of sixty-three young in seventy-four days has been reported for three females. At birth, the young measure 7 mm (0.3 in) long.

37 Terranatus dolichopterus (Sabre Fin)

37 Nothobranchius rachovii (Rachow's Egg-Laying Toothcarp)

37 Aphyosemion australe (Lyretail)

37 Jordanella floridae (American Flagfish)

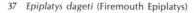
37 Nothobranchius korthause

37 Epiplatys dageti (Firemouth Epiplatys)

Size: 3.5 cm (1.4 in). *Distribution:* southern North America. *Temperament:* secretive, aggressive. *Water:* fresh and brackish, 20–24°C (68–75°F), medium hard.

Poecilia reticulata (Guppy, or Millions Fish)

Diagnosis: D.7–8, A.8–9. The male has a very swollen second ray on the pelvic fin, exhibits brilliant iridescence and a wide range of colours, and rarely resembles other males in appearance.

This little fish was named *Girardius guppii* by A.C. Gunther in 1866 after the Rev R.J.L. Guppy, who returned to the United Kingdom from Trinidad with specimens of it. But that name has led only to a common name for the fish, since it had already been described by W. Peters in 1859. The guppy is remarkable for its diversity of form and colour, and many varieties exist. Its natural habitat is in slow-moving fresh or brackish waters. Although an omnivore, it has gained a wide reputation as an effective insectivore in areas suffering from diseases spread by mosquitoes. The male's iridescent colours attract the female guppy. Courtship may begin with numerous behavioural patterns, two of which are known as "following" the female and "biting" at her genital region. In some of these actions, the male displays his median fins. If he succeeds in winning the female's attention, she responds by slowing her swimming. Then the male commences a series of sigmoid displays, bending his body into an S-shaped curve before the female, so that light reflects from his iridescent colours. It is during this final performance that he may make an attempt to copulate, manoeuvring into such a position that he can insert the tip of his gonopodium into the female's genital pore. The pair swim in a tight circle, with the female flanked by the male, while she arches her back to expose the genital region. The male transfers bundles of sperms which break up inside the female and migrate to a storage pouch near the ovary, where they are retained until required. The eggs mature in the ovary and are fertilized before being released, so that fertilization occurs prior to ovulation. As with the preceding species and many other poecilids, guppies can develop several broods of young at different stages simultaneously, a phenomenon known as superfoetation.

Poecilia reticulata (Yellow Double Swordtail Guppy and other varieties)

Diagnosis: See the diagnosis for the previous entry. This variety has an oval caudal fin whose outer upper and lower rays are extended to form two "swords". Their length should be about one and one-fifth times the body length. The dorsal fin is pointed and extends to one third of the length of the caudal fin.

This is amongst the many varieties which have been carefully bred by aquarists. The guppy's diversity is a major reason for its popularity, and numerous varieties as well as their genetic characteristics are well known. Societies are devoted to the keeping of them, and annual shows are held to exhibit those which have been bred to specific standards. About a dozen varieties with different dorsal and caudal fins are familiar, some examples being the spadetail, fantail, bottomsword, lyretail, and roundtail.

Size: 6 cm (2.4 in). *Distribution:* South America north of the Amazon, and Trinidad and Barbados. *Temperament:* active. *Water:* fresh and brackish, 16–30°C (61–86°F), not very soft.

Poecilia X (Hybrid Black Molly)

Diagnosis: Black molly hybrids have been produced for about fifty years by crossings from three species of *Poecilia*. These can be distinguished from each other, and from hybrids, by some of their meristics:

P. sphenops, D.8–11, LL.25–30, D. origin after A. origin; *P. latipinna,* D.13–16, LL. 26–30, D. origin before A. origin; *P. velifera,* D.18–19, LL.26–28, D. origin well before A. origin. Unless a hybrid has a known pedigree, its parentage is often difficult or impossible to determine.

The name "molly" is derived from the former generic name *Mollienesia,* a synonym of *Poecilia.* Originally, the black molly hybrid was produced by crossing *P. sphenops* with *P. latipinna,* but many varieties now exist due to crossing of all the above species, which can also produce partially or entirely melanistic (black) forms naturally and without crossing. It has even been suggested that *P. latipinna* and *P. velifera* are races of the same species, since they hybridize readily and their natural distributions meet. The black molly feeds omnivorously on small crustaceans and much vegetable matter. It breeds at an age of nine months to one year, and the gestation period lasts from six to eight weeks.

Size: 12 cm (4.8 in). *Distribution:* domestic (the parent species occur in southern North America). *Temperament:* peaceful. *Water:* brackish, 25–28°C (77–82.5°F), soft, slightly acid.

Xiphophorus helleri (Swordtail Fish)

Diagnosis: D.13–14, A.9–10, LL.26–29. The extended lower rays of the male's caudal fin form a long "sword".

This fish has a wide range of riverine habitats, from mountain sources to the slow-flowing junctions with swampy regions. It feeds on algae and various small animals. Breeding is typical of the family, and the females produce about 150 young per brood after a gestation period of four to six weeks. There are four subspecies, originating from different localities, and with distinctive structures at the tips of their gonopodia: *X. h. alvarezi, helleri, guentheri,* and *strigatus.* The fish is very popular in aquaria, and many varieties have been produced by crossing between its sub-species and with other species of *Xiphophorus.*

Size: 15 cm (6 in). *Distribution:* central America. *Temperament:* active, the males sometimes being aggressive. *Water:* fresh, 17–25°C (62.5–77°F), not critical in quality.

40 Melanotaeniidae (Rainbowfish family)

Diagnosis: The body is deep and laterally compressed, with a weakly developed lateral line and relatively large scales. The two dorsal fins are narrowly separated, and the anal-fin base is longer than the base of the second dorsal fin.

Distribution: New Guinea, Aru Island, and Australia.

This family contains about nineteen species, mostly freshwater.

Melanotaenia maccullochi (Dwarf Rainbowfish)

Diagnosis: 1D.IV–VII, 2D.I,8–10, A.I,14–15. The body is typical of the genus. The back is brown and the ventral side is pale yellow with seven horizontal stripes along the flank.

This fish swims in the middle water layers of weeded rivers. When preparing to spawn, it becomes reddish with greenish fins and has a brown or brick-red caudal fin. The female usually remains lighter in colour. When the eggs are laid, they have short filamentous processes with which they become attached to plants. The young hatch after about eight days, and are dark in colour.

Size: 8 cm (3.2 in). *Distribution:* northern Australia. *Temperament:* peaceful, shoaling. *Water:* fresh, 20–26°C (68–79°F), soft to medium hard.

41 Atherinidae (Silverside family)

Diagnosis: The body tends to be elongate, with two well-spaced dorsal fins and a broad horizontal silver band. The scales are relatively large and are either cycloid or ctenoid. The pelvic fins originate on the abdomen.

Distribution: Temperate and tropical regions.

Most of these fishes are marine, although some genera, such as *Chirostoma* and *Bedotia,* have freshwater species, and *Telmatherina* has brackish-water species. Many marine representatives swim in large shoals and are of economic importance. The eggs generally have several filamentous outgrowths which adhere to weeds and stones.

39 *Heterandria formosa* (Mosquito Fish)

39 *Poecilia reticulata* (Yellow Double Swordtail Guppy)

39 *Gambusia affinis* (Mosquito Fish)

39 *Poecilia reticulata* (Guppy, wild form)

39 *Poecilia reticulata* (Snakeskin Veiltail Guppy)

Bedotia geayi (Madagascar Rainbowfish)
Diagnosis: The body is fusiform, and the mouth is superior. The first of the two dorsal fins has its origin in the centre of the back, and the second is well separated, with a long base. The pectoral fins originate on the horizontal stripe and typically point upwards.

This fish keeps to the upper water layers, feeding on aquatic insects and their larvae. The caudal and anal fins of the male have a red border. Spawning is similar to that of the Celebes sailfish, described below.
Size: 15 cm (6 in). *Distribution:* Madagascar. *Temperament:* active, peaceful, shoaling. *Water:* fresh, 20–24°C (68–75°F), neutral to hard.

Telmatherina ladigesi (Celebes Sailfish)
Diagnosis: The body is elongate and compressed. The second dorsal fin is larger, and in a mature male, the rays are extended, the anal fin being similar. The first dorsal fin is black with white or yellow rays, and the second is orangey with the first ray black in the female but with the first two rays black in the male.

This species eats small animals. The female is more drab in colour than the male, and both are stimulated to spawn by the morning sunshine. After energetic driving, the two shed and fertilize their eggs, which collect amongst the roots of floating plants. The yellow eggs are vulnerable at this stage and are likely to be eaten if the parents are short of food. The eggs hatch after about ten days, and the fry remain on the surface, feeding upon micro-organisms. After seven months, they are generally mature enough to reproduce.
Size: 7 cm (2.8 in). *Distribution:* Celebes. *Temperament:* peaceful, shoaling. *Water:* brackish, 24–28°C (75–82.5°F).

42 Monocentridae
(Knightfish or Pinecone Fish family)

Diagnosis: The body is encased in heavy plate-like scales. The dorsal-fin spines are inclined to alternating sides, and the pelvic fins have one large spine and three soft rays. Two phosphorescent light organs below the lower jaw produce light by means of symbiotic bacteria.
Distribution: Indo-Pacific region.

This family contains two marine species in the same genus. The Australian species is *Monocentris gloriae-maris,* a yellow fish with markings of blue, red, orange, and white, which is often accidentally trawled up by fishermen.

Monocentrus japonicus (Knightfish or Pinecone Fish)
Diagnosis: D.V–VI,11–12, A.II,8, LL.13–16. The colouring is golden-yellow with black markings.

This fish has frequently been brought up from waters as deep as 200 m (656 ft). There, its light organs would be clearly visible in the darkness, and they may be used for attracting or seeing prey, although the fish's diet is unknown. Nothing is known of its breeding behaviour, but it is thought to live in shoals. In Japan, it is a popular food fish, and elsewhere, it is seldom seen in aquaria, but it has been presented as a gift by the Crown Prince of Japan to the Steinhart Aquarium in San Francisco.
Size: 16 cm (6.3 in). *Distribution:* Indo-Pacific, from scattered localities including Japan and South Africa. *Temperament:* peaceful, shoaling. *Water:* marine, 12–18°C (53.5–64.5°F).

43 Holocentridae
(Squirrelfish family)

Diagnosis: D.X–XIII and rays, Pel.I,5–8. All these fishes have a long-based dorsal fin, and most are red in colour. The body is covered with large rough scales, and the operculum has a spiny edge.
Distribution: Tropical oceans.

These marine fishes are mostly nocturnal. The adults tend to live near the bottom between the shoreline and a depth of 100 m (328 ft). During the day, they hide in crevices or under reef overhangs. The fry are planktonic. There are two subfamilies, one being the Holocentrinae (squirrelfishes) with a strong enlarged spine on the preoperculum, which in some species is toxic, and a long tubular swim-bladder that extends the length of the body. The second subfamily is the Myripristinae (soldierfishes) which lack the large spine and have a swim-bladder that is nearly divided into two separate chambers by a constriction.

Adioryx cornutum (White Squirrelfish)
Diagnosis: D.XI,12–13, A.IV,9, LL.35–36. The preopercular spine is smaller than the eye width. There are two opercular spines, the lower one being shorter. The third anal-fin spine is the largest. Dark spots are on the bases of the soft dorsal, anal, and caudal fins.

This fish is common on reefs, sheltering by day amongst the coral, and venturing out at night to feed on crustaceans. Like other members of the family, it is able to make loud noises by grunting and clicking.
Size: 20.3 cm (8 in). *Distribution:* east Africa, Queensland, and Melanesia. *Temperament:* secretive. *Water:* marine, 24–26°C (75–79°F).

44 Centriscidae
(Shrimpfish family)

Diagnosis: The body is very compressed and blade-like, with a sharp ventral edge and no lateral line. The snout is long and resembles a trumpet, with a small mouth. The fish is almost covered in horny, scale-like sutured plates, which are extensions of the vertebral column. Posteriorly, there is a sharp horizontal-pointing spine, which is the first dorsal spine.
Distribution: Indo-Pacific region.

This family consists of two genera, *Aeoliscus* and *Centriscus,* each with two species. These charming fishes swim in a nose-down vertical position, and swim horizontally only when trying to evade predators. Their tiny mouths and narrow snouts greatly limit the size of their food.

103

40 *Melanotaenia maccullochi* (Dwarf Rainbowfish)

41 *Telmatherina ladigesi* (Celebes Sailfish)

39 *Xiphophorus helleri* (Swordtail Fish)

39 *Poecilia X* (Hybrid Black Molly)

41 *Bedotia geayi* (Madagascar Rainbowfish)

Aeoliscus strigatus (Shrimpfish or Razorfish)
Diagnosis: The species in this genus are distinguished from those in the genus *Centriscus* by having a movable segment at the end of the dorsal spine and a space between the eyes which is striated instead of bearing a deep groove. This species has a smoky-black stripe along the flank, whereas the other species (*A. punctulatus*) has many little black spots instead.

These fishes find protection between the spines of the sea urchin *Diadema*. Many individuals may collect amongst the spines of one urchin, their dark stripes and semi-transparent bodies contributing to the camouflage. Their nose-down habit of swimming has sometimes been seen to change when they continue foraging for the minute marine life on which they feed, going up a vertical reef or along a cave ceiling. In these places, they maintain their bodies perpendicular to the substrate, and thus may appear to be suspended from a cave ceiling. The people of Palau Island in the Pacific Ocean are reported to use the dried bodies of these fishes as ornaments.
Size: 15 cm (6 in). *Distribution:* southeast Australian and New Guinea coasts and the Indo-Pacific. *Temperament:* peaceful, shoaling. *Water:* marine, 24–26°C (75–79°F).

45 Syngnathidae (Pipefish and Seahorse family)

Diagnosis: D.15–60. The elongate body is encased in bony plates that are beneath the skin. These fishes have a long snout, a small mouth, one dorsal fin, no pelvic fins, and a very small anal fin. Some species have no tail fin, and the caudal peduncle may be prehensile.
Distribution: Atlantic and Indo-Pacific regions.

These fishes live in shallow seas and inshore waters, a few species being found in fresh water. As they are well armoured, their body movements are minimal, and they swim by undulations of the fins. When spawning, the female transfers her eggs to the underbelly of the male, so that he can protect them until they hatch. There are two subfamilies: the Syngnathinae (pipefishes), in all kinds of water, and the Hippocampinae (seahorses), which are entirely marine.

Hippocampus kuda (Yellow Seahorse)
Diagnosis: D.16–18, A.4. The body has about thirty-six rings and is coloured yellow. The tail is mobile and prehensile, and the seahorse swims in an erect position.

This species is usually found out at sea and is attracted to the surface at night if lights are shining into the water. It can change its colour and does so during the excitement of spawning. The male and female approach each other while jerking their heads to produce a clicking sound, caused by a notch behind the head. They embrace, and the female places her enlarged oviduct into or against the male's pouch and transfers a few eggs. The pair then part, the male bending his body back and forth apparently to arrange the eggs. This process is repeated many times until 100–200 eggs have been

transferred. The male broods them, and, in about four or five weeks, the eggs hatch and the fry are released.
Size: 25.4 cm (10 in). *Distribution:* Indo-Pacific. *Temperament:* peaceful. *Water:* marine, 24–26°C (75–79°F).

Syngnathus pulcheris (African Freshwater Pipefish)
Diagnosis: D.25, A.2. There are forty-eight bony rings on the tail and trunk, the tail being very long. The colouring is grey or brown with blue highlights. The flanks are marbled, and black stripes radiate from the centre of the eye.

This fish occurs in brackish bays and estuaries, feeding on small invertebrates and fish fry. Like other members of the family, it can change its colour to match the surroundings. Its reproductive behaviour resembles that of other members, the female placing the eggs in the male's abdominal pouch. The eggs are then embedded in a spongy mass which is located on the ventral surface of the male.
Size: 15 cm (6 in). *Distribution:* Zaire and Ogowe Rivers. *Temperament:* peaceful. *Water:* fresh and brackish, 24–26°C (75–79°F), not critical in quality.

46 Gasterosteidae (Stickleback family)

Diagnosis: The body is fusiform in profile, and in some species the head is pointed. The skin is naked with vertical body plates. There are three or more erectile spines in front of the dorsal fin, and the anal fin is similar in shape to the dorsal fin.
Distribution: Widespread in the northern hemisphere.

These are active and alert fishes, feeding on small invertebrates. Many species build nests when spawning and have been studied intensively. All dwell in fresh or brackish water except the truly marine species *Spinachia spinachia*, the fifteen-spined stickleback.

Gasterosteus aculeatus (Three-Spined Stickleback)
Diagnosis: D.III–IV,8–14, A.I,6–11. Each of the three dorsal spines supports a sail-like membrane. The number of bony plates is variable and appears to be related to the salinity of the water, being greater in brackish than in fresh waters. The colouring is mottled green or brown on the back, or sometimes dark blue, fading to silver on the underside.

The species has been studied in detail (by Tinbergen and his colleagues), for example as regards its spawning, which is very like that of other members of the family. The male develops a red abdomen and establishes a territory where he builds a nest of weed. Upon seeing a ripe female, he courts her with a distinctive behaviour pattern. She is thus encouraged to lay her eggs in his nest, where he then fertilizes them. The male guards and fans them until they develop and hatch into fry.
Size: 10 cm (4 in). *Distribution:* Europe, northern Asia, Japan, and North America. *Temperament:* shoaling, territorial. *Water:* fresh, brackish, and marine, 4–20°C (39–68°F), not critical in quality.

47 Scorpaenidae (Scorpionfish family)

Diagnosis: Usually D.XI–XVII,8–18, A.I–III,3–9, Pel. I,2–5. The body is compressed and normally covered in ctenoid scales. The head has a bony ridge, or stay, running from the gill cover to below the eye, as well as other ridges and spines. There is usually one dorsal fin which has strong spines armed with venom glands. The anal and pelvic fins are present.
Distribution: Tropical and temperate seas, some Arctic waters.

This family is divided into eight subfamilies, some containing popular aquarium fishes. For example, the Pteroinae include the highly venomous *Pterois* species, whilst the Scorpaeninae include well-known species such as *Scorpaena* and *Scorpaenodes* (the scorpionfishes). Many members of the family are economically important, and the red fish from the north Atlantic (*Sebastes marinus*) is greatly exploited due to its excellent white flesh. Numerous species bear striking patterns, the predominant colour often being red. Most are fishes of moderate size, living cryptically amongst rocks and reefs or on beds of kelp, where they remain motionless for long periods. Here, they are well camouflaged and can be dangerous to humans who accidentally tread on them and are stung by their poisonous spines. The degree of danger varies with the species, but medical advice should always be sought by victims. The mode of reproduction is also variable, but *Sebastodes* and *Sebastes* both employ internal fertilization and reproduce ovoviviparously. The young are extruded at about the time of hatching, and it is thought probable that the young even hatch after the eggs have been laid. This occurs in the spring, at a depth of about 90 m (295 ft) on the western Atlantic coast. Other genera are known to fertilize the eggs externally.

Pterois volitans (Scorpionfish, Lionfish, or Turkeyfish)
Diagnosis: D.XII,10–11, A.III,6–7, Pect. 14. The fins are very extended, the dorsal spines being filamentous and as long as the body depth, and the pectoral fins having a feathered appearance. The body and head are patterned by twenty-four to thirty vertical stripes alternating with narrower white stripes. The soft dorsal, anal, and caudal fins have many dark spots.

This impressive species can inflict a painful injection of nerve toxin if the tip of a dorsal spine is touched. But the toxin is thermodegradable and may be treated like stings from the Dasyatidae (stingrays) and the Potamotrygonidae (river stingrays). The twelve dorsal spines each have a glandular groove which originates just below the spine base and extends along the entire length. The venom glands lie in this groove and may stretch for three-quarters of the length, the spine being covered in an integumentary sheath. The fish is often found on the undersides of reef overhangs, caves, or clefts in coral, where great care should be taken by divers. It is a voracious carnivore and feeds on shrimps, crabs, small fishes, and even the young

of its own kind. Despite its poisonous spines, it is a very popular aquarium fish.
Size: 30 cm (11.8 in). *Distribution:* tropical Indo-Pacific. *Temperament:* solitary. *Water:* marine, 24–26°C (75–79°F).

48 Centropomidae (Glassfish family)

Diagnosis: 1D.VII–IX, 2D.I,9–15, A.III,6–17, Pel.I,5. The lateral line extends onto the tail, and the body is relatively deep. A scaly process is usually present in the pelvic axis.
Distribution: Atlantic Ocean and Indo-Pacific region.

This family has nine genera and includes *Chanda,* the Asiatic glassfishes. In these fishes, the body is transparent, and the vertebral column and other internal structures can normally be seen. The family also contains *Lates niloticus,* the Nile perch, a well-known African freshwater fish.

Chanda ranga (Indian Glassfish)

Diagnosis: 1D.VII, 2D.I,12–15, A.III,13–15, LL.60–70. The body shape is typical of the family. The third ray of the anal fin is usually the longest, and the second dorsal fin edge is convex. The dorsal and anal fins have black rays and pale blue borders.

This fish lives in shoals when young but tends to be timid and solitary when mature. The female is paler and more yellow than the male. The pair is stimulated to spawn by sunshine and tends to do so in the morning. About four to six eggs are laid each time, and this is repeated until some 200 sticky eggs have been produced. These adhere to plants, and the young usually hatch within twenty-four hours. The fry swim independently after three or four days.
Size: 7 cm (2.8 in). *Distribution:* India, Burma, Thailand. *Temperament:* secretive. *Water:* fresh and brackish, 18–25°C (64.5–77°F), hard, alkaline.

49 Serranidae (Sea Bass, Grouper, or Rock Cod family)

Diagnosis: A.III, and rays, Pel.I,5. These fishes have robust bodies and large heads with three posteriorly pointing spines on the operculum. The lateral line is continuous and complete, and the scales are usually ctenoid, but sometimes cycloid. The caudal fin is truncate, rounded truncate, or lunate.
Distribution: Tropical and temperate regions.

This family contains numerous genera and totally about 370 species. A few of these are confined to fresh water, the remainder occurring in brackish estuaries and inshore waters. They are mostly benthic predatory fishes, some growing to well over 3.5 m (11.5 ft), such as *Epinephalus lanceolatus,* the grouper. Fishes of this size are greatly feared by divers but prized by anglers. Curiously, some species are hermaphroditic: although normally the fish passes through a female stage when it is young and develops later into a male, sometimes eggs and sperm develop at the same time in one individual. The eggs produced by the serranid fishes may float and be non-adhesive, or they may be demersal and adhesive, but in either case there appears to be no brood care of the eggs or fry.

Serranus scriba (Banded Seaperch, or Painted Comber)

Diagnosis: The fish is elongate, with a slightly rounded caudal fin, and a pectoral fin extending past the origin of the anal fin. It has a yellow-cream body with four to seven broad, brown, vertical stripes on the body and a scribbled pattern on the cheek. A large violet-blue patch is on the centre of the belly and extends midway up the flank.

This species is common along the rocky shores of the Mediterranean, where individuals establish a territory and defend it fiercely against other members of the species. Like most of the family, it is predatory and carefully stalks diverse prey such as species of *Atherina* (sand smelts), as well as eating molluscs and crustaceans. These fishes are hermaphroditic and spawn from May to August inshore, producing demersal adhesive eggs, which stick to rocks and stones.
Size: 25 cm (10 in). *Distribution:* Mediterranean, Black Sea, and the eastern Atlantic from the Bay of Biscay to South Africa. *Temperament:* aggressive, territorial. *Water:* marine, 18–26°C (64.5–79°F).

50 Grammistidae (Soapfish family)

Diagnosis: D.II–IX,12–27, A.0–III,8–17. The body is perch-like, elongate to oval, and compressed. It has scales on the head, and several large spines on the preoperculum and operculum. The mouth is superior and large, and there is a barbel on the chin.
Distribution: Atlantic and Indo-Pacific Oceans.

In this family are six genera of fishes of small to medium size, the maximum length being about 30 cm (12 in). Amongst others, they include the soapfishes of tropical America, named for the slippery mucus they produce, which makes the water frothy. All members of the family have toxic mucus glands in the skin, which secrete the bitter-tasting mucus that protects them from predation. Their bright colours are thought to be a warning of this danger.

Grammistes sexlineatus (Golden Striped Soapfish)

Diagnosis: 1D.VI–VIII,13–15, A.I–II,9–10, LL.63–72. This species has only a rudimentary barbel on its chin. The dorsal fin is contiguous. The preoperculum has three to four spines, and the operculum has three spines. The caudal fin is rounded, and the skin is characteristically slimy. The colour is reddish or brownish-black with three to nine yellowish-white horizontal stripes on the head and body. The juveniles have only three stripes.

This is an extremely wary fish which lives over coral reefs and in shallow lagoons, swimming alone or in twos or threes. It is always ready to dart into a crevice or other hiding place when disturbed. Like the rest of its family, it is covered in a bitter toxic slime which has been found to be repulsive to large

45 *Hippocampus kuda* (Yellow Seahorse, juvenile)
44 *Aeoliscus strigatus* (Shrimpfish)

predators and, in tests, lethal to small animals. Great care should be taken in a small aquarium, as the fish may be toxic to other species, especially if it is handled or frightened.

Size: 25.4 cm (10 in). *Distribution:* tropical Indo-Pacific. *Temperament:* aggressive. *Water:* marine, 24–26°C (75–79°F).

51 Grammidae (Basslet family)

Diagnosis: D.XI–XIII, and rays, Pel.I,5. The lateral line is divided and either extends to the full body length or is incomplete.

Distribution: Indo-Pacific and tropical west Atlantic.

These small, brightly coloured marine fishes were once classified with the sea basses (family Serranidae), to which they are closely related. They are now placed in a separate family including only about twelve species. Two genera (*Gramma* and *Lipogramma*) occur in the Caribbean Sea, and at least three more are in different areas of the Indo-Pacific. They are shy fishes and live in holes, caves, and crevices in coral reefs, sometimes using algae to make their own shelters. They feed on planktonic crustaceans and other plankton.

Gramma loreto (Fairy Basslet, or Royal Gramma)
Diagnosis: The species is identifiable by its spectacular colouring and by the black spot at the front of the dorsal fin.

This solitary fish usually lives in shallow waters at 12–24 m (40–80 ft) of depth. Individuals tend to inhabit a specific area of the reef and familiarize themselves with all its crevices and holes in order to use them for protection. When swimming under a reef overhang, they orientate themselves ventrally to the substrate. Sometimes, the juveniles clean parasites from other species. The adults mouth-brood the eggs, and this has been observed in captivity, although the eggs proved infertile. Basslets are able to jump, so it is advisable to cover their aquarium.

Size: 10 cm (4 in). *Distribution:* Caribbean. *Temperament:* peaceful, solitary. *Water:* marine, 24–26°C (75–79°F).

52 Theraponidae (Tigerperch family)

Diagnosis: D.XII–XIV,8–14, A.III,7–12. The body is oval and compressed. One or two spines are on the operculum, and the dorsal spines can be depressed into a groove. The pelvic-fin origin is behind the pectoral fins. The scales are finely ctenoid, and the lateral line is complete and continuous, with smaller scales than the rest of the body. Often, the body has conspicuous horizontal stripes.

Distribution: Indo-Pacific region.

This family is closely related to the sea basses (Serranidae), but it differs in breeding habits, in the number of dorsal spines, and in having a small mouth with many serrated teeth. There are fifteen species in three genera: *Helotes, Pelates,* and *Therapon.* Most of these occur in shallow marine waters, although some species penetrate estuaries

47 *Pterois volitans* (Scorpionfish)

43 *Adioryx cornutum* (White Squirrelfish)

and rivers, whilst others live solely in fresh water. Some of the larger species are locally valued as food fishes, and some are well known for grunting and croaking when removed from the water.

Therapon jarbua (Crescent Perch)
Diagnosis: D.XI–XII,10–11, A.III,7–9, LL.about 80. The preoperculum is serrated, and the caudal fin is distinctly emarginate. The colouring is brownish above and silver on the belly, with three curved brown-black horizontal lines, the upper line running from the front to the back of the dorsal fin. There are also dark marks on the dorsal and caudal fins when the fish is fully grown.

This is a predatory species and, when fully grown, will eat even quite large fish as well as smaller animals. It is known for the loud noises it can produce with its swim-bladder. It abundantly inhabits coastal waters and estuaries, often venturing far up rivers almost to fresh water. It has reportedly been seen to spawn in shallow places in the rivers of Sri Lanka. Here, at a depth of 15 cm (6 in), eggs are laid in hollows under stones or decaying wood. The adhesive eggs are guarded and tended by the male until they hatch. The juveniles are peaceful but active and collect in shoals but, as they mature, become more solitary and aggressive and, therefore, less popular for aquaria.
Size: 25.4 cm (10 in). *Distribution:* Indo-Pacific except Hawaii. *Temperament:* peaceful and shoaling when young, aggressive when mature. *Water:* brackish and marine, 24–26°C (75–79°F).

53 Centrarchidae
(Sunfish family)

Diagnosis: A.III plus, and rays. Most of these fishes are deep-bodied and strongly compressed, with an egg-shaped body profile, although the genera *Elassoma, Micropterus, Aplites,* and *Pomoxis* are more elongate. The lateral line is complete or nearly so, although it is absent in the genus *Elassoma.* The colouring is attractive in most juveniles but fades with age.
Distribution: North America.

This family lives in clear, weedy lowland waters, favouring a sandy substrate. Many of the larger species are solitary and predatory, whilst the smaller species tend to swim in groups. They feed mainly on insect larvae and other invertebrates.

Elassoma evergladei (Dwarf, or Pygmy, Sunfish)
Diagnosis: D.II–IV,8–9, A.III,5–7. The body is slightly elongate and compressed. There are large cycloid scales, and the colouring is grey with black spots.

This fish has an unusual method of moving over the substrate, by alternately using its pectoral fins. When spawning, the male becomes black with isolated silver scales. Spawning occurs after an interesting courtship, and thirty to sixty eggs are shed over the plant growth. The adults are not known to eat their young.
Size: 3.5 cm (1.4 in). *Distribution:* the Carolinas to Florida. *Temperament:* peaceful. *Water:* fresh, 4–30°C (39–86°F), soft, slightly acid.

54 Apogonidae
(Cardinalfish family)

Diagnosis: 1D.VI–VIII, 2D.1,8–14, A.II,8–18, LL.23–25. The body is laterally compressed, and the lateral line is simple and sometimes interrupted. The head, eyes, and mouth are large. Many species are red or bronze in body colour.
Distribution: Atlantic Ocean and Indo-Pacific region.

These are mostly marine fishes, some species occurring in fresh and brackish waters. They live around coral reefs and rocky outcrops, feeding on various small animals. Many species are nocturnal and rest during the day, hidden in dark caves or sometimes in sponges and molluscs. Such a relationship between animals, where the host gives only shelter, is known as endoecism.

Sphaeramia orbicularis (Polka-Dot Cardinalfish)
Diagnosis: A vertical stripe bisects the body, and dark spots are posterior to the stripe. There appear to be two similar forms or species, and some experts regard *S. nematopterus* as a distinct species, but others consider it to be the female of *S. orbicularis.*

This is a crepuscular fish which collects in small shoals around projecting heads of coral. It also occurs near mangroves and feeds on small crustaceans and other small animals. The eggs have long filaments and become entangled in a mass, which is brooded by the male.
Size: 10 cm (4 in). *Distribution:* Indian Ocean and western Pacific. *Temperament:* secretive, shoaling. *Water:* marine, 24–26°C (75–79°F).

55 Carangidae
(Jack and Pompano family)

Diagnosis: The compressed body varies in depth, and the skin may be naked or may bear small cycloid scales. The lateral line has spiny scutes. There are usually three anal spines, the first two being detached from the rest of the fin. The caudal peduncle is shallow, and the caudal fin is widely forked.
Distribution: Atlantic Ocean and Indo-Pacific region.

This family contains twenty-four genera, including many marine species and a few in brackish water. They are often important food fishes, such as the crevalle jack (*Caranx hippos*) in the tropical Atlantic and the Gulf of Mexico. Little is known about the breeding of any species in this family, although the common pilot fish (*Naucrates ductor*) is said to have demersal adhesive eggs. These have a fine entangling filament at one end which, it has been suggested, may become attached to sharks.

Gnathanodon speciosus (Kingfish, or Cavalla)
Diagnosis: 1D.I,VIII, 2D.I,18–21, A.II,I,15–17. When viewed laterally, the body is fusiform and very compressed. The colouring is characteristic in the young, which are yellow-silver and have about seven strong vertical stripes with paler ones between these. The stripes fade when the fish matures.

When young, these fishes are often encountered by divers in quiet lagoons, where small groups of them may swim alongside the diver for some distance. Another member of the family, the pilot fish (*Naucrates ductor*), exhibits similar behaviour and swims with sharks, often in front of them as if serving for guidance, a habit which explains its common name. When mature, the kingfish is more frequently found offshore, although occasionally caught in estuaries by anglers.
Size: 1 m (39 in). *Distribution:* Red Sea and Indo-Pacific region. *Temperament:* shoaling. *Water:* marine, 24–26°C (75–79°F).

56 Lutjanidae
(Snapper, or Seaperch, family)

Diagnosis: A.III and rays. These fishes have large canine teeth. The dorsal fin is continuous, and the pelvic fins are just below or slightly behind the base of the pectoral fins.
Distribution: Atlantic and Indo-Pacific Oceans.

Most of the snappers are brightly coloured, shoaling fishes which inhabit coral reefs and tropical lagoons. Some, like the beautiful blue-banded snapper (*Lutjanus kasmira*), congregate in shoals of well over 100 individuals, presenting a dramatic sight. Their common name is derived from their behaviour when removed from water, because they "snap" their jaws together with great force.

Little is known about their reproduction, but they are thought to produce large numbers of pelagic eggs and to perform no parental care. Most snappers provide good sport for fishermen and are excellent to eat, although some species have occasionally caused ciguatera, or tropical-fish poisoning. This has been found to occur between the latitudes of 34° north and south, due mainly to shore or reef fishes. The toxin is believed to pass through the food chain and to originate from some benthic organism eaten by herbivorous species which are in turn consumed by carnivorous fishes. Those at the top of the food chain somehow accumulate the poison without any known adverse effect upon themselves.

Lutjanus sebae (Red Emperor, or Red Snapper)
Diagnosis: The body is deep and compressed, with a large head having a steep dorsal profile. The adult is coloured white with three broad, vertical, dark brown bands. In juveniles, the ground colour is pink.

These predators feed upon fishes, crustaceans, and other small animals as well as vegetable matter. The juveniles seek protection amongst the spines of large sea urchins. They grow quickly and, when adult, form large shoals in the calmer areas of the reefs, becoming very prolific in some regions with abundant food.
Size: 60 cm (23.6 in). *Distribution:* tropical Indo-Pacific. *Temperament:* shoaling, peaceful when young. *Water:* marine, 24–26°C (75–79°F).

57 Lobotidae (Tripletail family)

Diagnosis: A.III and rays. The body is deep and compressed, with a short caudal peduncle. The rayed parts of the dorsal and anal fins are extended and rounded, so that the fish seems to have three tail-fins. The operculum has one or two spines.
Distribution: Atlantic Ocean and Indo-Pacific region.

This family contains about four species, and has two genera: *Lobotes*, with one marine species (*L. surinamensis*), and *Datnoides*, with brackish and freshwater species in southeast Asian river mouths. The juveniles are coloured so that they resemble leaves and complete the deception by drifting in the water on their sides with a slight curving of their bodies. All species are voracious predators when adult. They are thought to lay pelagic eggs.

Datnoides quadrifasciatus (Four-Banded Tripletail, or Tigerfish)

Diagnosis: D.XII,13–14, A.III,8–9, LL.55–62. The body bears eight to ten vertical or slanting stripes. Six of these are complete, and the four intermediate stripes are incomplete. The young have a black blotch on the operculum, and three stripes radiating from the eye.

This fish lives in the brackish waters of river estuaries, and the adults migrate upriver to spawn in fresh water.
Size: 30.5 cm (12 in). *Distribution:* southeast Asia. *Temperament:* aggressive, territorial. *Water:* fresh and brackish, 24–26°C (75–79°F), medium hard, slightly alkaline.

58 Pomadasyidae (Grunt family)

Diagnosis: A.III and rays. There is one dorsal fin. The body is laterally compressed, and most of the head and body are scaly, with a continuous lateral line.
Distribution: Atlantic Ocean and Indo-Pacific region.

Most species of grunts inhabit coral reefs, feeding on diverse planktonic and benthic invertebrates, whilst a few live in brackish or fresh water. Their common name is derived from a habit of rubbing their pharyngeal teeth together to produce a sound which is amplified in the adjacent swimbladder. Another odd trait is their "kissing" behaviour, in which two fishes approach each other and press their gaping mouths together. The significance of these acts is not understood.

Plectorhynchus orientalis (Oriental Sweetlips)

Diagnosis: D.XII–XIV,17–21, A.III,7–8, LL.about 80–85. The colouring is variable but, in adults, is usually yellow dorsally, with white flanks and three to four horizontal stripes, the middle stripe extending onto the tail. The dorsal fin is yellow with a black base, and the pectorals are black with a light edge. The young are chocolate-brown, with cream patches edged by yellow.

This species lives amongst the shallow coastal reefs, feeding like other marine members of the family. It is thought to produce pelagic eggs and to give no parental care.

52 *Therapon jarbua* (Crescent Perch)
48 *Chanda* species (Glassfish)

51 *Gramma loreto* (Fairy Basslet) 53 *Elassoma evergladei* (Dwarf Sunfish)

58 *Plectorhynchus orientalis* (Oriental Sweetlips)

54 *Sphaeramia orbicularius* (Polka-Dot
Cardinalfish)

56 *Lutjanus sebae* (Red Emperor)

Size: 40 cm (15.7 in). *Distribution:* Indo-Australian
archipelago and Indian Ocean. *Temperament:*
active. *Water:* marine, 24–26°C (75–79°F).

59 Sciaenidae
(Drum, or Croaker, family)

Diagnosis: A.I–II and rays. The spines are usually
weak, and the dorsal fin is contiguous or divided
into two fins. The lateral line extends to the end of
the caudal fin, which is either truncate or rounded.
Distribution: South and North American fresh
waters, Atlantic Ocean and Indo-Pacific region.

This family consists mostly of marine species,
with some fresh and brackish representatives,
totalling about 160 species in twenty-eight genera.
Some species have a patch of small barbels or a
single barbel on the chin. The swim-bladder, when
present, has many branches and is used as a
resonating chamber for producing sounds. The
family is of great interest because of these noises,
which are created by muscles adjacent to the swim-
bladder, supplemented in some species by the
grinding of the pharyngeal teeth.

Many species live in very turbid waters, and it
has been suggested that such noises are used for
navigation and communication, especially during
mating. Certain drumfishes are notably vocal when
exhibiting defensive and aggressive behaviour.
During and after the Second World War, it was
reported (by M.W. Johnson at the Scripps Institute
of Oceanography in California) that, from April
to September, drumfishes were largely responsible
for an underwater "dusk chorus", which began
about sunset and continued for several hours, and
consisted of frog-like croaks and soft drumming
sounds.

Most marine species spawn in relatively shallow
waters, and the larvae then move inshore to spend
their first summer in brackish water. They are
bottom-living species, some moving from a soft
muddy substrate to a rockier environment as they
mature.

Equetus lanceolatus (Jackknife Fish)

Diagnosis: 1D.XIV–XVI, 2D.I,53, A.II,5. The spiny
anterior part of the dorsal fin is very high and pointed, the rays becoming very extended in the adults.
The body colour is white, with three dark stripes,
each bordered by silver. The first stripe drops vertically through the eye; the second runs posteriorly
from the head, above the eye, to the base of the
ventral fin; the third is V-shaped and covers the
anterior edge of the spinous part of the dorsal fin
and then runs from its base to the tip of the caudal
fin. This colouring fades as the fish matures.

These attractive fishes live in moderately deep
water around coral reefs, collecting in small shoals.
They are nocturnal, hiding by day under rocky
overhangs and caves, emerging at dusk to feed on
crustaceans, such as crabs and shrimps, and on
other invertebrates. Little is known about their
reproduction.
Size: 23 cm (9.4 in). *Distribution:* Caribbean Sea to
Florida. *Temperament:* peaceful. *Water:* marine,
24–26°C (75–79°F).

60 Monodactylidae (Fingerfish, or Moonfish, family)

Diagnosis: D.V–VIII and rays, A.III and rays. The body is deep and very compressed. The dorsal fin has a very long fin base covered in scales, as does the anal fin. The pelvic fins are vestigial or quite small.

Distribution: West Africa and the Indo-Pacific region.

These beautiful shoaling fishes live in brackish and marine waters, sometimes entering rivers where they may even go upstream beyond the tidal influence. They often occur near sewerage outlets, feeding omnivorously. Their name derives from two Greek words and means "single finger", referring to the shape of the dorsal and anal fins.

Monodactylus sebae (Striped Fingerfish)

Diagnosis: D.VIII,32–36, A.III,37. The body is very compressed and appears to be even deeper than usual because of the scales covering the dorsal and anal fin bases. The pectoral fins are reduced to a few small rays. At least three dark vertical stripes are on the body and head, and the strongest one runs from the dorsal-fin lobe to the anal-fin lobe.

This is one of two species in the family which are usually imported for the aquarist. The other is *M. argenteus,* from east Africa, Malaysia, and Polynesia, and normally has only two vertical stripes. Both are peaceful and shoaling. Little is known of their sexual dimorphisms or reproduction, although *M. sebae* has been reported to breed in fresh water. The eggs are small, round, and buoyant. The young resemble miniature adults and grow rapidly. In this species, the colouring can fade dramatically when the fish is disturbed or frightened.

Size: 20 cm (7.9 in). *Distribution:* tropical west Africa, between the Senegal and Zaire river mouths. *Temperament:* peaceful, shoaling. *Water:* fresh, brackish, and marine, 24–28°C (75–82.5°F), hard, alkaline.

61 Toxotidae (Archerfish, or Riflefish, family)

Diagnosis: D.IV–VI,11–14, A.III,12–18. The body is deep, compressed, and covered in ctenoid scales. The eyes are large, and the lower jaw protrudes. The upper profile from the snout to the dorsal fin is almost straight. The colouring ranges from olive and yellow to silver, boldly marked with black blotches and bars.

Distribution: Arabia to the central Indo-Pacific region.

The name "archerfish" derives from the fish's amazing ability to shoot down insects, even those in flight, by squirting water from its mouth. There are about five species in a single genus *Toxotes.* They favour mangrove swamps but are also found in fresh, brackish, and coastal marine waters.

Toxotes jaculator (Archerfish)

Diagnosis: D.IV and rays. The colouring is variable, but there are usually about five black triangular saddle-marks along the base. A similar species is *T. chatareus,* distinguished by the dorsal-fin spines (D.V and rays).

This fish lives near estuaries and inshore waters such as mangrove swamps, preferring areas with overhanging plants. The adults sometimes are revealed when the tips of their lower jaws ripple the water surface as they wait for prey. Usually, the fish sees an insect come to rest upon vegetation, spits some water to knock the insect down onto the surface, and eats it. The powerful jet is produced by contracting the gill covers to force water along a tube formed between the tongue and the roof of the mouth. The angle of squirting is controlled by the thin anterior end of the tongue. To gauge the distance and position of the prey, the fish uses its well-developed mobile eyes, which permit binocular vision towards the surface. Occasionally, it shoots down flying insects or even leaps from the water to catch them. Nothing is known of its breeding habits, but it is thought to spawn on coral reefs far from the coast. When young, it lives in small shoals and is yellow in colour with iridescent flecks on the back. This colouring is believed to help the fishes to maintain mutual contact in the turbid waters they inhabit. Their skill in shooting is not acquired until they are about half grown. The fish has been reported (by Hugh M. Smith, adviser to the government of Thailand in the late 1940s) as being good to eat and often caught by anglers.

Size: 24 cm (9.5 in). *Distribution:* southeast Asia to northeast Australia and Melanesia. *Temperament:* solitary when adult, shoaling when young. *Water:* brackish, and fresh when young, 25–28°C (77–82.5°F).

62 Ephippidae (Spadefish family)

Diagnosis: A.III and rays. These fishes have curious-looking, deep, and compressed bodies, with small mouths. The spinous part of the dorsal fin is distinct from the rayed part.

Distribution: Atlantic Ocean and Indo-Pacific region.

This marine family is divided into two subfamilies: Drepaninae, with one genus, including the sicklefish, or concertinafish *(Drepane punctata),* and Ephippinae, which includes the genus *Platax* (batfishes).

Platax teira (Roundfaced, or Longfinned, Batfish)

Diagnosis: This fish has the typical batfish shape, but the anterior lobes of the dorsal, anal, and pelvic fins are very extended in the juveniles, shortening with maturity. The young are grey to black, with three broad vertical stripes which disappear with age.

This species is usually found in mangrove swamps, where its extended form and markings resemble the plant roots. It also occurs in the murky waters of harbours. It is a voracious omnivore and, when fully grown, is considered a delicacy in some areas.

Size: 61 cm (24 in). *Distribution:* tropical Indo-Pacific. *Temperament:* peaceful. *Water:* brackish, marine, 22–27°C (71.5–80.5°F).

63 Scatophagidae (Scat family)

Diagnosis: A.III and rays. These fishes are disc-shaped, with deep and very compressed bodies. They have small ctenoid scales which cover the bases of the soft anal and dorsal fins. The lateral line is distinct, complete, and curved. The mouth is terminal and not protractile.

Distribution: Indo-Pacific region.

The two genera in this family, *Prenes* and *Scatophagus,* live in marine and brackish waters. Their young pass through a larval stage, when a strong bony covering on the head is developed. This stage is called a "tholichthys", and later, the covering regresses.

Scatophagus argus (Argus Fish, or Scat)

Diagnosis: LL.100 plus. The body shape is typical of the genus, and the colouring is very variable, depending on the fish's origin. When young, it is quite dark, but from a size of about 5 cm (2 in), it becomes greenish, bluish, or brownish with a silver sheen. Vertical rows of large spots or lines are on the flanks of the body, and there are often brown and black markings on the fins. Such fishes found in marine waters usually have more brilliant colours.

This fish lives in coastal waters, river estuaries, and fresh water. Its name *Scatophagus* means "dung-eating" and refers to its habit of feeding on decomposing material near the sewerage outlets of large towns. The young can be found in fresh and brackish waters, where they grow rapidly. The sexual differences have not yet been recorded, and little is known of the breeding behaviour. But it has been suggested that the courtship resembles that of the cichlids, the male and female performing the same kind of brood care.

Size: 30 cm (11.8 in). *Distribution:* tropical Indo-Pacific. *Temperament:* active, peaceful, shoaling. *Water:* fresh, brackish, and marine, 20–28°C (68–82.5°F), medium hard.

64 Chaetodontidae (Butterflyfish and Angelfish family)

Diagnosis: The body is small, deep, and compressed, with a small mouth normally having bristle-like teeth. The caudal fin is emarginate to round, and the median fins are densely scaled.

Distribution: Atlantic Ocean and Indo-Pacific region.

These agile and brightly coloured fishes live mainly over coral reefs. They are divided into two subfamilies. Firstly, the Chaetodontinae (butterflyfishes) have no strong spines at the angle of the preoperculum but have a pelvic axillary process. Secondly, the Pomacanthinae (angelfishes) have a strong preopercular spine as well as a clear axillary process. Most species are elaborately marked, and some undergo changes in this respect as they mature. The juvenile stage of one species of angelfish bears patterns similar to Arabic script on the caudal fin, which have reportedly been read—on a specimen from Zanzibar—as religious messages.

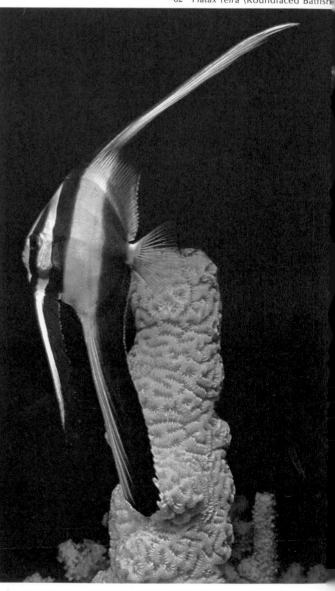

When fully grown, most species are valued as food fishes. Most are similar in shape and can be distinguished by their markings. When swimming, they use the caudal fin as a rudder and stabilizer, the motive force being provided by a rowing action of the pectoral fins. Little is known about their breeding behaviour.

Chaetodon auriga (Threadfin Coralfish)

Diagnosis: LL.26–30. This species has a deeply concave profile and a strongly projecting, conical snout. The fifth and sixth rays of its dorsal fin are extended into long free filaments. When the fish is immature, there is a large black spot on the soft part of the dorsal fin below the filament.

The name *Chaetodon* is derived from two Greek words meaning bristle and tooth, referring to the form of this family's teeth. These are used to strip polyps from the coral or small anemones from the rocks. Most species in this genus have a dark stripe to camouflage the eye. It has been suggested that some species, such as this one, have an eyespot on the dorsal fin in order to deceive predators about the body's orientation, enabling the fish to take evasive action. In certain species, the eyespots are thought to function as important social signals. This species is common within its distribution and is usually found singly or in pairs at a depth of about 1–10 m (3–33 ft). There are two subspecies, *C. a. auriga* originating from the Red Sea, and *C. a. setifer* found from the region of Australia and New Guinea to the entire Indo-Pacific. *Size:* 22.9 cm (9 in). *Distribution:* from the Red Sea to the Indo-Pacific. *Temperament:* active. *Water:* marine, 24–26°C (75–79°F).

Forcipiger flavissimus (Longnosed Butterflyfish, or Longbill)

Diagnosis: D.XII and rays. This fish closely resembles another species, *F. longirostris,* which has a longer snout and D.X–XI and rays.

The fish is widely distributed and much more common than its close relative mentioned above. It is usually found at depths of 1–30 m (3–99 ft) on coral growth. It swims either alone or in groups of up to five individuals. By using its long snout, it can probe into crevices in the coral for crustaceans, worms, and other small animals. *Size:* 13 cm (5.1 in). *Distribution:* Red Sea to Australia, Hawaii, and southern California. *Temperament:* active. *Water:* marine, 24–26°C (75–79°F).

Heniochus acuminatus (Pennant Coralfish, or Longfin Bannerfish)

Diagnosis: D.XI–XII,24–27, A.III,16–19. The length of the base of the spiny part on the dorsal fin equals the length of the rayed part. The fourth dorsal spine is very extended into a trailing filament, which is as long as the body. The colouring is also characteristic. This species develops with age a slight protuberance between the eyes.

The fish occurs on both offshore and inshore reefs. A common species, it is called the poor man's Moorish idol, due to its superficial resemblance to the Moorish idol (*Zanclus cornutus*) as regards the dorsal-fin length and the markings. Unlike many

64 *Chaetodon auriga* (Threadfin Coralfish)

63 *Scatophagus argus* (Argus Fish)

64 *Chelmon rostatus* (Copperbanded Butterflyfish)

64 *Heniochus acuminatus* (Pennant Coralfish)

64 *Pomacanthus imperator* (Emperor Angelfish)

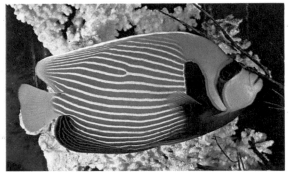

66　*Apistogramma ramirezi* (Ramirez Dwarf Cichlid)

66　*Astronotus ocellatus* (Oscar's Cichlid)

members of the family, it retains its juvenile colouring as it matures, but the elongated dorsal-fin ray and the interorbital protuberance develop further with age. This fish occurs individually, in pairs, or in small groups.
Size: 25.4 cm (10 in). *Distribution:* from the Red Sea to the Australian Great Barrier Reef and Hawaii. *Temperament:* peaceful, shoaling. *Water:* marine, 24–26°C (75–79°F).

Pomacanthus imperator (Emperor, or Imperial, Angelfish)
Diagnosis: D.XIV,19–21, A.III,18–21. The pattern and colouring are very distinctive in the adult. The young are dark blue, with a series of concentric white rings, which slowly change as the fish matures.

At the juvenile stage, this species is often found in the shallower parts of lagoons and the quieter waters around reefs. It then seems to be territorial and has been observed in the same place on a reef over a long period. When adult, it is frequently seen alone or in pairs at the entrances of caves or near overhangs, where it can hide quickly in case of danger. It feeds omnivorously on algae, coral polyps, and crustaceans. If frightened, it makes an unusual noise. Mature specimens are identifiable by an extension of some of the soft dorsal-fin rays.
Size: 30.5 cm (12 in). *Distribution:* Red Sea, Indo-Pacific region to Polynesia and Japan. *Temperament:* peaceful, but aggressive to its own species. *Water:* marine, 24–26°C (75–79°F).

65 Nandidae (Leaffish family)

Diagnosis: The head is usually large with a deeply cleft mouth. The dorsal-fin base is long, and the caudal fin is rounded.
Distribution: Northeastern America, southeast Asia, and west Africa.

These fishes are very voracious and aggressive predators, able to kill prey up to two-thirds of their own size. They favour quite shaded waters where they can successfully hide while awaiting their prey. Some species, such as Schomburgk's leaffish *(Polycentrus schomburgki),* closely resemble a leaf. Most species spawn in hollows, but *Polycentropsis abbreviata,* which is similar to the previous species, builds a bubble nest.

Badis badis (Badis)
Diagnosis: D.VI–VIII,6–10, LL.26–33. The body is elongate with a relatively small mouth. The lateral line is interrupted, and the dorsal-fin base is very long. A black stripe runs from the mouth, through the eye, to the origin of the dorsal fin.

This is the most peaceful member of the family. A beautifully coloured fish, it has a remarkable ability to change its colouring rapidly. It feeds on small invertebrates. The spawn is usually shed on the upper surface of a stone, and the male guards the brood.
Size: 8 cm (3.2 in). *Distribution:* India. *Temperament:* secretive. *Water:* fresh, 25–27°C (77–80.5°F), not critical in quality.

66 Cichlidae (Cichlid family)

Diagnosis: A.III or plus, and rays. These fishes are also distinguished from the perches by having only one pair of nostrils and a divided lateral line. The body shape is very variable but usually deep and compressed, as in the genus *Cichlasoma.* It may be disc-shaped, with high sail-like fins, as in *Pterophyllum,* or elongate, as in *Julidochromis.*
Distribution: Central and South America, West Indies, Africa, Madagascar, Syria, and coastal India.

This family contains about eighty-five genera and 700 species in both fresh and brackish waters. They are well represented in Africa, comprising

most of the species in the three large lakes: over 200 in Lake Malawi, at least 170 in Lake Victoria, and about 200 in Lake Tanganyika, whilst new species are still being discovered. Many of these cichlid species are difficult to identify, because they have evolved considerably from one or more ancestral species and adapted to different ecological niches. In the great African lakes, most species live along the shore in sluggish or standing waters and isolated pools. Some are herbivorous, but most are predatory and feed in diverse and sometimes quite specialized ways, ranging from a diet of small fishes, insects, and other animals to eating only parts of fishes. In the last case, parasitic species are known as eye-biters and scale-eaters.

About twenty genera with 150 species exist in South America. Like the African species, they have undergone much evolution. Many cichlids are popular aquarium species, such as *Symphysodon* and *Pterophyllum,* whilst others are good sport and food fishes, such as *Cichla ocellaris,* the largest cichlid, which can weigh over 8 kg (17.5 lb). Most species live in rivers and still by-waters, and a few hardy species inhabit headwaters. The cichlids exhibit highly organized breeding behaviour: some species mouth-brood, but usually the adults take a direct part in protecting their young and eggs. Many species exhibit a variety of colour patterns, which are associated with their main activities.

Apistogramma ramirezi (Ramirez Dwarf Cichlid)
Diagnosis: D.XIV–XV,9, A.III,8, LL.26–29. The body is deep and strongly compressed, with a tall dorsal fin which has several of the anterior spines extended. There are black stripes on the cheeks and a spot on the centre of the body. As with similar genera, the colouring varies with the fish's mood and age.

This beautiful cichlid derives its name from its courtship dance. It is an "open-breeding" species,

66 *Cichlasoma meeki* (Firemouth Cichlid)

using round stones or depressions in the substrate on which to place its eggs. The parents usually raise the brood together in a territory common to both. They normally produce 150–400 eggs, and the fry hatch after two days. The brood is carried by either of the parents into one of the pits that have been excavated previously, and here, the fry adsorb their yolk sacs within about six days. When the fry can swim freely, they follow the parents, who continue to watch over and protect them until they are quite large.
Size: 6 cm (2.4 in). *Distribution:* Bolivia, Venezuela, tributaries of the Rivers Apure and Meta. *Temperament:* peaceful. *Water:* fresh, 22–26°C (71.5–79°F), soft, with added peat.

Astronotus ocellatus (Oscar's Cichlid, or Velvet Cichlid)
Diagnosis: The body is deep and moderately compressed. The head is blunt with a large, protruding lower jaw. The colouring is variable, usually olive, grey, and orange in the adult but with a large, round, black mark edged by red on the caudal peduncle.

This is a robust, omnivorous fish that lives in diverse waters. It becomes sexually mature at a length of 10–12 cm (4.0–4.8 in), when the male is distinguished by three black marks on the dorsal-fin base. The eggs are laid and fertilized, and are placed in concentric circles on a flat stone. These fishes are excellent parents, transferring the fry after about three days to a carefully excavated trench in the sandy substrate, where the fry stay until able to swim freely. The young fishes are dark with pale marbling and change to the adult colouring when they are about 7.5 cm (3 in) long.
Size: 30 cm (11.8 in). *Distribution:* northern South America. *Temperament:* peaceful, except older specimens which may be aggressive. *Water:* fresh, 20–25°C (68–77°F), not critical in quality.

Cichlasoma meeki (Firemouth Cichlid)
Diagnosis: The body is deep and compressed. It has a blue-violet back, a red throat and belly, and numerous broad vertical stripes. All the scales are edged with red, and there are dark marks edged with gold on the gill covers, the centre of the back, and the tail base, which are joined by a dark horizontal stripe.

This species belongs to the largest genus of South American cichlids, whose approximately sixty species show a broad range of temperaments. They inhabit shaded waters, feeding mainly on invertebrates and plant debris. The sexes of this species are similar and pair up for mating when the water temperature is about 24–25°C (75–77°F). The female, which is usually a bit smaller and duller in colour, sometimes develops a white belly and shows her willingness to mate by protruding her ovipositor. The male becomes even more strongly coloured and begins to excavate a depression, usually under a stone, in which the eggs can be laid and protected. After several days of courting by the male, the female inspects the depression and, normally in the evening, about 200 eggs are laid and fertilized. The eggs are carefully tended by the female while the male defends the territory. When the fry are ready to hatch, the female helps them to emerge from the eggs by freeing the egg-cases with her mouth and spitting the fry into a safe corner of the depression. By the fifth day, they are swimming freely, but every night, they are guided back into a safe hollow and protected by the parent.
Size: 10 cm (4 in). *Distribution:* Central America. *Temperament:* territorial. *Water:* fresh, 20–25°C (68–77°F), soft, slightly acid.

Haplochromis venustus
Diagnosis: This fish is characterized by its colouring. Adult males have a sulphur-yellow flash extending between the eyes and over the nape to the dorsal fin, whose edge is pale yellow. The female has a series of pale, diagonally crossing stripes on the flank, which give the appearance of regular dark blotches. The young also have these marks, but the males soon lose them.

This species belongs to the largest genus of cichlids. It feeds omnivorously and is found over watery grass beds and sandy bottoms. Its breeding habits are typical of the genus. First, the male digs a hole in the substrate into which the eggs are laid. Then, the female takes them into her mouth and nudges the male's vent to encourage him to release his milt. The eggs are fertilized in her mouth, where they remain until they hatch, which usually takes about three weeks. During this period, the female is unable to feed and becomes very weak.
Size: 20 cm (7.9 in). *Distribution:* Lake Malawi. *Temperament:* aggressive. *Water:* fresh, 20–27.5°C (68–81.5°F), hard, slightly alkaline.

Hemichromis bimaculatus (Jewel Cichlid, or Red Cichlid)
Diagnosis: The body is deep and slightly compressed. The colouring is variable, but generally, the back is olive-brown and the flanks are pale yellow-green, fading to yellow on the belly and fins. The body is also flecked with green spots.

This species establishes a large territory in the still and flowing waters it inhabits, feeding on small animals. It is known to be an intelligent fish, with interesting brood-care behaviour which has been recorded in detail (by Konrad Lorenz in the book *King Solomon's Ring*). After a flamboyant courtship, the eggs are laid on a flat stone until they hatch. The female can then signal with her dorsal fin to the young fry when she wishes to gather them under her protection before settling into the nesting hole for the night. Meanwhile, the male parent searches the vicinity for any stragglers and inhales them into his mouth, carries them back to

the female's protection, and blows them into the nest.
Size: 15 cm (6 in). *Distribution:* tropical Africa. *Temperament:* active, aggressive when adult. *Water:* fresh, 24–26°C (75–79°F), not critical in quality.

Julidochromis ornatus (Golden Julie)
Diagnosis: The body is elongate and very compressed. The dorsal fin has a very long base, reaching nearly to the rounded caudal fin. The base colour is orange and, unlike a similar species (*J. marlieri),* the fish has three black or dark-brown horizontal stripes running from the snout to the tail.

The slim shape of this species is well adapted to its rocky habitat and enables it, especially when spawning and feeding, to move easily amongst the rocks. It feeds omnivorously on small animals and algae growing on the rocks. The male is slimmer and shorter than the female. When he has selected his territory, usually a rock, he excavates under it to form a cave. He swims with the female in circles around it until she turns upside-down and releases her eggs, usually about 100–150, on the underside of the rock. The male then fertilizes them and, within five days, the fry hatch and are swimming freely.
Size: 11 cm (4.3 in). *Distribution:* southern Lake Tanganyika. *Temperament:* territorial. *Water:* fresh, 22–25°C (71.5–77°F), slightly hard.

Pelvicachromis pulcher
Diagnosis: The body is laterally compressed and elongate, with a long dorsal-fin base. Its colouring is very variable and changes both as it ages and when it exhibits behaviour such as aggression, submission, sexual display, and brood care.

This fish lives near the bottom of fast-flowing rivers and searches the bottom for small animals to eat. It favours the edges of rivers where the current is slowed by dense vegetation. Here, it builds a cave underneath a stone in which to spawn. It then proceeds in a manner very similar to the species described last and lays about 200–300 eggs, which are brooded by the female. When the young hatch (in a week or so), the male helps to care for them. They are usually mature sexually in as little as seven to eight months. The male can sometimes be distinguished from the female as he is larger and has elongate and pointed anal and dorsal fins.
Size: 9 cm (3.5 in). *Distribution:* Africa, notably the Niger delta and basin and Cameroun. *Temperament:* active, peaceful. *Water:* brackish, 23–27°C (73.5–80.5°F), not critical in quality.

Pseudotropheus zebra (Nyasa Cichlid, or Malawi Blue Cichlid)
Diagnosis: The body is deep and compressed, and the rays of the dorsal and anal fins are long. The colouring is variable, but there are usually six to eight vertical stripes on the grey flanks, and two incomplete stripes on the head. The male's anal fin bears several round spots. Both sexes appear in a blue form.

This large and aggressive fish lives in the mid-

dle and lower water layers of the edge of Lake Malawi. Although found in crowded communities, it tends to be territorial, especially when spawning and feeding. It is omnivorous and, as with other members of the genus, it is a mouth-brooder. Little is known of its spawning behaviour, but this is thought to be like that of other mouth-brooders, the female carefully carrying the eggs in her mouth from the time of their fertilization until the fry can swim.
Size: 15 cm (6 in). *Distribution:* Lake Malawi. *Temperament:* active, aggressive. *Water:* fresh, 22–25°C (71.5–77°F), hard, neutral.

Pterophyllum scalare (Common Silver Angelfish, or Scalare)
Diagnosis: A.III plus, and rays. Another characteristic of the species in this genus is a compressed, disc-shaped body, which in the present case is slightly longer than deep, and which has a pointed snout. The dorsal and anal fins are very developed, and the pelvic fins are extended into long streamers. The colouring includes four vertical stripes, of which usually only one is complete and prominent, and descends from the middle of the dorsal fin to the middle of the anal fin. Many varieties now exist, due to hybridization.

This elegant, omnivorous fish lives in sluggish and overgrown waters. Spawning is reported to occur in January when the Amazon level begins to rise. The fishes collect in large numbers in recently flooded areas and prepare to spawn on the vegetation. Both sexes develop breeding tubes: the male's is smaller and pointed slightly forwards, while the female's is wider. After cleaning the chosen site, the pair spawn between 300 and 400 eggs, and sometimes several spawnings take place in one year. The parents brood the eggs and fry carefully, relocating them often before they are large enough to swim away freely.
Size: 15 cm (6 in). *Distribution:* Amazon basin. *Temperament:* peaceful. *Water:* fresh, 22–30°C (71.5–86°F), not critical in quality.

Symphysodon aequifasciata (Discus or Pompadour)
Diagnosis: LL.52–61. As with the other species in this genus, the body is very deep and compressed, forming a disc shape. It has small ctenoid scales which cover the cheek and operculum, and a small terminal mouth. It is slightly shorter in length than a similar species, *S. discus.* The colouring varies between individuals and between subspecies.

This species contains a number of colour varieties which have been regarded as adaptations to habitats. But according to some research (by L.P. Schultz), they indicate the beginning of speciation and are divisible into several subspecies. These are *S. a. aequifasciata* (green discus), *S. a. haraldi* (blue discus), and *S. a. axelrodi* (brown discus), the latter being probably the most commonly kept in aquaria. Recently, other varieties have been named from naturally occurring strains, such as the red discus, whilst other strains have been bred and named from fish in captivity. Discus fishes are found in slow-flowing waters, often in the bends of rivers and where the water is warm. They feed on

various small animals and plant matter. Spawning takes place in winter or during the early spring and is typical of cichlids, involving the careful cleaning of a chosen site, which is usually a stone or large leaf. The young hatch after about two days and are then transferred by the parents to leaves, where the fry hang from short threads while being fanned by the parents. When the young have adsorbed their egg sacs and can swim freely, they attach themselves to the parents, usually the female. It is thought that they feed initially on a milky skin secretion produced by the parent. Both parents are very attentive and, if one of the young becomes detached, it is quickly retrieved by one of the parents and re-attached. Within a few days, the young become independent, and after about three months, the true disc shape is developed, but sexual maturity is not reached for over two years.
Size: 18 cm (7.5 in). *Distribution:* the Amazon and its tributaries. *Temperament:* peaceful, sometimes shoaling. *Water:* fresh, 26–30°C (79–86°F), very soft, slightly acid, with added peat.

67 Pomacentridae (Damselfish family)
Diagnosis: D.IX–XIV,11–18, A.II–III, and rays. The body is deep and compressed, and the mouth is small. The dorsal fin is continuous, and the lateral line is either interrupted or incomplete.
Distribution: All tropical seas.

This family contains four subfamilies and is largely marine, but has some brackish representatives. It causes problems of classification due to the many varieties which occur in certain species. One subfamily, Premninae, includes *Premnas biaculeatus,* the sabrecheeked tomato clownfish, which has a sharp spine behind the eye and lives amongst the tentacles of a sea anemone. In the second subfamily is *Amphiprion ocellaris,* the clown anemone fish, having a commensal relationship with sea anemones. The subfamily Pomacentrinae comprises genera such as *Pomacentrus* and *Eupomacentrus* (damselfishes) and *Abudefduf* (sergeant-major fishes). Finally, the subfamily Chrominae includes the genera *Chromis* (chromis and demoiselles) and *Dascyllus,* the humbugs, which are also commensals with sea anemones and coral.

Amphiprion ocellaris (Clown Anemone Fish)
Diagnosis: D.XI,14–15, A.II,11–13, LL.29–38. This species is very similar to the less common *A. percula,* which differs in having D.IX–X and rays, and in being more black on the dorsal fin and between the first and second white bands on the body.

This fish is well known for its commensal relationship with sea anemones. It usually swims in small shoals and is never far from an anemone in which to seek refuge if danger threatens. But it also benefits the anemone by bringing food and removing parasites from the anemone's tentacles. To avoid being stung and eaten, the fish secretes anemone slime and cannot be distinguished by the anemone from its own body. Apparently, after a

66 *Hemichromis bimaculatus* (Jewel Cichlid)

66 *Julidochromis ornatus* (Golden Julie)

66 *Haplochromis venustus*

66 *Pseudotropheus zebra* (Nyasa Cichlid)

66 *Pelvicachromis pulcher*

short association with the anemone, the fish is able to secrete the correct mucus, but it will cease to do so if deprived of the anemone. The female fish is larger than the male, and more aggressive during courtship. A chosen nesting area is carefully cleaned of algae and the eggs are laid, usually at night, being attached to the substrate by short pedestals near the base of the anemone. The male performs most of the brood-care duties, which involve fanning and cleaning the eggs, and nipping or rubbing the anemone to encourage it to hang its tentacles over the eggs for their protection. The eggs number some 200 and hatch in about seven days. As soon as the larvae are free, they rise to the surface and live planktonically. These fishes can be kept in an aquarium without an anemone, but it is generally considered beneficial to keep them with one.

Size: 8 cm (3.2 in). *Distribution:* Indo-Pacific region from India to northern Australia. *Temperament:* shoaling. *Water:* marine, 24–26°C (75–79°F).

Chromis cyanea (Blue Chromis)

Diagnosis: D.XII,12, A.II,12, LL.16–18. The body is moderately elongate and has a terminal oblique mouth. The caudal fin has long filamentous tips on its lobes. Also characteristic is the brilliant blue colouring.

This species is usually found on outer reefs and in small shoals, feeding on zooplankton. It moves freely over the reef but, when preparing to spawn, the male acquires a solitary territory for the duration of the spawning period or even for the entire year. From here, he courts passing females and signals to them in two ways. Firstly, he changes colour, his back becoming black and his belly fading to white. Then, he performs a signal jump, swimming from the surface of the reef towards the female, looping over her, and returning to his territory. As his excitement increases, he repeats this action more rapidly until he attracts the female to a prepared spawning site. The female develops a small round tube through which she lays the eggs, and the male follows her to fertilize the eggs with milt that passes through his slightly more pointed breeding tube. After spawning with several different females in this manner, the male guards the eggs, which hatch within about three days.

Size: 12.7 cm (5 in). *Distribution:* Bermuda, southern Florida, and the Caribbean Sea. *Temperament:* active, shoaling. *Water:* marine, 24–26°C (75–79°F).

Dascyllus aruanus (Whitetailed Humbug)

Diagnosis: D.XII,12–13, A.II,12–13, LL.16–18. This species has a white caudal fin, and the first broad vertical black stripe runs onto the front of the dorsal fin. Otherwise, it is similar in appearance to the blacktailed humbug, *D. melanurus.*

This is a common species throughout the Indo-Pacific region and is usually found in small shoals over certain kinds of coral. It has also been seen diving amongst the tentacles of some sea anemones, and the anemone is suspected of ridding the fish of some of its parasites. It feeds on small crustaceans upon the coral.

66 *Symphysodon aequifasciata* (Discus)

66 *Pterophyllum scalare* (Common Silver Angelfish)

Size: 8 cm (3.2 in). *Distribution:* Indo-Pacific Ocean, including Hawaii. *Temperament:* peaceful. *Water:* marine, 24–26°C (76–79°F).

68 Labridae (Wrasse family)

Diagnosis: D.VIII–XXI, and rays, A.III,7–18. This family shows great diversity of shape and size. The mouth is protractile, with thick, fleshy lips, and there are usually teeth suitable for crushing crustaceans and molluscs. The scales are cycloid, and the lateral line is interrupted in many species.

Distribution: Atlantic Ocean and Indo-Pacific region.

This family has fifty-eight genera with about 500 species. These are most abundant in tropical regions with profuse weed growth and shallow coral reefs. They occur either individually or in pairs, and are diurnal. Most species adopt some mode of protection before sleeping at night: some bury themselves halfway or entirely in the sand, and others position themselves between rocky crevices. One species uses the same method as certain parrotfishes (Scaridae), making a mucous envelope in which to sleep. Some of the smaller species and the young of others act as cleaners, eating the external parasites and fungi which live on other fishes. Many are brightly coloured and patterned, and some exhibit dramatic changes of colour due to age or to a change of sex. The variation or polymorphism in some species has caused complications in classifying and naming them. In several species, it is known that the females become males, and it has been suggested that many species undergo a sex change.

Coris gaimardi (Gaimard's, or Tomato, Rainbow-fish)

Diagnosis: D.IX,12–13, A.III,12–13, LL.70–80 and abruptly bent. The first and second dorsal spines are longer than the others and are pliable. The adult fish is dark olive to brown on the body and profusely spotted with blue, or else the dorsal and anal fins are red with two or three horizontal blue lines. The juveniles are red with white patches edged by black on the back and dorsal-fin base.

This species is found mainly in coastal waters and over or around coral reefs. The juveniles are often seen in shallow rock pools. They retain their pattern until reaching a length of 6 cm (2.4 in), then adopt an intermediate pattern until they reach 10 cm (4 in). The fish has an unusual wriggling method of swimming and lies on its side upon the bottom when resting or when sleeping at night.

Size: 30 cm (11.8 in). *Distribution:* central and eastern areas of Indo-Pacific Ocean to Hawaii. *Temperament:* solitary. *Water:* marine, 24–26°C (75–79°F).

Gomphosus varius (Clubnosed Wrasse, or Beakfish)

Diagnosis: D.VIII,13, A.III,10–12, LL.26–30. The snout is tube-like. The caudal fin is rounded in the young and becomes truncate with slightly extended outer rays. The colouring is predominantly green in adult males and brown in females.

This fish is omnivorous and occurs in coastal

waters around reefs, using its snout to seek food between rocks and in coral crevices.
Size: 25.4 cm (10 in). *Distribution:* Indo-Pacific region from Hawaii to South Africa. *Temperament:* peaceful. *Water:* marine, 24–26°C (75–79°F).

Labroides dimidiatus (Cleaner Wrasse)
Diagnosis: D.IX,10–11, A.III,10, LL.47–53. The colouring varies with the age and mood of the fish. In small specimens, the horizontal black stripe is broader and the blue is brighter.

This fish inhabits coral reefs and tidal pools. It is welcomed by larger fishes as a cleaner of parasites and fungi from their bodies. It also cleans their mouths and gills, removing particles of food from the teeth as well as other debris. Even large and voracious fishes hold their mouths open for the fish's attention. Certain fishes are able to exploit the cleaner wrasse's behaviour by imitating its appearance but not its purpose. An example is *Aspidontus taeniatus,* the sabretoothed blenny, which takes bites out of the unsuspecting host instead of benefitting it. These wrasses have been observed to change sex if there is a shortage of nearby males or females.
Size: 10 cm (4 in). *Distribution:* Indo-Pacific except Hawaii. *Temperament:* peaceful. *Water:* marine, 24–26°C (75–79°F).

Crenilabrus mediterraneus (Axillary Wrasse)
Diagnosis: The body is elongate and compressed, with a deep caudal peduncle. There are three or four rows of scales on the cheek, and two prominent teeth on the upper jaw. The pectoral-fin base has a conspicuous jet-black spot extending onto the fin, and a large mark is at the caudal-fin base. The male is brownish green with a blue belly and throat. The cheeks are red, and there are pale horizontal stripes over the cheeks and back. Females and immature males do not have these stripes and are flesh-pink or light brown, with a black genital papilla.

This fish usually swims alone but is sometimes seen feeding with other species of *Crenilabrus* on invertebrates, particularly echinoderms. In early summer, the large males prepare to spawn by building nests from heaps of seaweed sprinkled with sand, usually between a sandy and a rocky area on the substrate. After the brood is laid in this nest, it is aggressively protected by the male.
Size: 17 cm (6.7 in). *Distribution:* Mediterranean. *Temperament:* active, territorial. *Water:* marine, 18–23°C (64.5–73.5°F).

69 Scaridae (Parrotfish family)
Diagnosis: D.IX,9–10, A.III,9, Pel.I,5. The body is elongate to oval and compressed. The mouth is non-protractile and has fused teeth which seem to resemble a parrot's beak. The scales are large and ctenoid, and there are usually twenty-two to twenty-four scales in the lateral line, which is interrupted below the dorsal-fin termination.
Distribution: Atlantic Ocean and Indo-Pacific region.

This family occurs mainly in tropical waters. It consists of two subfamilies with about sixty-eight species. The first subfamily differs from the second in having two to four rows of scales on the cheek below the eye, instead of a single row. All these fishes are colourful and usually the sexes are chromatically dimorphic. The use of colouring to identify species, because of their similar meristics, has caused great confusion in taxonomy. The close relationship of these fishes to the wrasses is noticeable in their behaviour. They are diurnal and, at night, sleep while wrapped up in weeds or buried in the sand, some species enclosing themselves in a loose cocoon of mucus. They are regarded as excellent food fishes in many countries, but as poisonous in some localities at certain times of year. Parrotfishes feed on vegetable matter, small molluscs, crustaceans, and coral, for which their teeth are perfectly adapted. They make a considerable noise when rasping coral, and their tooth-marks can be seen clearly in the coral. When they breed, the mating is either between one male and one female (pair-spawning) or between three or more individuals (group-spawning).

Bolbometopon bicolor (Two-Coloured Parrotfish)
Diagnosis: D.IX,9–10, A.III,9. When juvenile, the fish has a creamy colour with a broad vertical orange stripe on the head, an orange tail, and a black spot with an orange edge on the spiny part of the dorsal fin. When half-grown, it is pale grey with an orange head and black fins, unlike the adult.

These fishes are typical of their family and usually occur in small schools when young, older males becoming solitary. By day, they are very active, mainly in seeking food on coral reefs.
Size: 1.2 m (3.9 ft). *Distribution:* Red Sea, Indo-Pacific except Hawaii. *Temperament:* shoaling when young. *Water:* marine, 24–26°C (75–79°F).

70 Opisthognathidae (Jawfish family)
Diagnosis: The body is elongate and slightly compressed. The head and mouth are large, and small cycloid scales cover the body. The dorsal fin originates just behind the head, and the pelvic fins are in front of the pectorals. The lateral line is high and ends near the middle of the dorsal fin.
Distribution: Western and central Atlantic, Indian Ocean, Gulf of California.

This marine family consists of about thirty species of bottom-living fishes. They are usually found on sandy or coral-rubble substrates, where some species inhabit wormholes. Others excavate their own holes by using their jaws and line the entrances with small stones or shells. Here, the fish rests in a vertical position, awaiting the approach of suitable prey such as small crustaceans and fishes. Jawfishes are shy and quickly retreat into their holes at the first sign of danger. Some species are solitary or occur in small groups, as in the genus *Lonchopisthus,* whilst other species, such as *Opisthognathus aurifrons,* the yellowhead, are very social and live in colonies of up to seventy individuals. In many species, it is very difficult to

67 *Chromis cyanea* (Blue Chromis)

67 *Amphiprion ocellaris* (Clown Anemone Fish)
67 *Dascyllus aruanus* (Whitetailed Humbug)

68 *Labroides dimidiatus* (Cleaner Wrasse) on *Amphiprion frenatus*

distinguish the male from the female, but in other species, the sexes are chromatically dimorphic. The males of many species have been observed to mouth-brood the eggs.

Opisthognathus aurifrons (Yellowhead)

Diagnosis: D.XI,15–17, A.III,14–16. This fish is elongate and compressed with long flowing fins. The colouring is variable but is usually pale yellow with blue-tinged fins. Specimens from Florida have a bright yellow head with black pupils in blue irises. In the Bahamas, the head is white with dark grey in the form of a halo.

This fish is considered the most attractive of its genus. It usually lives at depths of over 30 m (100 ft), hovering vertically about 1 m (3 ft) above the bottom and immediately over its burrow. It surveys the surrounding water with its large eyes, for plankton and other small animals to be eaten. As they live in colonies of between three and seventy, the yellowheads can make an impressive sight when feeding in this manner. The only external sexual difference is in the upper jaw bone, or maxilla, which extends to well behind the eye in a male, and reaches to the front edge of the eye in a female. Spawning usually occurs at dawn or dusk. The male courts the female dramatically by arching his back and hovering above the bottom. He then leads her to either his own burrow or another "neutral" burrow, which he encourages her to enter, and follows her in. Because the actual mating takes place in the burrow, it has not been observed. But shortly after the female leaves, the male departs with the brood of eggs in his mouth, where they remain throughout the incubation period.
Size: 10 cm (4 in). *Distribution:* Bahamas, West Indies, and Florida. *Temperament:* peaceful. *Water:* marine, 24–26°C (75–79°F).

71 Blennidae (Combtooth Blenny family)

Diagnosis: D.III–XVII,9–119, Pect.10–18, Pel. I,2–4. These fishes are small and have either no scales or only vestigial ones. The head is blunt, often with cirri and tufts on it, which are important features for identifying species. The teeth are comb-like, some being quite large and resembling canine teeth.
Distribution: Tropical and temperate waters.

This family contains forty-six genera with over 276 species. Most occur in the sea, but a few are found in fresh and brackish waters. They are carnivorous and tend to live secretively in shallow water, over rock or coral formations or in rocky pools. Their colouring is usually drab and serves as camouflage, and they are abundant throughout their distribution. When breeding, they normally deposit the spawn in a well-hidden place, where it is cared for by one or both parents. The juvenile stage is often planktonic, and some of the young become pelagic.

Aspidontus taeniatus (Sabretoothed Blenny, or False Cleaner Fish)

Diagnosis: D.XI,26, A.26. The body is elongate and

68 Coris gaimardi (Gaimard's Rainbowfish, juvenile)

68 Gomphosus varius (Clubnosed Wrasse)

68 Halichoeres biocellatus

70 Opisthognathus aurifrons (Yellowhead)

69 Bolbometopon bicolor (Two-Coloured Parrotfish)

compressed. The mouth is ventral and carries two large teeth pointing forward. The basic colouring is blue when young, fading with maturity. A broad dark stripe runs from the snout to the caudal fin.

This fish is renowned for its resemblance to *Labroides dimidiatus* (the cleaner wrasse) in form, colour, and swimming action. By mimicking that beneficial species, it can approach larger fishes safely and, when close enough, bite pieces of fins, scales, and skin out of them. When not feeding, it is very shy and hides in coral crevices. It is also less common than the cleaner wrasse, as a mimic depends for its success upon being less common than the species mimicked: otherwise, the fishes being cleaned would learn to avoid both the mimic and its model, so as not to be attacked by the former. As has been pointed out (by J.E. Randall), the mimic preys mainly on young fishes, whilst older ones appear to avoid it. Since the sabretoothed blenny is one of the most exact mimics known, this raises an interesting question as to whether, and how, the victims learn to distinguish between the mimic and the cleaner. The answer may lie in observations that the sabretoothed blenny is territorial and that it bites a fish differently. The cleaner approaches a host from any side, including the front, and the host learns to offer its head to the cleaner. But the mimic approaches from behind and usually bites the tail of the host, retreating to wait for another opportunity if the victim turns toward it. These habits would enable an experienced fish to be wary of the mimic.
Size: 12 cm (4.8 in). *Distribution:* Indo-Pacific. *Temperament:* aggressive, solitary. *Water:* marine, 24–26°C (75–79°F).

Ophioblennius atlanticus (Atlantic, or Redlip, Blenny)
Diagnosis: D.XII,19–21, A.II,20–21, Pect.14–16, Pel.I,4. The lateral line is interrupted about midway along the body. The head has a very steep profile, a group of cirri on the margin of the anterior nostril, and an unbranched tentacle above each eye. The main body colouring varies from brown to olive or light grey.

This is one of the most abundant species in the offshore reef waters of the West Indies, where it occurs down to a depth of 8 m (26 ft). It is herbivorous and feeds chiefly on filamentous algae. Spawning takes place over coral, and the eggs are laid in crevices, being protected by the male until they hatch. The fry are pelagic and, unlike adults, have a pale colour and long canine teeth.
Size: 11.4 cm (4.5 in). *Distribution:* western Atlantic and the Gulf of Mexico. *Temperament:* secretive. *Water:* marine, 24–26°C (75–79°F).

72 Gobiidae (Goby family)

Diagnosis: 1D.II–VIII. These fishes have a sucking disc which is made of the united lateral edges of the pelvic fins. They also possess two dorsal fins, which, in some species, are continuous.
Distribution: Temperate, subtropical, and tropical waters.

This is one of the largest families of fishes, con-

taining about 800 species. These are mostly marine but also occur in brackish and fresh waters, some of the latter being catadromous (spawning in marine water). In the Philippines, the resulting fry are called "ipon" and measure only 1.25 cm (0.5 in) long. Upon returning to the mouths of rivers, they are caught in huge numbers by fishermen. The abundance of the marine species in tropical reef waters is an important aspect of benthic ecology. Many species live in close association with other animals: for example, those of the genus *Smilogobius* act as "watchdogs" for the snapping shrimp. While the shrimp excavates and maintains a burrow, the gobies keep watch, usually in pairs. When danger threatens, they raise an alarm by diving into the burrow, followed by the shrimp, which does not emerge until the gobies have resumed their post. Another close relationship is shown by neon gobies, which clean external parasites from larger fishes. Some of the most extraordinary gobies are the mudskippers, which include *Periophthalmus barbarus*. The smallest known fish is said to be *Pandaka pygmaea,* a freshwater goby in the Philippines, less than 1.25 cm (0.5 in) long when fully grown; it is also considered to be the smallest vertebrate. Most gobies lay elongated eggs, which are attached to the substrate, branches of coral, or plants by means of a small stalk and are often protected by the parents.

Brachygobius xanthozona (Bumblebee Fish)
Diagnosis: 2D.I,7, A.I,7. This species has a cylindrical cross-section which becomes compressed posteriorly. It is distinguished from similar species by having four dark-brown, vertical stripes which are as wide as the yellow stripes between them. The dorsal and anal fins are black.

This fish lives in river mouths as well as farther upstream. It lives benthically, feeding on various small animals and hiding under stones at any sign of danger. When spawning, the females are usually distinguished by their rounder bodies and less intense colouring. The eggs are large, being laid under a stone where the male guards them until they hatch in about five days. Soon, the juveniles acquire the characteristic markings. They swim in mid-water when young but move down to a benthic existence as they mature.
Size: 5 cm (2 in). *Distribution:* Sumatra, Borneo, and Java. *Temperament:* peaceful. *Water:* brackish, 24–30°C (75–86°F).

Elacatinus oceanops (Neon Goby)
Diagnosis: A broad electric-blue stripe runs along the flank of the black body, from just in front of the eyes to the caudal-fin base. The body colour covers the snout, and this feature is important in identifying the species.

This species is a cleaner, feeding on copepods and other external parasites on fishes. It also eats other crustaceans found on rocks and coral, as well as planktonic animals. It usually stays near its refuge, which consists of a worm-hole or a crevice in a shallow cave. This is also used for depositing and protecting its eggs. These fishes are usually seen in pairs and spawn after they are six to eight

months old. When beginning courtship, the male becomes darker. He anchors himself to the substrate with his sucking disc and moves his body as if swimming. If the female is receptive, she joins in this activity for some time, and after a few hours, the pair retire to the male's pre-selected spawning hole. Several hundred eggs are laid on the walls of the hole, which the male guards until they hatch in seven to twelve days. The fry are transparent and have a large yolk sac which is adsorbed within about twelve hours. Then, the fry become planktonic and feed on tiny organisms. After twenty days or so, they have usually developed to a benthic stage and acquired a dark lateral stripe. After three or four months, they are nearly mature, and within several months, they are preparing to spawn.
Size: 3.8 cm (1.5 in). *Distribution:* Florida to the West Indies. *Temperament:* active, peaceful. *Water:* marine, 24–26°C (75–79°F).

Periophthalmus barbarus (Mudskipper, or Mudhopper)
Diagnosis: The body is elongate and posteriorly compressed. The line of the back is almost straight from the eyes to the caudal fin. The head is large, with protruding and dorsally located eyes. The two dorsal fins are separated, and the pectoral fins are very powerful and used for terrestrial locomotion. Unlike other species in the genus, this has pelvic fins which are only incompletely joined by a small fold of skin at the posterior bases.

This species spends most of its time out of the water on mud flats where, as long as its skin and gills are kept moist, it can respire. Its usual habitat is in shallow brackish pools and ditches which rapidly dry out and become isolated during low tides. It can then raise itself upon its pectoral fins to survey the area with its dorsally positioned eyes. It is able to travel over land for some distance by using its pectoral fins. It is also a spectacular leaper, sometimes jumping as far as 2 m (6.5 ft). The sex distinctions are unknown, but spawning is thought to occur in holes in mud, after which the female probably cares for the brood. It is important to note that this fish is kept in a vivarium and not in a conventional aquarium.
Size: 15 cm (6 in). *Distribution:* east Africa and Madagascar, the Red Sea, and east India. *Temperament:* territorial. *Water:* brackish, 24–30°C (75–86°F).

73 Acanthuridae (Surgeonfish family)

Diagnosis: The body is deep and compressed, with a small mouth and an elongated nasal bone which forms the high head profile. There is only one dorsal fin, with both spines and rays.
Distribution: All tropical seas.

This family consists of marine herbivores which feed mainly on algae. They pass through an unusual planktonic larval stage, called the "acronurus" stage, in which the larvae have transparent bodies with vertical ridges. There are twelve genera in the two subfamilies. Firstly, the Acanthurinae

72 *Elacatinus oceanops* (Neon Goby)

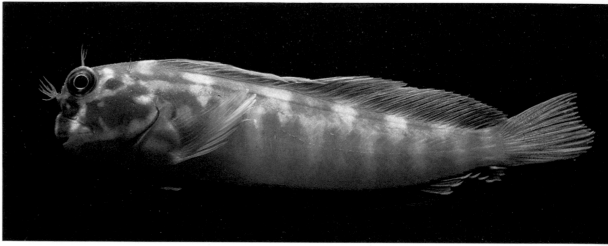

71 *Ophioblennius atlanticus* (Atlantic Blenny)

(surgeonfishes) have one or more spines on each side of the caudal peduncle, which can be extended to function as sharp "knives" or "scalpels" and are used as weapons. Secondly, the Zanclinae (Moorish idols) consists of only one genus and species, which does not have spines on its caudal peduncle.

Acanthurus leucosternon (Powderblue Surgeonfish)

Diagnosis: D.VII–IX,26–29, A.III,25–26. This species is readily identified by its beautiful colouring.

This fish swims either alone or in small groups over coral reefs, grazing on plants and sometimes foraging for small animals. Its colouring apparently serves to draw attention to the spine on its caudal peduncle, which is usually employed in disputes with members of its own species over territorial dominance, although occasionally used for defence against predators. Spawning tends to occur in the early evening, and pelagic eggs are produced, each of which contains a tiny drop of oil to provide buoyancy. The eggs hatch within a day or so, yielding laterally compressed diamond-shaped larvae with large eyes and pectoral fins. The dorsal fins soon develop, and the caudal fin changes from a small flap of skin to a tail. The scales develop, but the caudal spines do not show until the larvae have grown to about 1.3 cm (0.5 in). The larvae drift inshore at this acronurus stage to complete their development. Sexual maturity is thought to be reached after about a year, but they probably do not reproduce until the following season.

Size: 30 cm (11.8 in). *Distribution:* Indo-Pacific region. *Temperament:* aggressive to its own species, territorial. *Water:* marine, 24–26°C (75–79°F).

Zanclus cornutus (Moorish Idol)

Diagnosis: D.VII,38–41, A.III,32–35. The third dorsal spine is extended into a long, graceful filament which may be twice as long as the body. Both the shape and the colouring are very distinctive.

The juvenile of this fish was once thought to be a different species, named *Z. canescans*, because it has a spine at each corner of the mouth. As the fish matures, it loses these spines and develops an osseous spine, or horn, in front of each eye, so that it looks significantly different. No sexual differences have been recorded, and little is known about the reproductive behaviour.

Size: 24 cm (9.4 in). *Distribution:* Indo-Pacific region. *Temperament:* shoaling. *Water:* marine, 24–26°C (75–79°F).

74 Siganidae (Rabbitfish family)

Diagnosis: A.VII and rays, Pel.II,3. The body is oval and compressed with very tiny scales. The dorsal fin is preceded by a single procumbent spine. The spines of the fins are poisonous. The lateral line is complete.

Distribution: Eastern Mediterranean and the Indo-Pacific region.

The rabbit-like appearance of the mouth and the rounded nose give these fishes their common name. They are herbivores and usually swim in small groups over weed beds in shallow waters. The spines on the dorsal, anal, and pelvic fins are very sharp and have grooves down the sides containing venom sacs, and so are able to inflict a painful wound. Most of these fishes are similar in appearance and have spots or a reticulated pattern on their bodies, except *Lo vulpinus* (the foxface), which bears dramatic markings and a tubular snout and is placed in a separate genus. In some areas, they are important food fishes, whilst elsewhere, they are thought undesirable and poisonous. Although most species are marine, some, such as *Siganus vermiculatus*, occasionally move into brackish waters and rivers.

Lo vulpinus (Foxface, or Lo)

Diagnosis: D.VIII,10, A.VII,9. This species has a distinctive tubular snout and displays characteristic colouring.

This is a shy fish which prefers to stay near crevices and small caves in coral reefs, where it can take refuge. It also raises its spines if threatened, and great care should be taken when handling it. It grazes on algae.

Size: 23 cm (9 in). *Distribution:* southwest Pacific. *Temperament:* peaceful. *Water:* marine, 24–26°C (75–79°F).

75 Anabantidae (Labyrinth Fish, or Climbing Gourami, family)

Diagnosis: The superior mouth is relatively large. A respiratory organ is situated internally behind the eyes and is called a labyrinthic organ. There are usually elongate, thread-like pectoral fins and a rounded caudal fin.

Distribution: Africa and India to the Philippines.

These fishes live mainly in fresh water and occur rarely in brackish. Their three genera are *Anabas*, *Ctenopoma*, and *Sandelia*. The main feature shared by both African and Asian species of the family is the respiratory organ behind the eyes. It consists of many thin plates of tissue in the gill cavities, well supplied with blood vessels. Its resemblance to a maze, or labyrinth, explains the fish's popular name. The labyrinthic organ is used for extracting oxygen from the air, which is forced past these plates when the fish "breathes" at the water surface. Due to this ability, the fish can survive in water which has very little dissolved oxygen. The thread-like pectoral fins can move independently of each other and are used as touch and taste organs. The single genus in Africa, *Ctenopoma*, has a much smaller labyrinthic organ than do the other genera.

72 *Periophthalmus barbarus* (Mudskipper)

73 *Zanclus cornutus* (Moorish Idol)

73 *Acanthurus leucosternon* (Powderblue Surgeonfish)

Anabas testudineus (Climbing Perch)
Diagnosis: D.XVI–XIX,7–10, A.IX–XI,8–11, LL.26–31. The body is deep, posteriorly compressed, and elongate. The dorsal and anal fins are very long, and the mouth is obliquely superior. The body colour is olive-brown, younger specimens having darker spots on the caudal peduncle and head, with vertical stripes on the body.

This species is said to be the only member of its family that climbs out of the water and is also a very good jumper. Gathered in groups, these fishes often move as far as several hundred metres (or yards) in search of better waters or, sometimes, to forage for earthworms. They usually do so during a rain shower. At times of drought, they can burrow into the mud and aestivate like the lungfishes. Spawning occurs in shallow streams or rice fields, where up to 1,000 eggs are laid and fertilized and then float up to the water surface. The young hatch after twenty-four to thirty-six hours and are able to swim freely.
Size: 25 cm (9.8 in). *Distribution:* India, Sri Lanka, Malay archipelago, Philippines, south China. *Temperament:* aggressive. *Water:* fresh, 15–30°C (59–86°F), not critical in quality.

76 Belontiidae (Gourami family)

Diagnosis: D.less than 10. Many species have extended fins. The lateral line is vestigial or absent, and a labyrinthic organ is used to aid respiration.
Distribution: West Africa, India to Malaysia and Korea.

This is a freshwater family including many popular aquarium species. It is divided into three subfamilies. Belontiinae are the combtail gouramies, one of which is *Belontia signata* from Sri Lanka, the males having very extended fins. Macropodinae contains the Siamese fighting fish and the paradise fish. Trichogasterinae comprises the gouramies.

Betta splendens (Siamese Fighting Fish)
Diagnosis: D.I,8–9, A.II–IV,21–24, LL.30–32. The body is elongate and slightly compressed. The anal fin has a very long base reaching from behind the head to the tail, and the dorsal fin is set far back. The colouring varies with the specimen's origin and the degree of its selective breeding.

In the wild, this fish inhabits clear flowing water and irrigation ditches, feeding on small insects. It has been used in the sport of fish fighting for centuries in Thailand but was described only in 1909 by Regan. When preparing to spawn, the male builds a bubble nest by blowing mucus-covered bubbles onto the surface. He then entices a chosen female to the nest and, by biting and circling her, he induces her to lay on his nest, turning her upside-down. After she has laid ten to twenty eggs, he releases her and, while she remains motionless as though paralyzed, he swims to catch the falling eggs in his mouth and places them carefully in the bubbles. This process is repeated several times, and the female is then aggressively chased away by the male. He looks after the eggs and fry for some time after they have hatched, but he gradually loses interest and leaves them to fend for themselves.
Size: 6 cm (2.4 in). *Distribution:* southeast Asia. *Temperament:* aggressive. *Water:* fresh, 26–30°C (79–86°F), not critical in quality.

Macropodus opercularis (Paradise Fish)
Diagnosis: D.XIII–XVII,6–8, A.XVII–XX,11–15, LL.28–31. The body is elongate and compressed. The dorsal, anal, caudal, and pelvic fins are very extended. The basic body colour is brown to green with a black marbling on the back. The flanks have blue-green and red vertical stripes. A large, elongate, dark-brown blotch is on the gill covers. The fins are red to brown, the caudal and pelvic fins being predominantly red.

This fish is very aggressive to members of its own and other species. It occurs in many kinds of waters and feeds omnivorously on small animals and plant matter. Its spawning resembles that of the preceding species, although its bubble nest is often built under a leaf. The male can be distinguished from the female by his stronger colouring and the very extended soft rays of the dorsal and anal fins. The outer rays of the caudal fin are also extended, giving the tail a lyre shape. The fish has been kept as a pet for centuries in China and was probably first imported to Europe in the seventeenth century.
Size: 9 cm (3.5 in). *Distribution:* Korea, China, South Vietnam. *Temperament:* aggressive. *Water:* fresh, 15–24°C (59–75°F), not critical in quality.

Trichogaster leeri (Pearl, or Mosaic, Gourami)
Diagnosis: D.V–VII,8–10, A.XII,25–30, Pect.9, LL. 44–50. The body is elongate and compressed. The dorsal-fin base is short, and the pelvic fin is thread-like and very extended. The colouring is variable, but there are many small pale spots, a dark stripe running from the snout through the eye and nearly to the tail, and a dark spot on the caudal peduncle.

This beautiful fish is found in small streams, where it feeds on small animals. The male builds a large bubble nest, and the spawning is similar to that of *Betta splendens*.
Size: 11 cm (4.3 in). *Distribution:* Thailand. *Temperament:* peaceful. *Water:* fresh, 23–30°C (73.5–86°F), not critical in quality.

77 Helostomatidae

This family has only one species.

Helostoma temmincki (Kissing Gourami)
Diagnosis: The lateral line is divided below the first soft rays of the dorsal fin. The body is elongate and very compressed. The colouring is variable, usually either yellowish brown—with numerous round

76 *Betta splendens* (Siamese Fighting Fish)

whitish spots on the flanks and fins—or a uniform pale pink. There is a labyrinthic organ.

This timid fish lives in shaded waters and is primarily a herbivore. Its lips have horny teeth for scraping algae from stones and other surfaces. Its popular name derives from the way in which individuals press their lips together, appearing to kiss, although this is thought to be a threat display. Little is known of the breeding behaviour, but H. Berg observed in 1944 that the fishes embraced and allowed the spawn to float on the surface, just as the Anabantidae do. The young hatch within forty-eight hours and apparently receive no parental care.

Size: 11 cm (4.3 in). *Distribution:* Malay peninsula, Thailand, Sumatra, Borneo. *Temperament:* peaceful. *Water:* fresh, 20–28°C (68–82.5°F), not critical in quality.

78 Osphronemidae
This family has only one species.

Osphronemus goramy (Giant Gourami)
Diagnosis: D.XII–XIII,11–13, A.IX–XI,19–21, LL.30–33. The lateral line is continuous. The body is compressed, with a small head, and the pelvic fins are extended as fine threads. The colouring is brownish red with a lighter belly, and the head and body are covered in small black spots. The pelvic fins are orange, and the other fins are blue. There is a labyrinthic organ.

This fish lives in waters with abundant plant growth. It feeds on insects and other small animals

and plants. A favourite food fish for the local inhabitants, it was studied intensively by French scientists who tried unsuccessfully to acclimatize it in France and the Americas. Before spawning, the male builds a nest by weaving aquatic plants, usually bulrushes, to form a basket-like structure, which is strengthened with grasses and twigs and a few mucous bubbles. The breeding season is long but reaches a peak between March and May. Up to 1,000 eggs may be placed in depressions in the nest. The eggs are not adhesive but have the same specific gravity as the water and so remain under the nest. The nest, eggs, and young are protected mainly by the male.

Size: 60 cm (23.6 in). *Distribution:* Thailand to the Malay archipelago. *Temperament:* peaceful, shoaling. *Water:* fresh, 18–26°C (64.5–79°F), not critical in quality.

79 Mastacembelidae (Spiny Eel family)

Diagnosis: D.XIV–XXXV usually, and rays, A.II–III,30–130. These fishes have an elongate head and body with no pelvic fins. The dorsal fin is preceded by a series of isolated spines. The caudal fin is continuous with the dorsal and anal fins as in the African species, but it is separate and rounded in some of the Oriental species. The snout bears a proboscis-like appendage, and the scales covering the body are small.

Distribution: Tropical Africa, through Syria, to the Malay archipelago and China.

This family consists of two genera, *Macrognathus* and *Mastacembelus,* with about fifty species in fresh and brackish waters. All are attractively coloured and have a snout which is supported by cartilage. At its tip is a pair of tubular nostrils (in addition to a pair of nostrils near the eyes) that form a trilobate appendage which is used to find and suck in prey. This is usually a diet of small insects and crustaceans, which are sought after dusk. These fishes favour weedy waters over a muddy or sandy bottom, where they hide during the day by burrowing with a rocking and wriggling movement. Only their eyes and snout can then be seen above the surface of the sand. Many are able to survive in waters with very little dissolved oxygen for long periods. But it has been reported that some species will suffocate if they are prevented from obtaining air at the water surface.

When caught by fishermen, they wriggle violently and erect their dorsal spines, which can inflict unpleasant wounds. Usually, they swim through the water with an elegant snake-like motion of the body and with undulations of the anal and caudal fins. Most studies of reproduction in this family have been made with *Mastacembelus pancalus.* This species lives in the large rivers and coastal waters of India and has been reported to spawn near Calcutta at the beginning of the monsoon. The fish did not build a nest but found some algal moss in a convenient position below the water surface, and the female laid about ten to twenty eggs at a time, which were immediately fertilized by the male. The eggs were not protected, and hatched after some thirty-six hours.

74 *Lo vulpinus* (Foxface)

76 *Macropodus opercularis* (Paradise Fish)

***Macrognathus aculeatus* (Elephant Trunkfish)**
Diagnosis: D.XIV–XV,50–55, A.II,49–53. The body is elongate and, in older fishes, quite deep. It has a long and mobile appendage on the snout, which is corrugated on the underside. The brown dorsal fin has eyespots at the base, and the caudal fin has several vertical stripes.

This species lives in diverse habitats, from the coast to river estuaries as well as inland freshwater lakes, ditches, and turbid swamps. It is very typical of the family but, as its common name implies, it has a particularly long snout. The female is much more robust and rounded than the male during the breeding season. They are thought to reproduce in the manner of *Mastacembelus pancalus*, but the eggs are green and about 1.25 mm (.05 in) in diameter.
Size: 35 cm (13.8 in). *Distribution:* southern Asia, Malay archipelago, the Moluccas. *Temperament:* secretive. *Water:* fresh and brackish, 22–28°C (71.5–82.5°F), not critical in quality.

80 Callionymidae (Dragonet family)

Diagnosis: D. usually IV, 2D.6–11, A.4–10. The body is elongate and sometimes slightly depressed. The gill opening is reduced to a small pore-like hole, or spiracle, on the upper side of the head. A spine is on the preoperculum, and the mouth is terminal or slightly inferior.
Distribution: Indo-Pacific region and tropical and temperate seas.

This family contains about forty species of small bottom-living marine fishes. They usually live inshore on shallow reefs or in tidal pools, but some inhabit deeper waters. In certain species, much sexual dimorphism occurs, and the mating behaviour is very involved. Pelagic eggs are produced.

***Synchiropus picturatus* (Psychedelic Fish)**
Diagnosis: 2D.9, Pect.30–32. The colouring is characteristic, notably the black ocelli ringed with blue, black, and pink on the back and flanks. The preopercular spine has two terminal spines and another on the middle of the upper margin.

Both this species and the mandarinfish *(S. splendidus)* are admired for their dramatic colours and patterns. This is the less common of the two species. It feeds on small worms and other invertebrates upon the bottom.
Size: 10 cm (4 in). *Distribution:* Philippines and Melanesia. *Temperament:* peaceful. *Water:* marine, 24–26°C (75–79°F).

81 Soleidae (Sole family)

Diagnosis: Adults are very compressed and are bilaterally asymmetric. They swim on one side and have dextral eyes (on the right side).
Distribution: Temperate and tropical regions.

These flatfishes live in marine, brackish, and fresh waters. They are divided into two subfamilies. The Achirinae live on both sides of America and include the genus *Achirus*. Their dorsal and anal fins are free of the caudal fin. The Soleinae occur mainly in Europe, Australia, and Japan, and have the dorsal and anal fins united with the caudal fin.

***Achirus fasciatus* (Hog-Choker Sole)**
Diagnosis: D.50–56, A.36–42. This fish has a deep round body in profile. The right, or coloured, side is dusky brown with seven or eight black vertical stripes. The left, or blind, side is white or, more frequently, brownish.

This species is said to have acquired its name from the fact that hogs, which once ate fishes discarded on beaches, had great difficulty in swallowing the sole because of its rough hard scales. The main food of the hog-choker consists of annelids, small crustaceans, and algae. Spawning is thought to occur during the late spring and summer, and the eggs are small and numerous. The larval stage has one eye on each side of the head but, as the fish matures, the eye migrates until both eyes arrive at a position on the right side.
Size: 15 cm (6 in). *Distribution:* Atlantic coast of North America from Massachusetts to Panama. *Temperament:* peaceful when small, aggressive when adult. *Water:* fresh, brackish and marine, 5–25°C (41–77°F).

82 Balistidae (Triggerfish and Filefish family)

Diagnosis: D.I–III and rays. The body is deep and compressed, with no pelvic fins but possibly a pelvic spine. In one subfamily, the spines of the

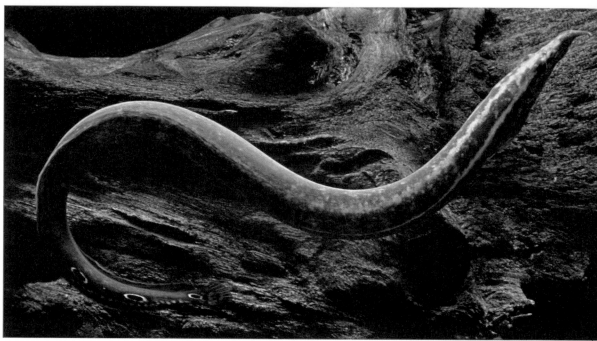

77 *Helostoma temmincki* (Kissing Gourami)   79 *Macrognathus aculeatus* (Elephant Trunkfish)
82 *Pervagor spilosoma* (Fantailed Filefish)   76 *Trichogaster leeri* (Pearl Gourami)

80 *Synchiropus picturatus* (Psychedelic Fish)

dorsal fin can be raised and locked in position, the second spine forming a locking mechanism for the first. The eyes can be rotated independently of each other.
Distribution: Atlantic Ocean and Indo-Pacific region.

This is an entirely marine family consisting of two subfamilies. The Balistinae (triggerfishes) have the ability to lock their dorsal-fin spines, which has given the family its name. They include numerous colourful species, and many of these are favoured by aquarists. The Monocanthinae (filefishes) have only two dorsal-fin spines, and sometimes, the second spine is absent or greatly reduced.

Pervagor spilosoma (Fantailed Filefish)
Diagnosis: D.I,38, A.35–36. The pelvic spine is movable. This fish is easily identified by its colouring.

Filefishes are named not for their spiny dorsal fin, but for the texture of their skin, which is very abrasive. It has many tiny scales, and in some places, especially near the tail, each scale bears a little spine. The caudal fin is alternately opened and closed like a fan as the fish swims. These fishes inhabit shallow waters over coral reefs, feeding omnivorously on small animals and algae. Little is known of their reproductive behaviour, but the eggs and larvae float near the surface.
Size: 13 cm (5.1 in). *Distribution:* tropical Pacific, the East Indies, and Hawaii. *Temperament:* peaceful. *Water:* marine, 24–26°C (75–79°F).

Rhinecanthus aculeatus (Whitebarred Triggerfish)
Diagnosis: D.III,24–25, A.21–23. There are three rows of horizontal spines on the caudal peduncle. The colouring is very distinctive.

This species is quite common throughout its distribution. Sometimes, it occurs in shallow tidal pools or over coral reefs where, if frightened, it will wedge itself securely into a crevice by locking its dorsal spine. When in this position, it cannot be dislodged easily and may inflict a painful bite if it is carelessly handled. As with other members of the family, it feeds on diverse small animals and algae. In Hawaii, the local name for this beautiful fish is *humuhumu-nukunuku-a-puas*.
Size: 30 cm (11.8 in). *Distribution:* Indo-Pacific region. *Temperament:* peaceful when young, aggressive when adult. *Water:* marine, 24–26°C (75–79°F).

83 Ostraciontidae (Boxfish, Cowfish, and Trunkfish family)
Diagnosis: The body is encased in a carapace made of numerous bony plates. There are no spines on the dorsal fin, and the mouth is not protractile.
Distribution: Atlantic Ocean and Indo-Pacific region.

These fishes are divided into two subfamilies. The Aracaninae, with nine species, have a carapace which is open behind the dorsal and anal fins. The carapace is closed in the Ostraciontinae, whose fifteen species include the boxfish (*Ostracion meleagris*), scrawled cowfish (*Acanthostracion quadricornis*), and longhorned cowfish (*Lactoria cornuta*). All members of the family are herbivores and live in the shallow waters of coral reefs. In some genera, they produce a toxic lathery secretion when frightened. Thus, in the confined environment of an aquarium, if such an individual is attacked by another species and responds by secreting its toxin, all the fishes will probably die, including the boxfish itself.

Lactoria cornuta (Longhorned Cowfish)
Diagnosis: D.9, A.8–9. There are protruding horns above the eyes and on each side of the anal-fin origin. The length of the tail increases proportionally with age.

This strange-looking fish lives on tropical reefs amongst marine vegetation, feeding on algae and microscopic animals. After the female has laid the eggs and they have been fertilized by the male, they float to the surface where they hatch in about five days and feed on plankton.
Size: 50 cm (19.7 in). *Distribution:* Indo-Pacific region. *Temperament: peaceful. Water:* marine, 24–26°C (75–79°F).

84 Tetraodontidae (Pufferfish, or Globefish, family)
Diagnosis: D.7–12, A.7–12 usually. The body is rounded, inflatable, and either naked or scattered with small prickles. The teeth are fused to form grinding plates. There are no pectoral fins.
Distribution: Atlantic Ocean and Indo-Pacific region.

These fishes occur primarily in warm seas, although some can be found in brackish and fresh waters. The family name derives from their four tooth-plates, used to grind up and eat snails. The flesh of certain pufferfishes contains a deadly alkaloid poison called tetraodotoxin. This exists in the gonads, liver, and intestines, and its concentration apparently varies with the changes in the reproductive cycle, being greatest before spawning. The Japanese eat such fishes in restaurants where qualified "fugu" cooks prepare the meat by removing the toxic parts, but careless preparation causes about twenty deaths annually there, just over three-fifths of the reported cases of tetraodon poisoning. Two subfamilies are recognized, the Tetraodontinae, with nine genera, including *Tetraodon*, and the Canthigasterinae (sharpnose puffers), which have deeper bodies and contain species that are popular in aquaria because of their small size.

Tetraodon fluviatilis (Green Pufferfish)
Diagnosis: D.14–16, A.12–15. There are two forked nasal tentacles, and the body is covered with small spines. The colouring is variable, but generally, the back is green with large black spots having pale borders. The underside is usually white or grey.

This fish swims by moving its powerful pectoral fins in a screw-like manner, using the tail and anal fins for steering. When attacked or frightened, it inflates its body by filling the sac-like diverticulum of its gullet with air or water. This not only increases the fish's volume, but also erects the body spines, thus serving as a defence mechanism. There are no known external sexual differences. When courting, the male and female circle each other near the bottom, then lay and fertilize 200-300 eggs on a rock. The male guards the eggs, sometimes resting over them in order to hide them from predators. They hatch in about six to nine days, and the male moves the young to a depression in the sand, continuing to guard them while they adsorb their yolk sacs. These fishes are very intelligent and can become quite tame in captivity.
Size: 18 cm (7 in). *Distribution:* southeast Asia. *Temperament:* active, aggressive. *Water:* fresh and brackish, 22–26°C (71.5–79°F), not critical in quality.

85 Diodontidae (Porcupinefish family)
Diagnosis: The body is rounded and covered by sharp spines, with no lateral line. There are two dental plates composed of fused teeth.
Distribution: Atlantic Ocean and Indo-Pacific region.

Members of this family are well known for being able to inflate themselves with air or water when alarmed. This causes their spines to become erect, making them undesirable for any predator. They comprise fifteen species, inhabiting inshore waters and usually living over weed or amongst coral. Often, they are found resting in caves, under coral ledges, or in weedy areas searching for food. Little is known of their reproductive behaviour, but they are thought to lay demersal non-adhesive eggs.

Diodon hystrix (Spotted Porcupinefish)
Diagnosis: D.12, A.12. The spines on the head are shorter than those on the body. The eyes protrude and can see in all directions.

This is the commonest and largest of its family. It has powerful jaws, which enable it to feed on small gastropods and echinoderms. Unfortunately, when it inflates, it often finds the process of deflating to be difficult. This frequently leads to its death and its being washed up on beaches. Its flesh is highly poisonous and, as with members of the family Tetraodontidae, has been proved to cause instances of poisoning by tetraodon, the most lethal of all toxins in fish flesh.
Size: 91 cm (35.8 in). *Distribution:* Atlantic and Indo-Pacific. *Temperament:* peaceful. *Water:* marine, 24–26°C (75–79°F).

82 *Rhinecanthus aculeatus* (Whitebarred Triggerfish)

82 *Amanses sandwichiensis* (Leopard Filefish)

83 *Lactoria cornuta* (Longhorned Cowfish)

85 *Diodon hystrix* (Spotted Porcupinefish)

84 *Tetraodon fluviatilis* (Green Pufferfish)

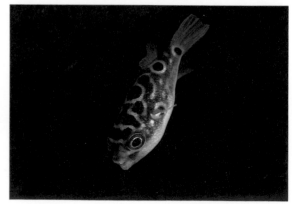

4 The Aquarium Environment

Aquatic habitats and their particular communities of living organisms have been examined in the preceding chapters. Life and health in such an environment depend upon specific physical and chemical conditions—with organic material created by sunlight reaching green plants, or supplied by the surroundings. The aquarium is a limited system which functions vitally in a similar manner. Its components are controlled to provide suitable circumstances for the various occupants. The first step towards its successful maintenance is, therefore, an understanding of the problems and possibilities involved.

The healthy aquarium

An aquarist's primary objective is to keep aquatic organisms alive in captivity. These animals and plants may come from any of the watery places on earth and may be adopted as individual specimens, in colonies of a single species, or in mixed communities. Their proper environment must be established initially, by setting up the aquarium with several general factors in mind: the physical space available, the influences of temperature and light, and the quality of water. Subsequently, the same conditions have to be sustained for an indefinite period, despite many processes which occur independently of the organisms or because of their activities. The keeper's duty is to know what happens inside the aquarium, and to regulate any undesirable changes that arise.

Living space

The basic space for life in an aquarium is the volume of water. Its size and shape are of great importance to the captive organisms, as well as to the owner. From each point of view, different preferences may exist. For example, stable conditions are usually easiest to maintain in a large body of water, whilst practical and aesthetic considerations often demand a small one. The latter requirements will be discussed later on, and the needs of organisms concern three aspects of this living space—its surrounding surfaces, biological contents, and moving water.

Vital surfaces

A principal feature of the aquarium's shape is the area of the water surface. This has a great influence upon the direct illumination of the water, and upon the exchanges of gas and heat between the water and air. An aquarium tank must also be shallow enough for the light from above to reach all depths in adequate strength, but it should remain sufficiently deep to allow healthy animal movement and plant growth, depending on the sizes and habits of the organisms present.

Life in an aquarium involves the continual transformation of energy and matter. Arrows showing movement here are green for dead organic material, blue for oxygen (O_2) and carbon dioxide (CO_2), yellow for nitrogen products, and red for inorganic nutrients.

Several processes combine to create a healthy balance in the aquarium life. (a) Plant photosynthesis under the influence of artificial and natural light takes in CO_2 and releases O_2. (b) Respiration has opposite effects and is the source of heat energy for the plant. (c) The grazing fish takes up organic material from the plant and from food supplied artificially. (d) Excrement and uneaten food collect in the sediment and are decomposed by bacteria. (e) Ammonia and urea, also excreted, and (f) dead plants, are broken down similarly. This bacterial activity consumes O_2 and releases CO_2 and other nutrients which are taken up by the roots and leaves of plants, so the cycle of processes is complete.

The tank interior is diversified by its background and base substrates, as well as by large plants and attached animals, in addition to water currents and air bubbles. Its physical structures are important, as they provide the organisms with a foundation to fix upon, a surface to crawl over, a medium to root or burrow in, or a region to hide against or shelter within. Aquarium substrates include the tank walls and windows, any rocks, shell, coral, wood, or plastic objects, and particles of sand, gravel, and detritus. The plants and animals themselves may also create surfaces, cavities, and tissues for occupation by others. These materials differ in shape, texture, colour, density, and further characteristics, which must be taken into account by the designer.

In the aquarium, as in nature, deposits of sand and shell fragments or gravel are valuable, as porous media that can be penetrated by organisms. Such sediments are able to hold the roots of higher plants, to be adapted as dwellings by animals, to attract widespread colonization by microscopic creatures, and to filter fine particles of detritus or silt from the water flowing through. Sediments range from coarse gravel to the finest sand, silt, and detritus. The size, roughness, and mixture of the particles determine the useful properties of the sediment—its density, porosity, and mobility.

For a given volume of sediment, the total area of particle surfaces will increase as the fineness becomes greater. But so will the restriction of water flowing through, and the sediment may stagnate because its interstitial channels are easily clogged by detritus. A good compromise between high through-flow and maximum surface area is obtained by a mixture of gravels of 2–6 mm (0.08–0.24 in) in diameter. This is the optimum grade of deposit for a bacterial filter. In the aquarium, a bottom sediment is often used as such a filter bed. Large populations of bacteria, which decompose organic and inorganic substances carried by water into the sediment, thrive on the angular surfaces of gravel and other particles.

Rooted plants can also prosper in this type of sediment. They must be able to extend their roots into a fairly clean medium where oxygen is available for aerobic decomposition by bacteria. Burrowing animals have more varied requirements. Many fish and crustaceans find a coarse mixture of stones, gravel, and shell to be suitable for shallow burrowing. Polychaete worms which make permanent burrows (such as the species *Arenicola marina*) need a fine sandy substrate that will not collapse behind them. And like bivalves, they need to push their way through the deposit, which must, therefore, be somewhat fluid or "thixotropic" (with reduced resistance when pressure is increased).

Biological capacity
Every animal or plant needs space in which to find nutrients, light, oxygen, mates, and social or tactile stimuli, and in which to leave waste products, secretions, and offspring. Since the volume of an aquarium is tiny in comparison to natural water bodies, there is a limit to the mass and numbers of organisms that can be kept healthily in its artificial system.

For animals, this limit is usually determined by the supply of oxygen—or by the rate of removal of a toxic waste product, normally ammonia. Overcrowding which causes oxygen shortage or excessive ammonia will lead to stress, illness, and fatalities. Plant growth is generally limited by the amount of light, or by the availability of carbon dioxide, nitrogen, or phosphorus.

Awareness of these factors should allow the aquarist to maintain a relatively high biological capacity, with a proportional degree of dependence upon equipment and management. Oxygen can be replenished rapidly by mechanical aeration. Metabolic wastes are removed by changing, filtering, or otherwise treating the water. Plant life is aided by increasing the intensity and duration of illumination, or by adding selected supplementary nutrients.

Although the extent of these manipulations will govern the capacity of a particular system, extremes should be avoided. In most aquaria, the aim is to display a group of specimens in the best possible condition. Stress must be minimized, and crowding prevented completely. Practical experimentation with any system is advisable, beginning with just enough specimens to create a community, then increasing their quantity over a period of months unless signs of overcrowding appear.

Water movement
The space inside an aquarium is effectively increased by moving water. A fish may swim for miles against a current without travelling through the tank at all. Water can even be driven around a circular or annular tank, to make an underwater "treadmill" for actively swimming animals.

Turbulent water flow, and circulation throughout the aquarium, are vital processes. They ensure the even mixing of heat and of many substances—nutrients, food particles, waste products—as well as the efficient exchange of gases between air and water. Water moving quickly carries more of a dissolved or suspended substance to an organism, and this can be important at low concentrations of the substance.

In addition to being the essential medium of the aquarium, water plays a fundamental role in various biochemical reactions. Molecules of water are split by light energy, in plant cells during photosynthesis, to release oxygen and, moreover, the hydrogen which becomes a reducer of carbon dioxide and carbohydrates. Water is also formed, during respiration, by the combination of hydrogen and oxygen.

Maintaining adequate circulation of water in an aquarium might involve the positioning of directional inlets and outlets, the lifting of water from bottom to top of a tank, the blowing of air across a surface, or the stirring of an entire body of water. Such methods of moving water, and their use in treating aquarium solutions, will be examined in detail later on.

Temperature
The temperature of the environment is one of the most important influences upon biological activity and the distribution of species. Each kind of living organism, having evolved in a particular locality, is adapted genetically to the local temperature régime—the actual levels of warmth and the size and rate of their changes with time. In most natural bodies of water, temperature fluctuates slowly and through a small range, due to the great volume of liquid and to the high specific heat of water.

The majority of aquatic organisms, therefore, can tolerate only gradual temperature changes within narrow limits. Marine and tropical environments are relatively stable, and their species require a very small range of temperatures (stenothermal) compared to that of temperate freshwater species. Such a range is centred about a definite optimum temperature which the aquarist must keep in mind.

Effects of heat and cold

Except for birds and mammals, all animals—fishes, invertebrates, amphibians, and reptiles, are poikilothermic: they have little control over their body heat, which thus increases or decreases as the ambient temperature changes. The water temperature affects an aquatic poikilotherm both directly, by governing the speed of all its biochemical reactions, and indirectly, by regulating factors such as the solubility of gases and the behaviour of nearby organisms.

With a fall in ambient temperature, the animal's rate of metabolism decreases, and it is generally less active. Below a certain minimum temperature, an essential chemical reaction will proceed too slowly, and the animal dies. With a rise in temperature, the metabolic rate speeds up, doubling or trebling for each 10°C (18°F). This increases the need of energy and, therefore, the respiration of organic material. The latter may be used up faster than it can be obtained, leading to starvation.

Above the normal range of temperatures, respiratory problems begin. Oxygen consumption must be increased, but the chemical haemoglobin in an organism has a reduced affinity for oxygen, so that the external concentration of oxygen should be ever higher. The oxygen content of warmer water is reduced as well, and the animal may suffocate. At an extreme upper temperature, essential organic molecules are damaged, and death results.

Adjustment to small changes in water temperature involves the modification of many of the body's protein and lipid substances, and particularly of the enzymes—organic protein molecules which catalyze metabolic reactions. This is why acclimatization to a different temperature must be achieved slowly. It may be days or weeks before a fully balanced metabolism is restored, and during this period, the animal is under stress. When conditions are unstable for a long time, the continual stress can cause illness and death. Consequently, the importance of temperature stability cannot be overemphasized.

Aquarium conditions

A vital aspect of aquarium management is to learn, and then to maintain, a suitable temperature régime for the chosen community. Since genetic adaptation in these artificial surroundings is virtually impossible, the régime must reflect the temperatures prevailing in the natural habitats of the species concerned.

For this purpose, an aquarium is frequently kept at a temperature above or below the external ambient level. Loss or gain of heat, due to contact with the air, must be controlled. One method of doing so is by a continuous inflow of water at the correct temperature, in an open system of water circulation. Techniques of direct heating or cooling are employed in relatively closed systems, to be described later.

Regulation of the aquarium's water temperature is made difficult by its small volume, and by the rapid exchange of heat with the air, in comparison to natural bodies of water. Insulation is important, and the mechanism of temperature control must be sensitive enough to counteract even tiny changes of around 1°C (1.8°F), at least when delicate specimens are present. In all cases, efficient circulation of water is essential, as heat distribution in the aquarium depends upon water movement.

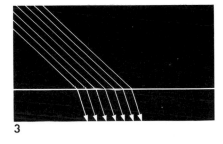

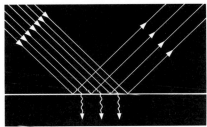

Light hitting a surface such as an aquarium window is affected by (1) reflection, (2) absorption, and (3) refraction. The apparent colour of a surface usually depends upon which colours in the light are reflected so that they can be seen.

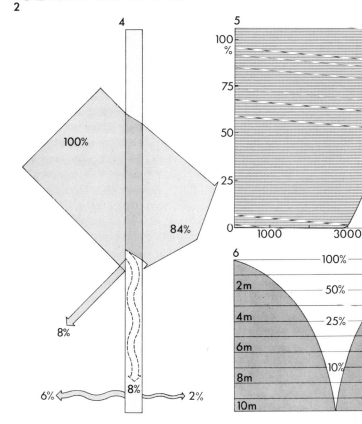

(4) Light passing through a window is partly reflected and partly absorbed, but mostly transmitted with a little refraction. The absorbed light becomes heat, is conducted away in the glass, and is radiated out on both sides. Shown here is the fate of light hitting a thin aquarium window: 84 per cent is transmitted, 2 per cent is radiated in, 8 per cent is reflected, and 6 per cent is radiated out.

The percentage of transmittance of light depends on its colour and the kind and thickness of the medium it passes through. (5) The graph shows that little or no ultraviolet light, at wavelengths below 3,900 angstroms, goes through ordinary glass. (6) Light in water is progressively absorbed. Turbidity increases the absorption rate.

131

A temperate, freshwater aquarium, based on a pond or on a quiet backwater of the lower reaches of a river. The general impression that this display should give is one of still, clear water with shelter, and with light broken by overhanging vegetation. The many organisms require different living spaces, with hard and soft substrates, and floating and rooted tall plants. The substrates are composed of dark-coloured, shallow, coarse gravel with pockets of sand. The odd outcrop of rock conceals small plant-holders. No heating or cooling is necessary, as regular, partial water changes will keep the water at the required temperature, 8–15°C (46–59°F). Neither is a filtration unit needed, whilst aeration and circulation are provided for by air-lift pumps and diffusers. Natural lighting is used, so the tank should be placed where it will receive enough bright light to keep the plants healthy and growing. Medium-hard water with a pH of 6.5–7.0 should be maintained.

The fishes stocked in the aquarium shown here are: (a) eel (*Anguilla anguilla*), (b) rudd (*Scardinius erythrophthalmus*), (c) roach (*Rutilus rutilus*), (d) stickleback (*Gasterosteus aculeatus*), and (e) goldfish (*Carassius auratus*). Of the wide variety of plants that could be included in such a habitat, the following have been chosen: (f) water milfoil (species of *Myriophyllum*), (g) water-lily (*Nymphaea alba*), (h) water

There is wide variation between species in speed and ability to acclimatize to temperature changes. But as a general guideline for the aquarist in minimizing stress, any temperature rise should be at a maximum rate of 2°C (3.6°F), and any decrease at less than 1°C (1.8°F), per period of twenty-four hours. The most natural conditions, as well as being economical, are established by imposing a daily or seasonal pattern on the aquarium environment, through slow changes in water temperature and other influences.

Thermal energy

Heat is a form of energy within a substance, measured by its temperature. This is proportional to the movement of its microscopic particles—atoms or molecules—which may travel freely or vibrate in definite positions. The substance may gain or lose heat in several ways that are relevant to aquarium management: radiation, conduction, convection, and evaporation or condensation.

Radiation usually means the transmission of electromagnetic waves. These include visible light, in a small range of the "spectrum" of all such wavelengths. At somewhat longer wavelengths, in the infrared range, the radiation is sensed as heat. Radiant heat can pass through some substances like air and glass, but not through water. Water absorbs the radiant energy and its temperature increases. The surface layers of natural waters are heated mainly by radiation. So is the surface of an aquarium which has a lamp or other source of heat above it.

Conduction is the transfer of heat by physical contact between the particles of a substance. It is proportional to the area of contact, and to the temperature gradient—or difference of heat between the portions in contact. Some materials, such as air and water, are very poor conductors of heat. The different rates at which materials conduct heat are used to calculate an aquarium's requirements for heating or cooling, as will be seen. This is especially true of solid materials which are good heat conductors and are needed to build aquaria.

Convection is the movement of heat by actual flow of a gas or liquid. As the substance becomes hotter or cooler, it can expand or contract in volume, thus moving under its own pressure and carrying energy with it. This happens continually in air or water which is not of uniform temperature, or is in contact with a relatively hot or cool body. By far the greatest amount of heat transfer in water is by currents of convection, and this has extremely important effects upon living organisms.

Evaporation is the change of a substance into its gaseous form, as when boiling water becomes steam. Particles may evaporate from a material at any temperature, and they take away heat energy in order to escape. Most heat loss from a body of water occurs in this way, and little heat may return by the opposite process of condensation. The amount of heat needed to evaporate boiling water at sea level, for example, is more than five times the amount needed to bring the water from its freezing to its boiling point. Large quantities of water may evaporate from the open surface of an aquarium, wasting considerable heat and requiring a constant source of supply.

Heat energy is often calculated in terms of a unit called the calorie. This is the amount necessary to raise the temperature of one gram (0.0022 pound) of water by 1°C (1.8°F). About 0.24 calorie per second is supplied by an energy source of one watt, equivalent to $\frac{1}{746}$ horsepower.

moss (*Fontinalis antipyretica*), *(i)* duckweed (*Lemna minor*), *(j)* frogbit (*Hydrocharis morsus-ranae*), *(k)* Canadian water weed (*Elodea canadensis*), and *(l)* pondweed (*Potamogeton densus*). The invertebrates shown are: *(m)* water spider (*Argyroneta aquatica*), *(n)* great silver beetle (*Hydrophilus piceus*), *(o)* great pond snail (*Lymnaea stagnalis*), *(p)* water louse (*Asellus aquaticus*), *(q)* painter's mussel (*Unio pictorum*), *(r)* white ramshorn snail (*Planorbis albus*), and *(s)* horse leech (*Haemopis sanguisuga*). The amphibians are: *(t)* common newt (*Triturus vulgaris*), *(u)* crested newt (*Triturus cristatus*), and *(v)* common frog (*Rana temporaria*).

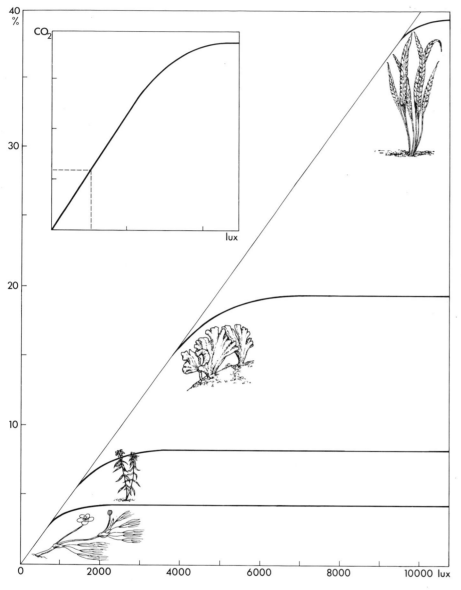

Illumination

An aquarium requires light for the viewing of its contents, the photosynthesis of plants, and the normal health of animal occupants. Intensity, colour, and periodicity are the characteristics of illumination, which must be controlled to produce the proper light régime for a given community.

Light in the aquarium

Light may shine into the aquarium from above—through the water surface—and from the front or sides through transparent walls. It may also be generated within the tank by underwater lamps or by luminescent animals. But when entering and travelling through the aquarium, light is altered in intensity and colour by various optical phenomena, whose importance for the designer will soon become evident.

Light is absorbed and scattered in water, greatly by suspensions of solid particles and micro-organisms, and to a lesser extent by dissolved substances and the water molecules themselves. Different wavelengths of light are affected at unequal rates, so that the apparent colour of light changes as it penetrates the water. The primary reason for minimizing these processes in an aquarium is that high clarity of vision must usually be maintained, to help both the animals and the observers. Consequently, very low turbidities in aquarium water are specified and can be achieved with methods of treatment such as filtration.

The aquarium surfaces also influence light. Any surface returns or "reflects" some of the radiation hitting it, and bends or "refracts" the radiation passing obliquely through it, as well as absorbing the rest of the radiant energy. Reflection ranges from the regular image in a smooth mirror to the diffuse appearance of rough objects. Refraction may be almost unnoticeable, for example through a fine window, or may be extreme, as in a distorted lens. Once again, each wavelength of light is affected differently, resulting in a change of colour. Thus, an aquarium combining the surfaces between air, water, glass, plastic, and other materials, can seem more complicated to the eye than it did to the planner. But in general, such effects are predictable and should be taken into account during initial construction.

The needs of plants

Light is the basic energy source of plants and, therefore, of all living organisms. It not only powers the synthesis of organic molecules from simple chemicals (photosynthesis), but also stimulates the movements of growing plant leaves and stems (phototropism), and is important in many species as a regulator of flower and seed formation (photoperiodism).

For healthy plant growth, light must reach the sensitive chlorophyll molecules with an adequate intensity and duration. The chosen régime should approximately match the natural light conditions to which the given species are adapted, as already described. Shallow open-water species are provided with 5,000–10,000 lux, whilst plants from deep-water or densely shaded habitats may need only 1,000 lux.

Insufficient "day-length" is probably a major cause of poor health in aquarium plants. For a normal display community, between eight and fifteen hours of illumination per day are essential. Tropical habitats require about twelve hours of light daily, throughout the year. A seasonal pattern may be of particular benefit to species from tem-

The large graph shows how the rate at which a plant grows (measured on the vertical axis in relative percentage) depends upon the intensity of light reaching the plant (measured on the horizontal axis in lux). The rate is controlled by the speeds of chemical reactions within the plant, notably photosynthesis by chlorophyll. In dim light, plants respond similarly to an increase of light, growing faster. But in brighter light, some plants cannot use such an increase, and continue to grow at their highest possible rate. This "saturation level" is shown for four general kinds of plants, using light in the four ranges of intensity advised by Chapter 2. The exemplary species are (from bottom) *Ranunculus fluitans, Callitriche palustris, Ulva lactuca,* and *Aponogeton crispus.*

Plants need a minimum amount of useful light as well as the maximum. To grow by photosynthesis, they must absorb carbon dioxide from the surroundings more rapidly than they lose it through respiration. The inset graph shows how such an absorption rate changes with light intensity. Below a "compensation level" of light, as in the sea beneath its euphotic zone, a plant cannot grow.

perate habitats, varying the length of day between winter and summer. To culture plants with maximum assimilation and production—for example, in a method of water filtration—continuous illumination is often employed, although a short interval of darkness in each day could be valuable.

A combination of artificial lights, possibly with natural light as well, is used to provide the best quality and control of illumination. As a general rule of efficiency, the light should include colours which have the greatest effect upon chlorophyll: blue-green (between 3800 and 4800 angstroms in wavelength) and orange-red (between 6000 and 7000 angstroms). Plants respond only gradually to light as their photosynthetic operations begin.

Lighting for animals
Less obviously than in the case of plants, light is an important factor in the lives of most aquatic animals. Many species have been found to depend upon a suitable light régime for normal orientation, movement, colouring, feeding, avoidance of predators, and social interactions. Various physiological functions, including vitamin synthesis, also require a certain amount of light. In fish, gonad ripening and the entire reproductive cycle are adjusted to the natural light intensity and day-length, whilst many freshwater tropical fish show increased sexual activity in the spring.

Animals may respond much more strongly to light than do plants. Sudden spotlighting sometimes causes fishes to panic and attempt escape, and a great shock can be fatal. Similar reactions are frequently produced by the sudden casting of a shadow after steady bright illumination. Excessive light has even been known to cause blindness in fishes. Little systematic research is yet done in this field, and scientific observations by the aquarist are to be encouraged.

The general guideline for an aquarium is to imitate nature. With natural lighting, dawn and dusk will pass fairly slowly. With artificial lighting, dimmer and time switches may be used to achieve similar effects. In nature, there is still some light at night, and it is often wise to employ night-lights in an aquarium for low illumination throughout the night, so that active animals will not be damaged by swimming into obstructions.

Sound and noise
The natural world is by no means silent underwater. Pressure waves, which travel outwards from a vibrating object, can be detected or heard as sound. Sound waves travel easily through water, with little deviation and loss as compared to sound in air. The crunching, grunting, and groaning of fishes, the stridulations of lobsters, the snapping and crackling of certain shrimp species, and many other sounds combine to create a continuous "bio-noise". Even limpets make a rasping sound as they constantly scrape algae from rocks.

Much of this noise is unimportant, for example in fishes which eat by crunching food or grinding their teeth, particularly those species having pharyngeal teeth and muscles near a swim-bladder that functions as a sound-box. But in a school of fishes, the rhythmic beating of tails generates a low-frequency sound, which may enable a formation to be kept or, indeed, may attract a predator. Many other sounds are made deliberately by underwater animals, often for communication and navigation. However, most species have not been studied in these

respects, and the controlled environment of the aquarium is promising for research here as well.

An aquarium's water will relay any sounds or vibrations reaching its surface, walls, or supports. Fishes respond to a regular sound stimulus, as is obvious at times of feeding. This habit might be developed by the aquarist into a complex routine of behaviour among the specimens. But the effects of excessive noise are largely unknown. Disturbance and stress are caused to sensitive organisms, particularly by sudden loud noise.

Aquarium chemistry
Plants and animals which live in water are far more attuned to the quality of their surroundings than are non-aquatic organisms. They have been adapted by evolution to a particular chemical environment, and they obtain raw materials from the watery solution as well as depositing waste products in it. The chemical conditions in an aquarium must be managed so as to resemble the natural habitat of the given species, and to prevent depletion of vital substances or accumulation of toxic ones.

Basic substances
Chemistry concerns the combinations of about a hundred basic elements that make up matter. The aquarium is an enclosed assortment of such substances and derives much value from being relatively self-contained: a dynamic system, small enough to be manipulated, with limited inputs and interactions and outflows of material. Its main constituents are compounds of hydrogen and oxygen (including water), carbon (called organic), nitrogen, and various metals. The last belong largely to dissolved salts, and salinity is the major factor dividing aquatic habitats—into salty and fresh, or hard and soft, waters.

Water salinity
A salt consists of particles which have both a metallic and a non-metallic component. The salinity of a body of water is its total concentration of dissolved salts, their amount per unit volume of water. These salts may vary in their relative individual concentrations, as well as in total amount. Sea water has a comparatively high and uniform content of salts, chiefly "common salt" (sodium chloride). Inland waters are much more diverse but, generally, quite low in salinity. Between the two extremes lie brackish waters, usually of sea water diluted by fresh water and, therefore, most similar to the sea in salt content. Some brackish waters, in addition to "hypersaline" inland lakes, are created by evaporation, resulting in peculiar local concentrations of salts.

A healthy aquatic organism maintains a balance between its internal fluids and the external solution, for example by drinking water and excreting salts, or by excreting water and absorbing certain salts. If the organism is placed in a strange solution, to whose salt content it is not physiologically adapted, its regulatory mechanisms may break down. Species differ widely in such tolerance: some can live happily in both fresh and sea waters, whilst others require a definite type of salinity. This is shown by the range of natural habitats for plants and animals in the preceding chapters, and of corresponding régimes for aquarium communities in the present chapter.

The average salinity of sea water is about 35 parts per thousand (grams per litre, or ounces per cubic foot). In a closed aquarium system, as water evaporates from the surface, sea water will increase in salinity, because the salts remain in the solution. This tendency puts a strain upon the community and should be corrected by periodically adding fresh water—as opposed to "topping up" with more sea water, which does not prevent the increase of salinity.

Inland waters are about one hundred times less saline than sea water, apart from the exceptional hypersaline or "soda" lakes. Of the diverse substances in natural fresh waters, eighty per cent are due to the weathering and dissolution of rocks and soil, whereas others—notably of sodium and chloride—are brought by wind and rain from the sea. The most abundant compounds in such water are bicarbonates, as a result of plentiful carbon dioxide and its effect on calcareous rocks. Also important are chlorides, sulphates, and nitrates, combined with metallic calcium, sodium, magnesium, potassium, and iron.

Hard and soft waters

Some salts produce insoluble materials in water when it is very hot or contains soap. They are especially noticeable in fresh waters, although absent in rain, and make the water "hard" to varying degrees. Mainly the bicarbonates and sulphates of calcium and magnesium, but also chloride and nitrate salts, are responsible. The bicarbonates cause temporary hardness, removed by heating the water to produce an insoluble precipitate, whilst other hardness is permanent unless the water is distilled or treated chemically. Hardness can be measured by the concentration of the calcium carbonate—"soft" water may contain up to fifty parts per million—or else by that of all the calcium and magnesium in the solution.

The degree of hardness has several biological effects upon aquatic life. Bicarbonates tend to prevent a solution from changing in acidity. Soft water, lacking this protection, may become particularly acidic when much carbon dioxide is present. Such a change creates stress for organisms, and the importance of acidity levels will be emphasized below. The proper growth of various plants, for example the stoneworts (species of *Chara*), is a further benefit of hard water rich in calcium.

Excessive hardness, on the other hand, causes an organism problems in absorbing substances through its delicate membranes. This is most true of the sensitive naked cells of eggs and sperm, so that soft water has been found to play a vital role in the successful reproduction of many species of freshwater fishes. Thus, at least for purposes such as fish breeding, a soft solution is desirable.

In a freshwater aquarium, water of medium hardness will generally be appropriate. Special requirements of animals and plants should be followed where they are known, as indicated in the previous chapters. To maintain soft water, all sources of calcium carbonate must be kept out of the aquarium system—calcareous rocks, gravels, coral, broken shells, and algae—whilst using only soft water initially and during changes or topping up. Conversely, the presence of such sources will preserve the water's hardness.

Elements of life

Aquatic plants and some micro-organisms, which turn inorganic elements into complex materials for living, must satisfy all their requirements through the surrounding solution. Plants absorb considerable amounts of nitrogen, carbon, hydrogen, and oxygen, along with

An aquarium habitat that suits the cichlids of Lake Tanganyika, one of the African Rift lakes, would be formed as shown, by large slabs of rock that make caves, ledges, and overhangs. A fairly large tank is recommended, as some of the fishes can become quite big and many have a territorial nature. The rocks give protection, and much of the cichlid's food—algae and crustaceans, for example—is found on or under the rocks. Many species spawn on rocks or under outcrops. Underwater vegetation is sparse in Lake Tanganyika, and the plants usually grow in isolated groups in sand and gravel, so fine sand (2 mm,

or $\frac{1}{12}$ in) should form the base substrate and fill any ledges where plants are to be sown. Two submersible pumps are used here to keep the water circulating at a high rate, so that the surface is agitated. High-intensity overall lighting (level 4 and over) and bright, angled spotlighting shine through the waves to produce dancing light. The water should be very hard (over 300 ppm), with a pH of 8.0–9.0 and a temperature of 23–25°C (73–77°F). An external mechanical and bacterial filter, backed up if necessary by activated-charcoal and diatomaceous-earth filtration, will keep the water clean and clear. The cichlids shown are: (a) *Tropheus duboisi*, (b) *Tropheus moorei*, (c) *Haplochromis burtoni*, (d) *Julidochromis ornatus*, (e) *Limnochromis auritus*, and (f) *Julidochromis regani*. The plants stocked are pondweed (*Potamogeton natans*) and water milfoil (species of *Myriophyllum*).

smaller quantities of many other elements. Animals need a similar range of substances, obtained mainly by eating food but also by direct absorption from the water. Altogether, twenty-five elements have been shown essential to life. These will now be listed with some principal functions, except for the elements named above, as well as boron and vanadium which are not fully understood.

Phosphorus	bones, molecules for energy transfer and nucleotides
Calcium	bones, enzymes, cell walls, fluids
Potassium	nerves, regulation of osmosis (absorption) in cells
Sulphur	proteins, vitamins
Sodium	blood, tissues, processes outside cells
Magnesium	bones, enzymes, chlorophyll
Chlorine	osmotic regulation
Fluorine	bones, teeth
Silicon	bones, spicules of sponges, cases of diatoms
Chromium	insulin
Manganese	enzymes, excretion
Iron	enzymes, haemoglobin, energy transfer
Cobalt	enzymes, vitamins
Copper	enzymes, photosynthesis, invertebrate blood
Zinc	enzymes, protein synthesis, respiration
Selenium	enzymes as in liver
Molybdenum	enzymes, nitrate utilization
Tin	hormones
Iodine	hormones

An aquarium solution does not need to be supplemented with mixtures of vital raw elements, if there is satisfactory release and recycling of chemicals, decomposition of substances by bacteria, and routine partial changing of the water. But in certain systems, it may be necessary to add inorganic fertilizers or doses of trace elements. Even solutions of sea water, despite their high concentrations of many elements, may lack some which are important to the living occupants.

When plants are cultivated intensively, major nutrients such as nitrogen or phosphorus can be depleted, limiting production. Elsewhere, elements required in small amounts can become trapped chemically within the organic detritus, and removed as the system is cleaned. Frequently, a process of water treatment—foam fractionation, and filtration through activated carbon or ion exchangers—is efficient at removing some elements from the aquarium, often because they are absorbed onto the dissolved organic substances being treated. Such effects must be counteracted in maintaining a vital solution.

Biological processes

The living community in an aquarium influences its environment continuously by respiration, photosynthesis, feeding, excretion, secretion, death, and decomposition. These changes create four main problems. First, oxygen is removed from the solution by respiration, and its solubility in water is rather limited as well.

Secondly, carbon dioxide is expired by all organisms and is highly soluble in water. It affects many biochemical reactions, either directly or by controlling the acidity of the solution. Third, the primary waste products of animal metabolism—notably ammonia—are toxic to most animals and must be minimized, since they are excreted into the aquarium water. Finally, dead organic material, in the form of detritus and dissolved compounds, tends to accumulate in the aquarium system. This is a rich source of food energy for bacteria, whose respiration removes much oxygen from the water.

Oxygen requirements
The amount of oxygen needed by an aquatic organism depends upon its species, the degree of its activity or stress, and the water temperature. Increased activity or stress makes an animal consume more oxygen, due to greater metabolism. Higher temperature also raises the metabolic rate and oxygen consumption of a poikilothermic animal. In an aquarium, the oxygen used by bacteria may be equal to that required by the specimens on display, thus doubling the total demand. In extreme circumstances, suffocation can occur in spite of apparently large amounts of dissolved oxygen.

The most complex animals are least tolerant of low oxygen. Whilst many crustaceans and molluscs can endure short exposure to a low level, under two or three parts per million, only some fish species can survive concentrations of less than five parts per million. But the majority of aquatic organisms are able to live with oxygen levels above five parts per million, given other favourable conditions.

Compared to an organism breathing air, one which breathes water is much more likely to find the oxygen level critically low. To extract a similar quantity of oxygen, some twenty to thirty times more water must be breathed than air, even if the solution is saturated with oxygen. In addition, breathing of water is far more strenuous, since water is about fifty times more dense and eight hundred times more viscous than air.

Sources in the aquarium
The solubility of oxygen in water varies with the temperature, salinity, and pressure. Its maximum point is the concentration which "saturates" the solution 100 per cent. For example, at the normal atmospheric pressure of sea-level, and at 27°C (81°F), this point is 6.5 parts of oxygen per million of sea water, or 8 parts per million of fresh water. An aquarium system is kept at a specific temperature and salinity, which set the limit to maximum oxygen levels. Moreover, the aquarium community removes oxygen at a rate proportional to the mass and number of occupants. This loss must be balanced or exceeded by replenishing the oxygen constantly.

Oxygen enters the water in two natural ways: from the atmosphere and by underwater photosynthesis of plants. Each process can be promoted artificially. Mechanical aeration of the water, especially through turbulence, increases the effective surface area between air and water. Illumination of the aquatic plants will release large amounts of oxygen into the water and can even temporarily supersaturate the solution, although the excess oxygen passes gradually into the atmosphere. Efficient methods of aeration and plant usage for these purposes will be described in the following chapters.

Carbon compounds
Carbon has a unique ability to form huge molecules shaped as chains or rings of atoms. This produces hundreds of thousands of organic compounds, including the three main kinds of living matter—

carbohydrates, fats, and proteins. Their manufacture, use, and decomposition belong to a vital process known as the carbon cycle.

The cycle begins with carbon dioxide being fixed into organic molecules, by the energy of sunlight hitting plants in photosynthesis. Plant materials, when eaten by animals, are recombined to create further carbon compounds necessary for life: body structures made during growth, as well as hormones, enzymes, and nucleic substances for control and coordination, besides fragments that are oxidized in respiration to provide energy. As the organism respires, and once it decomposes, carbon dioxide is released to complete the cycle.

Carbon dioxide, therefore, is one of the most important chemicals in the biological world. Normally an unnoticeable gas, it forms a tiny proportion of the atmosphere, but dissolves readily in water and influences processes ranging from the blood transport of oxygen to the production of flowers and seeds. Carbon dioxide and water combine to yield particles of hydrogen, carbonate, and bicarbonate, which largely determine the acidity of the solution.

Acidity and alkalinity
Pure water is a mixture of electrically charged particles, or ions, of hydrogen, having a positive charge, and of hydroxyl (hydrogen with oxygen), having a negative charge. Its concentration of hydrogen ions is said to characterize a neutral solution. Any substance dissolving in the water which adds hydrogen ions is called an acid. A substance whose dissolved ions react to neutralize an acid, or in general to decrease the concentration of hydrogen ions, is known as an alkali, or base. Thus, acidic and alkaline solutions are chemically opposite.

Carbon dioxide in water forms a weak acid termed carbonic. It has the "buffer" effect of preventing a further increase in acidity. For if hydrogen ions are added, they tend to react with its bicarbonate component, yielding free carbon dioxide and water. A similar reaction is produced by any mineral carbonates present, so that rocks such as limestone (calcium carbonate) can maintain a neutral or alkaline solution in an aquarium. These carbonates are especially valuable because the respiration of animals, bacteria, and plants often creates excessive carbon dioxide in the aquarium. This increases the concentration of hydrogen ions, and minerals are needed to prevent gradual acidification.

On the other hand, photosynthesis by plants will remove carbon dioxide from the solution, increasing the relative amount of hydroxyl ions and, therefore, tending towards alkalinity. But hydroxyl and bicarbonate ions react to produce insoluble substances, such as calcium carbonate. The presence of minerals will, then, again provide some buffering to maintain constant conditions. However, a long period of intensive photosynthesis can create an alkaline solution in an aquarium which is densely planted.

In both natural waters and aquaria, with organic life and good daytime illumination, there is a daily cycle in the levels of carbon dioxide and acidity. During darkness, only respiratory release of carbon dioxide into the water occurs. Acidity increases somewhat, but this is counteracted by underwater carbonates that dissolve. During the light period, photosynthesis removes carbon dioxide, but a rise in alkalinity is cancelled by the reaction which deposits carbonates.

The acidity or alkalinity of a solution is measured by its pH value. This ranges from about 0 to 14 and is the negative logarithm of the

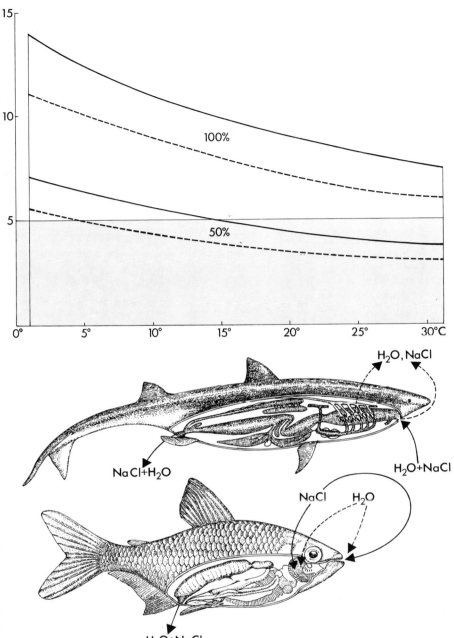

Salts in the water greatly influence its effects on living organisms. The graph above shows how the dissolved oxygen concentration (measured on the vertical axis in parts per million) varies with temperature (on the horizontal axis in degrees Centigrade), in either fresh water (solid lines) or sea water (dotted lines), which is either 50 or 100 per cent saturated by oxygen at the normal atmospheric pressure. The level of 5 parts per million is the minimum need of oxygen for most aquatic organisms.

In a fish's body, the concentration of salts (such as NaCl) is higher than in fresh water but less than in sea water. And water (H_2O) passes by osmosis into the region of greatest concentration, notably through the gills and mouth. So a marine fish (illustrated above) normally loses water, and must drink sea water while excreting or expiring the dissolved salt. A freshwater fish (below) gains water, and must excrete the excess with some dissolved salt, while taking in salt to replace this.

The hill streams of southeast Asia are the natural environment upon which this freshwater aquarium habitat has been modelled. The bottom has a substrate of coarse gravel (6 mm, or $\frac{1}{4}$ in) with pockets of sand where the plants are growing. Water-worn slabs of rock, as if they had fallen in the river, fill part of the bottom and provide shelter for the fishes. At the back is a bank of non-calcareous light-coloured rock. The water must be clean, clear, and lively, so the appropriate hardware should be chosen. Base-gravel filtration through an internal filter pump that pumps out the water well under the surface has been chosen, as it not only filters the water but also creates a turbulent circulation. An external plant filter unit with the water running through a marshy basin could also be used. The water is kept clear by a foam-fractionation unit. Other circulation and aeration hardware is not shown, as it is the make-up of the actual habitat that is of prime interest; however, the necessary hardware to create the optimum water conditions would be air-lift pumps, air injectors, inlets, and surface agitators. The water clarity is highlighted by the use of a bright and sparkling light (level 3–4). The water should be kept soft

(50–100 ppm), at a temperature of 24–28°C (75–82°F), and at a pH of 6.5–7.0.

The fish species chosen for this community are (a) red-tailed black shark (Labeo bicolor), (b) red, or rosy, barb (Barbus conchonius), (c) pearl danio (Brachydanio albolineatus), (d) green puffer (Tetraodon fluviatilis), (e) clown loach (Botia macracantha), (f) Celebes sailfish (Telmatherina ladigesi), (g) sucker loach (Gyrinocheilus aymonieri), (h) coolie loach (Acanthophthalmus kuhlii), and (i) zebra danio (Brachydanio rerio). The selection of plants shown consists of (j) Cryptocoryne balansae, (k) Java fern (Microsorium pteropus), (l) water milfoil (species of Myriophyllum), and (m) Aponogeton undulatus.

hydrogen-ion concentration. A neutral solution contains a ten-millionth of a gram per litre (ounce per cubic foot) and has a pH of 7. Acids contain a greater amount and have lower pH values, whilst the opposite is true for alkalis. Any change by one point on the scale—for example, from 6.5 to 5.5 in pH—means a difference of ten times in the hydrogen-ion concentration. Most natural waters are between 6 and 9 in pH, few being as acidic as 2–3 or as alkaline as 12, and the pH of sea water is fairly uniform around 7.5–8.3.

The pH level of a solution is very important to aquatic organisms. It has a wide influence upon their biochemical reactions, particularly in tissues which maintain direct contact with the water. This is most evident in microscopic protozoans and flatworms, gill tissues, and egg or sperm cells with a high ratio of naked surface area to volume.

Metabolic wastes

Throughout its life, an animal consumes organic material as food. Following digestion and absorption, organic molecules are respired to provide energy. Then, carbon dioxide is released as a waste product, and protein fragments which cannot be utilized are broken down to be excreted as ammonia, urea, or uric acid.

Ammonia is the most poisonous of these wastes. It is generated continuously, and in fairly large quantities, in an aquarium—and its

concentration must be strictly controlled. Tolerance of ammonia varies considerably between species. Fishes appear to be much less tolerant than invertebrates: prolonged exposure, even to very little ammonia, can cause poor growth and impaired resistance to disease. Gill and liver tissues are rapidly damaged, and the blood's ability to carry oxygen is greatly reduced.

Ammonia is a compound of nitrogen and hydrogen, normally a colourless gas. Highly soluble in water, it acts as a weak alkali by combining with hydrogen ions, to form relatively harmless ions of ammonium. But this process is hindered as the temperature or the pH value rises, so that the proportion of toxic ammonia increases. Thus, in marine aquaria, which usually have a pH around 8, ammonia is a greater potential problem than in freshwater aquaria, whose pH is generally 7 or less.

In any aquarium, the level of un-ionized ammonia should always be kept below 0.01 parts per million. This can be ensured by monitoring the total concentration of ammonia, and by seeing that it does not exceed a maximum permissible level which depends upon the given temperature and pH value.

Control of ammonia

Minimum levels of ammonia may be achieved through avoidance of an

excessive animal population, and through methods of treatment such as ozonation, ion exchange, foam fractionation, and partial water changes. An aquarium system can also be designed and managed so as to encourage the natural processes which remove ammonia. These are nitrification by bacteria, and assimilation by plants.

Nitrification is the removal of dissolved ammonia by special bacteria which oxidize it into nitrite and nitrate substances. This process is promoted in the aquarium by providing a large surface area of gravel and sand on which the bacteria can attach and multiply, with adequate oxygenation through the bed of bacteria, whilst maintaining suitable conditions of temperature, pH, and salinity. The main genera of nitrifying bacteria are *Nitrosomonas* and *Nitrosococcus*, which convert ammonia to nitrite, and *Nitrobacter* and *Nitrocystis*, which then change the nitrite into nitrate. They obtain food energy in these ways.

Nitrite is toxic like ammonia, and especially for freshwater organisms, to which it may cause stress and even death at concentrations as low as 0.2 parts per million—whereas several hundred parts per million can be tolerated by certain species in sea water. The recommended maximum level of nitrite in the aquarium is 0.10 to 0.15 parts per million, and efficient nitrification usually maintains levels below this.

Nitrate ions, the final product of nitrification, tend to accumulate in a closed aquarium system and, without changes of water, may reach several hundred parts per million. This increase forms a typical "nitrate curve" during the first few months of life in an aquarium. Although nitrate is not toxic for most species, some animals are sensitive to high levels, and it is recommended that levels be kept below 20 to 40 parts per million. The simplest way of reducing nitrate levels, replacement of old by new water, occurs continuously in an open aquarium system, but can be achieved periodically in a closed system. Two natural processes also remove nitrate ions: assimilation by photosynthesizing plants, and dissimilation by anaerobic bacteria.

Assimilation is the absorption of nitrate or ammonia, or of urea in some species, by plants for protein synthesis. It is one beneficial effect of plants in the aquarium and is the basis of the plant filter, in which plants are grown rapidly by saturation with light and carbon dioxide, maximizing their consumption of dissolved nutrients.

Dissimilation is the use of nitrate as a source of oxygen, by heterotrophic bacteria under anoxic conditions, in the respiratory breakdown of organic compounds. In this process of "nitrate respiration", nitrate is reduced to nitrite, ammonia, or nitrogen, depending upon the species of bacteria involved. The process occurs in aquarium systems despite their predominantly aerobic state. Anoxic conditions develop in small pockets within the gravel and detritus. As a result, nitrate levels are gradually stabilized in an old aquarium solution. But such conditions should not be allowed to arise, since low oxygen is more harmful than high nitrate to the aquarium community.

Dead organic material

Aquatic environments contain organic compounds which remain free, in the solution or in deposits, rather than being bound into living plants or animals. These compounds originate from the organisms and occur in dissolved form or as particles of detritus in suspension and sediments.

Dissolved organic materials are released into the water when cells die and rupture, as well as by secretion and by leakage through membranes. Their concentrations may be high enough to stain the aquarium water, reducing even the effectiveness of water treatment with ozone or ultraviolet light. But the dissolved molecules coalesce at an interface between water and air, forming tiny particles. Thus, an increase of the interface area, for example by bubbling, produces a scum or fine deposit which can be removed. This is the basis of water treatment by foam fractionation. Another appropriate method of removing such materials is adsorption onto activated charcoal.

Detritus is disintegrated and fairly amorphous, and includes tissues, cells, and dead bodies from plankton and larger organisms, or from faeces and uneaten food. The particles settle out as a fine deposit, or mulm, and may be transported by even slight water turbulence. Suspended detritus causes much of the turbidity in water, and a display aquarium must have facilities for removing it. Filtration through a bacterial bed, or through diatomaceous earth, is a suitable treatment process. Moreover, deposits of detritus are very beneficial to bacteria, as sources of food and surfaces for colonization. Excessive deposits can lead to enormous populations of bacteria, which deplete the oxygen in the aquarium, endangering higher forms of life.

Detritus and nutrients

On the other hand, inorganic substances such as phosphate and metals—including copper used as a medicament—are adsorbed onto detritus. These are returned to the solution when detritus decomposes during bacterial filtration. But they are lost if the detritus is simply removed. In addition, many aquatic animals feed on detritus, notably various species of fishes, worms, snails, bivalves, insect larvae, crabs, prawns, starfishes, and holothurians. Perhaps ten per cent of all fishes are nourished by bottom deposits rich in detritus, as is illustrated by certain carp (of the family Cyprinidae), suckers (Catastomidae), flatfishes (Pleuronectidae), mullet (Mugilidae), and gobies (Gobidae).

Aquarium habitats and communities

The choice of environments and occupants which can be established in an aquarium is virtually endless. Any aquatic organism might be coaxed into leading a healthy life in captivity, although numerous practical problems may arise. The prime rule is to create conditions which are physically, chemically, and biologically correct for the organisms concerned, by using as models the natural ecosystems described in Chapter 1. In the present chapter, a selection of such aquaria is presented, five in visual form, and five with detailed specifications. These embrace a wide range of natural situations, in terms of climatic zone, water chemistry, turbulence and flow, substrates, and living communities.

Each of the proposed aquaria has the appearance of a particular wild habitat and locality. Its scene is appropriate with the given suggestions for décor, lighting, and water systems. The physical and chemical requirements are suitable for the animal and plant species indicated. These species reflect not only geographical authenticity, but also the mutual compatibility of organisms, and their general advisability for the type of display envisaged, including factors of size, life-style, and delicacy.

Species from a particular kind of habitat, but from different geographical areas, may be kept in the same aquarium environment with no ill effects. Thus, the information provided will enable the aquarist to invent communities which cut across the regional boundaries, and to explore alternative display themes without basically departing from natural conditions. For example, the rocky shore pool is described with northwest European species, and the aquarist in a comparable climatic zone—such as North America, Japan, or New Zealand—can find ecologically similar animals and plants on local shores, supplying the population for a familiar tidal-pool scene.

Simplicity for starters

When an individual's first aquarium is being considered, and if expert assistance with installation and management is not available, a fairly simple system should be planned, so as to minimize the potential problems. For the inexperienced aquarist, an optimum size of tank or system must be adequate as regards the intended purpose, a reasonable lifetime, sensible costs of purchase and operation, quantity of livestock required, complexity of support equipment, and a sufficient capacity to reduce fluctuations of water quality—particularly in temperature. Initially, a tank of about 100–150 litres (25–35 gallons) may be advisable in the home, whilst a larger display might begin as a group of tanks which are easy to set up and manage.

Similarly, it is wise to start with a community of species that are readily obtainable and will accept a tank environment that can be created and maintained easily. This may involve collection of specimens from a neighbouring habitat, to develop a display of the local aquatic fauna and flora. Water taken from the same site should be usable as well. Room temperatures and natural lighting are permissible for the simplest aquaria. The freshwater temperate pond and the rocky shore pool are good examples to follow with such an aquarium and would also suit a school classroom or a small museum of natural history.

In the descriptions of habitats below, reference will be made to light levels as defined in the previous chapters, and to equipment which is discussed in the next chapters. The mutual compatibility of the fish species suggested for each habitat depends partly upon their temperaments, which should be studied, as in Chapter 3.

A European upland river

General impression: cold, very clear water; turbulent, bubbling, and sparkling effects; eroded, smooth rocks, forming backwaters.

Substrates: rounded rocks and boulders; many holes and crevices; patches of gravel with contrasting colours; a background of bedrock reaching above the water surface.

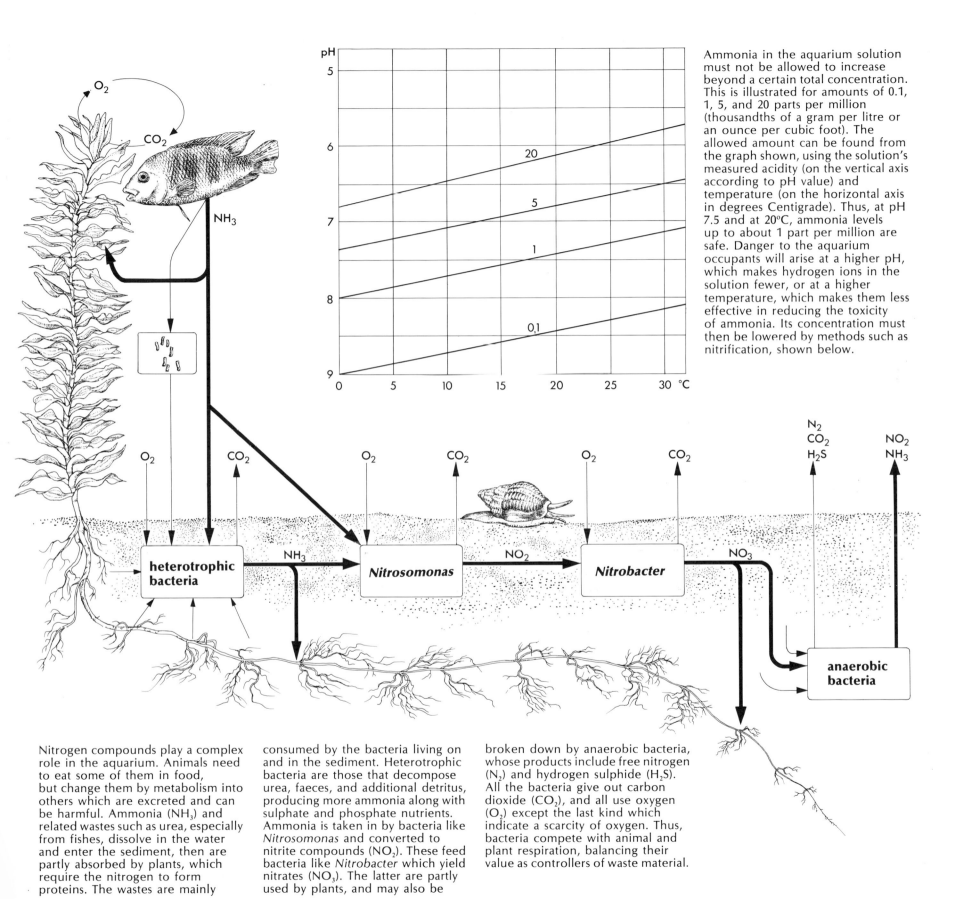

Ammonia in the aquarium solution must not be allowed to increase beyond a certain total concentration. This is illustrated for amounts of 0.1, 1, 5, and 20 parts per million (thousandths of a gram per litre or an ounce per cubic foot). The allowed amount can be found from the graph shown, using the solution's measured acidity (on the vertical axis according to pH value) and temperature (on the horizontal axis in degrees Centigrade). Thus, at pH 7.5 and at 20°C, ammonia levels up to about 1 part per million are safe. Danger to the aquarium occupants will arise at a higher pH, which makes hydrogen ions in the solution fewer, or at a higher temperature, which makes them less effective in reducing the toxicity of ammonia. Its concentration must then be lowered by methods such as nitrification, shown below.

Nitrogen compounds play a complex role in the aquarium. Animals need to eat some of them in food, but change them by metabolism into others which are excreted and can be harmful. Ammonia (NH_3) and related wastes such as urea, especially from fishes, dissolve in the water and enter the sediment, then are partly absorbed by plants, which require the nitrogen to form proteins. The wastes are mainly consumed by the bacteria living on and in the sediment. Heterotrophic bacteria are those that decompose urea, faeces, and additional detritus, producing more ammonia along with sulphate and phosphate nutrients. Ammonia is taken in by bacteria like *Nitrosomonas* and converted to nitrite compounds (NO_2). These feed bacteria like *Nitrobacter* which yield nitrates (NO_3). The latter are partly used by plants, and may also be broken down by anaerobic bacteria, whose products include free nitrogen (N_2) and hydrogen sulphide (H_2S). All the bacteria give out carbon dioxide (CO_2), and all use oxygen (O_2) except the last kind which indicate a scarcity of oxygen. Thus, bacteria compete with animal and plant respiration, balancing their value as controllers of waste material.

A brackish-water aquarium based on the type of environment found in an estuary in Florida or the Caribbean. The overall effect to aim at is one of an extensive habitat with a steady flow of water along the entire length of the tank, but no surface agitation. The system necessary is an external pressure filter and external aeration, heating, and foam fractionation in a reservoir chamber. Mangrove roots and eel grass dominate the scene, with the occasional flat stone lying on dark-coloured sand of 1–2 mm (0.04–0.08 in) diameter. The water should have a salinity of 10 ppt, a pH of 7.2–7.4, and a temperature of 25ºC (77ºF). Lighting should be moderate (level 2–3) and steady, casting shadows among the mangrove roots.

The species that might stock this tank are *(a)* mosquito fish (*Gambusia affinis*), *(b)* American flagfish (*Jordanella floridae*), *(c)* mosquito fish (*Heterandia formosa*), *(d)* molly (*Poecilia latipinna*), *(e)* bluegill (*Lepomis macrochirus*), *(f)* golden-ear killifish (*Fundulus chrysotus*), *(g)* frillfin goby (*Bathygobius soporator*), *(h)* fiddler crab (species of *Uca*), *(i)* spotted snake eel (*Ophichthys ophis*).

Water quality: fresh, 7.0–7.5 in pH, at 10–15°C (50–59°F), with medium hardness (about 200 parts per million), and moderate light (level 2).

Water movement: turbulent surface agitation, by gushing air-lifts onto rocks; high overall circulation around the tank; maximum aeration and bubbles.

Suggested systems: several air-lift pumps with directional outlets; base-gravel filtration; powered foam fractionation; additional water circulation; water chilling.

Sample species:

FISHES	*Thymallus thymallus*	Grayling
	Phoxinus phoxinus	Minnow
	Leuciscus leuciscus	Dace
	Cottus gobio	Bullhead
	Noemacheilus barbatulus	Stone loach
INVERTEBRATES	*Astacus fluviatilis*	Freshwater crayfish
PLANTS	*Ranunculus fluitans*	Crowfoot
	Callitriche platycarpa	Starwort

The Amazon river margin

General impression: very clear water; dappled, diverse light; a densely vegetated pool, with shadowy and secretive appearance.

Substrates: black basalt pebbles, over siliceous sand (2–4 mm, or 0.08–0.16 in, size of grains); planting in hidden peat plugs; dense bottom vegetation; waterlogged roots and branches.

Water quality: fresh, 6.0–6.5 in pH (no calcareous material), at 25–28°C (77–82°F), very soft (less than 50 parts per million in hardness); overall shady light (level 2–3), with some angled rays reaching the substrate.

Water movement: good but unobtrusive general circulation; aeration by a hidden air-lift.

Suggested systems: base-gravel filter, with air-lift power; also, an external powered mixed-media filter, if required.

Sample species:

FISHES	*Abramites microcephalus*	Headstander
	Anostomus anostomus	Striped headstander
	Poecilobrycon unifasciatus	One-line pencilfish
	Hemigrammus erythrozonus	Glowlight tetra
	Hyphessobrycon ornatus	Tetra
	Hyphessobrycon pulchripinnis	Lemon tetra
	Thayeria obliqua	Penguinfish
	Corydoras arcuatus	Arched catfish
	Corydoras julii	Leopard catfish
	Cichlasoma severum	Banded cichlid
	Astronotus ocellatus	Velvet cichlid
	Pterophyllum scalare	Angelfish
	Symphysodon discus	Discus
PLANTS	*Echinodorus amazonicus*	Sword plant
	Echinodorus parviflorus	Sword plant
	Echinodorus tenellus	Sword plant
	Echinodorus quadricostatus	Sword plant
	Pistia stratiotes	Water cabbage
	Azolla filiculoides	Fern

Cabomba aquatica	Fanwort
Cabomba piauhyensis	Fanwort
Eleocharis minima	Spike rush
Heteranthera zosterifolia	Mud plantain

A rocky shore pool

General impression: hard, water-worn rocks; turbulent water; dappled light with angled rays and contrasting shade.

Substrates: base of shell fragments and gravel about 6 mm (0.24 in) diameter; smooth, rounded, light-coloured cobbles; large rocks in the background with holes, ledges, and overhangs.

Water quality: full sea water, around 8.0 in pH, at 8–15°C (46–59°F), with bright light (level 4).

Water movement: high surface agitation, with strong air-lift and large bubbles; rapid circulation throughout tank, with directional inlets (if an external filter is used) and air-lift outflows.

Suggested system: base-gravel filter, with air-lift.

Sample species:

FISHES	*Blennius pholis*	Shanny, Blenny
	Gobius flavescens	Spotted goby
	Gobius paganellus	Rock goby
	Taurulus bubalis	Sea scorpion
	Nerophis lumbricoformis	Worm pipefish
	Pholis gunnelus	Butterfish, Gunnel
INVERTEBRATES	*Actinia equina*	Beadlet anemone
	Anemonia sulcata	Snakelocks anemone
	Littorina littorea	Periwinkle
	Gibbula cineraria	Topshell
	Patella aspera	Limpet
	Mytilus edulis	Mussel
	Eupagurus bernhardus	Hermit crab
PLANTS	*Enteromorpha* species	Green algae
	Ulva lactuca	Sea lettuce
	Cladophora species	Blanketweed

An Indian Ocean coral reef

General impression: bright, colourful sea-bed community; diverse background and species, with much activity and movement.

Substrates: dead shells, whole and crushed; clean coral sand and gravel, 2–4 mm (0.08–0.16 in) diameter; calcareous rock or coral skeleton.

Water quality: full sea water, 8.2–8.4 in pH, at 24–28°C (75–82°F), with bright flickering light (level 4).

Water movement: high surface agitation and turbulence, with underwater bubbles; efficient circulation and turnover.

Suggested systems: external powered mechanical filter; internal foam fractionation; sterilization by ultraviolet light.

Sample species:

FISHES	*Dasyatis kuhlii*	Blue-spotted stingray
	Caranx speciosus	Jack
	Heniochus acuminatus	Pennant coralfish
	Balistoides niger	White-blotched triggerfish
	Holocentrus ruber	Red squirrelfish
	Pterois volitans	Lionfish

If one uses the shallow sea bed of the Mediterranean as a model for an aquarium environment, the overall impression to be created is that of detailed variety, with a diversity of invertebrates. Weathered chunks of soft calcareous or sandstone rock build small caves and clefts, and a coarse to medium (4–6 mm, or $\frac{1}{6} - \frac{1}{4}$ in) light-coloured sand forms the base substrate. A bright light level (3–4) through surface waves produces dappled, dancing light. The sea water should have a pH of 8.0–8.3, and a temperature of 18–21°C (64–70°F).

The equipment necessary for this kind of environment consists of air-lift pumps, a foam-fractionation unit, and external biological, bacterial, and mechanical filtration with quick circulation. The surface choppiness can be caused by the flow from the air-lift pumps.

The choice of inhabitants for a Mediterranean shallow sea-bed community is vast. Here, the fishes chosen are: *(a)* common seahorse (*Hippocampus guttulatus*), *(b)* axillary wrasse (*Crenilabrus mediterraneus*), *(c)* damselfish (*Chromis chromis*), *(d)* peacock wrasse (*Thalassoma pavo*), *(e)* Anthias anthias, *(f)* black goby (*Gobius niger*), and *(g)* tompot blenny (*Blennius gattorugine*).

Of the wide variety of invertebrates that live in the Mediterranean, the following are shown: *(h)* anemone (*Cerianthus membranaceus*), *(i)* fan shell (*Pinna nobilis*), *(j)* sea urchin (*Cidaris cidaris*), *(k)* edible mussel (*Mytilus edulis*), *(l)* snakelocks anemone (*Anemonia sulcata*), *(m)* pilgrim scallop (*Pectens jacobens*), *(n)* coral (*Cladocora cespitosa*), *(o)* zoanthid (*Parazoanthus axinellae*), *(p)* tube-worm (*Spirographis spallanzani*), *(q)* soft coral (*Alcyonium palmatum*), and *(r)* erect sponge (*Axinella verrucosa*).

	Lutjanus species	Snappers
	Plectorhyncus species	Sweetlips, Grunts
	Chaetodon species	Butterflyfish
	Pomacanthus species	Angelfish
	Amphiprion species	Clownfish
	Abudefduf species	Sergeant-major
INVERTEBRATES	*Stoichactis* species	Sea anemone
	Stichopus species	Sea cucumber
	Tubastrea aurea	Stony corals
	Fungia fungites	Stony corals
	Palythoa tuberculosa	Stony corals
	Acropora species	Stony corals
	Porites species	Stony corals
	Cypraea tigris	Cowry
	Diadema setosum	Urchin
	Pentaceraster mammillatus	Starfish
	Fromia species	Starfish
	Aniculus maximus	Hermit crab
	Scyllarides species	Mole lobster

The North Atlantic seas

General impression: deep, dark, and mysterious; broad, obscure substrates with spotlighting.

Substrates: base of gravel or cobbles, with jumbled boulder cliffs; bedrock face of cliffs, with large holes for crustaceans, ledges for anemones and mussels; tunnels and overhangs, reaching close to surface.

Water quality: full sea water, 8.0–8.4 in pH, at 6–10°C (43–50°F); low, diffuse background lighting (level 1–2), with spotlights for particular ledges and the tank front.

Suggested systems: external gravity filter, bacterial and mechanical, incorporating a chiller; aeration, foam fractionation, and possibly ultraviolet sterilization.

Sample species:

FISHES	*Scyliorhinus canalicula*	Lesser spotted dogfish
	Raja clavata	Thornback ray
	Platichthys flesus	Flounder
	Lophius piscatorius	Angler
	Cyclopterus lumpus	Lumpsucker
	Trigla lucerna	Tub gurnard
	Labrus mixtus	Cuckoo wrasse
	Trisopterus minutus	Poor cod
	Pollachius pollachius	Pollack
	Conger conger	Conger eel
	Dicentrarchus labra	Bass
INVERTEBRATES	*Arctica islandica*	Black clam
	Pecten maximus	Scallop
	Modiolus modiolus	Horse mussel
	Tealia felina	Dahlia anemone
	Calliostoma zizyphinum	Painted topshell
	Cancer pagurus	Edible crab
	Palinurus elephas	Crawfish
	Eupagurus bernhardus	Hermit crab
	Galathea species	Squat lobster
	Psammechinus miliaris	Sea urchin
	Echinus esculentus	Edible urchin
	Holothuria forskali	Cotton spinner
	Ciona intestinalis	Sea squirt
	Metridium senile	Plumose anemone

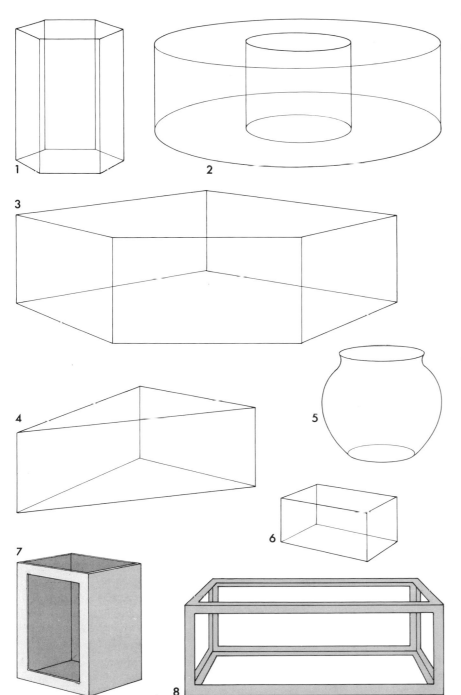

Aquarium Hardware

An aquarium is a system designed to maintain and exhibit aquatic organisms in captivity. The main elements are the display tank and units for controlling aeration, water movement, temperature, concentrations of dissolved and particulate matter, and illumination. There is a wide choice of types of equipment to perform each task. This chapter covers the range of hardware available, dealing with materials, construction, and principles of operation, and discusses the integration of different elements to form functioning aquarium systems.

Aquarium tanks

Any material which can be made waterproof, non–toxic to aquatic life, and strong enough to hold the weight of the water and the equipment used, is suitable for an aquarium tank. The tank must hold a volume of water which is sufficiently large, and appropriate in shape, for the living organisms. The underwater display has to be viewed, usually through transparent walls, but possibly through the water surface, or even by remote-control cameras.

Styles and materials

Aquarium shapes vary widely, from the traditional rectangles and spheres to L-shapes, triangles, bow-fronts, cylinders, and polygons, to glass-fronted rock pools and giant champagne glasses. Aquaria may be specially designed to accommodate most tastes and to suit all sorts of applications. Alternatively, many containers which were constructed for other purposes—such as industrial tanks, barrels, or basins—may be converted readily into aquarium tanks.

The most common and useful sizes are from about 50 to 1,500 litres (10 to 350 gallons). But capacity can range from $\frac{1}{4}$ litre ($\frac{1}{2}$ pint), as in a child's jam jar, to a display tank of one million or more litres (250,000 gallons) in a large public aquarium. Size, like shape, is governed partly by practical and aesthetic considerations of room setting, materials, and costs. The aquarist's choice must also take into account the requirements of the organisms to be housed, the intended function of the aquarium, and factors such as expertise and time available for management.

In addition to glass and the transparent plastics, which are essential for viewing panels, aquarium tanks are often made of GRP ("fibreglass"), wood, concrete, asbestos, or steel. These materials are all adequate in strength and rigidity to bear the contents of a tank.

Glass tanks

With the advent of silicone-rubber sealants in the 1960s, it became

Aquarium tanks can be made of glass, plastics, wood, steel, or concrete, in all sorts of shapes and sizes. Shown are a selection (not in scale). The appearance of the completed aquarium and the relationship between it and its setting are dependent mainly on the tank's specifications. (1) Hexagonal glass or acrylic tank. (2) Annular glass or acrylic tank. (3) Corner tank with three windows. (4) Triangular all-glass corner tank. (5) Goldfish bowl. (6) Conventional all-glass tank. (7) Wooden tank (can also be a large tin can) with one window. (8) Aluminium, steel, or plastic frame tank.

Building an all-glass aquarium to fit into a corner. The method can be used for other shapes and sizes, for instance those given in the main text. The glass should be bought ready-cut from the glazier. It may be helpful when designing the tank to make a dummy from stiff cardboard. In this way, the positioning and appearance of the tank in a room can be tested, and the most appropriate size can be determined precisely.

possible to make a very strong and watertight joint between two panes of glass, and to construct tanks without supporting frames. Such "all-glass" tanks can be made easily and rather cheaply, in diverse sizes and shapes, allowing a clear view from any direction. They involve no problems of corrosion, potentially toxic metals, drying putty, or cumbersome framing.

Silicone-glued glass needs to be slightly thicker than does glass set in a frame. An all-glass tank should also be supported firmly across the base, using a solid-topped stand, while cushioning and insulating the base on a sheet of expanded polystyrene or similar material. Whether the tank is in place or being transported, care must be taken not to knock its exposed glass corners, and it should be lifted only when empty or nearly so.

Framed glass tanks

Many tanks of small to medium size are made with glass panes sealed into a frame of welded angles of steel or, less often, of aluminium or plastic. These tanks are strong and have good viewing properties. Steel frames are vulnerable to rust, particularly when holding salt water. Several protective coatings are available, which galvanize or plate the steel with zinc, chrome, enamel, or a plastic such as nylon, and which vary in durability and cost. A stainless steel frame is common but relatively expensive, and even this may eventually rust in warm salty water. Plastic frames are obtainable for small aquaria, up to about 20

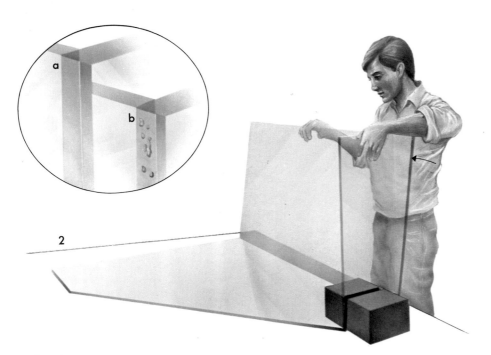

1 The clean, dry bottom panel is placed on a flat working surface and a thick string of silicone-rubber sealant is laid along all the edges except the front.
2 The first of the side panels is raised and pressed into the sealant on the bottom panel. Support blocks are used, if necessary. Next, the adjacent back panel is raised into place and pressed onto the sealant on the bottom panel and against the side panel. Tape the outside corner. (*Detail*) The sealant must be laid in a continuous string, making a bubble-free bond (*a*). If the bond is not bubble-free (*b*), leaks may occur.

3 The second back panel and the second side panel are raised, and the outside corners are taped.
4 All the inside joints are sealed (*a*) and the sealant is smoothed out with the finger (*b*). The sealant is left to harden for at least a day. Then, the front panel is added and sealed.

7 The thickness of glass required for an aquarium panel increases with the depth of the water and the length of the panel. The graph shows six thickness curves (a—f) against water depth (vertical axis) and length of panel (horizontal axis) in cms (multiply by 0.394 for inches).

The key to the graph is:

	vertical	base
a	4 mm ($\frac{1}{6}$ in)	6 mm ($\frac{1}{4}$ in)
b	5 mm ($\frac{1}{5}$ in)	6 mm ($\frac{1}{4}$ in)
c	6 mm ($\frac{1}{4}$ in)	10 mm ($\frac{2}{5}$ in)
d	10 mm ($\frac{2}{5}$ in)	12 mm ($\frac{1}{2}$ in)
e	12 mm ($\frac{1}{2}$ in)	15 mm ($\frac{3}{5}$ in)
f	15 mm ($\frac{3}{5}$ in)	20 mm ($\frac{4}{5}$ in)

For example, for a panel 70 cm (28 in) deep and 75 cm (30 in) long, the graph indicates thickness curve d as appropriate. This curve specifies a 10–mm ($\frac{2}{5}$in) thick vertical panel and a 12–mm ($\frac{1}{2}$in) thick base panel.

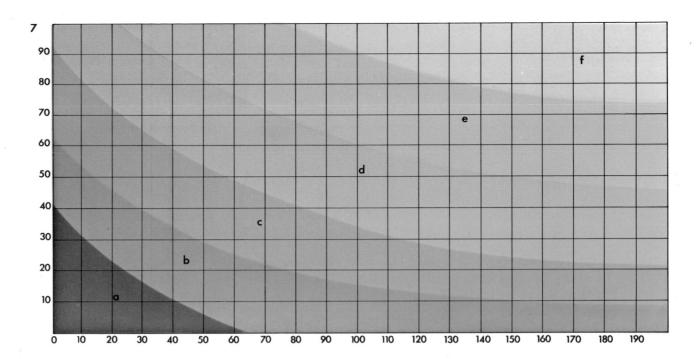

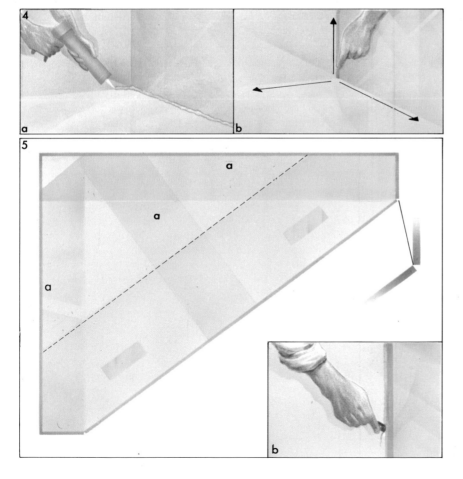

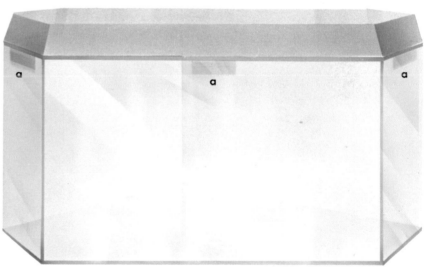

5 The view from the top shows how the various panels are joined and where cross-supports (a) may be put. The front part of the cover is indicated by the dotted line. The detail shows how the edges of the front panel form a V-shape with the edges of the side panels. This shape must be filled with sealant.

The inside angles must also be sealed, as shown. (b) A blade removes excess sealant from the outside joins.
6 The finished tank, with cover added. The glass ledges on which the cross-supports rest are shown (a). These ledges are glued on with sealant.

litres (50 gallons) in volume. They are attractive and non-corrosive, but lack the rigidity needed for larger tanks.

Types of glass
For clear viewing, glass composed of fused silica, soda, and lime is used. The commonest type, for panes up to 25 mm (1 in) of thickness, is *float* glass. Its undistorted sheets are produced by floating the glass on a bath of molten metal.

For very thick panes, *plate* glass may be employed. Although more expensive, it has almost perfect optical qualities. Each sheet is rolled, then ground and polished smooth. *Laminated* glass is manufactured by bonding alternate sheets of glass and thin plastic, such as polyvinylbutyral. Thus, extremely strong, even bullet-proof, panes can be made, up to 200 mm (7.8 in) thick.

Glass is *tempered* by a process of rapid cooling, to create a tough surface with high impact strength. It is generally unsuitable for the aquarium, as its great internal tension causes it to fragment when broken. *Wire reinforcement* does not increase the strenght of the glass sheet, but merely holds it together following breakage.

Glazing techniques
Successful installation of glass depends upon a correct choice and use of materials. Silicone rubbers, and some glues for acrylic sealants, remain elastic when set strongly. They are suitable for glazing into a frame which may expand or contract with changes in temperature. Most of them are translucent, and therefore unobtrusive between panes of glass or plastic, in frameless tanks. Linseed-oil putties and other standard glazing putties tend to dry out and crack in time, and should be painted over. Some contain toxins such as arsenates, so that it is necessary to check the putty before use.

When preparing the glass and surfaces, metal and wooden frames must be smoothed and primed. Plastic must be thoroughly degreased. In concrete or GRP tanks, the constructed rebate (rabbet) surfaces must be perfectly true. Sealing or priming may be required, too. The glass should be cut and edged professionally, avoiding flaws. Before installation, the pane must be cleaned, with water and detergent rinsed by clean water, or with a non-abrasive cleaner such as methylated spirit or carbon tetrachloride. The surfaces should be allowed to dry, and those to be bonded must not be subsequently touched.

The important point in aquarium glazing, after the materials have been chosen and prepared, is to apply the sealant with great care, ensuring a layer or bead of constant thickness which is free from air bubbles. The glass or plastic pane should be installed with uniform pressure across its surface and around its edges, maintained until the seal is completely cured. When a tank has been glazed, and particularly when the tank is deep, frequent changes in the pressure of water on the glass, by filling and draining, should be avoided. When emptying a large tank, the panes should be held firmly and uniformly against the rebate with shuttering.

Making an all-glass tank
The following specifications are for making a fairly small tank, of 90 litres (20 gallons) capacity, according to the method illustrated on pages 150–151. The same method may be used to construct other shapes and sizes of tanks, but careful calculation of panel sizes is essential. The required thickness of panels will increase with water depth and panel length, and is determinable from the graph shown. The tank base can be made of slightly thicker, yet cheaper, rough-cast glass, for greater strength and economy.

The external dimensions (length × width × depth) are 75 × 30 × 40 cm (29.5 × 11.8 × 15.7 in). The materials needed are:

Float glass, thickness 6 mm ($\frac{1}{4}$ in):

base	1 of 750 × 300 mm (29.5 × 11.8 in)
front, back	2 of 750 × 400 mm (29.5 × 15.7 in)
ends	2 of 288 × 400 mm (11.4 × 15.7 in)
top braces	2 of 750 × 50 mm (29.5 × 2 in).

Sealant, clear aquarium silicone rubber: 1 cartridge, 350 cc (12 oz).
Masking tape: 1 roll, width up to 50 mm (2 in).

Plastic tanks
Plastics are materials produced by polymerization—the formation of long chains of atoms—of diverse organic (carbon) chemicals, the majority of which are derived from petroleum. Among modern plastics are epoxy and polyester resins, acrylic, nylon, polyethylene, polyvinylacetate and -chloride, polystyrene, polypropylene, butyl and neoprene rubbers.

Generally, a plastic is a solid form. The term "resin" applies to liquid polymers, but some resins set rigidly when heated under pressure with a catalyst or hardener. With additional "accelerator" compounds, other resins set or cure rapidly even at room temperatures and atmospheric pressure. Many widely used resins are "cold-curing" polyesters which set hard in this way. Set polymers may be made tougher or harder by various reinforcing materials. For example, glass-fibre and carbon-reinforced plastics (GRP and CRP) contain very fine fibres of glass or carbon. Paper, cotton, asbestos, or wood powders are baked into durable protective laminates or strong fillers. Other additives, known as plasticizers, alter the flexibility of the finished product, for instance in PVC curtains and high-pressure piping.

Plastics in the aquarium
Plastics are characterized by imperviousness, general inertness, and, therefore, non-toxicity in water. Some plastics are as clear as glass. A further property of plastic, especially relevant to the manufacture of aquarium hardware, is its ability to be moulded or extruded into one-piece tanks, buckets, cases, boxes, enormous sheets, tubes, pipes, cylinders, and fittings of intricate design. Many standard household and industrial items of plastic may be put to good use in the aquarium, either directly or after do-it-yourself adaptation—such as bowls, food containers, sieves, and trays.

Acrylic plastics, notably Plexiglass and Perspex, are used increasingly as substitutes for glass. They are strong and can be moulded into any shape. They may be coloured, translucent, or of very good optical transparency. Many modern public aquaria are glazed with acrylic sheet: huge tank windows, 20 m (66 ft) or more in length and over 5 m (17 ft) high, are employed in several countries. Small aquarium tanks, mostly up to about 60 litres (15 gallons), are mass-produced by vacuum-moulding acrylic in one piece. These fully transparent tanks are lightweight, sterile, and cheap enough to be "semi-disposable". But due to lack of rigidity, they are limited in size and must be well supported. Certain acrylics are slightly less

Making a GRP tank. Firstly, the mould is made. The bottom of the mould should be somewhat less in area than the top, so that the mould can be removed more easily from the tank when the polyester has hardened. The mould's surface must be perfectly smooth, so all nails and screws must be countersunk, and the holes filled and sanded.

1 The mould is painted with the releasing agent.

2 Suitable lengths of GRP cloth are cut and fitted over the mould. The cloth is drenched with polyester resin and the resin is worked into it with a stiff brush *(a)* or a metal roller. No air bubbles should be left in the cloth. The various lengths of cloth are put on according to a pattern *(b, c)*.

3 When the resin has hardened, the mould is removed and holes are drilled at the corners of the planned window. A keyhole saw is used to cut out the window aperture, the edges of which are filed and sanded smooth.

4 The tank is turned on its side and a continuous string of silicone-rubber sealant is laid all around the inner edges of the aperture.

5 The tank is pulled half over the edge of the work bench and the window is inserted as indicated.

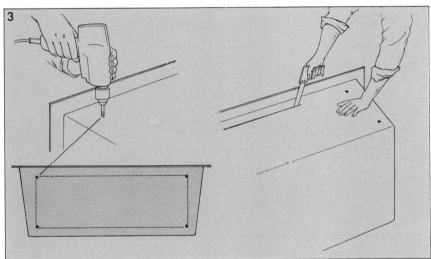

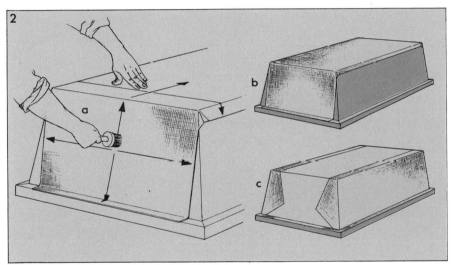

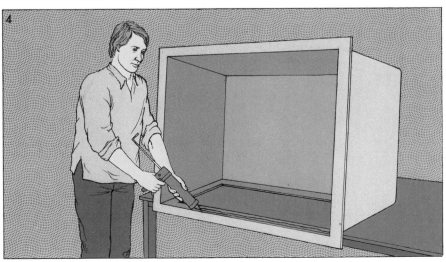

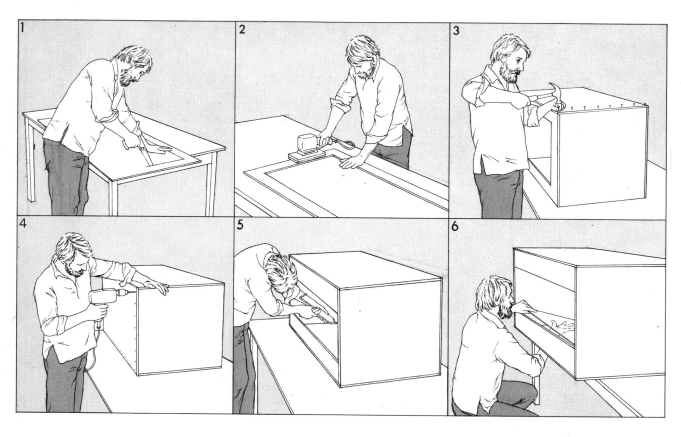

Building a wooden tank with one viewing window.

1 The window aperture is sawn from the front panel, leaving a margin of at least 7 cm (2.5 in) all round.

2 The sawn edges are sanded smooth.

3 The side, base, and rear panels are sawn, glued with waterproof wood adhesive, and pinned into position with panel pins. The sides are inset into the front and rear panels. The front and rear panels sit on the base.

4 When the glue is fully set, the pins are removed and holes are drilled every 10 cm (4 in) along the side and top of the front, base, and rear panels. Then, the tank is screwed together with brass screws. Holes for overflow, inflow, and air pipes are drilled, and the tank's inside is painted with two coats of varnish or pre-mixed resin and hardener.

5 When the second coat has dried, a bead of silicone-rubber sealant is run along the inside joins, and when that has hardened (after a day), a third coat is applied. This coat may be coloured, if desired.

6 Sealant is applied to the inside edges of the front panel and the glass is inserted.

7 Small battens are used to maintain uniform pressure on the glass while the sealant is hardening. If desired, a strip of veneer may be used to cover the screws. The detail shows how the base panel is screwed to the side panels and where the wood adhesive (a) and the silicone-rubber sealant (b) are applied.

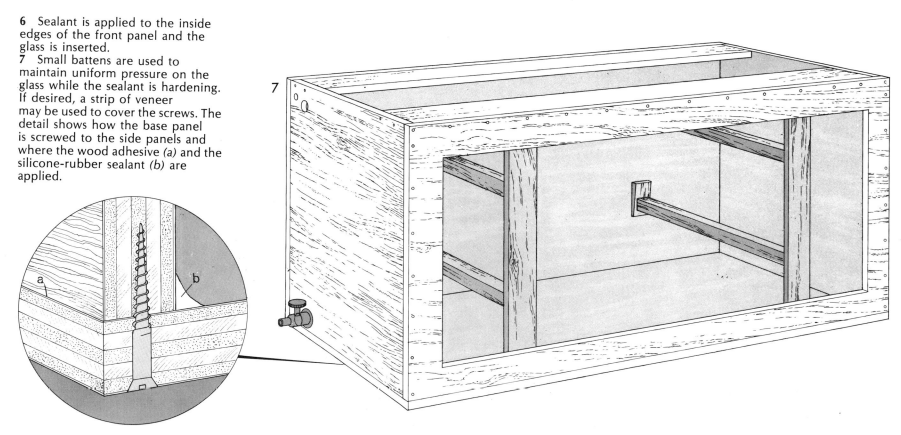

Using the methods shown on the opposite and previous pages, wood-and-glass tanks of all shapes may be designed to suit the aquarist's requirements. Here, for instance, is a wood-and-glass tank that has been designed for a right-angled corner. The sides against the wall, and the base, are wooden, whilst the other three sides are glass. A wooden flange is fitted round the top edges, base, and sides. The overhead view shows the top braces in position. The details show (a) the silicone-rubber sealant between the glass joins, and (b) how the flange is fitted to the base and how the sealant is laid between the base and the glass.

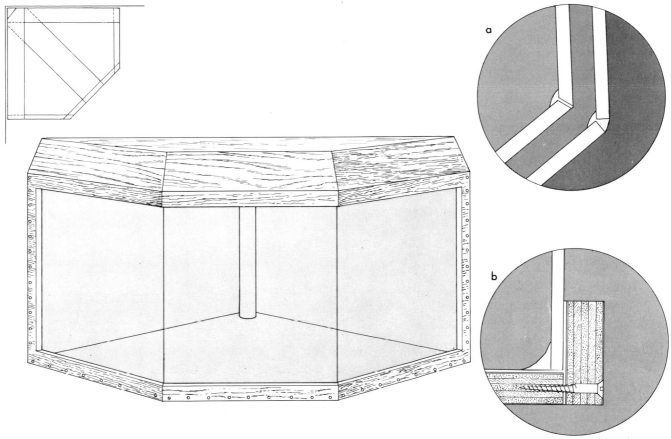

transparent than glass and, sometimes, "yellow" with age. Surfaces tend to be scratched more easily than glass, and algal films may be difficult to remove.

GRP: Glass-Fibre Reinforced Plastics

GRP combines the high strength of glass strands with the rigidity and other qualities of a set polymer. Its relatively low weight also makes it an excellent material for many structures. Its strength varies with the ratio of glass to plastic, the thickness, and the type of glass-fibre reinforcement employed—twisted lengths, woven cloth, or looser matting.

GRP is very simple to use: alternate coats of liquid polyester resin (with hardener added) and glass fibre are painted and laid onto a suitable mould. The mix is easy to manipulate in liquid form and is left to set hard without heat or pressure treatment. Given care, moderate dexterity, and access to the materials, all sorts of useful high-quality aquarium hardware can be made from GRP. It is best to begin by experimenting with a simple object, such as a trough for live food, before moving on to purpose-built display tanks, filter casings, hoods, plumbing, and imitation rockwork.

Fillers are inert powders for mixing with resin to increase its bulk, reinforce a solid shape, or give "through" colour. China clay, talc, mica, and surface-treated crystalline calcium carbonate are the usual fillers. Others include metal or vinyl powders or flakes for metallic or "opalescent" effects, and sawdust, which lends the set mix an

appearance of solid wood. Pigments may be added, normally only to the first (surface) layer of resin, the gel coat, to give colour to the GRP. Dyes are employed to colour resins in translucent or transparent mouldings and castings. The use of colour is particularly important to the aquarist wishing to create an attractive and realistic decoration or tank lining.

Making a GRP tank

Virtually any size and shape of tank can be made in GRP. The important point is to increase the thickness of walls, base, and stiffening flanges, when increasing the volume. Unsupported rims are particularly vulnerable, and top braces or reinforced lips should be built in. The finished tank has the advantages of lightness, transportability, simple installation of plumbing, and ease of repair.

The first step is to prepare a form to serve as a mould. A male mould is used to make a smooth internal surface. The outside will be slightly rough. Plywood is a suitable material. The following materials are required to build a tank of 900 litres (200 gallons), as shown on page 153.

Glass-fibre cloth: 1 roll, about 17 m × 10 cm (56 ft × 4 in).

Chopped-strand glass-fibre matting: 1 roll, about 20 m × 90 cm (66 × 3 ft).

Polyester resin: about 12 kg (26 lb). The amount of resin equals 2.5 times the total weight of matting, which is about 5 kg (11 lb) in the present example. This uses three layers, each of 5 grams per square decimetre (1.5 oz per square foot). Such a weight of matting per unit area indicates the thickness of the GRP.

Catalyst hardener.

Releasing agent (special wax polish or cellulose acetate spray, to pre-coat the mould and prevent adhesion).

Roller.

Wooden Aquaria

Wood is a fine material for making strong, attractive aquarium tanks in numerous shapes. Large tanks up to about 2 m (6.6 ft) deep, and tanks for special purposes such as transporting live specimens, may be constructed with simple tools and skills. Wood is widely available, durable, non-contaminating, and a good insulator, having excellent resilience and strength in relation to weight. Wooden aquaria are easy to fit with inlets, outlets, internal dividers, and so on, and are readily repaired.

Care must be taken to ensure that wood for an aquarium is thoroughly seasoned and sealed, both inside and out, to minimize warping and shrinkage, and to prevent rot and attack by aquatic organisms. Plywood sheeting is one of the most useful forms of wood, consisting of an odd number of thin layers, each with its grain at right angles to those of adjacent layers. The sheet is glued together under pressure. For aquarium construction, a marine or exterior grade of plywood, with waterproof adhesive, should be employed.

Making a wooden tank

The following materials are required for plywood construction of a display tank of 400 litres (100 gallons), as illustrated on page 154.

Marine-grade plywood, thickness 2 cm ($\frac{4}{5}$ in):

base	1 of 120 × 55 cm (47.2 × 21.7 in)
front, back	2 of 120 × 58 cm (47.2 × 22.8 in)
ends	2 of 58 × 51 cm (22.8 × 20.1 in)
top braces	2 of 116 × 7 cm (45.7 × 2.8 in).

Float glass, thickness 6 mm ($\frac{1}{4}$ in):

window	1 of 115 × 55.5 cm (45.3 × 21.9 in)

Sealant, clear aquarium silicone: 2 cartridges, each 350 cc (12 oz).
Brass wood screws, 4 cm (1.5 in) long, with countersunk heads.
Wood adhesive, waterproof.
Panel pins, 4 cm (1.5 in) long.
Epoxy or polyester resin for tank waterproofing.

Concrete tanks

Limestone, clay, gypsum, iron ore, and shale are ground together and baked to make cement powder. Concrete is cement, sand, and gravel mixed with water. This wet mix sets into a rock-like aggregate. Concrete is durable, versatile, water-resistant, and non-toxic once matured. It can be reinforced with various materials. In aquarium tanks, a framework of wire-mesh or steel rods wired together into the required form is most common. Glass fibre and asbestos fibre are also used: the mix can be sprayed into moulds to make tanks with thin rigid walls and light weight.

Reinforced concrete tanks can be built in virtually any shape and size. A mould, usually of wooden shuttering, constructed around the reinforcing frame, is used to produce the surfaces of the tank, which can thus be perfectly smooth, or textured as required. Fresh concrete

The circulation is as follows. Nutrient-rich water is pumped from beneath the bottom filter through a pipe (c) in which a diffuser stone (d) is fitted, up into the plant filter unit. Circulation within the display tank is aided by two air-lift pumps (e), also with diffuser stones. The temperature is kept at an appropriate level by the heater (f).

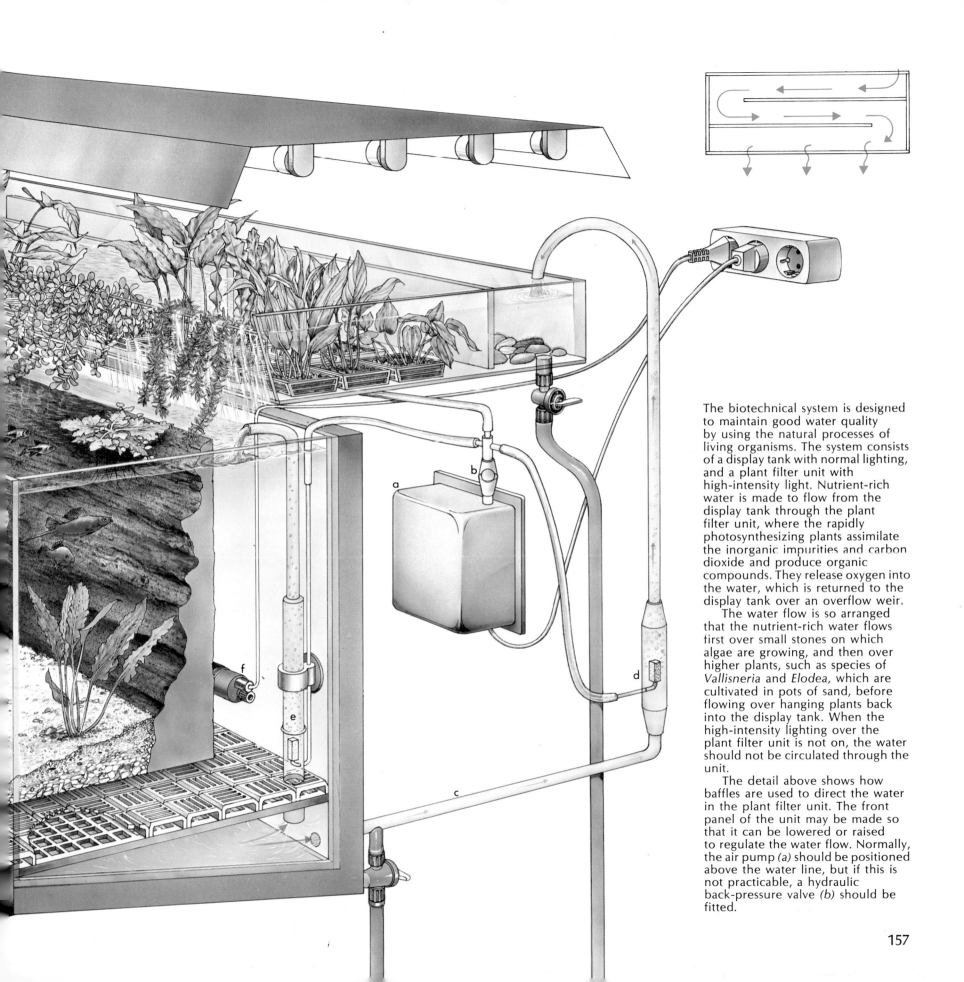

The biotechnical system is designed to maintain good water quality by using the natural processes of living organisms. The system consists of a display tank with normal lighting, and a plant filter unit with high-intensity light. Nutrient-rich water is made to flow from the display tank through the plant filter unit, where the rapidly photosynthesizing plants assimilate the inorganic impurities and carbon dioxide and produce organic compounds. They release oxygen into the water, which is returned to the display tank over an overflow weir.

The water flow is so arranged that the nutrient-rich water flows first over small stones on which algae are growing, and then over higher plants, such as species of *Vallisneria* and *Elodea,* which are cultivated in pots of sand, before flowing over hanging plants back into the display tank. When the high-intensity lighting over the plant filter unit is not on, the water should not be circulated through the unit.

The detail above shows how baffles are used to direct the water in the plant filter unit. The front panel of the unit may be made so that it can be lowered or raised to regulate the water flow. Normally, the air pump *(a)* should be positioned above the water line, but if this is not practicable, a hydraulic back-pressure valve *(b)* should be fitted.

The closed aquarium system is the basis of most small aquaria. An electric immersion heater (a) with thermostat regulates temperature. An air pump (b) draws water through the base filter (c) and the air-lift water pump (d), circulating and aerating the water. Diffuser stones (e) aid aeration. Illumination is provided by a fluorescent tube (f) in a reflector hood (g).

The low-technology system (opposite) uses natural lighting from, say, a window (a) and a skylight (b). A reflector (c) directs the light onto the surface (the aquarium cover is transparent). The tank has insulated walls and base, to reduce temperature fluctuations, which must be monitored carefully. The internal box filter (d) is powered by a small air-lift pump with a diffuser stone. An electric air pump provides air.

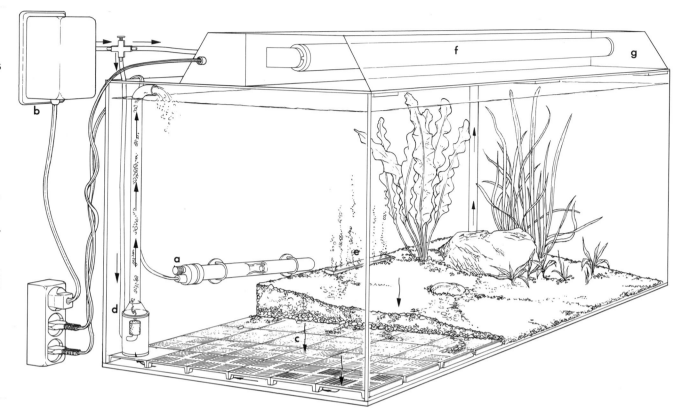

mix is poured into the mould and agitated briskly to remove air pockets, creating a good surface. Internal chambers and fittings, and suitable apertures for plumbed-in pipework, should be incorporated into the design and built into the mould. Concrete tanks which are to be glazed must be formed with perfect faces to the rebate, and this should be ensured when constructing the mould. But possible disadvantages are the relative thickness of concrete walls and window mullions, and the weight and immobility of the resultant tank.

It is advisable to coat a concrete tank with a waterproof material, such as the linings to be described below. This is particularly important on the inner faces of salt-water tanks, to prevent corrosion of the reinforcing steel and ensure maximum longevity for the tank. If not lined or otherwise sealed, the concrete tank must be treated prior to being used for aquatic organisms. Alkaline chemicals, which would otherwise leach into the aquarium water, must be dissolved out. The tank should be filled with fresh water and sufficient acetic, hydrochloric, or phosphoric acid to barely turn blue litmus paper red. If the litmus turns blue after twenty-four hours, more acid should be added, and any salt precipitate removed. The process should continue until the solution remains slightly acidic.

Steel tanks
Many kinds of steel drums, tins, and water tanks for industrial and domestic use are available in most parts of the world and can be converted into aquaria. Rusting is the main problem and must be prevented if the tank is to have a reasonable life. Accelerated rusting in salt water makes steel unsuitable for any marine or brackish-water aquarium.

For a freshwater aquarium, the steel tank or drum should be chosen carefully and cleaned thoroughly. A tank side or drum end can be cut out, ensuring that there is a minimum of 5 cm (2 in) surround, which is perfectly flat and smooth for glazing. After the glazing sealant has set, the container should be painted inside and out, preferably with epoxy resin, and left to cure before being checked for any leaks.

Tank linings
The many materials which may be used to construct strong forms for aquarium tanks do not always produce suitable internal surfaces. Important considerations include the surface's imperviousness to water and solutes, non-toxicity, resistance to damage by the aquarium occupants and by management operations, compatibility with the envisaged décor, colour, reflectivity, texture, and ease of cleaning, and the maintenance of these properties as the tank ages.

Of the materials described in this chapter, concrete, wood, asbestos, and steel may need to be lined. Suitable linings are rigid tiles of glass, stone (such as slate), ceramic, or flexible sheets of rubber or plastic material. These must be cemented onto the supporting tank form, as a thin "tank within a tank".

The lining must be strong enough to resist the water pressure, or plastic enough to "give" and retain integrity. There should be no large air pockets between the lining and the internal edge of the viewing panels. It may be better to line the rebate (in which case the perfect finish for glazing must not be spoiled), or to extend the lining onto the inside of the glass, or both. The choice depends upon the materials used, the effectiveness of bonding, and the order of steps followed in tank construction.

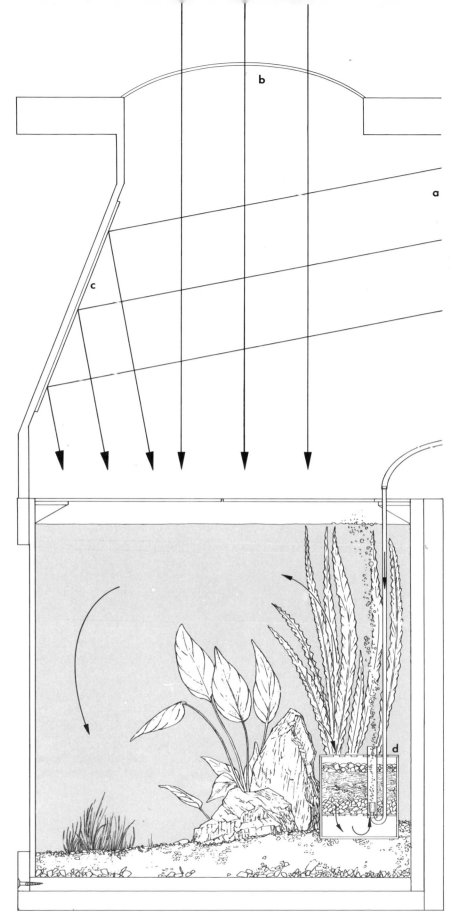

Aquarium systems

The health of the aquarium community demands maintenance of a proper environment. In any aquarium, conditions are subject to continual change: cooling and heating alter the water temperature; evaporation, dissolution, deposition, and adsorption alter the concentrations of both dissolved materials and suspended particles. In addition to these abiotic processes, the living inhabitants, through respiration, photosynthesis, food consumption, absorption, excretion, and secretion, are constantly introducing new substances to the water and removing others.

In the small and relatively self-contained volume of the aquarium, balanced conditions have to be ensured by counteracting the effects of such processes. The requirements of the organisms must be supplied and replenished, while accumulations of undesirable materials should be eliminated. For the long-term management of all aquaria, creation of a healthy environment and community depends upon artificial control of the changes which are taking place.

The illuminated display tank is the central unit and is connected to an integrated water-treatment system. Water treatment means circulation, aeration, temperature regulation, and purification. Items of hardware—such as pumps, heaters, and filters—govern these operations. The individual components are available in a wide range of types and sizes. Details of their construction and basic theory are discussed in the following sections. Aquarium systems built up from these components obey the same principles but vary in scale, cost, and technological complexity. A selection of different systems is illustrated.

Moving air and water

Many vital processes in the aquarium depend upon moving air and water. Water circulation is a particularly important aspect of the aquatic environment. It prevents local stagnation—the depletion of valuable substances and the accumulation of toxins. Exchanges of oxygen and carbon dioxide between the water and atmosphere are promoted when, for example, the water surface is agitated by air bubbles and turbulence. Practically all water-treatment methods involve movement of the water past an agent which can remove undesirable materials or replenish essential ones. This often calls for the use of a machine to pump air or water. Such machines are made in a wide range of types and sizes. The fundamental specification of a pump is its output, indicating the volume of fluid pumped per unit of time against a certain pressure.

Air pumps

Air pumps are helpful in every aquarium, both for introducing air into the water, and for mixing the water by turbulence which brings lower layers up to the surface. Certain types of pump, such as a rotary blower or turbine, push out large amounts of air, but only at low pressures: for instance, 25 cubic metres (883 cubic feet) per hour at 0.05 bar (or atmosphere). But a small sliding vane compressor may pump up to 1 bar and produce around 1 m³ (35 ft³) per hour of air, whilst a diaphragm pump may yield 0.5 m³ (18 ft³) per hour at 2 bars. A small piston air compressor may operate at over 5 bars, giving around 1.5 m³ (53 ft³) per hour of air.

In this order—from blower or turbine, sliding vane compressor, diaphragm pump, to piston air compressor—the tendency is towards

The high-technology system uses all the aquarium hardware necessary to maintain a healthy and attractive collection of, say, the type suggested for the coral-reef environment in Chapter 4. As coral reefs are brightly lit by sunshine for long periods, a high light intensity is required in the coral-reef aquarium, so the reflector hood (not shown here) should be fitted with both fluorescent tubes and spotlights. If the tank is big, a one-piece reflector hood and tank cover would be cumbersome and would make maintenance difficult, so a hood and cover that are sectioned are recommended.

The system shown consists of a long "peninsular" tank, with the two long sides made of glass. The machinery is left exposed, but it would normally be hidden in its own attractive box.

Beneath the tank is a return pipe (a), which carries the "used" water from the tank to the power filter (b). The filtered water is pumped down to the ultraviolet sterilization unit (c). From there, it is carried back to the tank through the foam-fractionation unit (d). The scum overflow from the foam-fractionation unit drains off into the drain pipe (e) beneath the tank. A large immersion heater (f) with a thermostat regulates the temperature and helps to keep the water circulating. An air-lift (g) is positioned so that its mouth is level with the water surface; this causes turbulence and circulation. (h) Drainage valve.

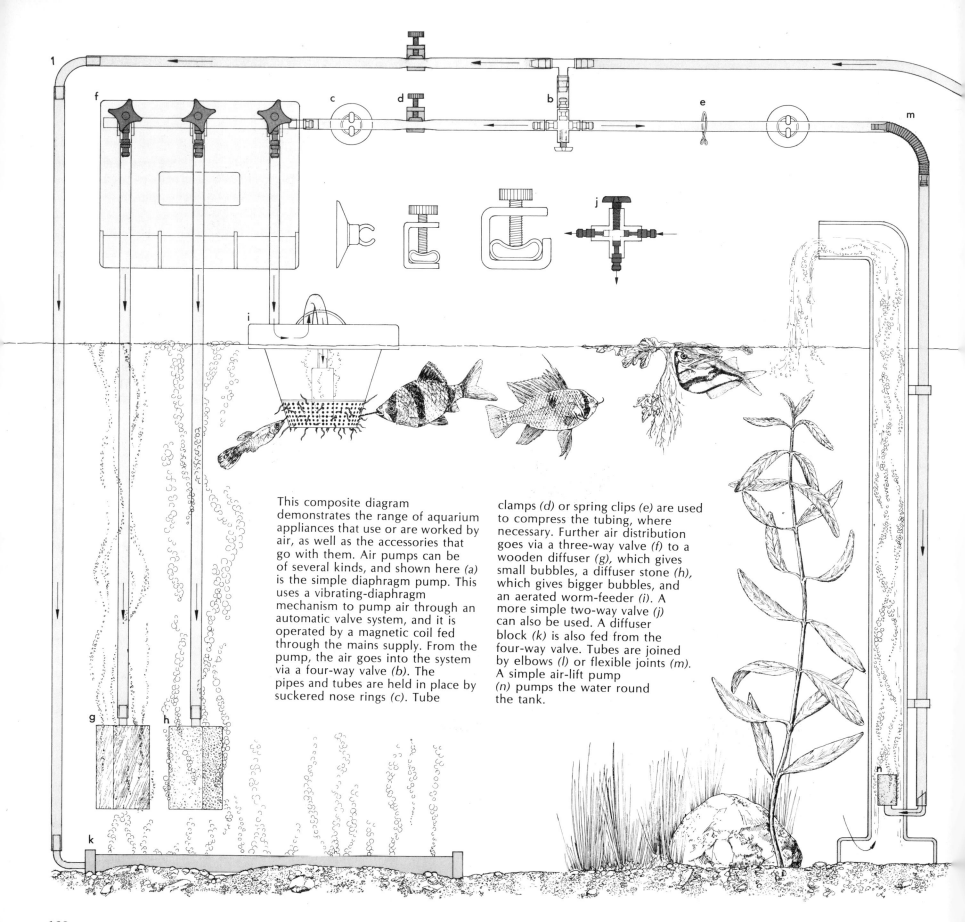

This composite diagram demonstrates the range of aquarium appliances that use or are worked by air, as well as the accessories that go with them. Air pumps can be of several kinds, and shown here (a) is the simple diaphragm pump. This uses a vibrating-diaphragm mechanism to pump air through an automatic valve system, and it is operated by a magnetic coil fed through the mains supply. From the pump, the air goes into the system via a four-way valve (b). The pipes and tubes are held in place by suckered nose rings (c). Tube clamps (d) or spring clips (e) are used to compress the tubing, where necessary. Further air distribution goes via a three-way valve (f) to a wooden diffuser (g), which gives small bubbles, a diffuser stone (h), which gives bigger bubbles, and an aerated worm-feeder (i). A more simple two-way valve (j) can also be used. A diffuser block (k) is also fed from the four-way valve. Tubes are joined by elbows (l) or flexible joints (m). A simple air-lift pump (n) pumps the water round the tank.

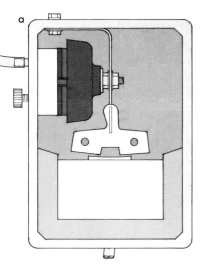

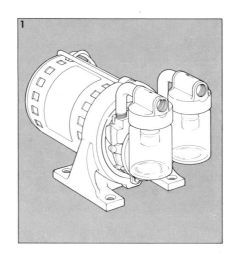

The diaphragm pump is suitable for most small to medium systems. For bigger systems with deep tanks, or with many tanks, the rotary vane pump (1) is suitable, as is the piston pump, the principle of which is shown here (2). At left is the down-stroke. Air in the lower chamber is pressed into the upper. At right,

the up-stroke pushes the air up and out through the system, while the valve at the end of the lower chamber is opened to admit more air.

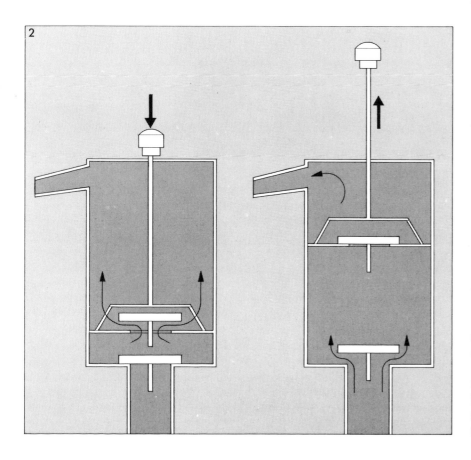

higher pressure capabilities. For each type of machine there are various models to suit every size of installation. A selection of these is illustrated.

Water pumps

Numerous mechanical water pumps are also available, the most common being small centrifugal pumps. But pumped air is used to power the water pump of widest currency: the air-lift. This type has several advantages—it has no moving parts, requires no lubrication, is simple to make and use, and provides aeration while it moves the water. Its principles are as follows.

Air, forced into a depth of water and released, rises quickly to the surface, dragging water upwards. An air-lift pump contains the air—water mixture in a tube, open-ended and partially submerged, which directs the flow. The mixture is less dense than water and will rise in the tube to above the water surface. From there the water can be allowed to gush out across the tank, or be channelled into another vessel.

Up to a certain point, water flow increases with the air input. When more than about ten per cent of the riser tube's volume is air, the pump spurts and flows unevenly, and the water-flow rate does not increase. But for a constant air input, water flow can be enhanced by increasing the submerged portion of the lift pipe. Ten to fifteen per cent of emergence is generally effective. Thus, in order to raise water at a reasonable rate to 20 cm (8 in) above the tank-water level, the riser pipe would have to be submerged to a depth of 150 to 200 cm (60 to 80 in), whilst in a tank of 50 cm (20 in) depth an air-lift could raise water by only about 5 cm (2 in) above it.

In an aquarium system, air-lift pumps are of great value; many aquaria operate with no other means of moving water. A central source can pump air at low pressure in large volumes, cheaply and efficiently, through a simple distribution network, to activate several appliances. Such steady and moderate circulation is essential to many kinds of water treatment and is suitable for diverse living organisms—plants, filter-feeders, and detritus-feeders, for example. Base-gravel filters, slow box filters, vacuum cleaners, foam-fractionation units, and other devices may be operated by means of air-lift pumps.

Connecting and siting a pump

From the pump, air or water is usually fed along a distribution system of pipes, bends, and valves to one or more appliances. In large systems, the frictional losses can be considerable, and these connections will increase the back-pressure. The nature of the lining, and the speed of flow, are especially important. In general, pipe bores should be as large as possible and smoothly lined; pipe lengths and bend angles should be minimized. The pressure reaching the appliance must be sufficient to make it work, and even a small air-diffuser will exert an appreciable back-pressure. In addition, the pump must be able to overcome the pressure of the depth of water into which it is pumping. Thus, pumps should be obtained with attention to the particular pipework, appliances, output rates, and tank depths employed.

The various outlets and devices must also be balanced in terms of their back-pressures. This is crucial in air systems. For example, two identical air-diffusers will receive different amounts of air from the same pump if they are fed by different lengths of piping. Similarly, an appliance requiring high pressure to operate will receive no air if it is

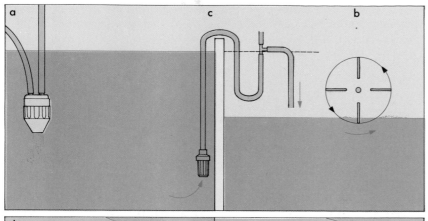

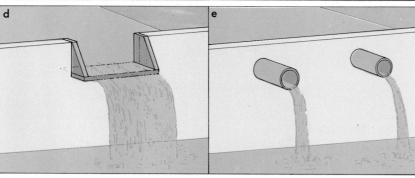

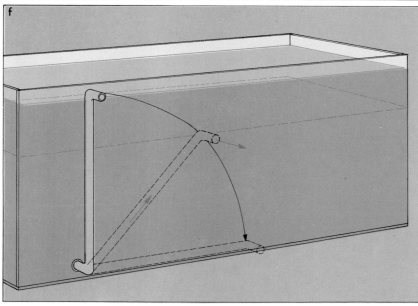

Methods of moving water and increasing its contact with the air are shown on this page. They serve especially for aeration, to replenish the oxygen in the aquarium solution. Examples are (a) injection of air with water, (b) surface agitation by a paddle-wheel (turned by a small electric motor), and flow of water to a lower level through (c) a siphon and cascade, (d) a shallow weir, or (e) a pipe overflow. An adjustable overflow (f) releases water when the level rises to its mouth, and can be used to drain the tank, being fed through a swivel joint near the base of the tank wall. A rotary pump (g) is most helpful when supplying air to several low-pressure appliances. It blows air out through a sound muffler, and can produce over 100 cubic metres per hour (or 1 cubic foot per second), giving less than $\frac{1}{4}$ of atmospheric pressure, and needing up to 1 kilowatt of electrical power. Such a pump can force air into water at a fair depth, since only about $\frac{1}{10}$ of atmospheric pressure is needed for each 100 cm (40 in) of depth.

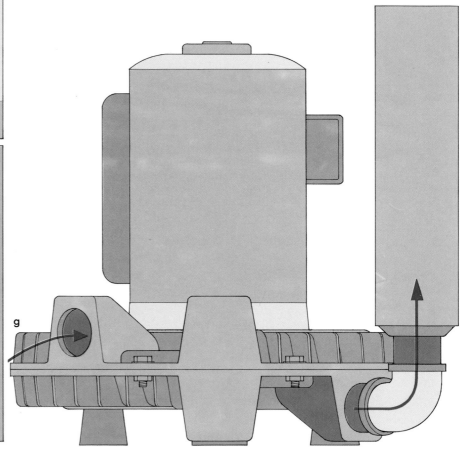

When an air-lift pump is used to move and aerate the water in an aquarium, it is important to know the rate at which the mixture of air bubbles and water will flow through the pump's lift pipe, or riser tube. This rate depends on the lift pipe's length, diameter, depth of submergence, and air input. The graphs at right show this rate (measured on the vertical axes in units of a litre, or about $\frac{1}{4}$ gallon, per minute) when the air input is adjusted to maximize it, as stated in the text. In the upper graph, the rate varies with pipe length (measured on the horizontal axis in centimetres) for four different diameters of pipe (equal to 0.4, 0.8, 1.2, and 1.6 in), and in each case for three different degrees of submergence (80, 90, and 100 per cent of the pipe length). In the lower graph, the rate varies with pipe diameter over a greater range (on the horizontal axis) for four different lengths of pipe (equal to 12, 20, 30, and 39 in), each having a different percentage of submergence. Further values can be estimated: for example, a pipe 100 cm long, 4 cm wide, and 85 percent underwater, yields about 58 litres per minute (1 quart per second).

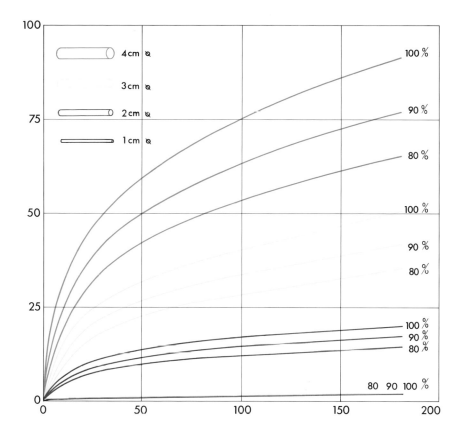

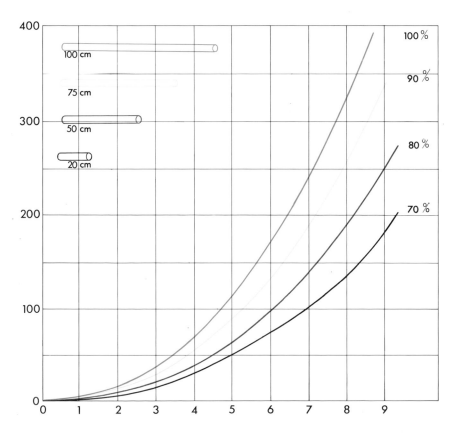

placed in line with a low-pressure unit. The pressure in the pipework must then be increased by placing a restrictive valve before the low-pressure outlet. The system of valves needed to distribute air evenly throughout a network will have to be checked regularly, as the back-pressure of the appliances may change with time—for instance, when stones in an air-diffuser become clogged with age.

Water and air pumps can be noisy devices. Large units should be firmly mounted on a solid base through a soundproofing material such as rubber. Small units can sometimes be suspended to avoid transmitting vibrations. The pumps must be sited carefully with respect to both the aquarium and the viewing areas, so that neither animals nor audience are disturbed.

Some air pumps reverse when they are switched off. Others do not actively suck water back, but water is drawn up from the aquarium when the air in the piping cools and contracts. If the air pump is situated below the water level in the tank, water may be siphoned over, flooding the pump and the floor. The pump should be sited above the level of the water in the tank. If this is impossible, or if a good safety measure is desired, a one-way valve can be fitted into the piping. Water pumps which are not self-priming are best situated below the water level in the tank, for easier restarting.

Water circulation systems

In most aquaria of moderate size, the water is circulated in a continuous cycle and forms a closed system, as in the examples illustrated. But in an open system, new water is run through the tank to become waste, at a rate which maintains the chemical quality of the solution. Thus, materials produced in the aquarium are simply flushed out, while those used up are replenished. Turnover rates of between twenty-five and one hundred per cent each hour may be employed.

An open system may require pre-treatment between the water source and the aquarium, to ensure that the influent water is of suitable temperature, clarity, and dissolved oxygen concentrations, and to control the entry of disease or predatory organisms. Incoming organisms may also settle in the system's pipework and reservoirs, to constitute a biological fouling problem. Yet these mainly planktonic organisms are a source of live food in the aquarium itself.

Any open system needs a reliable source of good water. There may be difficulties over the right to extract large quantities of water from a natural source. Another major factor in the design and operation of most open systems is the raising of water to a useful level. The water should be pumped only once if possible—from the source to a raised reservoir or feeder tank—from where it can flow through the aquarium display under the influence of gravity. Treatment inside the tank is usually limited to aerating and circulating the water before it overflows and runs to waste. Further problems may arise, particularly inland and with densely stocked systems, over allowing the aquarium effluent to run into a natural water body, without appropriate pollution control.

Mechanical aeration processes

Aeration serves primarily to replenish the dissolved oxygen in the aquarium water. It depends upon increasing the contact between the water and the air, as stressed in Chapter 4. The proportion of water-surface area to volume is very important but cannot be directly changed, and, in many aquaria, it is fairly limited. Consequently, the

Good insulation slows down heat transfer in either direction and reduces energy costs somewhat. An aquarium loses heat through the water surface, windows, walls, base and outside piping and equipment (such as an external filter). Tank covers should fit closely, as evaporative heat loss can be high. All pipes to and from external treatment units should be lagged (a), and the walls should be insulated with polystyrene or cork (b). Double glazing is essential in such a system, and hermetically sealed panes can be bought to size. The detail (c) shows how the aquarist can install his own double glazing and insulation. The front pane (d) is put in as on page 154, except that it is sealed to a ledge (e) made of a wooden lath. The inner base (f) has been screwed to the lath and the outside wall, and the second pane (g) is sealed to the inner base and the lath. The tank's outer base (h) is now screwed to the front, rear, and side walls, with the base insulation (i) inserted in between the two bases. The two panes of glass must be sealed at the top, and the detail (j) shows a well-fitting glass strip sealed to the tops of the panes. The sides and back of the aquarium must be sealed at the top, to prevent condensation getting into the insulation. The detail (k) shows the sealing operation, with a resin-and-hardener mixture being used.

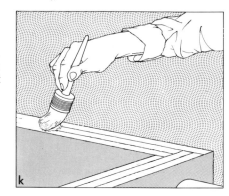

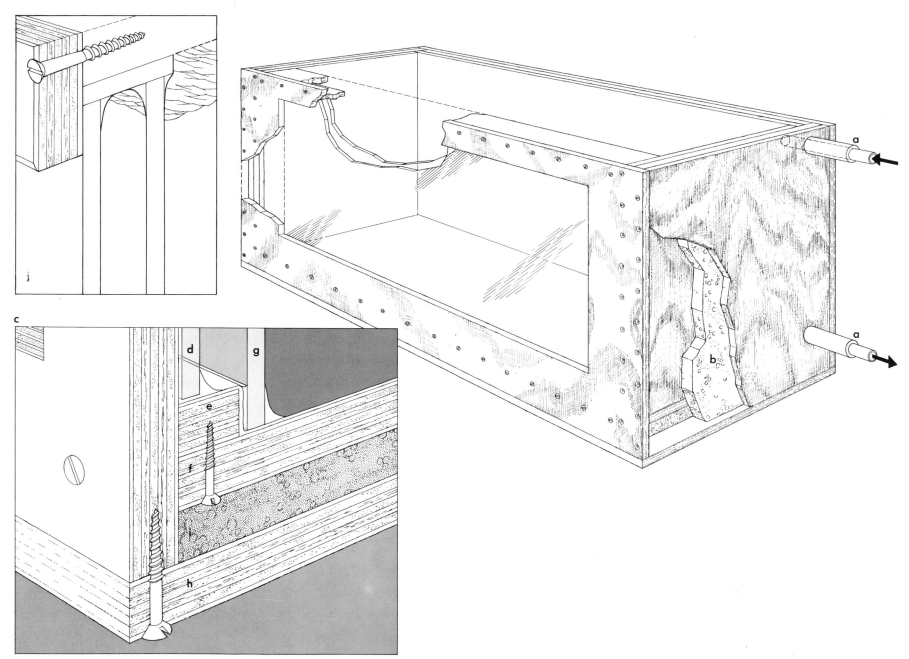

chief management operation is to increase the effective area of the air–water interface by promoting surface agitation and water turbulence. This may be done in various ways, as with the aquaria illustrated: a waterfall cascade, a shallow weir, streams of air bubbles, generation of waves, an air-lift pump, a foam-fractionation unit, or water–air injection.

Temperature regulation

Two aspects of temperature control in an aquarium are vital. The water temperature must be maintained within the optimum range of the particular captive community, and any change in temperature within this range must take place as slowly as possible. When ambient air temperatures fluctuate widely or are very different from the required water temperature, some form of heating or cooling must be employed, together with efficient insulation and a sensitive temperature-regulation system, to minimize short-term fluctuations. These principles apply primarily to closed, recycling water systems, but also to open systems when the temperature of the source water differs from the required aquarium temperature.

Heat and insulation

By maintaining a suitable temperature in the room housing the aquarium, the need to heat or cool the aquarium itself is lessened. Rooms and buildings should be insulated, draughts excluded or utilized to retain or disperse heat, and so on: this is basic energy conservation. A similar concept is seen in an intensive aquaculture unit, where human comfort is subordinated to efficient temperature regulation. Thus, it is possible to maintain large numbers of separate tanks at any constant temperature, by housing them in an insulated, centrally heated or cooled, room or building.

When the room's air temperature is lower or higher, or more variable, than the specified aquarium temperature, it is important to insulate the tank. Good insulation slows down heat transfer in either direction, reducing fluctuations in water temperature. Energy costs, and wear on heaters or coolers, are cut down. In addition, the tank is safeguarded against a possible failure of temperature-regulation machinery or power.

Evaporative heat loss can be very high and should be minimized by covering the entire tank top. Double glazing can reduce loss through tank windows by about 40 per cent, with an optimum width between panes of 12 to 20 mm ($\frac{1}{2}$ to $\frac{4}{5}$ in). Unglazed tank walls may be insulated with cork, expanded plastic foam, wood, or glass wool, on the outside: absorbent materials must not get wet by splashing. All components of a water-circulation system should be insulated—filter units, pipework, reservoirs.

Heating and cooling requirements

Heating or cooling is needed to balance the heat lost from, or gained by, the aquarium. If ambient temperatures were entirely suitable for the aquarium community, or if insulation could be completely effective, heating or cooling could be avoided once the specified temperature had been reached. But in practice, an aquarium loses or gains heat through the water surface, windows, walls, and base, in proportion to the surface areas and materials, to the temperature gradient between water and air, and to the degree of water-surface agitation and of air flow around the tank.

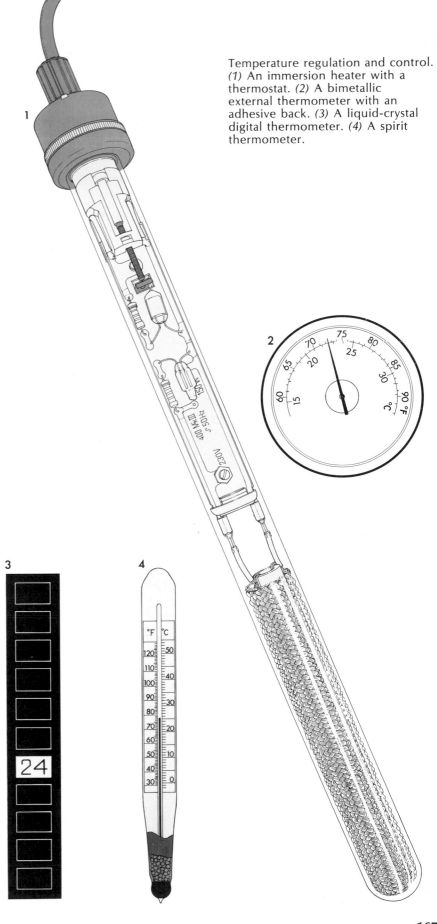

Temperature regulation and control. (1) An immersion heater with a thermostat. (2) A bimetallic external thermometer with an adhesive back. (3) A liquid-crystal digital thermometer. (4) A spirit thermometer.

1 How the bimetallic thermostat works. The bimetallic strip (a) curves out when heated above the pre-set temperature, thus breaking the circuit and turning off the heater (b). The dotted line shows the strip's position when the heater is on. The temperature required is pre-set by means of a screw adjustment (c).

2 Detail of a thermostat heater for heating water in an external filter, before the water is returned to the display tank.
3 The immersion heater (a) should be placed lengthways at the back of the tank and close to the bottom, where the circulation is good and will distribute the heat efficiently. The separate thermostat (b) is placed away from the heater so that it is not affected by direct heat from the heater. A thermometer (c) provides the possibility of checking the efficiency of the heater and the thermostat.

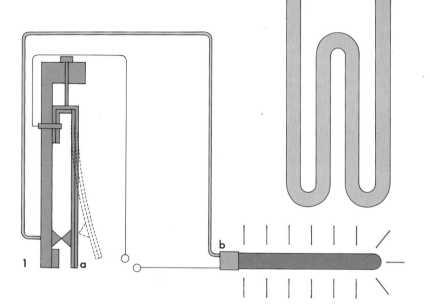

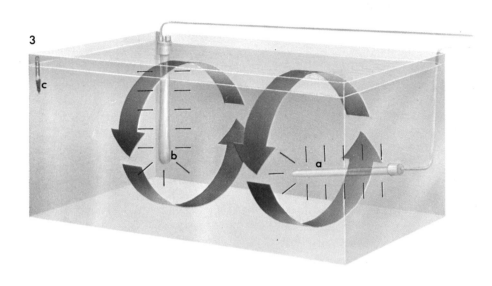

A simple calculation can be made of the power of a heater or cooler which would suffice for a particular aquarium. It is based upon the following equation:

heat required = heat lost or gained = (sa$_1$ × htr$_1$ + sa$_2$ × htr$_2$ + sa$_3$ × htr$_3$ ...) × temperature difference;

sa$_{1,2,3}$... are the surface areas of the water, glass windows, walls, and base;

htr$_{1,2,3}$... are the heat transfer rates through these surfaces.

Heat transfer rates may be expressed in watts per square centimetre per degree Centigrade (and multiplied by $\frac{1}{746}$ for horsepower, 6.5 for square inch, or 0.56 for degree Fahrenheit, as the units used). They are listed below for a variety of surface materials:

float glass, 4 mm ($\frac{1}{6}$ in) thick	6.5/10,000
double glass, with air space	4/10,000
plywood 2 cm ($\frac{4}{5}$ in) thick, with resin coating	3.5/10,000
glass-reinforced plastic, 1 cm ($\frac{2}{5}$ in) thick	2/10,000
concrete, 10 cm (4 in) thick	3/10,000
water surface	9.5/10,000

These values have been modified for heat transfer through the material which is bounded on one side by moving air, and on the other side by moving water. If the tank base is insulated or is placed on a solid support, or if the sides are insulated with 1 cm ($\frac{2}{5}$ in) thickness of insulation (such as cork or expanded polystyrene), the values can be divided by three.

As an example, we may consider a tank of 380 litres (95 gallons), made of plywood 2 cm ($\frac{4}{5}$ in) thick, standing on a solid platform. Its inner dimensions (length × width × depth) are 115 × 60 × 60 cm (45.3 × 23.6 × 23.6 in), and the water is 55 cm (21.7 in) deep; a viewing window of 100 × 45 cm (39.4 × 17.7 in) is centred in the front side. The temperature is 20°C (68°F) in the air and will be maintained at 28°C (82°F) in the water. We obtain the following amounts:

Surface	Area	Rate
water	115 × 60	9.5/10,000
glass	100 × 45	6.5/10,000
plywood: back	115 × 55	3.5/10,000
ends	2 × (60 × 55)	3.5/10,000
front surround	(15 × 55) + (100 × 10)	3.5/10,000
plywood base on solid platform	115 × 60	1/10,000

Multiplying across, adding the results downward, and finally multiplying by the temperature difference of 8°C, we find that the heat input required to maintain the water temperature is 123 watts. In practice, the heater should supply about three times this amount, so that it is not made to work continually. Thus, in the example above, two heaters of 150 and 200 watts would be suitable.

Thermostats

A thermostat is a heat-sensitive switch, based usually on a bimetallic strip. At certain temperatures, the strip curves sufficiently to make or break (turn on or off) the electric circuit of a heater or cooler. Also available are thermostatically controlled valves, to control flow through a pipe. The aquarium thermostat must be fairly sensitive: it should not allow the water temperature to rise or fall by more than one degree Centigrade (1.8°F).

A wide choice of models is designed specifically for aquarium use, varying in capacity from 100 to 2,000 watts. Some operate totally or partially submerged; others are mounted externally, and the water temperature is sensed through the tank wall, or by a probe. Some have an adjustable temperature range, but others are pre-fixed. Many have a neon light indicating when the contact is closed. Several heaters of the same wattage connected in series, or heating for bases and spaces in a multiple-tank system, may be controlled by a single thermostat.

Immersion heaters

Immersion heaters for aquaria usually consist of an electrical heating element, such as a coil of nichrome wire, wound on a ceramic former, inside a sealed protective tube of heat-resistant glass or plastic, or of stainless steel or aluminium. A range of powers from 25 to 300 watts, and various sizes and designs, are widely available.

The fully submerged tube heats the surrounding water, which is moved away by convection or by normal tank-water currents. Long, thin models give better heat dispersion than short, stubby versions, but may be more fragile. To avoid overheating and burning out the element, immersion heaters must be switched on only when underwater. Some heaters of higher wattage are fitted with two elements, insuring against excessive drops in temperature if an element should fail.

Many models, combining a heater and thermostat, are neat and easy to install, with fewer wires than separate units. Tubular immersion heaters should be positioned at the back or sides of the tank, close to the bottom but above the base substrate—and in an area where water circulation is good, but where the likelihood of being knocked by either aquarist or occupants is low. They can be attached by suckers to the tank wall, but not in direct contact with it, and preferably in a horizontal plane for efficient heat dispersion. The heaters may be used in an external filter, header, or reservoir tank, rather than in the main aquarium. This removes unsightly wires from the display, and separates hot elements from inquisitive specimens.

As an alternative to the wall-mounted tubular heater, there are low-wattage immersion heating coils designed to be buried in or below the aquarium gravel floor. These units may be rigid or flexible, and sealed inside resin, plastic, or rubber.

Heat from lamps

Electric lamps produce heat as well as light. Incandescent bulbs generate two or three times as much heat as do fluorescent ones. Where water temperatures are being maintained above ambient level, it is sensible to make use of this by-product heat by integrating the aquarium lighting and heating systems. This can be done very efficiently, with appropriately waterproofed and earthed fittings, by immersing the lamps in the water. Where excessive heating occurs, it is necessary to reduce the numbers or power of any incandescent lamps, or to insulate the water from the hot air around the lamps with a cover or by raising the lamps away from the water surface.

Base heating

In another method, hot water or air, steam, or electric heating elements may be run in channels or pipes beneath the aquarium tank, to warm the air around the base and sides. This form of heating is adequate and most economical for multiple-tank systems where uniform tank temperatures, not much above ambient, are required. The only in-tank fittings are those for thermostatic feedback control. Low heat is

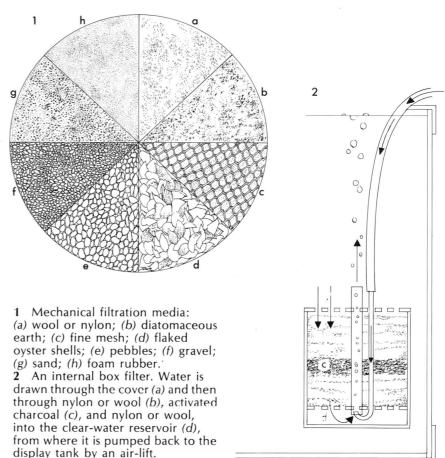

1 Mechanical filtration media: *(a)* wool or nylon; *(b)* diatomaceous earth; *(c)* fine mesh; *(d)* flaked oyster shells; *(e)* pebbles; *(f)* gravel; *(g)* sand; *(h)* foam rubber.
2 An internal box filter. Water is drawn through the cover *(a)* and then through nylon or wool *(b)*, activated charcoal *(c)*, and nylon or wool, into the clear-water reservoir *(d)*, from where it is pumped back to the display tank by an air-lift.
3 An external box filter. *(a)* Intake. *(b)* Base plate. *(c)* Filter. *(d)* Air-lift return. *(e)* Diffuser stone.

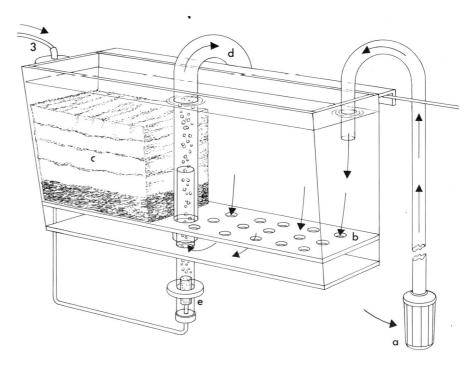

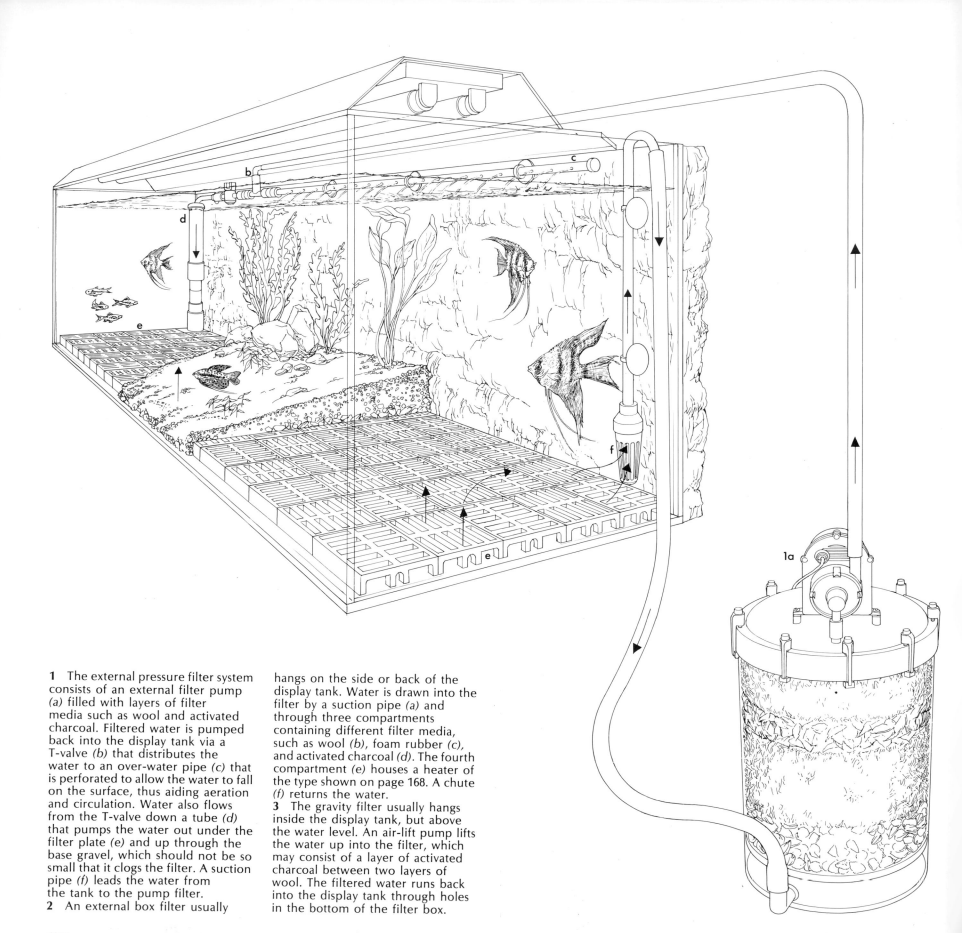

1 The external pressure filter system consists of an external filter pump (a) filled with layers of filter media such as wool and activated charcoal. Filtered water is pumped back into the display tank via a T-valve (b) that distributes the water to an over-water pipe (c) that is perforated to allow the water to fall on the surface, thus aiding aeration and circulation. Water also flows from the T-valve down a tube (d) that pumps the water out under the filter plate (e) and up through the base gravel, which should not be so small that it clogs the filter. A suction pipe (f) leads the water from the tank to the pump filter.

2 An external box filter usually hangs on the side or back of the display tank. Water is drawn into the filter by a suction pipe (a) and through three compartments containing different filter media, such as wool (b), foam rubber (c), and activated charcoal (d). The fourth compartment (e) houses a heater of the type shown on page 168. A chute (f) returns the water.

3 The gravity filter usually hangs inside the display tank, but above the water level. An air-lift pump lifts the water up into the filter, which may consist of a layer of activated charcoal between two layers of wool. The filtered water runs back into the display tank through holes in the bottom of the filter box.

applied, and temperature gradients are slight. The tank bases must be good conductors, and resistant to the heat: glass, steel, and slate are suitable materials. Any bottom gravel will impede heat transfer, unless a sub-gravel filter space is maintained. Water circulation throughout the tank and across the tank bottom must be efficient.

Exchange heating and cooling

In a heat exchanger, the aquarium water is brought into close contact with a second liquid, or with air, which has been heated or cooled. Coils or grids of pipework carrying the hot or cold fluid present a large surface for heat transfer and may be immersed directly into the aquarium—or somewhere else in the water circulation system, for instance in an external filter. Heat is transferred through the ducting walls to or from the aquarium water, with greatest efficiency when the water flow is rapid.

A wide range of fluid heaters or boilers is suitable for supplying the heat exchanger, in order to heat the aquarium. Solar heating panels can be connected to the exchanger, as an additional supply. This process is of particular relevance to a large system, with a central water circulation (closed or semi-closed) supplying sizeable or multiple tanks. A recent small-scale application of aquarium heat-exchanging is the use of the heat produced by an electrically powered apparatus, such as a water pump: the aquarium water is circulated through a pump-cooling jacket.

Most aquarium cooling involves heat-exchange apparatus. At a simple level, for occasional cooling of the water, a coil of plastic pipe is immersed in the aquarium, with one end connected to the main supply, and the other to a drain, while cold water is run through. In some coolers designed for small aquaria, the water is passed over a small evaporator unit. For larger systems, standard refrigerator or air-conditioner chillers can be adapted fairly easily, for plumbing into heat exchangers connected with the aquarium water circulation.

Most refrigerators and air-chiller units operate by successively compressing and evaporating fluid compounds called freons, in a circulating system. Compression raises the temperature and liquifies the freon. Reduction in pressure causes the liquid to evaporate, taking heat from the surrounding air or water. The evaporator side of the unit is expanded into coils to allow efficient heat transfer.

Water purification

Aquarium water-treatment systems usually include one or more kinds of filtration. This generally means the removal of undesirable matter as a filtrate, when the aquarium solution is passed through an appropriate substance or structure as the filter medium. The principal undesirables which have to be controlled are inorganic and organic particles in suspension, dissolved organic compounds, and dissolved nitrogenous waste products from living organisms. These can be removed from the aquarium by one or more of the main filtration processes: mechanical, biological (caused by bacteria or green plants), and physico-chemical.

Mechanical filtration

Particles are mechanically removed from suspension by straining the water through a mesh or bed of a suitable material. Mineral particles ranging from clay to sand, organic detritus, and living micro-organisms can be filtered out, using appropriate filter media and through-flow rates. Sands and gravels, diatomaceous earth, and synthetic matrices of

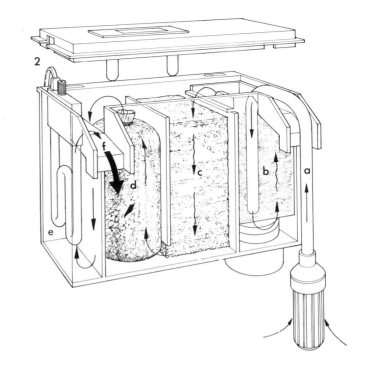

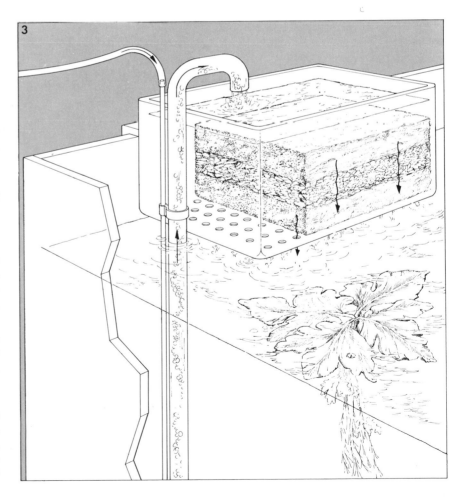

1 The principle of the ion exchanger, which is used to treat water from domestic sources or re-cycled water by exchanging its ions for ions of similar overall charge. Here, a cation exchanger (a) is coupled to an anion exchanger (b). The treated water contains virtually no biologically essential elements and should be mixed with water that has the necessary elements, or they should be added.

H^+ or Na^+
NH_4^+, Cu^+, Zn^+, Ca^+, or Mg^+
OH^- or Cl^-
NO_3^-, NO_2^-, PO_4^-, SO_4^-, or HCO_3^-

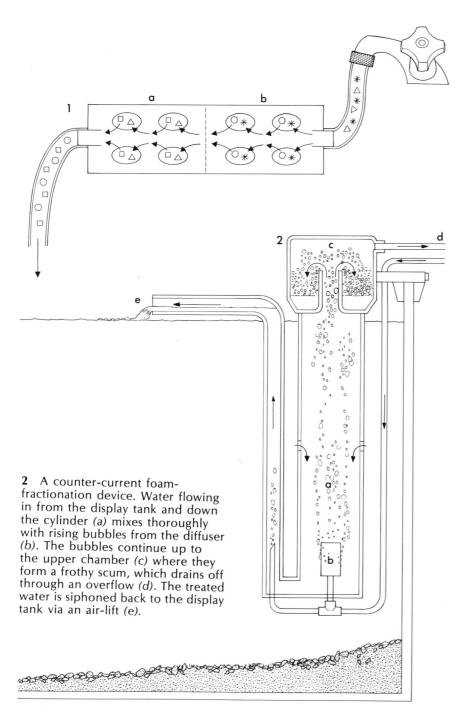

2 A counter-current foam-fractionation device. Water flowing in from the display tank and down the cylinder (a) mixes thoroughly with rising bubbles from the diffuser (b). The bubbles continue up to the upper chamber (c) where they form a frothy scum, which drains off through an overflow (d). The treated water is siphoned back to the display tank via an air-lift (e).

foam, wool, or plastic mesh are employed in aquarium mechanical filters.

Even packing of the material into the filter housing is very important, to ensure uniform density and resistance to water flow, and to avoid local stagnation. The size of pores through the filter medium increases with the coarseness of the medium. Filtering rates are high through coarse media, and in pressurized filters. Impurities are then carried far into the bed, and a deep bed must be used. To maintain high flow rates, periodic backwashing, or dismantling and cleaning of the entire bed, is essential.

Slow filtering rates occur where the medium is fine or the water pressure is low: in gravity filters, slow sand filters, base-gravel filters operated by air-lift, and trickle filters. In fine media, most of the filtrate is removed in the top few centimetres (one inch). A surface skin is created by the greatly reduced pore diameters and, with time, increasingly fine material is filtered out.

Particles which are even smaller than the pores through the filter, including colloidal material, can also be removed by a mechanical filter. This is due to complex interactions between the grains or meshes of a medium and the individual substances in suspension. Both physical and chemical processes may be involved, many of which are poorly understood, complicating the apparently simple picture of "mechanical" filtration. Moreover, an undisturbed mechanical filter will support a colony of bacteria on the surfaces of the medium, and will, therefore, filter biologically as well as mechanically. Whenever the medium is cleaned, a proportion of the bacteria is lost, so that a rapid or frequently washed filter will have little bacterial action.

Diatomaceous earth is used as a filter medium primarily when the water clarity must be kept high, or when bacteria in the water are to be minimized. Such earth consists of tiny aquatic plant fossils and is available commercially in various grades. Since its filtration is very fine, it serves only to treat water which is already fairly clean, as it clogs easily and cannot be reused. It may remove not only microscopic particles and parasites, but also useful nitrifying bacteria. To maintain its porosity, the filter should be pre-coated by circulating water through it, and be backwashed or renewed periodically.

Biological filtration

A biological filter removes or converts undesirable substances by the activity of living organisms. This is done by filtration through a bed of bacteria, or else through photosynthesizing plants.

Various species of live bacteria in the aquarium system will remove inorganic and organic materials from the water. A large and healthy colony of suitable bacteria is maintained, and the water to be treated is passed through the colony. A bed of any medium which provides a great area of surfaces on which the bacteria can grow, and which allows a reasonable rate of water through-flow, can be used. Thus, mechanical filters, and exhausted activated-carbon filters or ion-exchange resins, will become bacterial filters if the bacteria are given time to multiply, and if the water flow is suitable. Healthy bacteria are ensured in the same way as with the other aquarium occupants: by providing ample living space within the filter bed, supplying oxygen and regular food, diluting or removing wastes and toxins, and establishing proper temperatures, acidity, and salinity.

The bacterial processes by which substances are removed from the aquarium system, and others are added, are as follows. Excretion, secretion, and decay of organisms result in abundant particles of detritus, dissolved organic molecules (carbohydrate, protein, and fat fragments), and dissolved ammonia in the water. Special nitrifying bacteria obtain vital energy from the oxidation of ammonia to nitrites and thence to nitrates (see Chapter 4 on nitrification). Moreover, diverse heterotrophic bacteria absorb the organic matter as energy-rich food. This energy is released by respiration, with carbon dioxide and water as by-products, together with ammonia when the organic matter is proteinaceous (see Chapter 4 on ammonification).

These processes require a good supply of oxygen to the bacterial filter by aeration. Otherwise, the oxidation and respiration cannot continue. If conditions are allowed to stagnate with depletion of oxygen, many of the heterotrophic bacteria may instead use nitrate and sulphate to oxidize the organic matter. Sulphate is reduced to toxic hydrogen sulphide, while nitrate reduces to nitrite which is also toxic, and to molecular nitrogen which escapes into the atmosphere.

Plant filters

In light, plants assimilate inorganic compounds to form organic compounds—carbohydrates, proteins, and fats. This process of photosynthesis is the basis of the plant filter. A bed of algae or plants is grown under conditions which encourage maximum assimilation. Optimally high light and long day-lengths (about sixteen or more hours), and good water circulation to distribute nutrients and maximize uptake by the plant leaves, are maintained. Water depth is kept as shallow as possible to minimize light loss and maximize plant–water contact. The plants should be grown in small pockets of clean, coarse sand—or without any sediment, as is feasible with algae attached to stones.

The aquarium water is pumped through the bed. The influent from the display tank is high in carbon dioxide, ammonia, nitrate, and phosphate. These are taken up by the filter plants. Organic compounds and oxygen are produced, the oxygen is released into the water, and the plants grow. Periodic harvesting is necessary to maintain an optimum density. During periods of darkness, or if there is a power failure with no natural light, the aquarium water circulation should not pass through the plant filter, as no photosynthesis is taking place, and oxygen levels would fall and carbon dioxide increase through plant respiration.

Any attached plants capable of fast growth underwater are appropiate. Species will vary, of course, depending upon the salinity and temperature levels. In marine systems, species of green algae such as *Caulerpa, Ulva, Enteromorpha,* and *Cladophora* can be used. In fresh water, higher plant species such as *Elodea, Hygrophila, Ceratophyllum, Vallisneria,* and many others are permissible.

Physico-chemical filtration and fractionation

Certain substances, particularly organic molecules, are attracted out of solution onto a suitable water–air or water–solid interface. Both physical and chemical forces may be involved as a substance is adsorbed thus. This is the basis of physico-chemical treatment processes, which include filtration through activated carbon and ion-exchange resins, and foam fractionation.

Activated carbon

Activated carbon is used as a special filter medium, primarily to remove substances by adsorption. Its effect depends upon the highly porous nature of the activated-carbon structure, and the consequently great total surface area. One gram of activated carbon presents several hundred square metres of surface, providing an enormous expanse of water–solid interface. Such filtration will remove dissolved organic molecules, including acids from peat and protein breakdown, dyes, phenols, medicaments, and chlorine.

Grades of activated carbon differ in particle size, and in power and selectivity of adsorption. Wood and bone are the commonest sources; wood carbons are cheaper but have lower adsorptive powers. These are prepared by heating to redness in the absence of oxygen, and then activating the resultant charcoal by re-heating in oxygen to 900°C (1,652°F). Granules of diameter over 0.1 mm (0.004 in) and powders (less than 0.1 mm) are available, granules being more common, less likely to clog, and easier to handle.

A bed or column of activated carbon becomes "exhausted" after a time. This will occur progressively down the length of a column, until all available space is taken up by adsorbed materials. The time taken for a column in constant use to become exhausted depends upon the concentration of removable substances in the influent water and may be a matter of days or months. To test for exhaustion, a few drops of the dye "methylene blue" can be added to the influent. If the colour is not removed by the filter, the carbon should be re-activated. Re-activation entails baking at 500°C (932°F) in the absence of oxygen.

In a multi-stage aquarium water-treatment system, activated-carbon filtration should be preceded by mechanical and biological filtration, to remove the bulk of the suspended mineral and detrital matter. It should itself precede disinfection processes, as these are inefficient when dissolved organics are present.

Ion exchange

By a combination of absorbing into the structure and adsorbing onto the surface, various natural and synthetically prepared materials are able to remove ions from solution. They exchange these for ions of similar total electric charge, which are released from the exchange material into solution. Ion-exchange materials are often provided by natural zeolites and clays. But nowadays, most consist of an inert matrix of a polymer, such as polystyrene, onto which specific ion groups are loosely bound.

Cation or *acid-exchange resins* are charged with sodium (Na^+) or hydrogen (H^+) ions. They can be used in the aquarium to remove cations from the re-cycling solution, notably ammonium (NH_4^+) and metal ions (such as copper, Cu^+, and zinc, Zn^+) which are potentially toxic, and calcium (Ca^+) and magnesium (Mg^+) ions which are responsible for water hardness.

Anion-exchange resins are less widely used and studied. Specific kinds are available to remove nitrate (NO_3^-), nitrite (NO_2^-), phosphates (PO_4^-), sulphates (SO_4^-), and bicarbonates (HCO_3^-), in exchange for hydroxide (OH^-) or chloride (Cl^-) ions.

Highly specific resins can be prepared which will remove, for example, ammonium from sea water. But in general, ion exchanging is more applicable to freshwater systems, where there is less interference from non-target ions.

The resin is packed into a column (pre-packing in a cartridge is common) and plumbed in, either to the main water supply to obtain soft water for the aquarium, or to the aquarium circulation itself, following biological filtration to reduce the level of dissolved organics. Alternatively available are mats impregnated with exchange resins, which can be placed within a gravel filter bed. A resin becomes "exhausted" as exchange sites are used up or fouled by organic molecules. It may then be revitalized by treatment with a fairly concentrated solution of the ion that is depleted, for example hydrochloric or sulphuric acid to recharge the resin with H^+ ions, and sodium chloride or hydroxide to supply Na^+, Cl^-, or OH^-, depending upon the resin.

Foam fractionation

The surfaces of air bubbles in water attract dissolved molecules and suspended particles. Foam fractionation—also termed protein skimming, or air stripping—makes use of this fact. Rising bubbles are mixed thoroughly with the aquarium solution, preferably in a vertical cylinder with a downward current of water (the counter-current principle). As the bubbles burst at the water surface, any surface-adsorbed materials are left in an enriched film which forms a frothy scum. The froth is easily removed by an overflow.

This elegant process is particularly valuable in concentrating and removing organic molecules, including dyes and acids from humus or peat, plant-secreted proteins and lipids, and so on. Organic molecules are polarized: one end is attracted to water, and the other is repelled. The molecules "stick" at the interface between water and air. To make the process effective, the interface area is increased by injecting fine bubbles into the water. Finer bubbles increase the total surface area and, by slowing the speed of rising bubbles, increase the air–water contact time.

Foam fractionation removes other dissolved chemicals from the solution. Inorganic phosphates and metal ions, including Cu^+, Mg^{++}, Mn^{++}, and Ca^{++}, are attracted onto the organic molecules in solution and are removed with them in the froth. Particulate organic materials can be removed as well: fine particles of detritus, and even microscopic algal cells, accumulate at the air–water interface of bubbles and the tank surface. There, they coagulate as the bubbles burst, and either sink to the bottom or are removed with the froth.

Foam fractionation is especially useful in densely stocked closed systems, to keep dissolved organics at a reasonable level without frequent water changing. But there are possible problems in the process. It removes many medicaments and must, therefore, be halted during in-tank treatment. Moreover, very fine bubbles injected into the tank may cause gas-bubble disease.

Air filtration

It is equally important that air entering the aquarium be pure. Cigarette smoke, dust, noxious fumes, aerosols, and other pollutants may dissolve in the water and accumulate to levels dangerous to the inhabitants. Some types of pumps are lubricated with oil, another source of contamination.

Where contamination is suspected, an air filter should be used. Good-quality air pumps are fitted with small filters on both the inlet and outlet, to protect the pump as well as the aquarium contents. By bubbling the air through a wash bottle, many atmospheric pollutants are removed. Activated carbon removes oil vapour and other noxious gases or fumes. Silica gel and activated alumina are analogous filter media which remove water vapour.

Disinfection methods

Normally, an uncrowded aquarium, with adequate aeration and filtration, and with healthy livestock, does not require disinfection. However, under certain circumstances, it may be wise to include a disinfection stage in the water treatment: for example, when stocking densities are high, when infected specimens or water are introduced, or when intensive re-cycling or the occasional lapse in management leads to unhealthy conditions.

Disinfection kills bacteria, viruses, and other micro-organisms in the water. It may be particularly useful in systems for breeding, intensive culture, or delicate specimens. Common disinfection treatments for the aquarium include heat, ultraviolet irradiation, and ozonation. Each of these processes destroys living tissue, and rather unselectively. Suitable treatment can kill large percentages of any water-borne micro-organisms present. But one should note that a direct application of some treatments to tanks containing livestock may also kill or injure the aquarium specimens—and that all these processes kill useful bacteria, such as the nitrifiers, as well as potential pathogens.

Heat

When held at a high temperature for a suitable period, water is disinfected. Treatment of 60°C (140°F) for thirty minutes, or 70°C (158°F) for thirty seconds, will kill most bacteria, viruses, fungi, and protozoans. Heat treatment is suitable to sterilize small volumes of water, for use in quarantine tanks and for "topping up". The cost of heating is usually too high for large volumes to be treated economically in this way.

Ultraviolet irradiation

Ultraviolet light rays (UV), of wavelengths between 2,000 and 2,800 angstroms, destroy nucleic-acid molecules within cell nuclei, causing rapid death. Many bacteria, viruses, and other micro-organisms can be killed instantly by application of UV, making disinfection of water by UV a widespread treatment process in fish hatcheries and aquaculture units, as well as in aquaria.

Aquarium water can be UV-irradiated by suspending a UV-lamp over the tank itself, or by passing the water near a UV-lamp in an enclosed contact tube. The second method is preferable, being more efficient and easier to control. The effectiveness of disinfection by UV

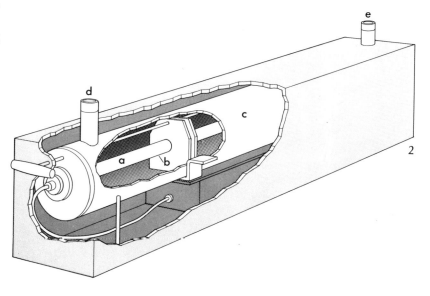

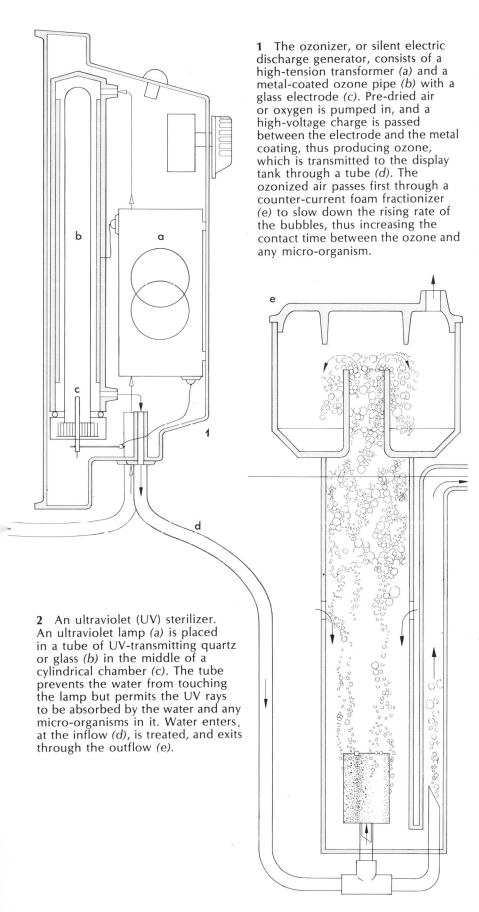

1 The ozonizer, or silent electric discharge generator, consists of a high-tension transformer (a) and a metal-coated ozone pipe (b) with a glass electrode (c). Pre-dried air or oxygen is pumped in, and a high-voltage charge is passed between the electrode and the metal coating, thus producing ozone, which is transmitted to the display tank through a tube (d). The ozonized air passes first through a counter-current foam fractionizer (e) to slow down the rising rate of the bubbles, thus increasing the contact time between the ozone and any micro-organism.

2 An ultraviolet (UV) sterilizer. An ultraviolet lamp (a) is placed in a tube of UV-transmitting quartz or glass (b) in the middle of a cylindrical chamber (c). The tube prevents the water from touching the lamp but permits the UV rays to be absorbed by the water and any micro-organisms in it. Water enters at the inflow (d), is treated, and exits through the outflow (e).

depends upon the turbidity of the water, the size of the target organism, the intensity of irradiation, and the contact time. UV penetration of water is reduced considerably by absorption in turbid, coloured (with organic acids) or, to a lesser extent, saline waters. Water must, therefore, be filtered before UV treatment, preferably by mechanical and biological means.

The intensity (or wattage) and duration of UV are multiplied to give the dosage. As a general rule, the minimum lethal dosage increases with the size of organism. However, some species and strains are more resistant than others. For example, using a wavelength of about 2,500 angstroms, the larger protozoa will be killed with a dosage equivalent to about one watt for one second. This amount can be divided by 10 for small protozoa and resistant fungi, by 70 for bacteria and other fungi, or by 300 for viruses. Once an adequate dosage is estimated, a suitable water-flow rate through a particular UV unit may be calculated. Since the unit emits UV at a specific intensity, variation of the flow rate increases or decreases the time for which each target organism is irradiated, and thus governs the total amount of UV it receives.

The effectiveness of direct irradiation of the display tank is limited by the poor penetration of the UV. Yet this ensures that the main concentration of "useful" bacteria—in the bottom sediments—is not irradiated and killed, and that the aquarium specimens receive only a moderate dose. There is some discussion today about damage and benefits from UV to "macroscopic" organisms, including the possibility of causing blindness in fishes and, on the other hand, of controlling skin parasites and cleansing abrasions or wounds where bacteria are prevalent.

Immersed UV units in constant use require cleaning, about once a month, to remove accumulations of mineral salts. The unit is disconnected and filled with dilute hydrochloric acid for an hour.

Ozone disinfection

Ozone is an unstable gas (O_3) and, in common with many disinfecting agents, is a powerful oxidizing agent. It is harmful to living organisms, including man. In the aquarium, small quantities, bubbled through the water, can be used to kill most micro-organisms in suspension. Ozone is toxic on contact, and disinfection increases with the concentration and contact time. The O_3 molecule dissociates readily back to oxygen (O_2), so the ozone must be generated when and where it is required.

For small aquarium systems, UV generators are most suitable: the UV splits O_2 molecules, and some of their atoms reform as O_3. When air passes over the UV-lamp, about half a gram ($\frac{1}{50}$ oz) of O_3 per hour is produced, at concentrations around 1 to 10 parts per million. For higher yields, up to five per cent of ozone, a silent electrical discharge generator can be used. In both cases, the feed gas (air or pure oxygen) must be thoroughly dried by pre-filtering and should be pre-cooled.

Contact time, between the ozonized air passed through the water and any suspended micro-organisms, may be increased by using baffle plates to slow the water flow, or a counter-current system and fine bubbling to slow the bubble rising rate. Ozone disinfection is less effective in water of high turbidity, or with high dissolved organics, as much of the oxidizing potential is spent on these impurities. For this reason, ozonation should be preceded in a water-treatment system by mechanical and biological or by physico-chemical filtration.

Aquarium lighting

The health of the living community and the visual impact of the display depend upon the maintenance of suitable illumination. Equally important are the quantity and quality of the light which reaches the absorbing and reflecting surfaces—leaves, skin, eyes, or the inanimate background.

Light quantity is a product of intensity and duration of the illumination. Intensity is reduced as the light passes through water: it is absorbed, mainly by mineral and detritus particles. This turbidity must be minimized by dilution and filtration. Light intensity may be increased artificially by the use of lamps and reflectors, as can the duration and timing of illumination.

Quality means the colour, or spectral composition (wavelengths), of the light. In addition to the effect of the light's colour upon the colouring of objects—an object's colour is the portion of incident light which is not absorbed but reflected—plant photosynthesis and animal vision (including that of humans) function most efficiently at certain wavelengths. The composition of the aquarium illumination may be controlled by using different types of lamps. Some slight modification occurs to both natural and artificial light, as it passes into and through the aquarium glass, plastic, and water: each filters out certain wavelengths more than others.

The conditions of illumination to which aquatic plants and animals are accustomed, and the lighting régimes to adopt for a selection of display aquarium communities, are discussed in Chapters 2, 3 and 4. The following sections cover the various types of lamps suitable for aquaria, and the choice of lighting systems.

Natural lighting

For many aquaria, it would be relatively simple to develop a lighting system which utilizes incident daylight. Such a system would direct the available natural light into the aquarium, through the water surface, at a correct angle. Reflective material can be used to focus the light and to screen the viewing area. The system is cheap to assemble and virtually free to operate, and provides light of spectral composition close to that of daylight. It would be adequate for most aquarium displays, and particularly for those of local flora and fauna.

Yet, the aquarist must beware of overheating in the summer and, in winter, might have to be content with a rather uninspiring display due to insufficient light. A natural lighting system is best used to supplement artificial sources. When ambient light is suitable, there is no need to burn electricity. But artificial illumination will ensure healthy growth all the year round, and a visually impressive display in any weather or time of night and day.

Artificial lighting

In order to satisfy the requirements of the captive plants and animals, most aquarium environments must be maintained under unusual régimes of light (and heat). With artificial electric lighting, the source is under complete control. Wavelengths, intensity, duration, and the distribution of light in the aquarium may all be altered to suit the particular specimens, and also enable a bright display to be created.

Choice of lamps

Two main types of lamps are available. An *incandescent* lamp is a bulb

Lamps for an aquarium must be selected with attention to their practical value as well as the quality of their light (which is shown on the opposite page). One may choose between an incandescent lamp with a tungsten filament of the *(F)* domestic or *(G)* halogen type, or a discharge lamp of the *(A–E)* fluorescent or *(H)* sodium-vapour type (of the last, a high-pressure version is illustrated). In this order, they tend to increase in cost, complexity of installation, size (varying from 3 to 250 cm, or 1 to 100 in, long), lifetime (500–8,000 hours), resistance to damage, efficacy of light production from electricity, coolness, and range of uses (notably in growing plants). They are available up to a power of at least 1,000 watts, except the fluorescent type (to 125 watts). Often a combination of different types is needed for maximum advantage.

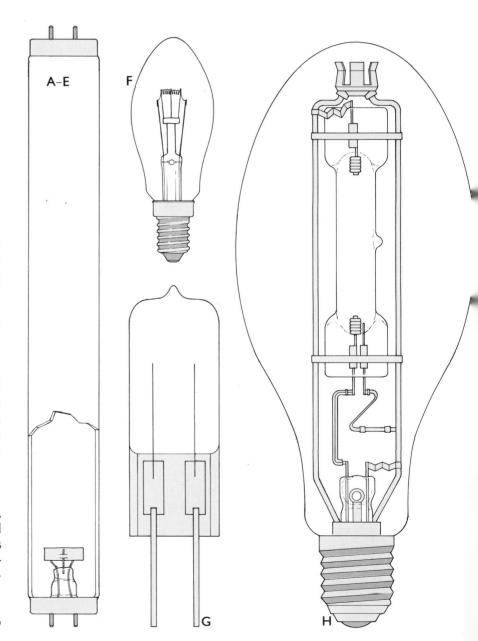

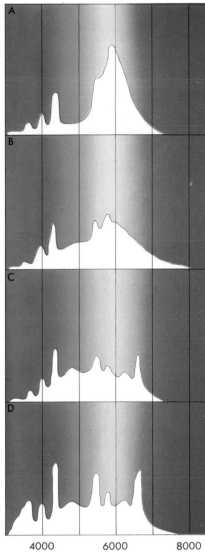

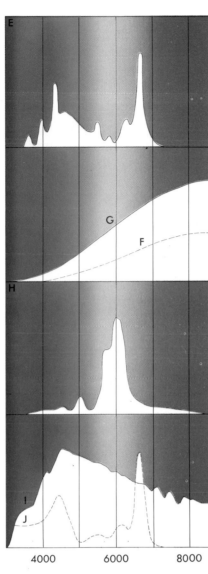

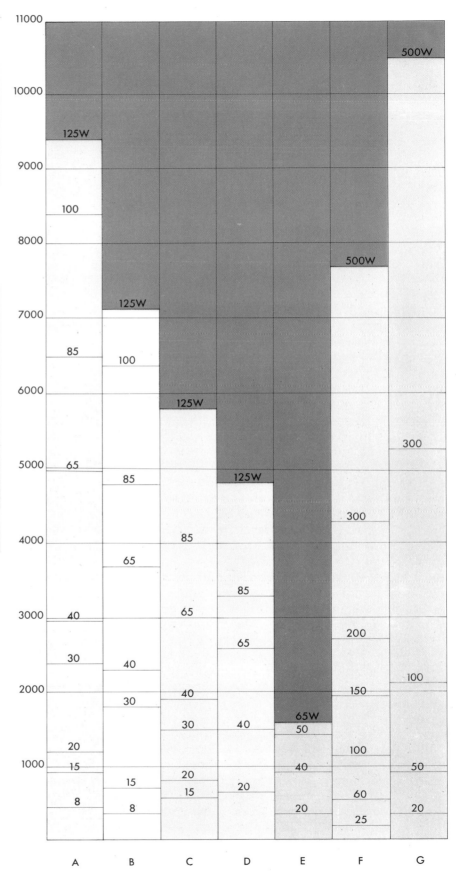

A lamp emits light of certain colours, or wavelengths, each with a definite proportion of its total power output, depending upon the material elements which produce the light. The resultant spectrum of emission is shown above for various kinds of lamp: the fluorescent (A) Warm White, (B) Natural, (C) Northlight, (D) Artificial Daylight, and (E) Grolux, the incandescent (F) domestic and (G) tungsten–halogen, and (H) the sodium-vapour high-pressure discharge. Graph (I) is the spectrum of natural daylight, and (J) shows the sensitivity of plants to light for photosynthesis. Wavelength is measured on the horizontal axis (in angstroms, or ten-billionths of a metre), and relative power on the vertical axis, in the visible range.

The chart at right shows, for each kind of lamp, the total amount of emitted light (in lumens on the vertical axis) at various typical levels of electrical power input (indicated in watts within each column). Dividing the number of lumens by that of watts will give the efficacy value of the lamp, which helps in determining the relative cost of its use for illumination. With the least efficient types of lamp, in (F–G), up to 75 per cent of the input is changed into heat energy. Such heat is also a factor in aquarium temperature control.

177

containing a conductor (usually a coiled tungsten filament) inside a vacuum or inert gas (such as argon). Electricity passes through the filament to heat it, producing light. A definite filament, or "colour", temperature is specified in degrees Kelvin (equal to Centigrade plus 273°). This is about 2,700°K for domestic lamps, and 3,000°K for high-wattage photographic or tungsten–halogen lamps, whilst natural daylight is equivalent to 6,500°K. Such lamps emit a continuous spectrum of wavelengths, at a constant intensity until they burn out and must be replaced. They can be dimmed by using domestic rheostat units. In tungsten–halogen lamps, the filament is made extremely hot and gives a strong white light. Some of its tungsten evaporates but, instead of blackening the bulb wall as in a conventional lamp, combines with the halogen (a small quantity of iodine or bromine) and is restored onto the filament, extending the life of the lamp.

A *discharge* lamp is normally a glass tube containing a conductive gas at low pressure. Electricity ionizes the gas to produce light of certain wavelengths, forming a discontinuous or line spectrum. The intensity decreases with long use, and such lamps must be replaced after a "rated lifetime". They require specially adapted units to be dimmed. In the most popular *fluorescent* lamps, light from mercury gas irradiates a coating of phosphor on the inside of the tube, which emits a steady visible light. These may resemble incandescent lamps in general colour, but their specific bands of wavelengths may colour objects quite differently. In a sodium-vapour lamp, metallic sodium on the tube is heated by an initial discharge through neon or xenon gas (with a red glow) for several minutes, and then emits yellow-orange light very efficiently.

The aquarium lamp, or combination of lamps, should be chosen according to the wavelengths desired. Illustrated here are the spectra of a selection of incandescent and fluorescent lamps. Both blue-green and orange-red wavebands must be supplied to promote the healthy growth of higher plants and algae. Grolux tubes, or a fluorescent "Daylight" combined with incandescent spotlamps, could be used. Some plant species benefit more than others from additional orange-red illumination.

Fluorescent light, with much green and blue colour, enhances the colouring of display specimens but is slightly harsh and "cold". For a natural light, lamps with a balanced output close to daylight, or a combination of lamps with complementary emissions (blue-green with warm white, for example), should be used.

Another main factor in choosing lamps is the desired visual effect of the illuminated display. Long fluorescent tubes, set in parallel, give even light with few shadows. Supplementary incandescent lamps can be employed for directional effects, to produce greater contrast between light and shadow, or to highlight particular features of the aquarium. Dichroic spotlamps are helpful, as they disperse heat in a different direction from that of the light.

Underwater and black light
Unreal and dramatic effects may be created by having a source of light under the water. Special underwater lamps can be used, set into watertight chambers in the tank wall, or as self-contained sealed units, with fully waterproofed cables and connectors leading to the surface. A low-voltage circuit is a good safety precaution. Fibre optics, based upon the total internal reflection of light shining down the length of a fine acrylic plastic fibre, might also be employed to create points of light underwater.

Ultraviolet radiation is invisible—hence the name "black light", which includes infrared or heat radiation. Yet it does have important applications in the aquarium. It is valuable not only for disinfection, as described above, but also for aquarium display. Animal and plant colours are somewhat enhanced by supplementary UV lighting. Many materials fluoresce—emitting visible light—when irradiated by UV, and a variety of animal species have been found to contain UV-activated luminous substances. An entire "black aquarium" can be created in a UV-illuminated tank, viewed from a darkened room, with mere glows of fluorescing animal shapes, and disembodied flashes from bioluminous organs.

Switches
The aquarium lighting system should include a separate switching arrangement, to maintain low illumination even during the night. This is of particular importance for many active fishes which, in total darkness, might swim into tank walls or other obstructions. It is also of value to the researcher or the insomniac aquarist who wishes to check on his charges' nocturnal activities without disturbing them. In general, light switches should be readily accessible, with minimal disturbance to other equipment or the aquarium itself.

As was noted in Chapter 4, a dimmer switch—a rheostat or similar device for governing the current through the circuit—can be used to raise or lower the light intensity slowly, over the dawn and dusk periods. An alternative system is to switch on a bank of lights, a few at a time, over ten to thirty minutes. Where minimal management is specified, for example during holiday periods, the lighting circuit may be automated with time switches: one should switch on and off some of the lamps, earlier and later than a second switch, which controls the remainder of the lamps.

The number of lamps required
The number of lamps needed for an aquarium lighting system may be calculated from the amount of light emitted per lamp, the area to be illuminated, and the intensity of light desired over that area. A lamp's emission is measured in *lumens* and is proportional to the electrical power input (in watts). The amount of lumens emitted per watt of input, indicating the lamp's efficacy, varies widely from about 10 to 150. An illustration shows the efficacy of various types of lamps.

The intensity of light shining onto a given area is measured in *lux,* or lumens per square metre. Chapter 4 discusses the level of intensity needed to illuminate an aquarium. Most critical are the requirements of the photosynthesizing plants. An average suitable level for a healthy planted aquarium is around 5,000 lux, although levels from 1,000 to 10,000 might be tested with diverse species.

Our calculation is thus expressed by a simple equation:

$(n_1 \times e_1 + n_2 \times e_2 ...) =$ intensity required (lux) $\times$ area to be lit (square metres) $\times$ correction factor;

$n_{1,2}...$ are the numbers of lamps of different types needed;

$e_{1,2}...$ are the emissions (in lumens) of those types of lamp.

The correction factor is determined as follows. Light produced by a lamp must be directed down into the aquarium, usually by a reflector which is not very efficient. Moreover, some of the light passing through the aquarium is absorbed by materials in suspension and

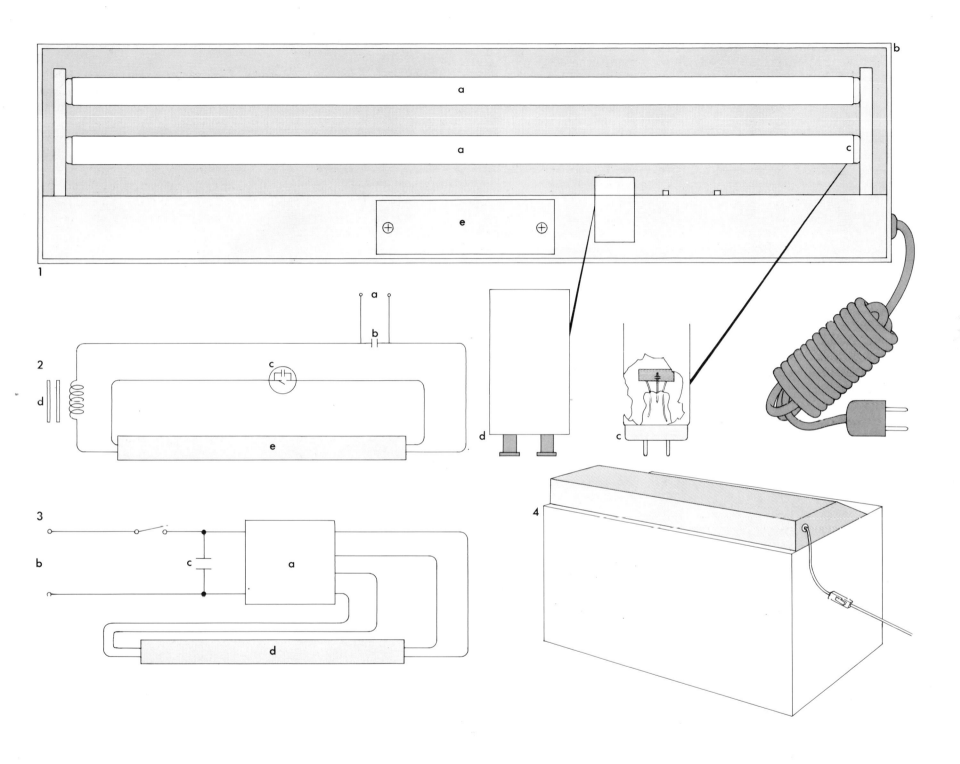

1 A typical fluorescent-tube fixture for a small aquarium. The tube (a) is fitted into a reflector hood (b). Mercury at low pressure, and some argon, fills the tube, at each end of which is a pin terminal (c) with a filament electrode which is coated with a material that emits electrons when heated. When the current is switched on, the filaments heat up, and the starter (d) automatically breaks the circuit, causing the choke, or ballast (e), to emit a high-voltage discharge. This causes first the argon and then the mercury to discharge. The ionized vapour's ultraviolet radiation falls on the inside of the tube, which is coated with a fluorescent material. This glows upon absorbing the ultraviolet, and the glow is seen as light.

2 A circuit diagram for a fluorescent tube. (a) Mains. (b) Capacitor. (c) Starter. (d) Choke. (e) Fluorescent tube.

3 A circuit diagram for a tube that has an autotransformer/choke (a), which obviates the need for a starter. (b) Mains. (c) Capacitor. (d) Fluorescent tube.

4 The aquarium tank with the reflector hood in place.

solution. These effects reduce the amount of light reaching the surface to be illuminated and are counteracted by increasing the amount of light supplied. This correction factor becomes greater with the depth and turbidity of water. Turbidity should be kept to a minimum by filtration. For clear colourless water, a factor of 2 may be used, growing to 3 or more with depths exceeding about 1 m (3 ft).

For example, let us consider a planted tank of dimensions $200 \times 70 \times 60$ cm ($78.7 \times 27.6 \times 23.6$ in). Its base area of 1.4 m², the required light intensity of 4,500 lux, and a correction factor of 2, are multiplied to show that the total light needed is 12,600 lumens. The lamps chosen may be incandescent (of 60 watts giving 600 lumens each), and fluorescent of the Natural (40 watts giving 2,300 lumens each) and Grolux (40 watts giving 900 lumens each) types. A suitable array would then be 5, 3, and 3 such lamps, which supplies exactly the total amount of light needed.

A simpler tank of dimensions $75 \times 30 \times 40$ cm ($29.5 \times 11.8 \times 15.7$ in), with a base area of 0.225 m², a required intensity of 2,000 lux, and the correction factor of 2, needs only 900 lumens of light. If the lamps chosen are one incandescent (of 40 watts giving 350 lumens) and one fluorescent of the Artificial Daylight type (20 watts giving 650 lumens), more than enough light would be available.

Reflectors, hoods, and lamp positioning

A good reflector should be used to direct as much light as possible onto the water surface. Suitable materials include polished aluminium, stainless or enamelled steel, mirrored glass or plastics. The shape of the reflector directs the light at various angles, to achieve particular lighting effects.

For even light distribution, the reflector should be large. On small tanks, it may be built into the hood, covering most of the tank top. As incandescent bulbs can be damaged by being moved or knocked, particularly when hot, it is a good idea to be able to raise a portion of the reflector hood, for feeding and other purposes, without disturbing the lamps. A hood will not only screen the tank surroundings from the bright aquarium lights, but also screen the water surface from outside illumination.

For maximum light to reach the water, lamps should be near the water surface. This also increases water heating. Remote spotlamps are useful for general illumination of the aquarium surroundings, rather than of the tank interior. For good access to the entire tank surface, as is sometimes necessary, one should be able to move lamp units well out of the way, using counter-weighted pivots, pulleys, or springs to handle them easily.

Covers

It is normally advisable to cover the entire aquarium top with a cover. This has the important benefits of reducing evaporation of water from the tank, and contamination of the aquarium by outside fumes, water, or alien organisms; of preventing the escape of restless captive specimens; and of protecting the tank's external fittings from corrosion and salt encrustation.

Lamps resistant to corrosion and water can be mounted between the tank cover and the water surface. But ordinarily, a transparent glass or acrylic plastic cover is used below the lamps. This reduces and slightly alters the light passing into the aquarium, so the cover must be kept clean and free from salt, algae, and other deposits.

1 Tank reflectors. Both reflectors shown have only one fluorescent tube, but the design of the reflector on the right is such that direct or reflected light shines on the whole surface.

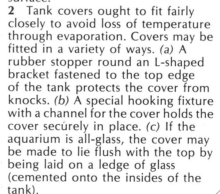

2 Tank covers ought to fit fairly closely to avoid loss of temperature through evaporation. Covers may be fitted in a variety of ways. (a) A rubber stopper round an L-shaped bracket fastened to the top edge of the tank protects the cover from knocks. (b) A special hooking fixture with a channel for the cover holds the cover securely in place. (c) If the aquarium is all-glass, the cover may be made to lie flush with the top by being laid on a ledge of glass (cemented onto the insides of the tank).

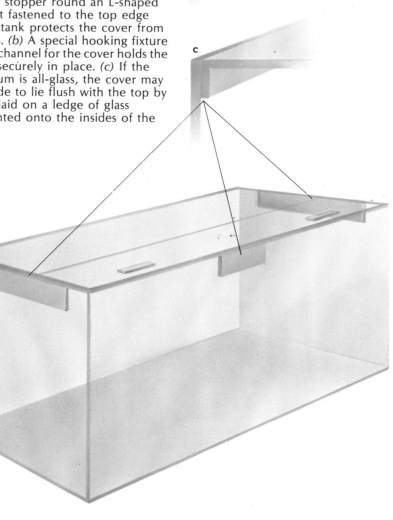

Setting Up an Aquarium

The two major influences upon the form of the aquarium are the designer and the *biota*—animal and plant life. The functioning unit may be a compromise between what the creator or purchaser originally wanted and what the captive organisms need. Balancing these objectives is the essence of setting up an aquarium properly.

Aquaria are built for specific purposes such as entertainment, education, and biological display. The designer's considerations include the space, materials, expertise, help, and time that are available, the sources of water and of specimens, and the costs of building, equipping, stocking, and running the aquarium. The species to be displayed should be decided upon at an early stage, as their individual characteristics will affect the system adopted. Over the life-span of an aquarium, expansion or changes in the display may be desirable, and this long-term goal should also be borne in mind.

Each of these factors must be explored thoroughly at the beginning, prior to any site work, purchasing, or collecting. The various requirements of the finished aquarium, in terms of viewing access, services, and support systems, should be checked against restrictions which arise. A programme of the entire operation, if sketched out in advance, enables one to proceed coherently and foresee problems, avoiding errors and disappointments.

Aquarium design

The range of possible tanks, styles, displays, and systems is so great that there is a suitable aquarium for virtually any setting. The two can be matched in both function and appearance from the start. The aquarium designer either has a setting into which one or more aquaria are to be fitted, or has an aquarium—if not simply a biological collection—which is to be installed and exhibited somewhere.

Space and location

When choosing an aquarium for a setting, it is important to consider the amount and shape of the space occupied by the tank and support systems, and needed by access for maintenance and viewing. To save space, the tank may be set flush into a wall, and serviced from either the front or rear, perhaps with an adjoining room for ancillary units such as filters and pumps. No extra floor space is required if an existing item of furniture, such as a little-used table, cupboard, or wall area, is adapted to hold the aquarium. Obsolete space can be revitalized by building a tank into an alcove, old doorway, or fireplace. A bank or

The design and setting up of an attractive aquarium environment like this takes a lot of planning. Consideration must be taken of the shape, size, mutual compatibility, and colour of the different plants and animals to be included, and the aquarist should plan from the beginning how he is going to light the display. The plants here form a fine background to the blue and red of the cardinal tetras, whilst the warmer colours of the Sumatra barb form a more sober contrast with the greenery.

The large cement aquarium shown above is built into a wall and is serviced from an adjoining room. It has the advantages of saving space, protecting the tank, separating its equipment (such as lamps) from the viewer, and creating a visual focus.

Many kinds of rooms for recreation or work can be divided attractively by an aquarium which has good all-round visibility and service access, with greater reliance on indirect lighting. Such a heavy and exposed tank requires strong flooring as well as caution in nearby activities.

grouping of several tanks may be designed as a compact integral unit, with common water-treatment and power-supply systems.

An attractive aquarium display is an eye-catching feature in an otherwise unused, dull corner. A triangular tank, or two tanks at right angles to each other, concealing ancillary equipment between or beneath them, may be installed here. The length of a wall can also be accentuated with a long tank. A focal point is created in a large open room by a free-standing, cylindrical aquarium, with its hardware hidden above or below in the central core. An aquarium might be built perpendicularly out from a wall as a room-divider, or a "living wall", viewed from both sides.

The weight of an aquarium must be calculated and allowed for initially. A floor has to bear—preferably with ease—the tank, water, fittings, décor, stand, cabinet, and other equipment, as well as any observers. The loading capacities of floors vary widely. In each case, this capacity should be assessed and checked against the aquarium's weight. If a floor is weak, the aquarium should be kept near a supporting wall; its weight should be across, rather than along, the floor joists; and lighter materials, less depth of water, or a smaller volume should be specified in designing it.

As in the example above, two or more aquaria can be combined in an angular setting to enhance the impression of natural surroundings. The tanks may show distinct habitats or incompatible species of animals, and a corner space between tanks can hide equipment such as filters used by both.

Illustrated below is a cylindrical aquarium with no obtrusive framework, and large enough to minimize optical distortion. Such a free-standing tank is serviced by removing a top panel, and its supporting base conceals the main equipment.

Services and access

The electrical power required for heating and lighting, and the water supply and drainage facilities needed for water changes and routine cleaning, must be estimated during planning. These services are to be provided at the chosen site.

Virtually all aquaria need electrical power. The supporting system may involve current for heating, and for pumping of air or water, as well as for lighting and various technological aids. The site supply must be of adequate capacity and reliability. An aquarium should be assigned its own electric circuit or sockets, and a separate emergency system, for greatest security.

Most small aquaria are self-contained, closed water systems, relying upon periodic and partial changes of water. For these, a bucket and siphon are usually adequate. Larger systems may incorporate independent water-treatment units, or may be plumbed into central facilities for supply and drainage which serve a series of tanks.

Good access for all servicing operations is essential. During the periods of setting up and livestocking an aquarium, it may be necessary to bring large and heavy containers of water, specimens, or rockwork to the tank. For convenience, this may involve fitting double doors, building ramps rather than steps, or installing a pulley device for lifting weights.

Regular cleaning and maintenance inside the tank—of windows, walls, substrates, and fittings—require comfortable access to the entire tank top. Any major tank operations concerning live specimens, such as catching them, are also made much easier in this way. Damage to specimens, and unnecessary stress, are inevitable when attempting to catch an animal from an awkward position, where equipment cannot be manipulated properly.

Tanks which are narrow enough to be reached across—an average arm length is about 70 cm (28 in)—may be worked upon adequately from above the back, front, or side, providing that sufficient head-room exists. When a tank is large, more than about 1.5 m (5 ft)

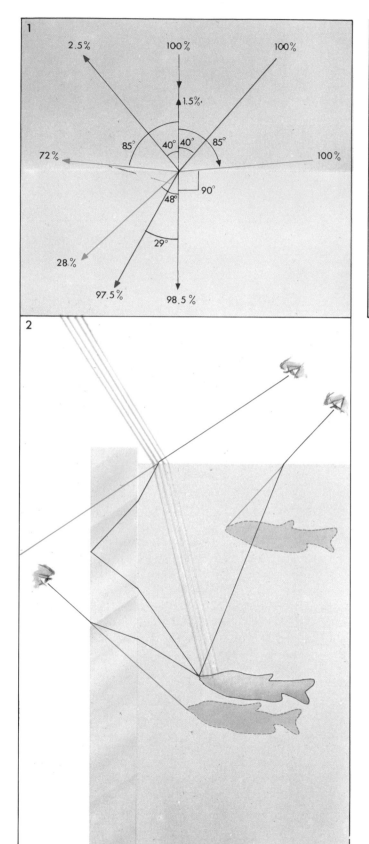

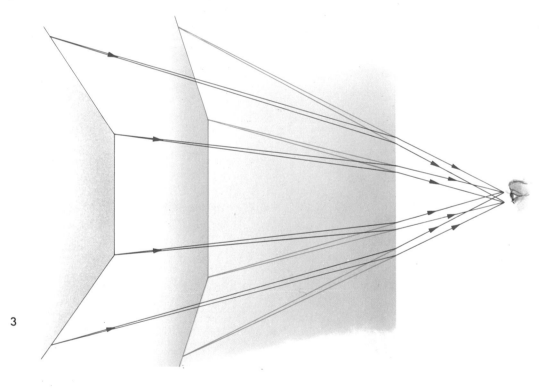

The light-ray diagrams on this page illustrate the optical properties of an aquarium.

1 Three rays hit the water surface with different angles of incidence. Each ray divides into a reflected and a refracted ray, the former becoming fainter and the latter brighter as the angle decreases. Angles of refraction are calculated exactly by the law given in the text (see page 187).

2 A fish in an aquarium appears slightly larger, closer, and in different positions as it is viewed from different directions, because of refraction—as well as total internal reflection in one case—through the water surface and the glass window.

3 Similar effects are shown for the rear of a tank interior, which looks somewhat flattened.

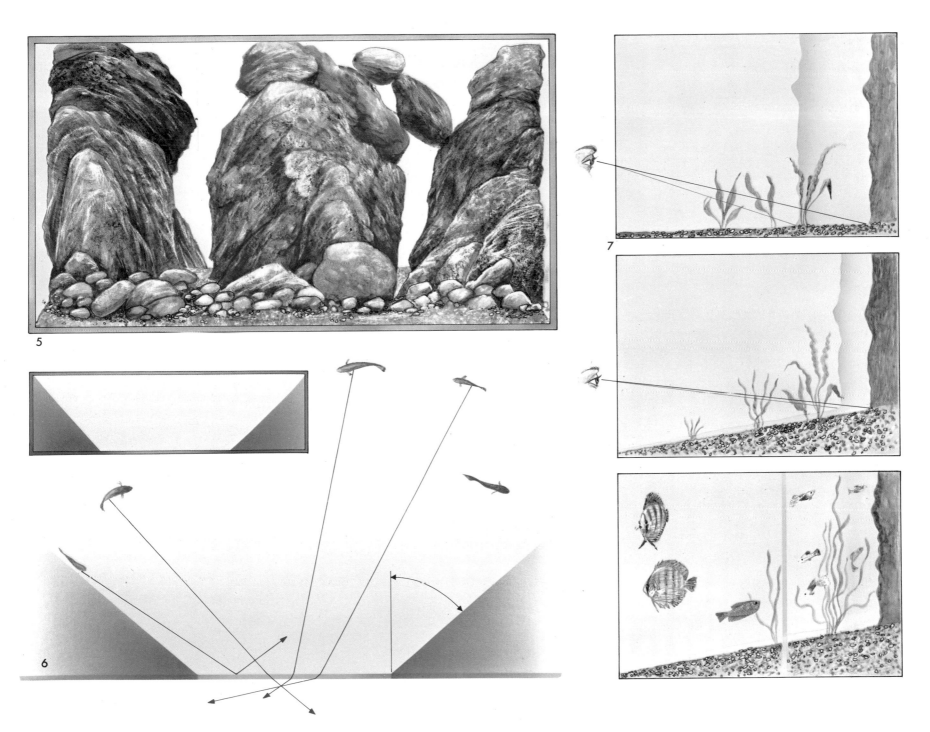

5

6

7

Since light refraction magnifies the contents of an aquarium and decreases the apparent space inside it, methods of increasing its depth of field are valuable. Several of these are shown here.

4 The rear wall of a tank is light-coloured or translucent behind rocky outcrops, giving a sense of distance through contrast. Similar effects can be achieved by introducing certain species of plants and animals which are partly translucent.

5 This tank has a more varied rocky landscape with crevices and channels, directing the viewer's eye into the distance.

6 This tank is built with inner walls which cannot be seen through a window, because they meet the window at an angle (50°) greater than the "critical angle": light from them and nearby objects is kept inside the tank by total internal reflection, while the light from other objects is refracted normally out of the tank.

7 The rear wall of a tank appears to be farther away if the tank bottom is sloped upward to meet it, thus decreasing the amount of light refraction. The tank may also be divided by a thin pane of glass, to form a rear compartment which contains relatively small animals and plants, so that it seems much more distant than the large organisms in front. A number of separate tanks may be lined up for the same purpose. Other methods include the use of coloured panes or lights, artificial backlighting, and a mirror in the rear wall, enhancing the impression of underwater volume.

185

wide, it must be worked from above. A clear standing room of 2 m (6.5 ft) above a service platform, around or across the top of the tank, should be allowed.

Light fittings, and other equipment suspended above the water surface, may need to be movable, on a pulleyed gantry or a spring-loaded pivot, to permit unhindered work. The most frequent attention to the aquarium—feeding, control of lighting, and temperature checks—should be the easiest to carry out. When a tank is completely hooded, a separate hinged flap should be fitted, through which food may be introduced. Switches, thermometers, and indicator lights must be fitted where they are simplest to reach and read. Particularly when the aquarium is built into a wall, provision should be made for periodically checking the external tank condition, for signs of corrosion or leakage.

Environmental influences

There are diverse two-way exchanges between the aquarium and its surroundings. For instance, light passing into the aquarium is partially absorbed, and partially reflected outward, with an altered spectrum of wavelengths. Heat passes from air to water, or conversely, depending upon the temperature gradient. The rate of heat transfer is governed by the tank's structural and insulating materials. The aquarium should not be exposed to cold or hot currents of air, which cause local heating or cooling. Careful siting is thus required, with respect to draughts, radiators, open fires, pipes, ventilators, and similar agents.

The aquarium must be installed away from doors and passageways, and from busy thoroughfares, in order to reduce the chances of accidental collision with the tank or stand. Vibrations and shocks are to be minimized by careful siting, or by strengthening and insulating the tank foundations. Any machine—from a dishwasher to a train—may be a source of disturbance. Indeed, the aquarium machinery may be noisy and need to be soundproofed or removed from the immediate vicinity. There should also be no possibility of contaminating the aquarium water or air systems with smoke, fumes, dirt, extraneous water, or other liquids.

On the other hand, an aquarium may affect its setting in ways additional to being an attractive source of interest. It may produce highly humid conditions in the areas of viewing and service, especially when water temperatures are above the ambient level and the tank is uncovered. Moreover, low tank temperatures and high ambient humidity can cause condensation on the aquarium glass, sides, and pipework. This may become a serious nuisance, damaging decorations and obscuring the view. Consequently, the tank should be covered and, if necessary, insulated and double-glazed. A second partial solution is to separate the viewing area from the service area.

Viewing the aquarium

The living display, and the appearance of the visible portions of the tank, must be designed with the observer in mind. Height and horizontal distance between the display and the observer are important. Will the observers be standing or seated, short or tall, and many at a time? Is it necessary to plan for a sensible visitor-flow pattern? Is the room sufficiently large for an observer to move back from the tank and appreciate the overall effect of the aquarium?

The ambient or room lighting is also significant. The tank viewing window must be shielded from direct or bright external light; otherwise, the view into the tank may be obscured by reflections. This might be a particular problem when the ambient light cannot be controlled easily—for example, outdoors. A further advantage of subdued lighting in the viewing area is the increased clarity and visual impact of the illuminated tank interior.

The room decoration and furnishings, and the aquarium tank, may be designed to complement each other. Shapes, colours, texture, materials, and lighting should be chosen and blended to achieve a general impression. A good display makes optimum use of the aquarium's internal shape and optical properties, in relation to each aspect of the design—decoration, illumination, and living contents.

Lighting installations

Lamps and their reflectors should be designed and positioned so as to maximize the amount of light entering the aquarium. When light hits a water or glass surface perpendicularly, the loss caused by reflection from the surface is minimized. The light should also be directed downward and slightly backward away from the main viewing window, to reduce shadowing on the ventral and near sides of swimming specimens.

The translucence of some animals and plants—anemones, ascidians, medusae, red algae, and certain egg-cases of molluscs and dogfishes—may be viewed most effectively against back-lighting. The iridescent and silvery-blue colouring of many open-water fishes, created by interference between different wavelengths of light passing through special cells or crystals in the scales, is best seen under unidirectional spotlighting.

The tank background formations and base substrates interact with the pattern of illumination, producing shadows, black "caves", bright areas or "pools" of light, and exaggerated surface textures. Water movement, and especially surface agitation and choppy waves, yield a flickering or "dancing" underwater illumination, as the convex and concave surfaces of waves focus and disperse the light. Mirrors and spotlights may be used to further diversify the aquarium scene. Unusual effects can be provided by combining side-lighting, underwater lamps, coloured lamps or filters, and fibre optics, as well as by employing internal reflections by the tank windows and water surface.

Optical properties

The behaviour of light in an aquarium is governed by two basic laws of physical optics. These involve relationships between the angles at which light enters or leaves a surface of water or glass. Such an angle is always measured between the light ray and the direction perpendicular to the surface. The laws also concern the relative amounts of light entering and leaving. When light is incident upon a surface, some of it is reflected back, and the rest is refracted through the surface. The amounts of reflected and refracted light depend on the angles, and on the kinds of materials that make up the surface.

According to the law of reflection, the angles of incident and reflected light are equal—and on opposite sides of the direction perpendicular to the surface. Thus, the light simply bounces off the surface like a ball. As the angles increase, an increasing amount of the incident light is reflected. If the light is going from a less dense material into a more dense one, for example from air into water or glass, nearly all of the light will be reflected when it is shining almost parallel to the surface. This "mirror" effect would make external lighting useless to illuminate the interior of an aquarium.

According to the law of refraction (known as Snell's Law), the angles of incident and refracted light are different—unless the light hits the surface perpendicularly, when both angles are zero. Thus, the light is "bent" as it passes obliquely through the surface. The angle of light in the less dense material is greater than that in the more dense one. If light goes from air into water or glass, or from water into glass, it bends toward the perpendicular; if in the reverse direction, it bends oppositely. The angles may be calculated exactly with an equation:

$n_1 \times$ sine of angle$_1 = n_2 \times$ sine of angle$_2$;

$n_{1,2}$ are the indexes of refraction of the two materials,
    usually expressed by numbers between 1 and 2
    (such as 1.0 for air, 1.33 for water, 1.5 for glass);

the sines of angles are numbers between 0 and 1, given by
    a table of trigonometric functions.

As these angles increase, a decreasing amount of the incident light is refracted. Light which hits a more dense material, even at a large angle, will always be partially refracted into it. But light hitting a less dense material will not be refracted at all, if the angle of incidence is greater than a certain value. At this value, called the *critical angle*, any refracted light would be bent parallel to the surface and could not escape. So at this and every larger angle, the light undergoes *total internal reflection* back into the denser material. For light travelling in water or glass toward a surface of air, the above equation shows that the critical angle is around 45°.

Illusions in the aquarium

The foregoing laws create peculiar effects for the observer of an aquarium. For instance, refraction makes an object in the water look closer and bigger than it actually is. Even the width of the tank, or depth of view, appears foreshortened. This impression can be counteracted in designing the aquarium display, by using a variety of techniques as well as individual ingenuity. Thus, the tank may be given a light-coloured rear wall which is visible between rocky outcrops. Small fishes or plants may be kept in a rear section inside the tank, separated by plain or frosted glass or by plastic. A distinct tank, or a dry "diorama" compartment, may be installed behind the rear wall of an all-glass tank. The result is to emphasize objects which are farthest away from the viewer, lending depth to the scene.

Total internal reflection limits the volume of the aquarium that is visible from outside. When looking through a particular point of the window or water surface, one can only see objects within a cone-shaped volume, whose edges meet that surface at less than the critical angle of about 45° (measured from the perpendicular to the surface). Even the inner surfaces of the tank are hidden from view if they do not lie within this cone, creating the illusion of an underwater scene which extends indefinitely. The side walls can thus be "lost" by building them at a divergent angle, or else by reducing their length in relation to the window length. In a straight-sided octagonal tank, the walls meet at an angle of 135°, or 45° more than the perpendicular, and are just beyond the visible region as one looks through a wall toward an adjacent wall. Similarly, the water surface can be hidden by placing the entire window well below it, to produce the appearance of a deep-sea habitat.

When an inner surface of the tank does remain visible through a window, it may resemble a mirror, even if it is actually transparent. This occurs when it lies at an angle, relative to the window, of about 90° or more (the perpendicular). No light which is refracted through that surface from outside the tank can then hit the window at less than the critical angle. Thus, one cannot see right through the tank in that direction, and only internal reflections will appear. Here, the aquarist finds an advantage: the water surface seems opaque when viewed through vertical windows, and the typical tangle of wires, lamps, or tubes above it is hidden. In aquaria of the commonest shapes, such as simple rectangularity, sighting between opposite windows is the sole means of seeing through the tank.

Decorating the tank

The interior set, or décor, is perhaps the most important element of the aquarium display. It is not only the visible landscape, but also the physical environment in which the captive animals and plants spend their lives. The majority of aquatic organisms are closely associated with the structure of their environment. Clear regions of water are essential to the normal behaviour of free-swimming and shoaling creatures, whilst—at the other extreme—access to "land" is necessary for amphibians and certain fishes, crustaceans, and gastropods which leave the water temporarily.

Many algae, bacteria, and invertebrate animals must attach to a firm surface. Some species of plants and animals need a particular quality of sediment into which to root or burrow. Rock and coral-reef fishes experience stress if removed from the dense and intricate cover of their natural surroundings. Freshwater and marine animals often have specific requirements for dark overhangs, private caves, or territorial space amongst plants or rocks, and for spawning sites under leaves, stones, or shells.

The main features of internal décor are formations of rock or wood, sediments on the base, and relatively static organisms such as plants. Also to be considered below are artificial scenes, built either inside or outside the tank. Generally, the décor should be kept simple, and the landscape constructed thoughtfully. Clutter is worth avoiding, and inaccessible corners or crevices will obstruct cleaning, gather detritus, stagnate, look unsightly, waste space, or otherwise detract from the effectiveness of the display. All in-tank materials must, of course, be non-toxic and properly prepared before installation.

When planning an interior set for a particular aquarium, natural habitats should be examined, either in the field or in books, and used as references. An appropriate site should be chosen, and its rocks, sediments, vegetation, fauna, and overall appearance should be systematically studied. If possible, photographs and sketches of a relevant field location must be made. River-banks and sea-shores are easiest to visit, and diving gear is helpful for exploring underwater environments.

Natural materials

Impressive aquarium landscapes are dominated by areas of stone, coral, or wood. These serve as focal points in the display and establish its basic character. Such solid structures may also be used to emphasize

The display in an aquarium is greatly affected by the kinds and arrangements of lighting employed, as can be seen on this and the next page. All views are of the same tank of 200 litres (about 50 gallons) volume, with a front-to-back depth of 35 cm (14 in) and a backcloth made of sculpted cork in a separate box behind the tank. The main plants, from left to right, are species of *Limnophila, Ludwigia, Myriophyllum, Echinodorus,* and again *Limnophila.* Smaller species in the foreground are of *Cryptocoryne* and *Micranthemum,* with *Anubias nana* and *Nymphoides aquatica.*

1

2

1 The simplest arrangement is direct illumination from above, with fairly intense lighting by four fluorescent lamps of 40 watts each. Many shadows are cast and the visual character of the backcloth is minimized.
2 The foreground is emphasized by a strong fluorescent lamp, while the rest of the tank top is covered and a part of the background at right is exposed by a spotlight of 100 watts.

the three dimensions of the scene. As explained previously, refraction tends to flatten and restrict the view through the tank, and can be counteracted. Special methods of doing this are readily discovered, for example by constructing a crevice in a rear cliff reaching to the water surface, or by arranging a tree stump to jut forward. In cylindrical, annular, or angular tanks with all-round transparency, a conspicuous pinnacle, reef, or tree stump may stand freely near the centre, supported by a length of pipe with an air-lift, filter, or water duct concealed inside it.

Rockwork
Rocks suitable for the aquarium are available virtually everywhere. The three major types differ in chemical and physical properties. They are sedimentary, igneous, and metamorphic rock.

Sedimentary rock is a sediment which has become hardened, usually by pressure or chemical cementation. Sandstones, shales, and conglomerates are thus formed respectively by deposits of sand, mud, and gravel. They are generally the softest and most easily eroded rocks. Organic limestones are hardened deposits of calcareous animal and plant shells, skeletons, and cell walls.

Igneous rocks are solidified molten magma from deep inside the earth. They are mixtures of crystals of different minerals fused together, and tend to be the hardest and most inert of rocks. Metamorphic rocks are igneous or sedimentary rocks which have been altered by increased pressure or temperature. For example, marble is limestone which has been metamorphosed by great heat. These rocks are normally quite resistant to weathering.

3 The strong lighting into the front quarter of the tank is maintained, and the spotlight on the background shines towards the left. Another spotlight is directed onto the *Myriophyllum*, and this contrast increases the apparent front-to-back distance in the tank.

3

4

4 The tank hood is opened and tilted so that its lamps give a general light towards the background. To preserve the clarity of plants in front, spotlights are directed onto the *Limnophila* at left and the *Myriophyllum,* while the *Ludwigia* is illuminated more softly by an ordinary incandescent 40-watt bulb. A similar 60-watt bulb is placed in the backcloth box to illuminate it further.

Rockwork is a key element in many aquarium displays. Its physical structure, texture, and overall appearance are of highest significance to the designer, but its chemical properties must also be borne in mind. Different types of rock should be studied in the field, to learn how they vary in position, wearing by water or wind, colour, and formation.

In the aquarium, garish and unrealistic combinations should be avoided, using only one or two types of rock. Before starting construction, sufficient raw material for the entire display should be assembled in a "dry run" test, referring to field photographs and sketches. In small aquaria, single natural slabs or chunks of rock may be large enough to form complete features. Split, layered rocks can be set on edge, if necessary in a small concrete base for stability, as jagged outcrops standing over the base gravel. Larger rock formations require

greater artistry and skill. Slabs and boulders can be piled up carefully or fastened together into more elaborate structures with the aid of concrete or GRP. Solid stone or concrete features must not be made too massive to be lifted into position safely, accurately, and rather easily.
Chemical precautions
Unless collected specifically because of its attachment of living organisms, all rock for the aquarium should be cleaned and sterilized. Dirt or debris must be scrubbed off. Thickly encrusted pieces may be soaked in a bleach solution of 30 per cent for one or two days between scrubbings, and afterwards, soaked or boiled in fresh water. Rocks which are highly porous, crumbly, or composed of possibly harmful metal oxides must be thoroughly cleaned, dried, and given two or more coats of clear resin varnish.

189

Using rocks to create an attractive and practical setting in the aquarium involves several operations which are illustrated on this and the next page.

1 It is essential to clean all stony material, including sands and gravels to be employed as sediments, so that undesirable substances on or within them are removed. The specific type of water quality to be maintained in the tank should also be decided initially because it determines the kinds of materials which are selected, notably as regards their calcareous content. Calcareous rocks such as many sandstones, limestone, dolomite, and marble may be chosen for their light colouring but are unsuitable in water that is fresh, soft, and not buffered against changes in acidity.

2 An appropriate sediment is laid on the tank bottom and shaped to produce a good visual impression as well as to serve the aquatic organisms.

3 When positioning heavier rocks, a slab may be balanced upon other stones as if fallen, to avoid an artificial appearance and to provide shelter for animals that need it.

4 A rocky landscape can not only be dramatic, and similar to the natural habitat of the organisms, but conceal equipment such as pipes and filters. All large rocks should be put directly on the tank floor, and any unstable structures should be secured with a solid base; otherwise, they may collapse due to animal activity and cause damage.

5 Some kinds of common rock that can easily be found are: *(a)* sedimentary sandstone, *(b)* igneous basalt and *(c)* granite, and *(d)* metamorphic slate in a cement base.

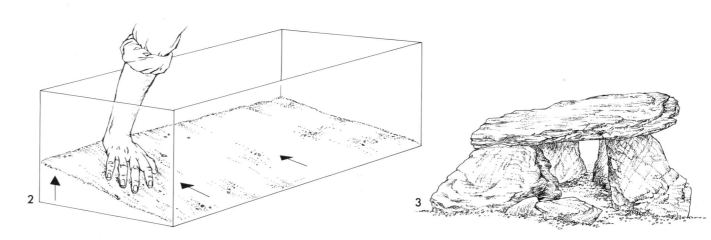

It is important to know whether a rock or gravel is calcareous. This determines its suitability for a buffered hard-water system, including sea waters, or for a relatively unbuffered soft-water system. Calcareous material is often apparent in a rock as white or pale streaking. A simple test is to pour a little dilute hydrochloric acid or vinegar (acetic acid) onto the rock surface. Effervescence or fizzing—the escape of carbon-dioxide gas bubbles—indicates the presence of calcareous material.

Living organisms on rock

Rocks collected underwater or low down on the shore, in fresh or marine waters, are likely to be covered with living creatures. Porous, broken rock will also contain animals. Some calcareous rock is formed by the inhabitants themselves and may be termed biogenic or "living" rock. Chunks of such rock colonies can be sought especially to be kept alive as aquarium specimens. They may hold encrusting algae, bryozoans, hydroids, polychaetes, sponges, bivalves, and tunicates. Algae in general are most satisfactorily collected in this way, still attached to their stone or shell.

The amount of living material in, and upon, even small pieces of porous rock may be considerable. These organisms will have been taken from an environment with high turbulence and good quality of water. This character must be maintained in order to keep the colony alive in the aquarium. Any lapse will result in oxygen shortage, suffocation, and decomposition, and the entire structure may become a smelly black mass.

Skeletons and shells

Corals, molluscs, and bryozoans are amongst the organisms which, when alive, produce stony shell or skeletal material to support and protect their soft tissues. Some of the beautifully sculpted structures which these animals lay down, in particular the calcareous "skeletons" of stony corals, the horny "skeletons" of sea fans, and large molluscan shells, can be used —when dead— to create an interesting landscape in the aquarium.

Most of the specimens are collected in the wild as live animals, allowed to die, then bleached and marketed. This trade caters rather exclusively to the aquarist. These materials produced by live animals should not be wasted or treated carelessly. The structures are fragile, and it is often best to use one piece as a form for a mould, manufacturing a series of replicas which are more durable and easily cleaned.

Sediments

The sediment on the base of an aquarium is of great importance, both visually to the observer, and vitally to the animals, plants, and bacteria in the tank. As part of the décor, a sediment should complement the other features and be matched to the chosen illumination. Bottom-living animals must be provided with a sediment which is suitable for their camouflage, attachment, or burrowing habits. Higher plants need to be able to root firmly into the sediment. Bacteria should be encouraged, particularly in systems which employ their decomposing and nitrifying activities, by providing a base sediment with a large area of surfaces—and with good interstitial (between the grains) water quality, which means good circulation. Thus, sediment for an aquarium must be selected carefully, with attention to the grains' colours, sizes, shapes, type, texture, and degree of intermixing.

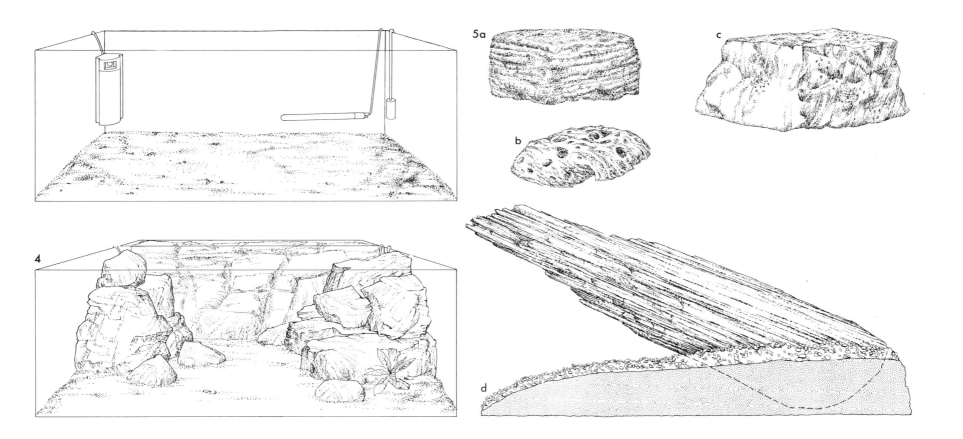

When base-gravel filtration is used, the sediment should be a graded gravel, with grains between 2 and 6 mm (0.08–0.24 in) in diameter. This is an optimum compromise between water flow-through rate and total surface area. A shallow base layer of small pebbles or stones is easy to keep clean, by periodically siphoning between the stones, but is not suitable for base filtration. At the other extreme, fine sandy sediments tend to stagnate because of poor interstitial circulation, and the tiny particles can easily become waterborne, subsequently settling upon leaves, rocks, and animals.

Sands and gravels are weathered fragments of rock or coral. Many are made predominantly of quartz, others of basalt or flint. These are all non-calcareous and, therefore, are suitable for maintaining soft water conditions in the aquarium. For sea-water and hard-water aquaria, calcareous sediments should be used, to increase the buffering capacity of the system. Sands, grits, and gravels of calcium carbonate include marble, dolomite, crushed coral, and broken shells. Calcareous sediments are generally light in colour and may be darkened if necessary by adding some darker, silica-based material.

All sands and gravels, collected in the wild or bought, must be washed thoroughly before use, to remove dust and any toxic or organic contaminants. Small amounts should be washed at a time, after sieving and soaking if necessary, using plenty of clean water.

Wood

Formations of overhanging branches, fallen tree trunks and stumps, protruding roots, and so on, are of great value in creating aquarium displays which represent streams, rivers, swamps, and other sheltered tree-lined shallows. All sound and water-resistant woods are suitable, including most heartwoods and hardwoods, gnarled oak roots, trailing branches or fibrous root systems of pine, ivy, willow, or alder. Sometimes, a thoroughly waterlogged or partially petrified stump or branch is found in a bog or on the shore of a lake, river, or sea. Fantastically twisted and intricate shapes can be particularly effective in an underwater scene.

Wood is an organic material and, without preservation, may decompose in the aquarium. The right size and shape for each piece displayed must be chosen. To prepare the piece for installation, unwanted side-shoots are removed, and any desired cutting to shape is carried out. Surface dirt must be cleaned off, and the entire piece should be soaked in fresh water for several weeks, as well as boiled if feasible, to remove soluble substances, including tannins. Following this treatment, the wood may be sufficiently sound for use. Otherwise, it should first be thoroughly dried, then sealed or impregnated with varnish or resin.

As a fallen tree stump or branch, or as roots protruding from an eroded river-bank display, the sculpted and prepared wood can be positioned on the base of the tank, or attached to a side or rear wall. This can be particularly effective in a deep tank. The root or branch is sealed onto a flat base, of suitably camouflaged and waterproofed wood, GRP, concrete, or asbestos sheet, which is fixed firmly to the wall.

The bark of the cork oak has a beautifully convoluted surface and is naturally resistant to decomposition in water. Properly weighted, it

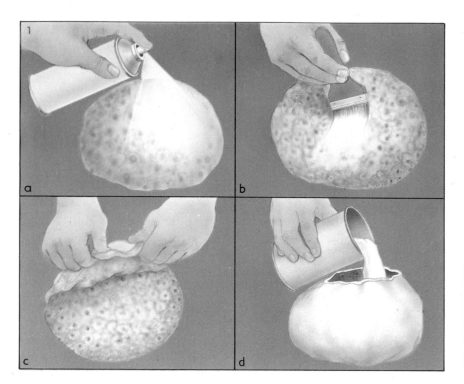

Many features of aquarium decoration can be made artificially by moulding and casting.

1 Shown is a simple way of producing duplicates of a piece of natural coral: (a) spray the piece lightly with a releasing agent such as silicone; (b) cover it with a layer of liquid rubber which fills the surface details; (c) when this has dried, free the edges of the rubber all round and peel it from the coral; (d) use the rubber as a mould in the same manner, spraying its inner surface, applying a mixture such as resin that sets hard, and peeling off the mould.

2 A larger display like the hanging roots of a tree or mangrove should be attached to a wall of the tank, with good sealing to avoid pockets of poor water flow and stagnation.

3 Objects may also be fixed into a slab of concrete which stands against the rear wall of the tank. This panel is easily cast in a wooden frame, and can conceal water pipes as well.

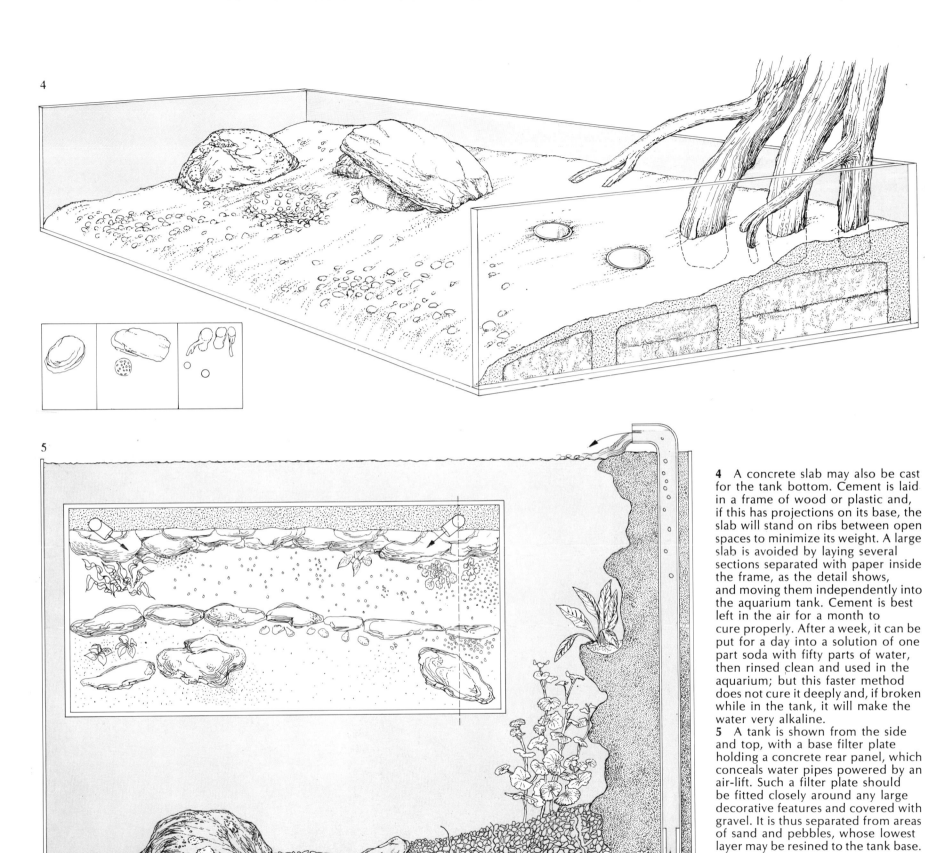

4 A concrete slab may also be cast for the tank bottom. Cement is laid in a frame of wood or plastic and, if this has projections on its base, the slab will stand on ribs between open spaces to minimize its weight. A large slab is avoided by laying several sections separated with paper inside the frame, as the detail shows, and moving them independently into the aquarium tank. Cement is best left in the air for a month to cure properly. After a week, it can be put for a day into a solution of one part soda with fifty parts of water, then rinsed clean and used in the aquarium; but this faster method does not cure it deeply and, if broken while in the tank, it will make the water very alkaline.

5 A tank is shown from the side and top, with a base filter plate holding a concrete rear panel, which conceals water pipes powered by an air-lift. Such a filter plate should be fitted closely around any large decorative features and covered with gravel. It is thus separated from areas of sand and pebbles, whose lowest layer may be resined to the tank base.

Decorations placed behind the aquarium tank and seen through it can add much to its interest and apparent volume. At right, a backcloth made of rigid material is attached to the rear wall after being sculpted and painted as a scene appropriate to freshwater life. Below, a diorama compartment is filled with coral to enhance a marine habitat. This space should be illuminated well, and its solid back is curved to give an impression of varying distances.

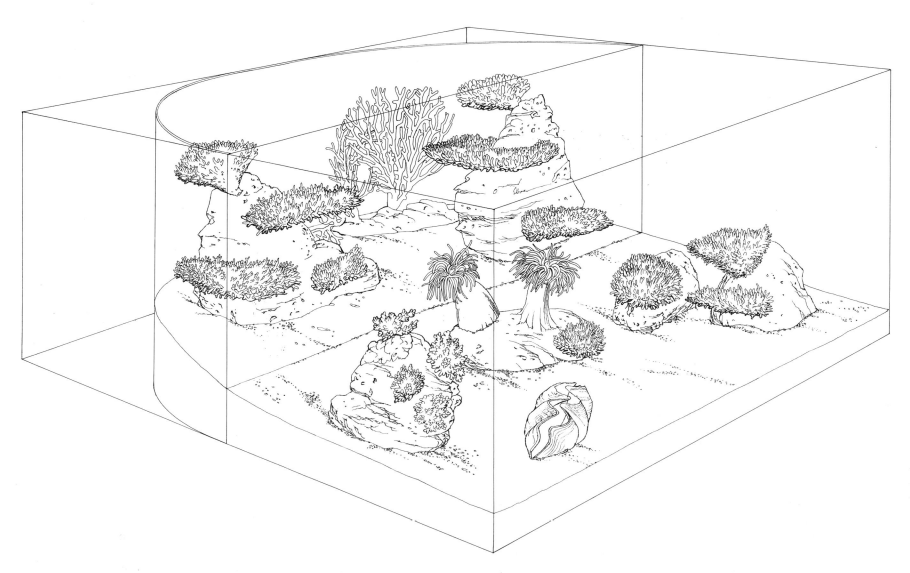

can be used inside the aquarium to represent a submerged branch or tree trunk, protruding from the base gravel. Alternatively, it may be employed externally as part of the display backcloth or in a diorama.

Artificial materials

As with rocks and corals, natural wood surfaces and forms can be valuable as patterns or moulds, from which to make artificial wood from concrete, clay, plaster, or plastics. Such materials are more resistant to decay, but care is needed to achieve an authentic appearance with them.

Sculpting and moulding

For medium and large tanks, a decorative slab or panel can be made to fill all or most of an internal wall face. The back of the slab is sealed against the tank wall, and the front is fashioned into a three-dimensional feature, with the appearance of a natural cliff, bank, or slope, formed of bedrock, boulders, compacted clay, eroded soil, or other elements.

The panel may be built—either entirely, or as a matrix into which natural materials such as stones and reeds will be set—from concrete, plaster, GRP, or clay. These substances can be worked easily in semi-liquid form before they set rigidly, or can be sculpted after setting. The decorative panel may be pre-cast outside the tank, and fixed into place once it is cured. Panels can be used singly, or in interlocking groups to cover a large wall area.

The greatest care must be taken to produce a satisfactory visible face. Overall shape, surface texture, and colouring are all-important. If a mould is used, the fluid mortar or resin mix will be poured into a "female" mould or applied—for example with a brush—over the surface of a "male" mould. The type of mould to use depends upon the side of the panel which is to be the good visible face. This is normally the side in contact with the mould.

The usual process is to prepare a natural boulder, rock face, piece of coral, shell, or tree stump, or an artificial form upon which to construct a mould, or which might itself be a mould. Moulds may be made from GRP, latex rubber, plasticine, sand, foamed plastics, wood such as balsa, hardboard, plaster, or papier-maché. Making the mould is the major task requiring time and attention. Before using it, one must fill all spaces or cracks in the mould which may prevent detachment of the finished panel, or may allow the panel to trap dirt and stagnate when underwater. Appropriate releasing agents should be applied between the mould and panel. Dyes or paints may be used to colour the decorative face of the panel, but only non-toxic and leach-proof materials should be employed.

As an alternative to pre-casting the slab outside the tank, it can be made when in position, by directly applying layers of the mortar or plastic mix to the prepared tank wall, using a brush, hand, or special gun. Natural stones, shoots, or roots may be held in place on the panel by a temporary framework, until the mortar has set. In this way, ridges, ledges, overhangs, and other features can be built up.

Coloured glass and plastics

Thus far, our emphasis has been upon materials which are natural, or are fashionable into representations of natural features. But any non-toxic, insoluble, non-porous materials which can yield suitable shapes are useful in aquarium decoration. Glass, and transparent plastics such as acrylic, may be dyed with bright colours and employed as a bizarre contrast to natural décor.

Translucent acrylic ledges, caves, and cliffs, or reefs of rough lumpy glass streaked with colour, are especially effective in bright displays with spotlighting and plenty of surface-water agitation. Air might be bubbled through a maze of glass or plastic tubing, to lead the observer's eyes around this fantasy aquarium.

Artefacts and imitations

In large aquarium displays, suitable artefacts such as part of a wrecked ship, an anchor, or an amphora vase, can provide impressive focal points. Genuine articles may be used after proper cleaning and treatment to prevent corrosion, leaching, and attack by the aquarium inmates. Alternatively, replicas can be made from cement, GRP, or clay.

For the smaller aquarium, many miniature models of treasure chests, divers, galleons, gnomes, frogs, and other objects, are produced commercially. Some are fairly grotesque, and all should be deployed with discretion. But they are often useful as sterile substitutes. Plastic plants, in particular, are valuable for sheltering animals which breed, or for protection of quarantine plants, and are also interesting to employ during the period before natural plants become established.

Backcloths and dioramas

A tank with a transparent rear wall may be decorated behind, rather than inside, the tank. As they are not immersed in water, materials such as paper, wood, cloth, cork, and polystyrene are all suitable, without waterproofing, for being cut and formed into a wide variety of decorative backcloths. Even water-soluble and toxic substances, including paints, can be used. Paints are applicable directly onto the outside of the tank glass.

A good backcloth gives extra diversity and "depth of field" to the aquarium display and takes up no tank space. If sufficient space behind the tank is available, the backcloth can be moved away from the rear wall to form a dry compartment. Within this area, a miniature three-dimensional scene may be created, known as a *diorama*. The rear wall can be painted with a natural underwater view or pattern, or a frieze can be built on it. Clay, plaster, papier-maché, plasticine, and plastics might be moulded onto a rear wall of plywood, hardboard, cardboard, or transparent sheeting, and even decorated with natural materials—pebbles, dried reeds, bamboo, driftwood—to represent a cliff face or river-bank, curving along the back of the aquarium display. The illusion of looking through a distance of water may be increased by leaving gaps in the "cliff face" and painting the background with a translucent green or blue colour.

The backcloth or diorama must, of course, match the interior set of the aquarium, and both should be appropriate to the specific captive community. This consistency should extend to the use of similar sand or gravel on the bases of the diorama and the tank, matching their levels carefully.

Establishing life

The aquarium is above all a habitat for living organisms, and it requires careful provision for them at the outset. This preparation mainly concerns the three basic components: water, plants, and animals, besides useful bacteria.

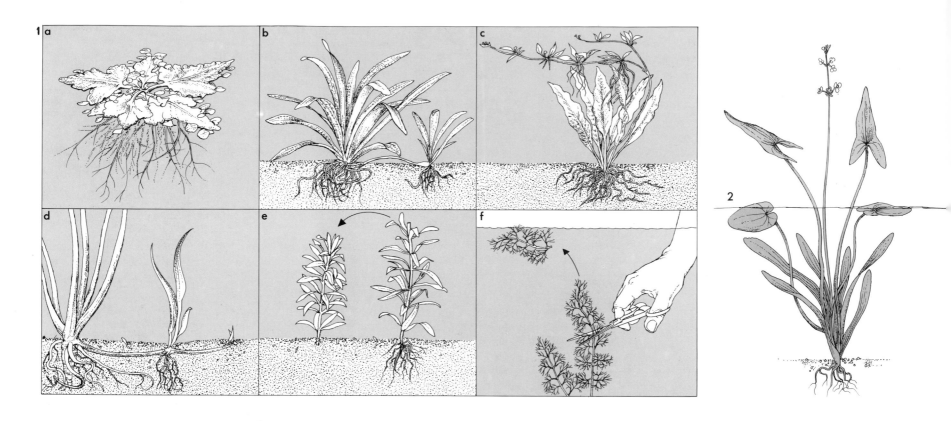

1 The following propagation methods are common amongst aquarium plants. *(a)* A bud sprouts in an old leaf, roots develop, and the young plant is separated and planted. If the plant is floating, then the young plant is left floating. *(b)* A side runner grows out from the crown, and a new shoot grows and roots. *(c)* New shoots grow from the flower and are cut and planted. *(d)* A shoot grows from a lateral root. *(e)* A top cutting is planted directly. *(f)* A top cutting may also be left floating until roots develop.

2 Many aquarium plants have varying leaves: *Sagittaria latifolia* has ribbon-shaped underwater leaves, roundish floating leaves, and arrow-shaped over-water leaves.

3 When choosing plants, the aquarist should consider their suitability to the animal life, mutual compatibility, and size. The range shown here depicts the following: *(a) Vesicularia dubyana, (b)* species of *Vallisneria, (c) Echinodorus paniculatus, (d)* species of *Cabomba, (e) Hygrophila polysperma, (f) Cryptocoryne griffithi, (g) C. balansae, (h) Microsorium pteropus, (i) Cryptocoryne affinis, (j) Echinodorus cordifolius, (k) E. latifolius, (l) Cryptocoryne nevillii,*

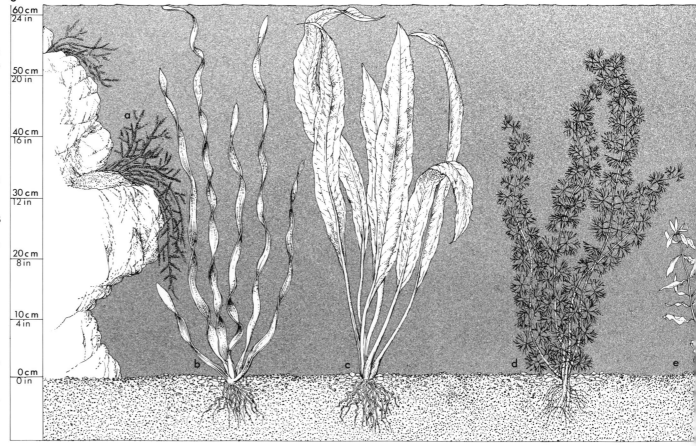

(m) Echinodorus tenellus, (n) Riccia fluitans, (o) Ceratopteris cornuta, (p) Lemna minor, and *(q) Pistia stratiotes.*

4 Planting is best done by hand, as a planting-stick can damage the plant. *(a)* Handle the plant gently, holding the crown between thumb and forefinger. *(b)* Place the plant in a hole of appropriate size, so that the roots are spread out. When planted, the crown should be just above the gravel. *(c)* Planting on ledges gives the impression of a river or pond bank with luxuriant growth. *(d)* A fine visual effect is obtained by letting the leaves of a plant such as *Vallisneria* stream out with the current from a hidden pump outlet. *(e)* A plant that needs nutrients from soil can be planted in a sand/soil mixture in a pot, which can then be covered with stones and gravel.

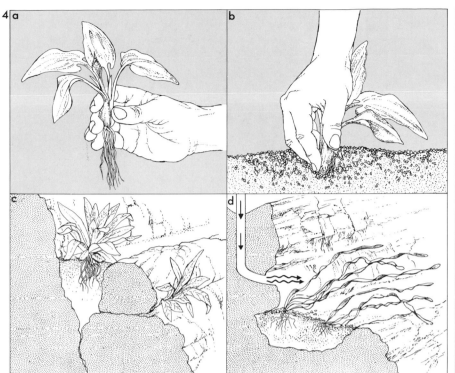

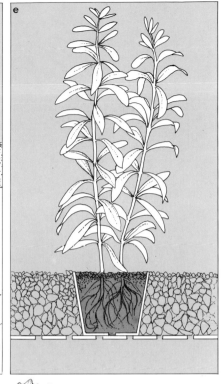

Water sources

The chief sources of water for aquaria are untreated natural bodies—lakes, streams, wells, or the sea—and the treated "domestic" supply on tap in homes. For a large-scale, open aquarium system, whose water is not re-cycled, the source of water must be reliable and reasonably constant during the entire year, as well as cheap and easy to extract. Great volumes may be needed, and natural sources requiring little pre-treatment are best. A simple method of pre-treatment is to draw the water from the natural body through a bed of sand.

If the quality of the water is poor or inconsistent, then a closed system with re-cycling and treatment should be considered. Closed and semi-closed systems require smaller volumes of new water, and only at intervals when a partial change of water is made or when the tank level needs to be topped up. A regular supply of good water is essential.

Natural fresh waters

Local sources of fresh water in nature must be assessed for their availability, seasonal constancy, and quality. The latter factor includes temperature, salinity, hardness, acidity, turbidity, and contamination. Pollution, by industrial wastes, urban discharges, or run-off from farmland, can require complex treatment in obtaining water of a suitable quality, and this is usually too costly. Rocks of limestone or chalk in the catchment area may produce water which is hard and alkaline, whilst siliceous rocks will create soft and neutral or slightly acidic waters.

Rain water is a good source of soft, neutral, or slightly acidic water. It should be collected from a thoroughly cleaned surface, and only after the first half hour of rainfall has cleansed the atmosphere to some extent, reducing possible contamination by mineral salts, pollutants, or aerial bacteria.

Tap water

The domestic water supply is a convenient source of clean fresh water. Its salinity, hardness, and acidity depend upon the geology of the supply area. Tap water is usually free from infectious agents such as bacteria, as it has been treated with chlorine or fluorine. These chemicals, however, must be removed before the water is added to an aquarium. This may be done fairly easily, by aerating and agitating the water briskly for twenty-four hours, by filtering it through activated carbon, or by neutralizing the chemicals with sodium thiosulphate. For the latter treatment, one gram (0.035 oz) of the neutralizer is added to each 100 litres (about 25 gallons) of the water, which is then stirred and left for five minutes. Next, five cubic centimetres (0.2 oz) of a fifteen per cent solution of hydrogen peroxide is added to that volume and stirred.

Excessively hard water may be softened, either by boiling, diluting with distilled water, or filtering through a water-softener (ion-exchanger) or through peat. Contamination from metal piping, especially of copper, can be a serious danger in new domestic water systems, and in using hot-water systems. Thus, domestic hot-water supplies should not be used, and cold water should be run from the tap for ten minutes or so before use.

Planting in the aquarium

The diverse kingdom of plants includes delicate ferns, mosses, liverworts, simple but variable algae, the highly evolved and beautifully structured flowering plants (angiosperms), and minute *Euglenas*, flagellates, and diatoms. Their forms, sizes, and life cycles in water are discussed in Chapter 2.

With fresh water, in the aquarium as in natural habitats, the higher plants are the most important. They are usually the main photosynthesizers, assimilating inorganic nutrients and releasing oxygen when illuminated. They provide different surfaces and shade for animals to attach to, rest and shelter in, and feed or spawn upon. In addition, they readily create a major and attractive element of the aquarium display. Suitable types range from those which trail long ribbon-like leaves in the current, and low tufted plants carpeting the stream bed, to thick bushy plants in still water, tall dense clumps dividing the water space, and floating rafts of leaves trailing fine roots.

For salt-water aquaria too, appropriate higher plants exist, notably the sea- or turtle-grasses (family Zosteraceae). But the algae are the dominant marine plants. Most commonly, the alga's base is attached firmly to a solid surface. As separation would damage the plant, algae must be collected with their attached substrates. Algae flourish on fairly sheltered shores, attached to stones and even dead shells. Some algae, for example *Ulva lactuca*, are able to live detached and floating at the water surface for a time, but generally, they do not re-attach. However, the Mediterranean alga, *Caulerpa*, "creeps" across a shell-gravel bed on root-like rhizoids, and fragments broken off will soon re-attach.

Choice and design

For aquarium display, suitable species of plants should be chosen for the particular environment and community which are planned. Each plant's expected growth and method of reproduction should be allowed for—a fast-growing plant with runners may soon spread over a large area. To resist destructive animals, varieties with tough leaves, roots, and fronds should be planted, or perhaps a few soft and succulent varieties to satisfy these animals.

The plant display should be simple in design, with a few groups of plants of one species. It is important to aim for good natural contrast in texture, form, and colouring. The arrangement of plants in the aquarium landscape is a matter of personal choice. A general rule is to place taller, denser plants at the rear or centre, and shorter ones at the front. When a living backdrop for the animal display is required, open areas of water should be reserved near the front and centre.

In communities dominated by algae, the type and size of the base to which the algae attach will limit the scope of the display designer. Specimens may have to be placed simply on different areas of the base sediment. Rather more elaborately, pockets can be made in a decorative rockwork panel, into which the stone base of the algae can be put.

With particular reference to freshwater communities, plants may be used to emphasize the full height and the depth of field of the display. The impression of luxuriant growth along the edge of a stream or lake bank can be enhanced by planting on raised terraces, in pockets, or in baskets or pots suspended over the side of the tank into the water. An attractive extension of the freshwater aquarium is to construct an area above the water surface as a planted marsh. Trays of peat and loam can be planted with a variety of wetland plants, which can be encouraged to trail down into the water along the edge of the tank.

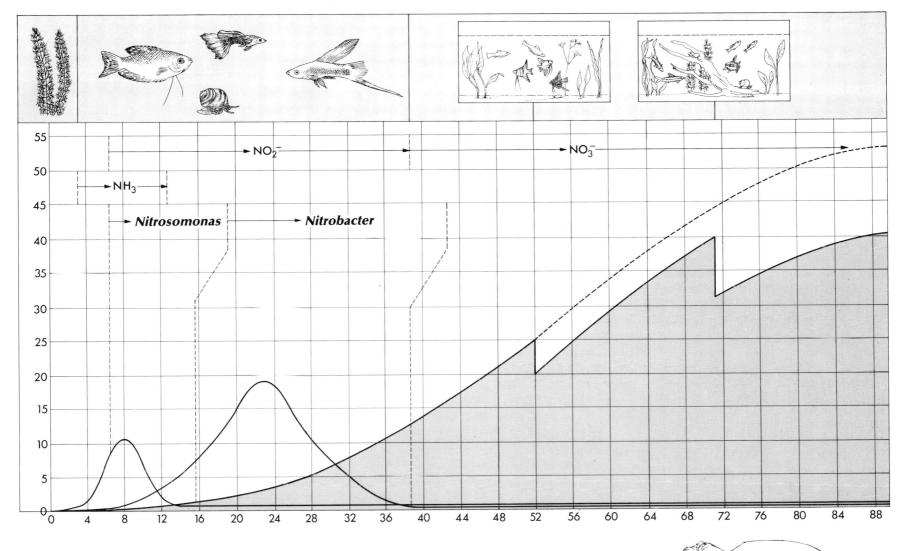

NO$_2^-$

NH$_3$

→ *Nitrosomonas* → *Nitrobacter*

NO$_3^-$

Above are shown the initial changes in amounts of toxic nitrogen compounds in an aquarium, due to increasing activity of bacteria such as *Nitrosomonas* and *Nitrobacter*. Days of operation are on the horizontal axis, and concentrations in parts per million are on the vertical axis. At first, animals are introduced which can tolerate water that is not critical in quality (see Chapter 3). Levels of ammonia (NH$_3$) and nitrite (NO$_2^-$) are reduced until more sensitive animals can be added. The rising level of nitrate (NO$_3^-$) may be controlled by periodically replacing some of the water, while removing excess detritus through a siphon as shown at right.

Guidelines for planting

Some plants acquired as cuttings can be buried in the gravel and left to form roots. Others should be floated on the water surface until roots are well developed, and then be planted. Most rooting aquatic plants will flourish in gravel of 2 to 6 mm (0.08 to 0.24 in) diameter. The depth of the bed must be adequate for the size of plant used, for it is worth remembering that the roots may be as voluminous as the shoots.

The more robust species, especially those with rhizomatous roots, will grow in clean tap water. Other species must obtain nutrients from the water and, when rooted, from the substrate, and they may not flourish in a newly established aquarium. After a few months, animals and bacteria will have produced more than enough nutrients for good plant growth.

When first setting up a tank, a planting medium of peat or loamy soil may help root development and provide nutrients. But later, the organic soil may hinder water circulation into the gravel, and will add a considerable load to any water-treatment system. If rooting is a problem, the plant can be placed in a small, individual plug of soil in a small basket which is buried in the gravel. Any excessively buoyant plant can be weighted in the desired position until firmly rooted, using ties or small stones, lead, concrete, or glass weights.

In a newly planted aquarium, the light may be left on for up to twenty hours a day, to encourage rapid establishment. Boisterous or destructive animals should not be introduced, or should be removed, until the plants are growing healthily.

Quarantine or disinfection

Plants from the wild, or any other source where parasitic, pathogenic, or otherwise undesirable organisms might be present on the specimen, should be cleaned carefully and quarantined or disinfected, before being introduced to the aquarium. Freshwater plants may be dipped, for only fifteen to thirty seconds, into a dilute salt solution, and then rinsed thoroughly in clean water. Alternatively, the plants should be maintained in an isolation tank for three weeks, or in a bath of potassium permanganate (solution of three parts per million) for two days.

Livestocking the aquarium

The choice of animal species must be made, at least in general terms, at an early stage of planning an aquarium display. The visible animals are usually the chief element of the scene and are also the most demanding as regards water quality, décor and substrates, and suitable plant types. Aquatic species include many strange invertebrate creatures and a vast range of fishes—each being unique in its typical size, shape, colour, movement, nutrition, growth rate, longevity, territoriality, gregariousness, breeding habits, and attitude towards offspring. Even within species, there is great variety with size and age, not to mention individual idiosyncracies.

The aquarist usually begins with a specific theme for the expected display, and a wish to explore or demonstrate a particular feature of aquatic animal life. He may be interested in a definite habitat or geographical area, or in fishes which breed in a certain way or make peculiar noises, or in gastropod snails that maintain miniature gardens of edible algae around them, or even in animals of a distinctive colour.

The species selected must all be suitable for keeping under the same conditions of water temperature, salinity, and acidity, in the same aquarium set of substrates, plants, illumination, and depth, volume, and movement of water. The community tank can be designed to house a variety of species with complementary life-styles. These might include shoaling and solitary species, animals which burrow and others which crawl over rock, highly active fishes and sessile invertebrates, piscivores, detritivores, herbivores, and so on.

The collected animals must be directly compatible with each other. Animals should not be held captive in conditions of stress, and the stress caused by animals amongst themselves can be just as real and damaging as is inadequate oxygen or excessive ammonia. In particular, predatory species must not be kept with animals upon which they prey, unless the latter are large enough to avoid harassment. The well-being of all vulnerable specimens should be ensured before placing them with other creatures in the aquarium, giving due attention to the power or aggressiveness of some species and the delicacy or submissiveness of others.

As a general rule, fish species which occupy closely similar niches in the wild—with the same feeding habits, shelter areas, and range of size or appearance, such as the juvenile chaetodontids (butterflyfishes)—should not be kept together in a small aquarium. If potential combatants are kept together, signs of aggressive territoriality or bullying must be noted, and the individuals separated if necessary. As well as tank size, the physical diversity of the aquarium environment is important: in a tank with many dividing lines formed by rock outcrops, plants, or water currents, there is likely to be more harmony and a healthier community.

Procuring specimens

When buying or being given animals for the aquarium, or collecting them in the wild, several basic points must be borne in mind. The origin of each specimen should be traced as far as possible, by recording the location, time, and method of capturing or raising, and of transporting, the animal. Many specimens are juveniles, and their growth rate and probable eventual size should be ascertained, for comparison to the space that will be available in the aquarium.

Each animal must be in good health, or at least the aquarist must be aware of its state of health. He should note carefully the conditions under which the animal has been living in captivity, as regards duration, temperature, salinity, acidity, and illumination, as well as the size of tank, choice of companions, and kind of water treatment. He should ask whether the animal has been ill, or received any prophylactic or other medication.

Whether an animal is healthy can be judged largely by its behaviour, when compared to other specimens of the same species, and to what is expected as normal activity. Rapid ventilation, air gulping, general lethargy, imbalance, restlessness, darting, unusual orientation or position in the tank, or poor relations with companions, should be looked for as indications of poor health or stressful conditions.

All new animals must be subjected to a quarantine period. Detailed procedures are discussed in Chapter 7, but the two general objectives are worth emphasizing. Any likelihood of introducing illness to the main aquarium should be minimized; and the animal must be given the best possible chance of recovering from previous mistreatment or stress, and of becoming accustomed to its new

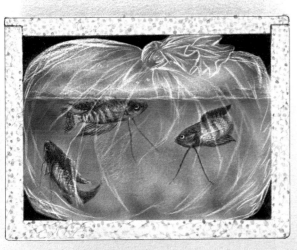

Careful transfer of fishes to the tank is very important. Shown at left is a standard method of transportation, as will be described in Chapter 7: a strong polystyrene box, its lid sealed by tape, holds a double polythene bag with no corners where a fish may become trapped. The bag must be tightly closed and is partly filled with pure oxygen to aerate the water. Below, the animals in such a bag are introduced slowly to their new home.

1 The bag, still closed, is placed directly into the tank water and is left until its own water temperature reaches that of the tank water.
2 Several small holes are pierced in the bag with a pin, so that the two waters mix gradually and equalize in quality, accustoming the animals to the aquarium solution.
3 A large hole may be cut in the bag, enabling fishes to swim out into the tank. Other animals can be removed from the bag underwater and placed on firm surfaces.

surroundings. Adjustment of water quality and development of satisfactory feeding are brought about during this crucial period.

Introducing animals to the tank

The animal should be transferred from a holding tank, or from the wild, in insulated polythene bags—possibly with excess oxygen and mild anaesthesia. It must be introduced into a quarantine tank which has been adjusted, as far as possible, to the temperature, salinity, and acidity of the holding tank or natural habitat. The water in the quarantine tank must be completely clean and well aerated.

During transportation, temperature control and insulation must be adequate to ensure that there is little difference in temperature between the animal and the quarantine tank. The transfer should be carried out gently, with as little disturbance to the animal as possible. It should be made in subdued lighting, and the quarantine lights should be kept dim for twelve hours or more after the animal has been introduced.

The same general procedures are to be followed when the animal has satisfactorily completed its quarantine period and is moved to the main aquarium tank. The quarantine and main tank conditions must be matched carefully, ensuring a high quality of water in the main tank.

But the animal is now being introduced to an established community of other organisms, as well as to a new physical environment, requiring further precautions to reduce stress.

The established animals may pester or attack a new arrival in various ways. In extreme cases, the animal may be bitten or even harried to death. Any newcomer is at a considerable disadvantage, being disturbed by the transfer operation and deposited in unfamiliar surroundings amongst potential aggressors. So the introduction should be made as advantageous to the new specimen as possible, by feeding the aquarium inhabitants little, dimming the lights, then placing the specimen in the tank quietly. Where trouble is anticipated, addition of more rocky shelters, or the rearrangement of some tank décor, will put the new arrival on a more equal basis with other occupants.

For the first week or two, newly introduced animals may require special attention, particularly during feeding. There are also unusual cases such as large anemones which arrive detached from any substrate: until they have satisfactorily attached, it may be useful to reduce the rates of aeration and water circulation. Animals which burrow into sand or gravel may be vulnerable to attack until they have dug a new hole or been provided with one.

Bacterial filtration and conditioning

Attention must also be paid to the proper development of the invisible bacteria which do so much to maintain the ambience of animals in the aquarium. Correct installation of a bacterial filter is the first step. The sub-gravel plate in the tank preserves a uniform water space between the gravel and the tank bottom, in order to ensure water flow through the gravel. This plate should fit the tank well, all round the edges, and should be sealed with tape or glue if necessary. It may cover the entire tank bottom, or only a portion thereof.

Fixed rockwork in the tank should be sealed to the tank bottom, and the filter plate should butt against and be sealed to the rocks. There should be no dead areas or crevices where detritus may accumulate and produce stagnation. The air-lift water pump should be fitted securely to the filter plate, with its diffuser stone and air-line in place. Next, the gravel should be mixed and sieved dry, thoroughly washed, and spread uniformly over the filter plate to the required depth.

The tank should now be filled with suitable aquarium water. Any rooting plants may be installed conveniently when the tank is partially filled. Water heating, aeration, and illumination should be switched on subsequently. Circulation of water begins through the base gravel, and the flow rates of air and water are adjusted. At this stage, there will be low numbers of bacteria in the system, particularly when precautions have been taken to disinfect the water and materials in the aquarium, minimizing the introduction of pathogenic bacteria and other parasites.

A conditioning process is necessary to build up large and healthy populations of nitrifying and decomposing bacteria in the aquarium filter bed. A "seed" colony of these bacteria may be introduced by adding a small amount of gravel and water from another aquarium which has been operating for some time. The latter must have similar temperature and salinity of water, if one is to avoid killing the bacteria by transferring them. Without seeding, the conditioning will take place but, due to the low starting numbers of bacteria, will take longer.

Nitrifying bacteria depend upon supplies of ammonia or nitrite, and of oxygen. Heterotrophic decomposing bacteria require continuous supplies of organic material as food. These materials begin to accumulate as soon as living animals enter the aquarium. Only a few specimens of hardy species should be introduced—the water conditions are not stable and, until the bacterial population has increased, toxins of ammonia and nitrite may rise to dangerous levels.

If the right conditions are maintained—good aeration, water circulation, and temperature—and if appropriate sources of food energy are supplied, the bacteria will flourish and multiply rapidly to colonize the extensive surfaces of the filter bed. Various typical changes occur during the first few months in the life of an aquarium. Ammonia and then nitrite will increase, and later decrease as the specific nitrifying bacterial populations grow to utilize these metabolic wastes. The end product, nitrate, increases and then stabilizes. Such changes should be monitored and plotted daily, so that the aquarist will know when it is safe to complete the livestocking of the new aquarium. This should be accomplished as gradually as possible, once ammonia and nitrite levels have stabilized to low values.

Aquarium Management

Management embraces all the tasks necessary to ensure that the entire aquarium system continues to function and develop in the best possible manner. It includes the aspects of planning ahead, obtaining new specimens, organizing expeditions to collect them, taking photographs, preparing for visitors, mending equipment, designing and building hardware, making scientific observations, recording events, and treating illness, as well as following a programme of routine checks and carrying out essential chores regularly.

Routine operations

In the fully functioning aquarium, it is important to devise and obey a schedule for management. The tank, contents, and support systems are sufficiently complex to justify working methodically through checklists. This should provide consistent attention and adequate care for the various components—structure, water, livestock, and technology.

The maintenance schedule

Ten main types of tasks for the aquarist are described below, with reference to their performance at daily, monthly, and yearly rates. These intervals and activities must be adapted to suit the particular requirements of each aquarium and its equipment.

Animals

Daily: feeding, three to seven times per week, in accordance with the details to be given later. Count all specimens and check their condition. Unusual, aggressive, or listless behaviour may call for measures such as the medical treatment to be discussed subsequently.

Monthly: stock the inventory of food—especially if live—and of materials for display, quarantine, or other needs.

Yearly: split or cull any excess populations. Assess the range of specimens, and procure additions if desired; methods of collecting and breeding fishes will conclude this chapter.

Plants

Daily: note the condition of all specimens, and look for uprooting, torn leaves or fronds, algal covering, and faded colour.

Monthly: stock the inventory. Thin out as necessary, including plants or algae used in a filter.

Yearly: split, and extensively crop away, any excess growth.

Tank interior

Daily: remove uneaten food, and clean windows as necessary. Viewing windows may have to be cleaned on both sides every day. Silt will settle upon tank walls and windows, whilst microscopic and filamentous

Modern aquarium accessories include various devices for cleaning the tank. Above, paired magnets with soft coatings are slid along opposite sides of a tank window, and the inner magnet serves as a rubber to remove algae.

Quantitative analysis of the aquarium water helps to keep it healthy.

1 A chemical titration set consists of a clamp stand (a) holding a burette tube (b) over a mixing bottle (c), with exact measurements on the glass containers for the test solution and substances added to it. These include a liquid of known concentration which reacts with the test solution, and an indicator whose colour is changed by the reaction. The concentration of the test solution can thus be estimated.

2 Titration may determine the acidity or alkalinity (pH value) of the test solution by treating a certain amount of it (a) with a fixed quantity of a mixture of the reagent and indicator (b), agitating the solution to give a uniform colour (c), and comparing this with a scale (d) to find the pH. The colour depends on the pH because the indicator shows how much of the reagent is used up by the reaction, and this proportion depends upon the concentration of the test solution.

3 Titration can measure water hardness by treating a certain amount of the test solution with drops of a reagent–indicator mixture until a change of colour is completed. The number of drops will show the degree of hardness because the amount of reagent needed is proportional to the concentration of the test solution. The colour range differs for (a) temporary hardness due to bicarbonates and (b) total hardness including permanent kinds. Typically, each drop is equivalent to the presence of about fifty millionths of a gram (or two millionths of an ounce) of calcium oxide in the volume of test solution.

4 Titration may require more than one reagent, as in this measurement of the toxic nitrite level. Two mixtures are added separately, the reaction ends after several minutes, and the test solution is compared to a colour scale which shows the nitrite concentration in parts per million.

5 Spectrophotometry is a more complex and accurate method of analysis. Light of certain wavelengths (measured in angstroms) is passed through the test solution to see how much its particles absorb (as shown by a light detector). This spectrum reveals their chemical nature and their concentration (as on the vertical graph axis illustrated).

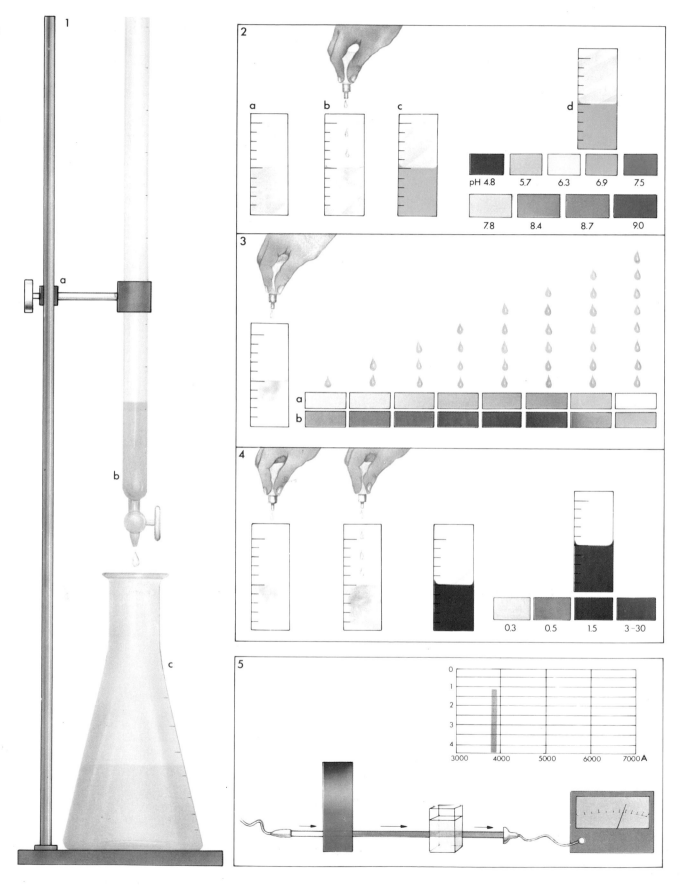

algae grow there, and greasy fingerprints smear the glass. Among the available appliances are plastic scourers, rubber pads, long-handled holders and blades, and paired magnets. Great care must be taken not to scratch the window surfaces. Some plastics are easily marked, and glass can be scratched by metal, glass, gravel or sand, or jewellery.

Monthly: siphon carefully the accumulated detritus from rocks, sediments, and leaves. Check and balance the water level, clean the cover glass, and put the physical set or décor in order as required.

Yearly: stir up the sediment gradually, siphoning off the fine top layer as it settles out. Fine detritus is dead organic matter, and must be removed periodically, by techniques ranging from the simple siphon to the use of dip tubes and vacuum cleaners, the last being powered by an air-lift or a small water pump.

Water quality

Daily: measure and record the water and air temperatures. Note any bad odours or excess turbidity. Check the water surface for a film of dust or oil.

Monthly: measure and record chemical factors, taking corrective measures when necessary, and change the water partially.

The quality of the solution in the aquarium changes with time, as materials and energy are removed and added by various inorganic or living processes. Important factors to measure are the temperature, acidity (pH), salinity (conductivity), hardness, and concentrations of substances such as oxygen, ammonia, and nitrate—as well as sound transmission and relative light intensity. Any analysis may be either qualitative or quantitative, for example in detecting the presence of a substance or measuring its actual amount. Quantitative methods are most useful but differ in sensitivity and complexity of the required equipment. This includes chemical titration, spectrophotometry, colorimetry, and specific electrode probes, all of which are illustrated here.

A partial change of the solution with clean fresh water is needed at intervals to maintain the quality of the aquarium water, particularly in a closed system with no biological filtration. This change serves to dilute the accumulated metabolic substances—nitrates, phosphates, ammonia, hydrogen ions—and to replace any trace elements depleted by the organisms. The proper rate of change should be determined, for a given system, by monitoring the water quality, especially in regard to nitrate and ammonia, and noting the rate of stagnation that must be balanced. As a general rule, about twenty per cent of the water might be changed every three to four weeks. Frequent small changes are wiser than a single flush, and minimum disturbance to the aquarium and livestock is essential. New water must be aerated thoroughly beforehand, at the required temperature, salinity, and purity. It should be added so as to keep the water level constant, while the old water is quietly siphoned from the tank bottom to remove deposited detritus.

Heaters and lamps

Daily: operate the lighting on and off, checking the switches and settings. Adjust controls for heating and cooling, if necessary.

Monthly: check that the dimmers, timers, thermostats, and other switches are fully operational. Correct the positioning of lamps and heaters. Inspect the equipment for overheating, wear, corrosion, blackening, salt incrustation, and algal growth.

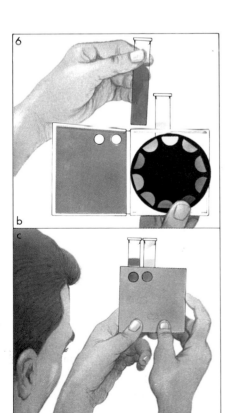

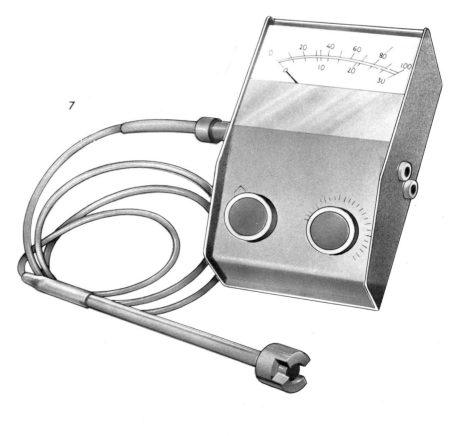

6 Colorimetry is an improved method of examining a test solution after adding an indicator.
A transparent plastic disc (a), before a tube of clear water next to the solution (b), is rotated until it colours the water just like the solution (c), whose concentration is shown on the disc near this colour.

7 A probe that detects a specific kind of chemical or energy can be placed in a solution to send direct readings of the concentration or intensity through an electrical cable to a meter.

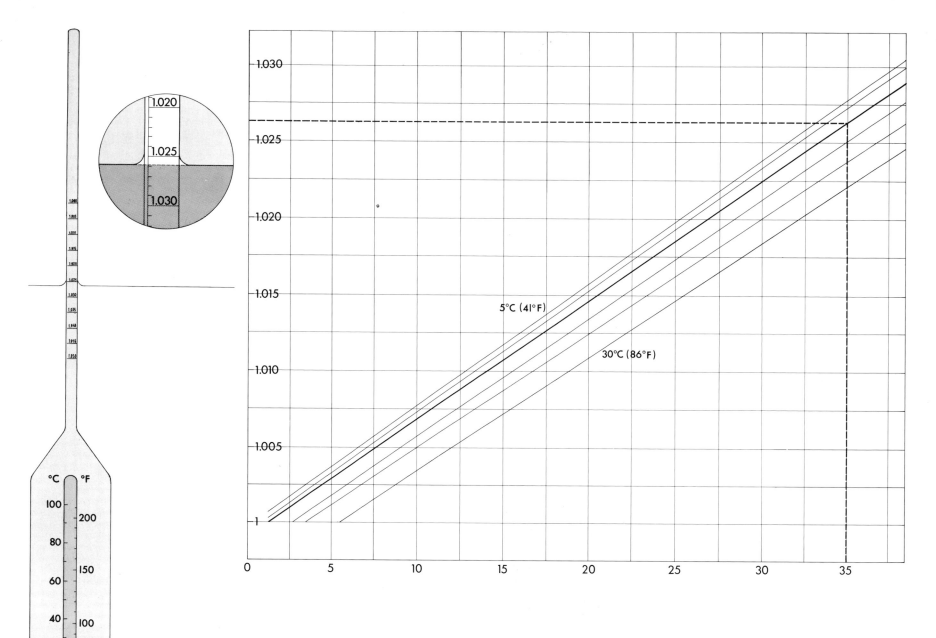

The hydrometer is a common device for determining the salinity of water in an aquarium. As shown at left, it is placed in the water and floats, with one end kept downwards by a ballast material in the bulb. The narrow tube end protrudes above the water surface and is calibrated. The reading on the scale should be made at the level of the surrounding water, not at the top of the curved meniscus where the water meets the tube due to surface tension. Such a reading is normally a value of "specific gravity". This is the ratio of the density of the water solution to the density of pure water. Density depends on the amount of dissolved salts, and on the temperature of the solution. Thus, by indirectly reading the density, at a known temperature, one can determine the total salinity.

The graph shown above is used for this purpose, with specific gravity values on the vertical axis, and levels of salinity on the horizontal axis in parts per thousand (grams per litre or ounces per cubic foot). The graph is drawn for temperatures at intervals of 5°C (9°F) between the extremes of 5°C (41°F) and 30°C (86°F). An example is shown for full sea water at 15°C (59°F). The hydrometer may contain a thermometer to measure temperatures, or may be calibrated directly to read the salinity at a single temperature. Hydrometers are based on Archimedes' principle that an object floats in a liquid to a depth which decreases as the density of the liquid increases. A small variation in density does not greatly change the object's submerged volume, but this change will be mainly in depth if the object is very narrow at the surface level, and will be seen more easily on the side of the object, so a sensitive hydrometer is one with a narrow tube compared to the bulb. Other methods of determining salinity include measurement of the solution's electrical conductivity or its index of light refraction.

Yearly: replace lamp elements, especially the fluorescent types, after their specified lifetimes.

Pumps and power units
Daily: ensure smooth running, without excess heat or noise, and at the required output of water, air, or power.
Monthly: check vulnerable components for wear, such as diaphragms in air pumps. Clean and lubricate as necessary, using alternative or duplicate units in the aquarium.
Yearly: full service every six to twenty-four months, depending upon the type of unit and the amount of usage.

Distribution and filtration systems
Daily: check the positioning and operation of directional water inlets, streams, weirs, channels, pipes, air-lifts, diffusers, and skimmers.
Monthly: clean air-lifts, diffusers, and all flow channels, as necessary. Check the circulation and flow of water and air. Clean and re-pack filters if required, except biological ones.
Yearly: dismantle, clean thoroughly, and refill non-biological filters.

Connection devices
Monthly: check wires, pipes, lines, and valves for any leaks, snags, rotting, or overheating. Clean submerged parts and check their routes.

Ancillary equipment
Daily: clean any used items such as food utensils.
Monthly: repair and store away the apparatus as necessary.
Yearly: recondition or replace the most heavily used items.

Tank structure and surroundings
Monthly: check the frame, supports, stands, joints, seals, and welds for corrosion or leakage, repairing as necessary. Clean all external units and surfaces with fresh water.
Yearly: inspect the entire installation and carry out any required repairs, sealing, or repainting.

Food and feeding

A good diet for the aquarium animals must be not only well balanced in nutritional contents, but also palatable and presentable in form. It provides each animal with energy to live healthily, and it might include supplementary components—such as vitamins, trace elements, or pigments—which are medicinal or can enhance colouring.

Much valuable information from aquaculture research on the feeding requirements of fishes is relevant to the aquarist. However, the aims of commercial aquaculture and of aquarium management are rather different. Aquarium specimens tend to have higher dietary needs than do farmed fishes, which demand optimum growth in relation to costs of food and heat input.

Nutrition
The food supplied must contain fats and carbohydrates for energy, as well as all the protein and fat which are essential for the replacement of cell materials, for normal growth, and in maintaining general metabolism, besides small amounts of vitamins and minerals.

Protein
In the diet of fishes, protein is of particular importance. Fish flesh consists largely of protein, and health depends upon a constantly high proportion of protein in the food. This should be around thirty to forty per cent, with variation according to the species, age, size, water quality, and temperature. The protein must also be in a digestible form: animal proteins are easier to digest than plant proteins, which are within tough cell walls, and carnivorous animals have shorter intestines than do herbivores.

Natural proteins, of either plant or animal origin, are compounds of carbon, nitrogen, oxygen, hydrogen, and some minor elements. They contain differing proportions of about twenty-five amino acids. Ten of these cannot be synthesized by the fish and must be supplied in its diet. If any of the essential amino acids is not available, body-protein manufacture stops. Thus, either unbalanced or inadequate protein in the diet may reduce growth, repair of damaged tissue, and resistance to infection. Poor energy content of a food may also lead to protein deficiency, by forcing the diversion of protein to energy production. On the other hand, any excess protein is excreted as toxic ammonia or urea.

Carbohydrates
The carbohydrates range from simple sugars, such as glucose, to complex polymers which include starch and cellulose. None are specifically essential to the animal. Carnivorous fishes cannot metabolize large quantities, and any excess is stored as glycogen in the liver and blood where—if extreme—it can lead to disease and death.

A dietary level of around forty per cent of carbohydrate seems to be suitable. Roughage, in the form of indigestible cellulose fibres, may be important to the correct functioning of the intestine (as it is in humans), and can safely constitute about four per cent of the diet.

Fats
Fats are the main source of energy in a fish's diet and are major components of living cell walls. The most important are simple, unsaturated fatty acids linked to glycerol molecules. These are fluid and utilizable at the generally low body temperatures of an aquatic poikilotherm.

The total fat content of the diet must be adequate for the animal's energy needs, in order to avoid "burning" proteins. A level of around eight per cent has been found suitable for several fish groups. An energy deficiency may lead to stunted growth, but excess fats are deposited about the viscera and can cause diseases of the liver, kidney, and heart. Some fatty acids must be supplied in proper amounts with the diet, as they cannot be synthesized by the fish. Fatty acid deficiencies have been linked to fin-rot and heart diseases, and to death.

Vitamins
The diverse organic substances known as vitamins are essential in small amounts for normal metabolism in animals. Many are not synthesized within the body and must be supplied in the diet. Necessary quantities have some probable variation between species: a fish seems to require higher amounts of vitamins than does a mammal, perhaps due to using them less efficiently.

Most compound foods, commercially available to the aquarist, contain mixed vitamin supplements, and live foods generally offer a suitable natural balance of vitamins. The following table summarizes the functions of fifteen vitamins which must be provided in the diet of aquarium fishes. The first four vitamins are fat-soluble and can be stored in the body, whilst the others are water-soluble.

Vitamin A	vision, formation of mucous membrane, development and maintenance of pigmentation (colouring)

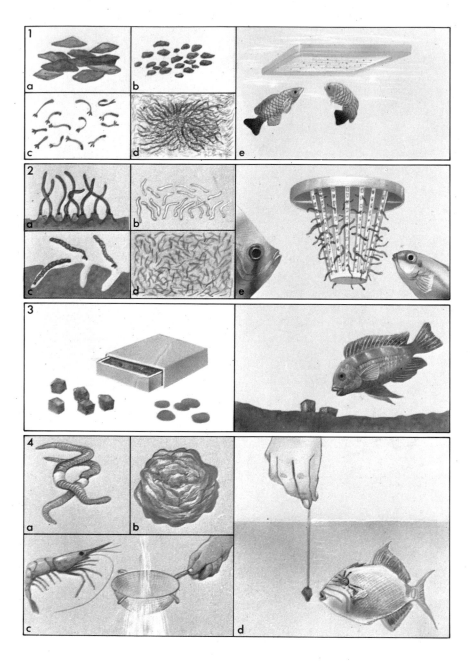

ROUGHAGE

FATS

VITAMINS AND MINERALS

PROTEIN

CARBOHYDRATES

5

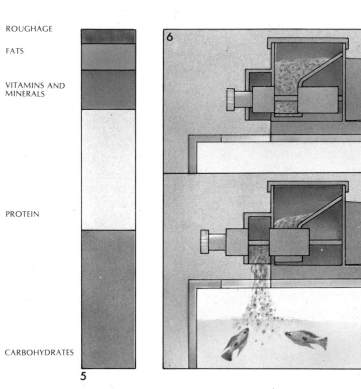

6

7

The diverse ways of feeding fishes in an aquarium are shown on these pages.

1 Compound foods can be purchased in forms such as *(a)* large and *(b)* small flakes for fishes of different sizes. So can whole foods, such as *(c)* dried mosquito larvae and *(d)* antiseptically dried and frozen tubifex worms. Many foods will float on the surface and can be kept within a plastic enclosure until they are eaten *(e)*.

2 Live foods such as *(a)* tubifex, *(b)* enchytrae, or grindal worms, *(c)* bloodworms, and *(d)* micronematodes for small fishes, can be eaten after they crawl through holes in a plastic feeder *(e)*, which may be separately aerated to prolong the worms' life.

3 Tablets and pellets of various sizes are available to suit feeding habits.

4 Larger foods such as *(a)* earthworms, *(b)* vegetables, and *(c)* prawns may be cut into pieces and cleaned with fresh water through a sieve. Moving a piece through the tank can encourage a wary fish to eat it *(d)*.

5 A balanced diet for many kinds of aquarium animals will have the total percentages of constituents shown.
6 An automatic feeder may be bought to ensure regular meals. The type shown here can drop flakes through a hole in the tank cover for a week or more. Its time-switch can also vary the aeration, filtration, or lights during feeding.

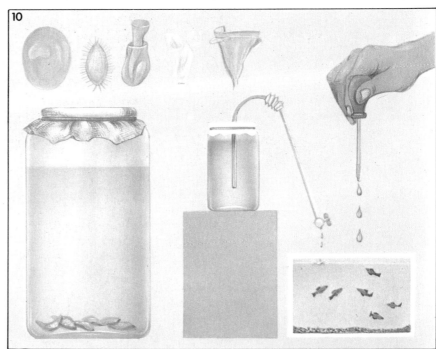

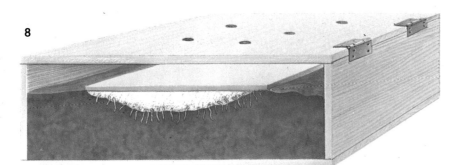

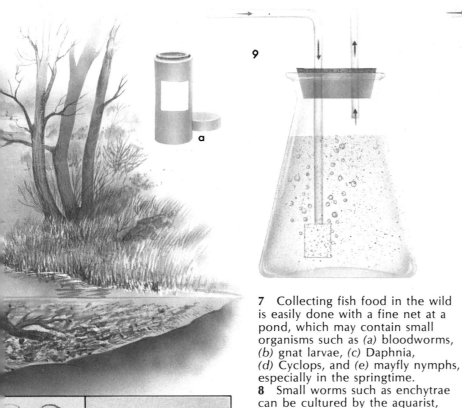

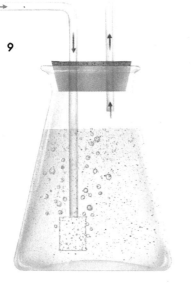

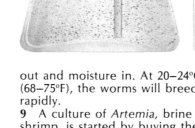

7 Collecting fish food in the wild is easily done with a fine net at a pond, which may contain small organisms such as *(a)* bloodworms, *(b)* gnat larvae, *(c)* Daphnia, *(d)* Cyclops, and *(e)* mayfly nymphs, especially in the springtime.
8 Small worms such as enchytrae can be cultured by the aquarist, starting with a collected sample. This is placed in a wooden box, on a layer of soil mixed with peat, and covered by a paste of oatmeal, beneath a glass sheet and enough paper or dark polythene to keep light

out and moisture in. At 20–24°C (68–75°F), the worms will breed rapidly.
9 A culture of *Artemia*, brine shrimp, is started by buying their eggs *(a)*. These are placed in a bottle of water solution of non-iodized salt (specific gravity about 1.024) at a temperature of 24–27°C (75–81°F) and well aerated. The eggs hatch after a day or so, and their shells float up to the surface. The live shrimp can be siphoned from the bottom and caught in a sieve. They will grow to 1.5 cm (0.6 in) long if put in a larger

tank with aeration and food such as algae or yeast.
10 Young fishes feed on microscopic infusorians such as protozoans and rotifers. These can be cultured in a closed flask of water with chopped vegetable matter, at 18–21°C (64–70°F) in dim light for 10–14 days. They are fed to the tank through a siphon with a tap, or through a dropper.

Vitamin D	regulation of calcium and phosphorus metabolism, bone formation in young		
Vitamin E	regulation of oxidative metabolism		
Vitamin K	blood clotting		
Vitamin B₁ (thiamine)	metabolic enzyme reactions		

Vitamin D — regulation of calcium and phosphorus metabolism, bone formation in young

Vitamin E — regulation of oxidative metabolism

Vitamin K — blood clotting

Vitamin B_1 (thiamine) — metabolic enzyme reactions

Vitamin B_2 (riboflavin) — vision, carbohydrate metabolism

Vitamin B_6 (pyridoxine) — vision, protein and fat metabolism

Pantothenic acid — cell growth, molecule transfer enzymes, development of central nervous system

Nicotinic acid (niacin) — cell growth, transfer enzymes

Biotin — fatty acid metabolism

Folic acid — transfer enzymes, blood cell formation and glucose regulation

Vitamin B_{12} (cyanoco-balamin) — protein metabolism, red blood corpuscle and nucleic acid formation

Vitamin C (ascorbic acid) — collagen synthesis, growth, tissue repair

Inositol — cell membrane formation

Choline — nervous system, fat transport

Minerals and other elements

In addition to the major components of organic matter—carbon, hydrogen, oxygen, and nitrogen—at least twenty more elements are vital to living processes, and some of their functions are summarized in Chapter 4. Aquatic plants satisfy all such requirements from the surrounding water or the substrate. Aquatic animals can absorb part of the necessary supply from this source as well. Thus, water salinity and hardness are important to the mineral demands of every organism.

An animal, however, obtains these elements mainly from its food. Each of them exists to some extent in many food ingredients and may be included with the vitamin supplement in compound foods. With few exceptions, a normal varied diet will supply the aquarium livestock with adequate concentrations of all essential elements.

Compound foods

Commercially prepared fish foods are dried into pellets, flakes, and powders. Convenient and widely available, they are blended to suit the nutritional requirements of fishes, and most aquatic animals will accept and thrive on them. Such compound foods differ in quality. The cheaper bulk foods are based upon grain, pulses, or meal, and are intended for use with a whole food supplement. Others are made with meat or vegetable proteins, and are designed scientifically to meet all nutritional needs.

Flaked foods provide a particularly wide variety of recipes, to be used for herbivores, the pre-spawning period, rapidly growing young, and so on. Flakes will float while dry, and sink slowly when saturated with water. Pellets are produced as "mouth-sized particles" for large fishes. Some pellets float for surface feeders, whilst others sink for mid-water and bottom feeders. Powdered foods are useful for young fry and suspension-feeding invertebrates.

Home-made food

Compound foods can also be prepared by the aquarist. It is most convenient to make a dry-base mixture in reasonably large quantities which are easily storable. The mixture could include high-protein wheat cereal, bran, soya-bean meal, dried skimmed milk, shrimp and fish meals, offering a balanced content of protein, fat, and carbohydrate. Starchy foods, such as biscuits, bread, and potatoes, should be avoided.

As a quantity of food is being prepared—for example, a supply lasting two weeks, which can be kept in the refrigerator—the dry base is added to an equal or slightly smaller amount of fresh protein purée. This can be made in an electric liquidizer–blender from fresh fish, meat, or vegetables such as spinach or alfalfa (lucerne). The resulting paste can be made into a variety of forms, depending upon the size and species of animals to be fed. It may be mixed with agar to produce a thick jelly, extruded and dried into pellets, smeared and dried onto small pieces of porous material (stone, pot, or coral) to tempt fine-toothed coral-reef fishes, or made into a block with plaster-of-paris for rock-grazers such as the parrotfishes.

Listed below are some ingredients suitable for home-made food, with their composition in percentages. The total percentage of each component in the resulting food must be calculated so as to obtain the required balance of protein, fat, and carbohydrate content.

Ingredient	Protein	Fat	Carbohydrate	Roughage	Minerals	Vitamins
Meat and bone meal	54	10	3	2	30	A,B,D
Fish and fish meal	70	7	3	1	15	A,B,D
Crustaceans and shrimp meal	54	3	2	12	—	A,B,D,K
Dried skimmed milk	35	1	55	0.2	8	B,C,D
Bran	18	4	60	10	6	B,E
High-protein cereals	20	4	57	15	3	B,E
Soya bean meal	49	10	17	4	6	B₂,K
Dried yeast	50	2	35	3	7	B,D
Green vegetables	16	2.5	44	28	9	A,C,E,K

Whole foods

Many whole foods—live or preserved animals, and algae or higher plants—are suitable for the aquarium. They contain balanced proportions of the essential components for healthy diets and are often more attractive to an animal which is difficult to feed. Possible problems are the collection of food organisms, which may not be convenient or feasible during the whole year, and the introduction of disease agents or other undesirables.

The culturing of a food organism, under controlled and hygienic conditions, can provide suitable live food continuously, cheaply, simply, and with a minimal risk of introducing parasites or disease. A variety of appropriate animal species is illustrated here. Some can be bought as eggs or young, but others are specially bred, and the methods or apparatuses employed are also diverse.

Live food may, instead, be collected in the wild. Organisms from non-aquatic sources, such as earthworms, aphids, caterpillars, and land snails, are free from possible pathogens which could harm the aquarium inhabitants. When collecting from aquatic sources, one should take precautions against introducing disease to the aquarium. If feasible, organisms collected in fresh water can be fed to marine animals, and vice versa. Freshwater foods are less likely to harbour fish parasites if collected from fish-free waters. Live foods must be cleaned thoroughly, and quarantined by isolation, if practicable, to kill parasites by denying them a host. Plants may be initially dipped in potassium per-

A variety of animals suitable as whole foods for the aquarium is illustrated, increasing in size from top to bottom with horizontal divisions at about 1, 2, 5, 10 and 25 mm (0.04–1.0 in): *(a)* microscopic infusorian, *(b)* Cyclops, *(c)* Daphnia water-flea, *(d)* aphid, *(e)* micronematode worm, *(f)* Calanus plankton, *(g)* mosquito larva, *(h)* grindal worm, *(i)* Artemia brine shrimp, *(j)* mayfly nymph, *(k)* Asellus louse, *(l)* tubifex worm, *(m)* Mysis shrimp, *(n)* caddisfly, *(o)* Gammarus shrimp, *(p)* marine ragworm, *(q)* stick insect, *(r)* bivalve mollusc, *(s)* earthworm, *(t)* gastropod snail, *(u)* crayfish. These may be served to animals of proportional size, but many can also be used easily to make compound foods in diverse forms.

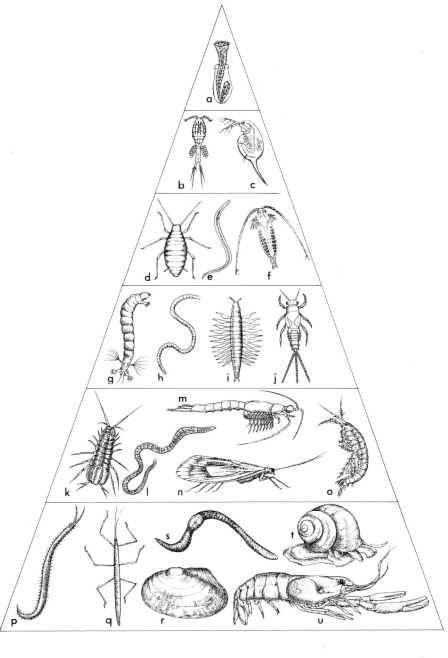

manganate and washed well. Alternatively, wild foods—especially if from dubious sources—can be disinfected by boiling in water and can then be used as dead nourishment.

Preservation

Whole foods—bought, collected, or cultured—may be preserved for long periods, if required, by drying or freezing. Drying can be done in an oven, the sunlight, an airstream, or a freeze-drying environment. Heat-drying reduces the food volume, flavour, and texture somewhat but is useful on a small scale. Excessive or prolonged heat reduces the nutritional value by denaturing proteins and vitamins. Freeze-drying involves special equipment to treat the food in a vacuum, so rapidly that few changes take place. Most commercially available whole foods are freeze-dried and do not need to be stored frozen.

Food that is frozen deep or wet will retain its nutritional value, colour, flavour, and texture. Commercial freezing processes also irradiate aquarium foods with gamma rays to kill freeze-resistant bacteria and spores. Wild or home-grown foods should first be blanched (immersed in boiling water), and then be frozen quickly as separate pieces or in convenient blocks. All preserved and stored packages and boxes of food must be labelled indelibly with contents and preparation dates.

Serving meals

The aquarium food must be formed and presented in a manner acceptable to each captive animal. The ways in which animals feed, and their foods in the wild, are very diverse, as is shown by the wide range of feeding habits that have evolved. The aquarist should contend with this diversity by using a technique and food which suit as many inhabitants as possible, and by dealing individually with the more difficult cases, generally through simulation of what the specimens are accustomed to eat.

Animals may often be tricked by preparing foods in disguised form. Physical properties, including buoyancy, texture, shape, and size, are as important as nutritional value in encouraging feeding. The food can even be given a life-like appearance to attract predatory animals, by moving it through the water or suspending fragments in a water current or a stream of air bubbles.

In the aquarium, sessile animals must have food supplied by hand or carried to them by a water current. Mobile animals will move after food, nibble at plants, graze on algae-covered rocks, chase food that floats on the surface or sinks through the water, or hunt for live prey in the open water or amongst the substrate materials.

Time and quantity

The timing and frequency of feeding must suit the inhabitants as well as the aquarist. Food should be added to the aquarium once or twice daily for the fish community, but once every two to four days for invertebrates. The feeding period should last between two and five minutes, with no food left uneaten in the tank at the end. Compound dried foods are in concentrated form and, therefore, easy to overfeed. Experience and acquaintance with the individual animals will indicate when to raise or lower the daily ration. Allowance must also be made for seasonal variation. In many natural habitats, and in aquaria kept to a natural temperature régime, the animals are less active in the winter, and need less food, than in the summer and particularly in pre-spawning periods.

The feeding habits of aquatic animals in nature are a guide to the aquarist.
1 A sea anemone stings a small fish with tentacle-cells and swallows it.
2 A bivalve filters suspended food from water passing through its gills.
3 A sea cucumber consumes detritus in the silt collected by its feeding-arms.
4 An octopus eats a lobster with the beak-like mouth between its strong tentacles.
5 A rabbitfish nibbles at algae on the stones in shallow sea waters.
6 The parrotfish has rasping teeth to eat small animals, plants, and coral.
7 A butterflyfish feeds in crevices with its long snout and fine teeth.
8 An archerfish shoots down insects with a jet of water from its mouth.
9 A goatfish hunts on the sea bottom with its sensitive chin barbels.
10 The lionfish stalks small fishes and is disguised by its splayed fins.
11 Freshwater species feeding near the surface are (a) the hatchetfish, and (b) halfbeak.
12 A catfish with a sucker mouth and barbels eats algae on a river bottom.

Feeding times provide the best opportunity for regularly checking the condition of the aquarium community. An animal's behaviour during such a period gives a useful indication of its health, and exposes any unusual patterns or lethargy. Attention must be paid to individuals which are low in the social hierarchy, or are slow to respond when feeding begins, so as to ensure that they obtain adequate food.

New specimens, particularly animals captured recently from the wild, may need careful weaning onto the established supply of food. They are possibly stressed by capture and transportation, and therefore require gentle and patient treatment. Feeding should be encouraged by experimenting with various preparations and techniques, including live foods and suitably shaped and sized whole foods.

Fish fry also demand special attention. They should be fed as much as they can eat, three to five times per day. Most grow very quickly, and a full complement of vitamins, amino and fatty acids, and mineral elements is vital for normal development. Food particles must be sufficiently small: the fry hatched recently from eggs need smaller particles than do fry born live, and the food size should increase with fry size. Suitable foods are live rotifers and protozoans (infusoria), pre-soaked and dried food powder, drops of liquidized whole foods, or hard-boiled egg yolk squeezed through a muslin bag. As the young fishes grow, the number of feeds can be reduced, with a gradual weaning onto the routine diet of convenience.

Diseases in the aquarium

The subject of aquatic diseases is complex, covering a wide array of agents, symptoms, and treatments. An aquarist's first priority is to reduce the likelihood of any illness, through healthy management. In addition, one must be aware of the more common ailments which may afflict the aquarium occupants, and of the appearance of the causes, so that appropriate action is not delayed. Equipment and knowledge should also be prepared for the administration of suitable treatment once a diagnosis has been made.

Preventive measures

It is far better to take all possible steps to prevent disease from arising in the aquarium than to try to cure it after its development. Disease prevention is based chiefly upon the maintenance of stress-free living conditions, good general hygiene, and routine procedures of quarantine and observation.

Avoiding stress

Animals which experience stress are susceptible to infection. Stress is caused largely by poor water quality, with an accumulation of toxins such as ammonia, an excess of carbon dioxide, fluctuating temperature, or inadequate oxygen. Further causes are physical injury, fright and shock during handling or chasing, confinement with a dominant or predatory animal, and overcrowding.

These factors produce serious changes in an organism's physiology. Its internal chemical balance is altered, and a struggle to regain equilibrium follows, reducing the natural resistance to infection. Such changes may last long after the cause of stress has been removed. For example, if a fish is caught by hand-netting, lifted out of the water and immediately put back, even into the same aquarium, the physiological effects will take several days to disappear.

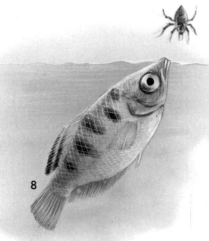

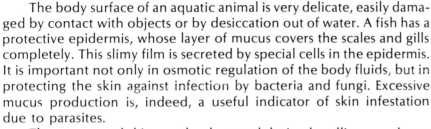

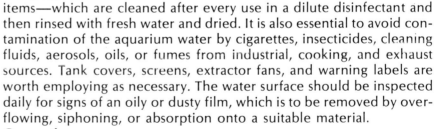

The body surface of an aquatic animal is very delicate, easily damaged by contact with objects or by desiccation out of water. A fish has a protective epidermis, whose layer of mucus covers the scales and gills completely. This slimy film is secreted by special cells in the epidermis. It is important not only in osmotic regulation of the body fluids, but in protecting the skin against infection by bacteria and fungi. Excessive mucus production is, indeed, a useful indicator of skin infestation due to parasites.

The mucus and skin may be damaged during handling, or when a fish is panicked and dashes against a stone. Fishes in traps often hurt the mouth and eyes by continually pushing at the walls. In an aquarium, some fishes wear away the skin entirely from a prominent area, such as the operculum (gill-cover), by habitually swimming along the window or walls and scraping that area. Physical injury, as well as mental stress, can also result from fighting between specimens, particularly those of territorial species, and some species are notorious for biting the fins of other inmates.

General hygiene

Good hygiene must be practised throughout the aquarium. Disease organisms and other causes of illness, such as toxins, can easily be transmitted in or on contaminated equipment, hands, food, animals, plants, or water. It is unwise to use foodstuffs that might be infected, to introduce any living organisms without quarantine, or to transfer aquarium water between tanks except for a purpose such as moving a specimen to the treatment tank.

Routine disinfection should be performed, with a set of labelled utensils for each tank—a bucket, net, cleaning instrument, and other items—which are cleaned after every use in a dilute disinfectant and then rinsed with fresh water and dried. It is also essential to avoid contamination of the aquarium water by cigarettes, insecticides, cleaning fluids, aerosols, oils, or fumes from industrial, cooking, and exhaust sources. Tank covers, screens, extractor fans, and warning labels are worth employing as necessary. The water surface should be inspected daily for signs of an oily or dusty film, which is to be removed by overflowing, siphoning, or absorption onto a suitable material.

Quarantine

Upon arrival, all animals and plants must undergo a strict period of isolation, during which they are accustomed to the régime of aquarium life and are observed closely—without disturbance—for signs of abnormality and illness. A similar precaution is to quarantine organisms during the transfer between tanks. The basic idea is to separate an organism long enough for any latent or developing disease to manifest itself. In addition, specimens, including plants and invertebrates, may be carrying potential pathogens, which do not make them ill but would infect the animals in an established aquarium.

During quarantine, a prophylactic medication is often a valuable safeguard. In a dilute treatment, it reduces the possibility of infection due, for example, to stress and damage of aquatic organisms during capture and transfer. If a number of similar fishes are being treated, the medication is best tried with one or two of them initially. Fishes should be observed during treatment and removed to well-oxygenated water at the same temperature if any signs of gasping or other stress occur.

Two such treatments are outlined below for fishes. The first (A) employs a medicine called formalin (in a solution at 80 parts per million), and also malachite green for large specimens (at 2 parts per million). The second (B) uses nitrofural (at 15 parts per million) or potassium dichromate (at 50 parts per million). An alternative in (A) for small specimens, and in (B), is methylene blue (at 2 parts per million). These treatments are generally suitable for either freshwater or marine fishes.

Day	Treatment A	Treatment B
1–3	Place fish in quarantine tank to become adjusted. Begin observations, and establish feeding, in either treatment.	
4	Give fish no food for twelve hours, then transfer to bath of formalin for one hour, but return it to quarantine tank before stress occurs.	Add medicine to tank (add nitrofural in three stages over three days), feed and observe fish.
5	Repeat formalin treatment.	
6–8	Allow fish to recover, with normal feeding.	
9	Give fish no food for twelve hours, then transfer to bath of malachite green or methylene blue for one hour, but return it to quarantine tank before stress occurs.	Change water in tank and add fresh medicine as before. Continue feeding and observation.
10	Repeat Day 9.	
11	Repeat Day 9.	
12–21	Continue to observe fish in quarantine tank.	On Day 14, change water in tank for fresh water.
21	If no signs of disease or abnormality have appeared, introduce fish into main aquarium.	

If a prophylactic medication is not used, the specimens should be placed in the quarantine tank for at least two weeks. This is done for all invertebrates as well as plants and many fishes. In the same period, satisfactory feeding should be established. If necessary, the water temperature is changed gradually during the period, from the previous acclimatization level to the temperature prevailing in the main aquarium tank.

A detailed record should be kept of each specimen's state of health and behaviour during quarantine, including its condition on arrival, colouring, movements, and so on. This begins a "case history" which is best compiled throughout the specimen's life in the aquarium. With specimens in quarantine, the experienced aquarist can also consult past records of other new arrivals of the same species, in order to foresee and cope with any problems.

Examination

Daily visual checking of the aquarium inhabitants is essential. It should include a brief note of any peculiar behaviour, feeding, cuts, colouring, and so on, for each specimen or species. Such abnormal occurrences are often the earliest warnings of illness. Among the most obvious indications of stress, irritation, or ailments are: darting, rubbing, erratic or unbalanced movement, quivering, lethargy, folding or twitching of fins, increased ventilation rate and gasping for air, loss of appetite or weight, loss of colour or general darkening, increased mucus secretion, unusual swellings, spots, haemorrhaging, open sores, frayed or eroded fins, and visible external parasites.

At the first suspicious signs, a full inspection of the aquarium and its population must be made, from the quality of water and equipment to the aggressiveness of animals. Recent events should be considered when seeking the causes, such as lapses in management routine, changes in diet, failure of equipment, prophylactic treatment, and addition of new specimens. The purpose is to correlate all available circumstances and reach a preliminary diagnosis. If this can be done with a fair confidence of accuracy, appropriate measures should be initiated without delay.

Accurate diagnosis often requires a closer examination of the sick fish than is possible when it remains free in the tank. It can be examined externally out of the tank, under mild anaesthesia if necessary, but must be kept warm and moist. Dead fishes should be examined internally as well, in order to identify the cause of death.

In a proper external examination, cuts and open wounds are inspected for fungus infection (strands resembling cotton–wool). Gills are studied for signs of haemorrhaging, whitened areas showing necrosis, cysts, sticking filaments, and damaged edges. Infected areas of skin or gills are scraped with a fine blade to obtain a sample of mucus, which is examined—in a drop of water on a slide—through a microscope to look for disease organisms. Large parasites are sought in the mouth, gills, and body crevices. Skeletal deformities are noted.

An internal examination of the animal by post-mortem dissection should be conducted as soon as possible. There is often no other way of discovering the cause of death, which will assist in prescribing treatment if the same external symptoms appear amongst further fishes. Inside the body cavity, parasites such as cestode worms, cysts due to bacteria, sporozoans, or trematodes, excessive fluid or mucus, or tumours may be found. Microscopic study of mucus smears, drops of fluid, or squashed tissue can reveal the causative organisms.

Non-infectious disorders

Several causes of illness in aquatic animals are not of the infectious kind transmitted by living organisms. They include chemical, genetic, and nutritional disorders, the most common being due to poisons.

Gas-bubble disease

This is a condition of fishes and may appear externally as small bubbles within the body or under the skin, particularly around the head and eyes—in which case it can cause protruding eyes (exophthalmus). It results from supersaturation of the water and the blood with dissolved nitrogen or oxygen. Supersaturation may be caused by heating the water, by injecting air into water at high pressure, or by great photosynthetic production of oxygen which precedes a decrease in oxygen due, for example, to greater aeration. In each case, the concentration of gas in the water falls rapidly, while the blood is still supersaturated, and the excess gas escapes from solution into bubbles rather than by slow diffusion. The bubbles may obstruct blood vessels, and the fish can die from "gas embolism". If an afflicted fish is placed in fresh water, the bubbles may dissolve again. And if damage is not extreme, the fish may recover.

Genetic abnormalities

In various species, genetic deformities of the skeleton, muscles, fins, and internal organization have been confirmed. These are the result of either direct mutation or inherited characteristics. However, similar occurrences are the basis of hybridization and selection in captive fishes: new strains of life are produced by keeping the "abnormalities" and breeding them.

Nutritional ailments

A diet which is unbalanced or deficient in any significant respect will cause disorders of another kind. Vitamin requirements have already been discussed in regard to food and feeding. Excessive fat in the diet, and overfeeding in general, can lead to degeneration and disease of the animal's liver, as well as increased susceptibility to infectious disease. Poor feeding, or the wrong types of food, may also result in problems such as emaciation, choking, and constipation.

Poisoning

Among the poisonous substances which may become dangerous in the aquarium are metals, including copper, zinc, and lead, in addition to common contaminants such as chlorine and ammonia. Possible sources of copper or lead are a medication—copper sulphate—and water pipes. The aquarium system should not use metal pipes, and its water must not be drawn from a main supply which employs copper or lead piping. Lead weights, to hold plants down until their roots grow, should not be left in the tank, especially in acidic fresh water. Zinc can usually be avoided, by keeping zinc-galvanized iron out of contact with the aquarium water, and by specifying medicinal compounds—particularly malachite green—as free of zinc. All paints, sealants, and similar materials which may contact the water must be metal-free, and it may be necessary to consult manufacturers or even to run careful tests. If metal has to be used in water, it should be coated completely with resin or rubber.

Heavy metal poisoning of fishes will cause severe damage, notably to gill tissue. Gill filaments stick together as the surrounding mucus coagulates. Early symptoms are an increased ventilation rate, inflamed gills, and gasping at the surface, with a danger of death by suffocation. The remedy is to put the fish in clean water immediately, trace and remove the metal source, and change the aquarium water entirely.

Chlorine is used to disinfect most domestic main water supplies, killing their bacteria, odours, and tastes. The chlorine must be removed before the water is employed in an aquarium. Fishes and invertebrates are irritated by chlorine, especially on the gills and skin, and plants may also be affected. Symptoms in fishes are restless movement and a loss of equilibrium. The chlorine damages both plant and animal enzymes, and the organisms may not recover even if transferred immediately to clean water.

Ammonia is produced in the aquarium as the principal result of animal excretion, and during bacterial decomposition of organic mat-

ter. It may also enter the aquarium from outside, due to nearby animals, fumes, contaminated water, or ammonia-based cleaners. As has been emphasized earlier, ammonia is very toxic. It destroys gill tissue, impairs growth, and reduces resistance to infection. Cases of bacterial infection of gills, fins, and tails are attributed to ammonia. The symptoms of ammonia poisoning include an increase in mucus production, swollen and fused gill filaments, and haemorrhaging spots.

Infectious organisms

The forms of life that can actively cause disease in an aquarium are protozoans, viruses, bacteria, fungi, and other parasites. Successful treatment of them depends upon a scientific knowledge of their nature and habits, which, in many cases, is not very extensive.

Protozoans

Microscopic protozoa occur abundantly in all natural waters. Many are free-living, nourished by bacteria and fine detritus, and some of these can be harmful as they attach to fishes. When very numerous, they make the fish uncomfortable, and it responds by secreting mucus copiously. Most such species of protozoa are parasitic, actually feeding on the fish. Some cause death directly, and others indirectly by opening wounds for secondary infection by bacteria or fungi.

Protozoa usually have motile, free-living offspring, which spread easily throughout the aquarium but can live only briefly without finding a suitable host. Generally, the protozoan may form a dormant stage that is not affected by medicines, so that a programme of repeated treatment is necessary.

Ciliates

A common skin disease of fishes is "white spot", or "ich", caused by the ciliate protozoan species *Ichthyophthirius multifiliis* in fresh water, and by *Cryptokaryon irritans* in sea water. It is seen as small white or off-white spots or soft cysts, about 1 mm (0.04 in) in diameter, formed where the ciliate has penetrated the epidermis and been enveloped by a layer of cells. A mucus scraping and microscopic examination reveals the slowly turning parasite. This feeds from tiny blood vessels and, when mature, bursts out of the fish through the skin, sinking to the bottom. Within a protective cyst, it divides into hundreds of young "ich" which, after thirty-six hours, are all capable of infecting new hosts. The fish is left weakened and susceptible to secondary infection. The disease may be introduced into the aquarium on fishes, food plants, or other animals.

These protozoans cannot be treated effectively while inside the fish or encysted on the bottom. But the free-swimming stage is sensitive to various medicaments, so that extended treatment in medicated water will eventually kill all the parasites. Methylene blue, malachite green, acriflavine, Neguvon, formalin, or antibiotics might be used effectively. The diseased fish should be isolated in a treatment tank with one of these solutions. The temperature can be raised by several degrees, to speed up the parasitic development. At 10°C (50°F), it takes weeks for the parasites to mature and leave the fish, compared to three or four days above 20°C (68°F). If all fishes are removed from the infected aquarium, it will be safe again after three days, as the young parasites will have failed to find a fish host and died.

Flagellates

Another ailment is "velvet (or gold dust) disease", caused by the

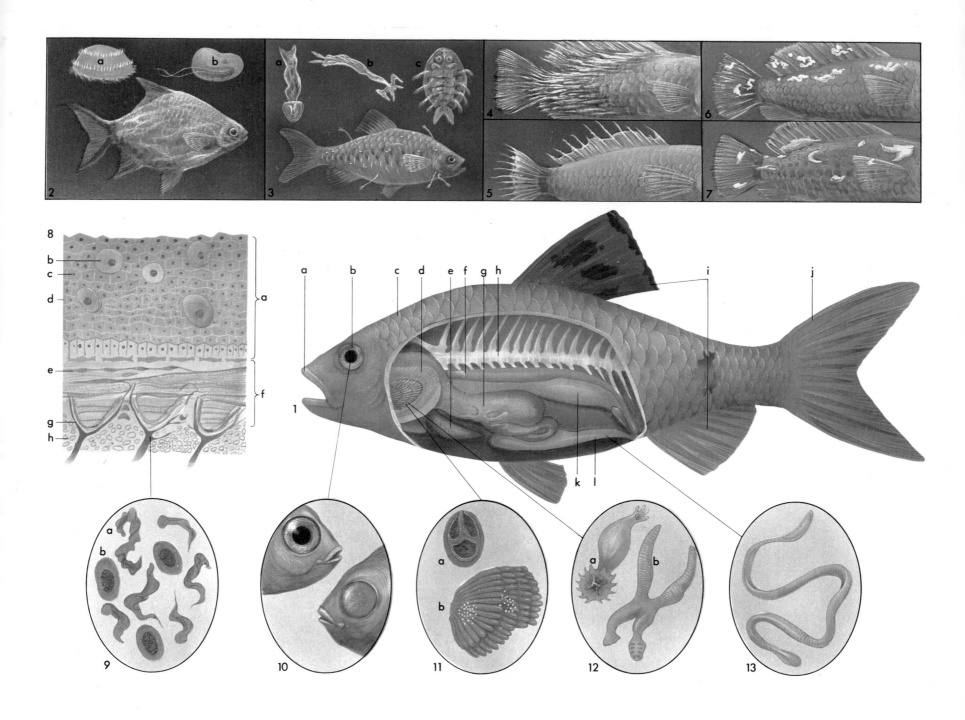

1   The anatomy of a typical aquarium fish shows several main areas where disease may occur: *(a)* mouth, *(b)* eye, *(c)* skin, *(d)* gills, *(e)* liver, *(f)* kidney, *(g)* stomach, *(h)* skeleton, *(i)* fins, *(j)* tail, *(k)* swim-bladder, *(l)* intestine, as well as the blood and tissues in general.
2   Two parasites that cause slimy skin are the protozoans *(a) Trichodina,* a ciliate, and *(b) Costia,* a flagellate.
3   Parasites on skin are *(a)* the fluke

Gyrodactylus and the crustaceans, *(b)* anchor worm and *(c)* fish louse.
4   Dermatomycosis on the surfaces of a fish is caused by a fungus, which may grow on dead food in the aquarium.
5   Fin rot is a bacterial infection, often promoted by unclean water.
6   Lymphocystis is the most familiar viral disease of aquarium fishes.
7   Also due to infection by a virus is pox, which spreads over the skin.

8   An enlarged section of a fish's skin shows the *(a)* epidermis, *(b)* slime cells, *(c)* cell nuclei, *(d)* epithelial cells, *(e)* chromatophora, *(f)* cutis, *(g)* blood vessels, *(h)* fat.
9   The blood of a fish may be attacked by flagellate trypanosomes *(a)* which destroy red corpuscles *(b)* and can be passed by flukes to other fishes.

10   The eye lens is susceptible to infection by *Diplostomum* flukes, which may even cause blindness.
11   Microscopic spores of *Myxobolus (a)* can produce cysts on the gills *(b)* as well as on the skin.
12   Parasitic flukes on the gills are *(a) Dactylogyrus* and *(b) Diplozoon.*
13   A tapeworm may live in the fish's intestine and use its nutrients.

The life cycle of a digenean trematode fluke involves a secondary host such as a gastropod snail. The fluke lives in a fish's intestine and the eggs are expelled in the faeces (a). Each egg hatches to produce a ciliated larva called a miracidium (b). This swims to find a host snail, bores into the soft flesh, and loses its cilia, becoming a sporocyst (c). The latter develops into larvae of another kind known as rediae (d), which form a further kind termed cercariae (e). These leave the snail and swim away, usually encysting in fishes and reaching the intestine to create eggs, completing the cycle. Therefore, wild snails should not be kept in an aquarium with fishes, as they may introduce such infection.

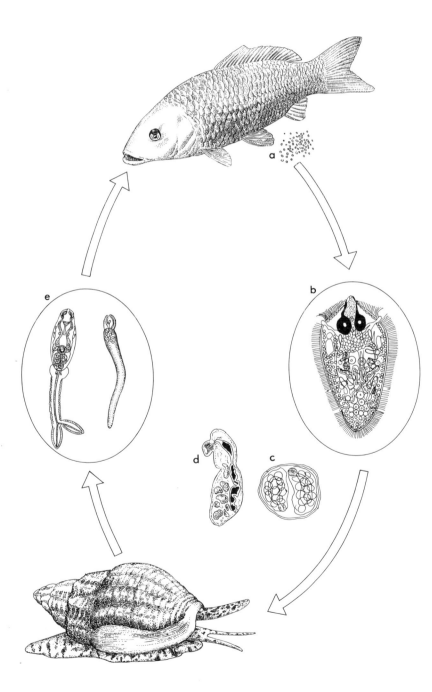

flagellate protozoan Oodinium limneticum, principally on the skin. Fishes in warm fresh water are affected most, particularly when young. A golden-yellow powder appears over the skin where the parasite has attached and grown into the epidermis. The parasite, feeding inside, is pear-shaped under a microscope. When mature, it encysts in the fish, dividing into two hundred or more young, which leave the cyst and settle again on a fish's skin or gills.

Similar is "pillularis disease", of the skin and occasionally the gills, caused by Oodinium pillularis, especially in tropical cyprinids. The small spots or dust on the skin are grey, and skin fragments may pull off. The parasite leaves the fish and encysts and multiplies on the bottom. Marine tropical fishes also suffer from a parasite, Oodinium ocellatum, which causes "coral fish disease", affecting mainly the gills but also the skin. Its early-warning signs include gasping at the surface for air, general weakness, and lethargy. It produces haemorrhaged spots, cysts, necrosis, and inflammation of the gills. Treatment must be rapid to be effective.

Several other species of protozoans, such as members of the genera Chilodonella, Trichodina, and Costia, browse over the skin or gills of fishes, feeding on epithelial cells, and on tissue around ulcers or wounds. The discomforted victim secretes much mucus, which can suffocate it in extreme cases. These parasites occur in fresh and marine waters alike and are able to infest many species of fishes.

As with the ciliates, medication must be prolonged or repeated in order to kill successive generations of flagellates. Methylene blue, malachite green, acriflavine, Neguvon, and copper sulphate are variably successful as bath solutions for isolated fishes. The main tank must remain free of fishes for at least fourteen days after an epidemic.

Sporozoans

The sporozoan protozoa are characterized by complex life cycles and the production of many tiny, infectious spores. Numerous species infect the visceral organs of fishes—kidneys, liver, gut, and gonads—as well as the blood, muscles, and other tissues. A healthy fish can restrict the growth and effect of these parasites, but in an unhealthy one with lowered resistance, they can reproduce very rapidly, erupting as large boils, pimples, knots, and cysts, to cause haemorrhaging, blocking of blood vessels, and consequent necrosis.

The coccidian sporozoans are common and dangerous parasites of the intestine, in both freshwater and marine fishes. They live attached to the gut wall, feeding until mature, when they encyst. The cysts leave the fish in its faeces and can remain dormant until eaten by another fish. The young sporozoans hatch out in the new host's intestine and attach to the lining. Signs of the disease include local swelling of the body wall, lethargic movement, and—with heavy infestation—poor growth, dull colour, and emaciation.

In fresh waters, a sporozoan species of Plistophora, responsible for "neon tetra disease", is often found in characoids and cyprinids. A pale white blemish on the fish's flank is usually the first sign of the disease and gradually grows round the body. Colours fade and the fish may become emaciated, behaving erratically. Cysts form in the muscles and internal organs, and necrosis leads to death.

Successful treatment of sporozoan diseases is difficult. The fish must be isolated immediately and given medication, maintaining strict hygiene. Malachite green can be an effective bath treatment and might

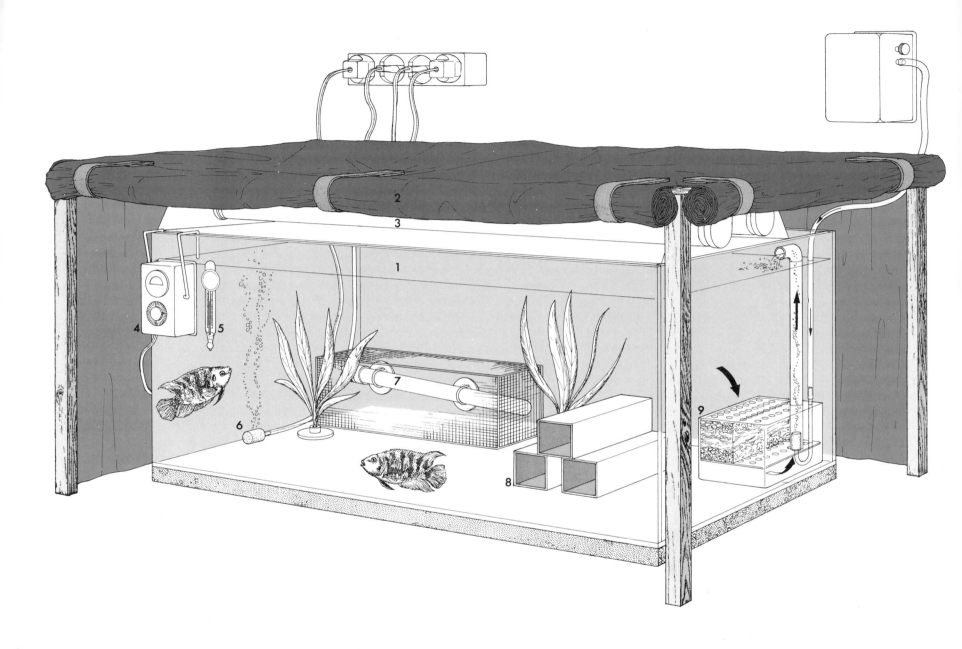

A tank for quarantine and treatment of aquatic organisms is built as follows.

1 The tank may be all-glass or made of moulded acrylic, with outer dimensions (length × width × depth) about 45 × 25 × 30 cm (18 × 10 × 12 in), of some 34 litres (8–9 gallons) volume. It rests on a base of insulating material but contains no substrate particles, and all the fittings should be sterilizable.

2 A canopy of black material, such as polythene, can be unrolled to cover the top and sides of a lightweight frame which surrounds the tank, isolating it from external influences if necessary.

3 Suspended from the frame above the tank are a fluorescent lamp and an ultraviolet lamp, with a reflector, for illumination and irradiation of the water when required.

4 A thermostat may be mounted outside the tank for convenient adjustment of the water temperature, or an internal type of thermostat can be used.

5 Temperature may be checked directly with a bulb thermometer in the water.

6 The water is aerated and circulated by a diffuser connected to an air pump.

7 A small immersion heater to warm the water is placed in a rear corner upon glass or rubber supports, shielded by a plastic grating, and its electrical wires are connected to the thermostat.

8 Shelter for animals is provided by plastic enclosures such as drainpipes, model reefs, or broken flower-pots, with a few plastic plants.

9 Mechanical filtration of the water occurs in a box filled with layers of gravel and wool, through which water is circulated by an air-lift.

also be used to control an outbreak in the main aquarium tank. Nitrofurazone may be used on isolated fishes affected by boils and knots on the skin, as a swab over infected areas. Large boils can be cut open, and scraped before swabbing. This medicament may also serve as a permanent bath and be fed to the fish with food. Normally, after a sporozoan epidemic, the entire tank should be disinfected to avoid a recurrence.

Viruses

Viruses are minute objects, similar in some ways to living creatures, and live in the cells of another organism. They use the cell to form more virus particles, which burst out of the cell and kill it. This leads to many viral diseases of plants and animals, including fishes. There are no effective cures for fish viral diseases, which are mostly contagious and often fatal. Some success has been obtained with acriflavine and various antibiotics. But infected specimens must be isolated, and destroyed if necessary. The tank should be thoroughly disinfected.

Dropsy is a disease condition probably caused by a virus. It tends to be aggravated by secondary bacterial infection, usually due to species of *Aeromonas*. Characterized by fluid accumulating within infected organs and tissues, it often causes a greatly distended belly, protruding scales, and bulging eyes. Pox is a viral disease in freshwater fishes, possibly following a faulty diet or skin damage. This condition appears as cloudy-white spots or growths on the skin surface, but they may drop off and heal if the water quality remains good, or they may become discoloured. Although the disease is seldom fatal, it can produce stunted growth and slight emaciation. Another such disease, chiefly of freshwater fishes, is lymphocystis. This yields heavy wart-like growths on the skin and fins, spreading slowly and leading to emaciation, even to death. Large growths may be removed by surgery.

Bacteria

Bacteria are microscopic organisms, from 0.5 to 10 micrometres (20 to 400 millionths of an inch) long. Many do not have characteristic shapes, and the organisms must be cultured in a laboratory for positive identification. Bacteria are ubiquitous in vast numbers. Often saprophytic—feeding on dead organic matter—and vital in nature, they bring about the re-cycling of inorganic nutrients. In the aquarium, nitrifying and decomposer bacteria are essential to filtration processes. Hence, it is important not to use medication in an aquarium system depending on healthy bacteria.

Many species are pathogenic and can thrive without hosts until they attack as secondary infectors—of wounds and sores (notably species of *Aeromonas* in fresh water and of *Vibrio* in sea water), or of animals weakened by stress or another infection. Pathogenic bacteria often produce distinctive symptoms of disease, and a diagnosis with appropriate treatment can be made rather easily. Antibiotics may prove to be the only cure, although success is sometimes found by treatments of malachite green, acriflavine, copper sulphate, nitrofurazone, potassium dichromate, and phenoxethol.

The "cotton–wool disease", or "columnaris", is caused by slime bacteria, *Chondrococcus* and *Cytophaga*, in both fresh and sea waters. Victims become lethargic and show woolly growths on the mouth, gradual erosion of the mouth and cheeks, and white spots on the head, fins, gills, and skin. The disease is contagious and often fatal. A condition known as tail and fin rot, caused by numerous species of bacteria, is common in marine and freshwater fishes. Its symptoms include haemorrhaging at the base of the tail and fins, with erosion of skin and flesh, often followed by a secondary infection of fungus.

Tuberculosis is the most frequent bacterial disease of the internal organs, infecting fishes in warm fresh water particularly. Due to species of *Mycobacterium*, it produces general signs of ill health, such as sluggishness and loss of weight and colour. Advanced signs are falling scales, folded fins, skin blood spots, and skeletal deformities. Positive diagnosis requires post-mortem examination. Small, knotty, grey cysts or tubercles are often found in the internal organs and in skin and muscle tissues. Fishes showing these signs must be isolated.

Fungi

Parasitic fungi occur in all fresh and marine waters. They are common secondary infectors of fishes, where mechanical damage, wounds due to protozoa, or bacterial ulcers have broken the skin, and the fish's natural resistance is lowered. Many species have highly resistant spores which can survive without a host, and this hinders disinfection treatments.

A frequent fungal disease of freshwater fishes is dermatomycosis. Caused by various members of the family Saprolegniacae, it is unsightly but usually not fatal. Infection appears as grey-white woolly growths of fungal threads on the skin, fins and, occasionally, gills. These "hyphae" are fed and supported by a matrix of "mycelium" threads, which grow into the fish's dermis and sometimes into the muscle. Members of the same family also attack the eyes of freshwater and marine fishes, again normally after abrasion or damage. The hyphae grow around and into the eye, so that treatment must be rapid to prevent the mycelium from damaging the eye and entering the brain.

Ichthyophonus disease is caused by a fungus species of the same name. It is widespread amongst marine and freshwater fishes, but is difficult to diagnose without laboratory facilities, as there are no distinctive external symptoms. The fish may show lethargy, skin darkening, emaciation, protruding eyes, and ulcers. The parasitic fungus penetrates the fish's skin and grows slowly throughout the body organs, gradually destroying them. Usually, treatment is effective only if the disease is at an early stage. Thus, as detection is difficult, the condition is often fatal.

Fungal infections should be treated by isolating the fish, and placing it in a bath of methylene blue, malachite green, acriflavine, potassium dichromate, or phenoxethol. Alternatively, small areas of infected skin can be swabbed directly with iodine or potassium dichromate. Ozone treatment of the water for a short period each day during ten days may also be effective.

Crustacean parasites

There are several types of crustacean fish parasites. The fish louse, a copepod crustacean, is one of the commonest and largest, 5 to 10 mm (0.2 to 0.4 in) long. A member of various species of *Argulus,* it occurs all over the world in fresh and sea waters. It infests both the skin and gills of a fish victim, attaching with suckers and hooks, and inserting its blood-sucking proboscis into the blood vessels of the dermis.

The anchor worm, a species of *Lernaea,* is another common parasitic copepod, especially of fishes in warm fresh water. It lives on the skin surface like *Argulus,* but only until mature. Then, the fertilized female loses her crustacean appearance and burrows deeply into the

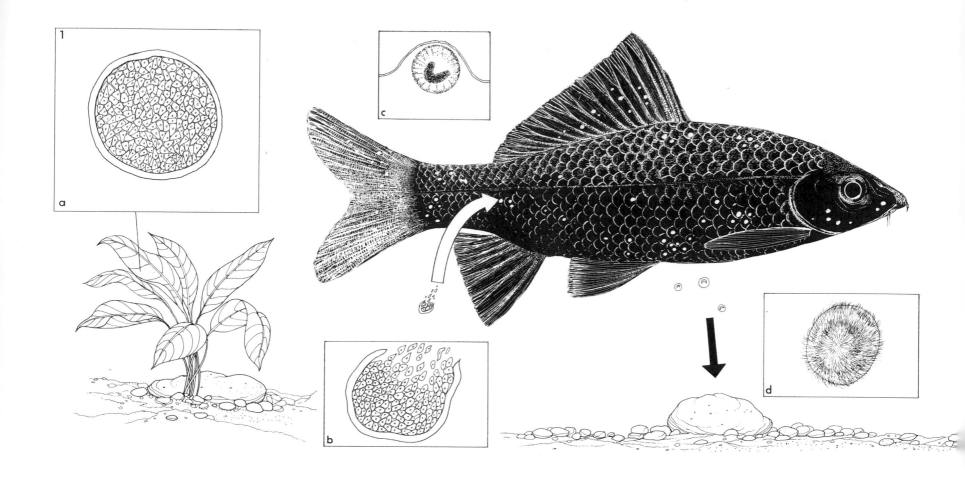

subcutaneous muscle, while only her eggs remain hanging free on the skin, and the fish is badly injured. Closely related to this type, and to anchor worms of *Lernaeocera* species which occur mainly in sea water, are copepods that parasitize the gills of fishes. These are frequently species of *Ergasilus,* and they have a pair of large hooks to dig into the fish's gill filaments. They infest sizeable fishes, and the signs include excessive mucus secretion, rubbing, darting, and flicking movements, as the fish tries to rid itself of the irritant.

Like other blood-suckers, copepod parasites can transmit viral and bacterial diseases, and leave the fish open to secondary infection by piercing the skin deeply. They are easily introduced on live food, plants, or fishes which have not been adequately quarantined. As for treatment, large fish lice can often be rubbed or pulled off the fish by hand, or may be dabbed directly with somewhat concentrated potassium permanganate. Alternatively, infested fishes should be dipped or bathed in a more dilute solution of that chemical, or in formalin or Neguvon. Sodium chloride (salt) as a dip may be useful against freshwater copepod parasites.

Trematode flukes

Many species of small, unsegmented flukes live as parasites of freshwater and marine fishes. The commonest of monogenean trematodes, often found together, are species of *Dactylogyrus* on the gills—about 1 mm (0.04 in) long—and of *Gyrodactylus* (more often on

the skin). These feed on epithelial cells, sometimes eating away large areas which form wounds open to infection by bacteria and fungi. The flukes are hard to see, being usually covered in mucus. Symptoms of infestation shown by the fish may include loss of colour, blood spots, drooping fins, increased mucus secretion, rubbing, and darting movements, followed by lethargy, exhaustion, and death if not treated. Flukes on the gills cause a great rise in the fish's ventilation rate. The operculum may be held open to expose swollen gills, and the fish may gasp for air at the surface.

Such flukes should be treated as soon as possible, by removal into a well-aerated bath of methylene blue, formalin, or acriflavine, or—for freshwater species—by dipping into a Neguvon or salt solution. The eggs produced by flukes are resistant, and the medication must be repeated to kill the young as they hatch. The aquarium itself can be treated with methylene blue, or left for three to seven days with no fishes inside it so that the hatching young will die after failing to find a host.

Digenean trematodes include species which are parasites of fishes, but require a secondary host—often a gastropod snail or a bivalve—to complete their life cycle. Hence, they are not infectious unless this host is present. Many of these flukes infest the intestine and blood, causing emaciation and lethargy, and cannot be treated effectively. Another, *Diplostomum,* attacks the eye lens: the eye becomes milky, then solid

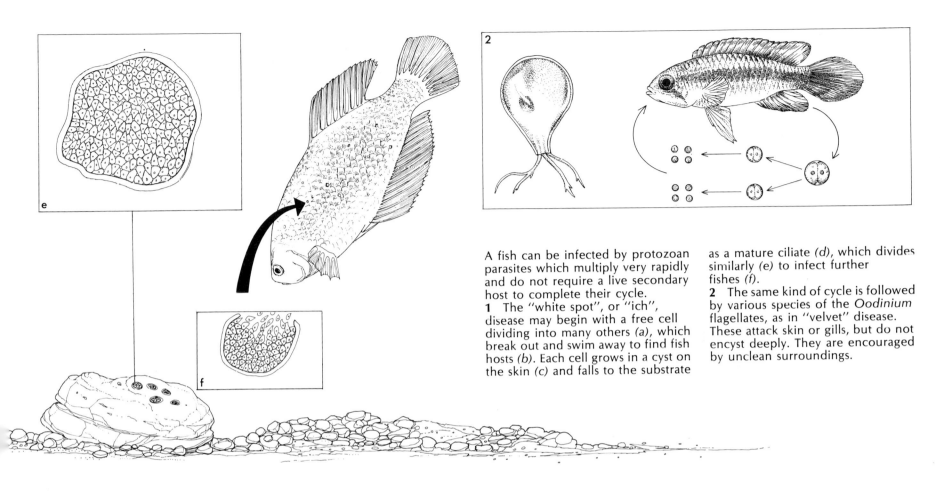

A fish can be infected by protozoan parasites which multiply very rapidly and do not require a live secondary host to complete their cycle.

1 The "white spot", or "ich", disease may begin with a free cell dividing into many others (a), which break out and swim away to find fish hosts (b). Each cell grows in a cyst on the skin (c) and falls to the substrate as a mature ciliate (d), which divides similarly (e) to infect further fishes (f).

2 The same kind of cycle is followed by various species of the *Oodinium* flagellates, as in "velvet" disease. These attack skin or gills, but do not encyst deeply. They are encouraged by unclean surroundings.

white, and fluid accumulates behind the cornea, which may burst. This allows secondary infection by bacteria or fungi, and death often results, although a suitable treatment is by phenoxethol in the food and bath.

Leeches

Leeches are segmented annelid worms, in fresh water and, less commonly, in sea water. When living parasitically on fishes, they cut through the skin and suck the blood, using an anticoagulant. Heavy infestation can cause severe anaemia and large, open wounds. Leeches are fairly big, averaging about 2 cm (0.8 in) long, and should be looked for when plants or fishes are collected in the wild. Symptomatic behaviour includes restless swimming and rubbing against the substrate. Leech-infested freshwater fishes must be treated by dipping in a salt solution for five to fifteen minutes, or in Neguvon.

Treatment of disease

In most cases, it is best to remove the sick animal from the aquarium into a carefully prepared tank, for treatment and observation. This facilitates handling and separates other aquarium inhabitants from the main source of infection as well as from any medications used.

Administering medicine

Medicaments are also potential toxins, and a slight error in measuring their concentrations may damage or kill the "patient". Their prepara-

tion and application, along with calculations of water volume and dosage, must be done with great care. It is best to make a dilute solution of the medicament in stock, for use either directly or after further dilution as required. Dry powders or crystals are dissolved in water to make the stock. Powders are somewhat easier to weigh and dissolve. Certain chemicals need to be dissolved in hot water. All glassware and instruments should be washed thoroughly before and just after use, in clean water.

The basic ways of applying a medicament are as follows. First, it can be added to the treatment tank in a concentration which is tolerable for several hours or days. Second, the specimen may be dipped into a more concentrated solution in a separate container, for between a few seconds and an hour. Third, as a swab, the concentrated solution is applied directly to an infected area or a large external parasite, using a small cotton pad or a fine brush. Fourth, food may be specially drugged by mixing or soaking it in the medicament. A fifth method, injection, should be attempted only by a competent person.

Several other factors must be borne in mind. To begin with, toxicity depends upon the varying sensitivity of species to chemicals. There is often a narrow difference between killing the disease agent and harming the fish. As mentioned already, a treatment should be initially assessed in a trial run with one or two specimens, and those under treatment must be watched closely, being removed into clean water if stress appears.

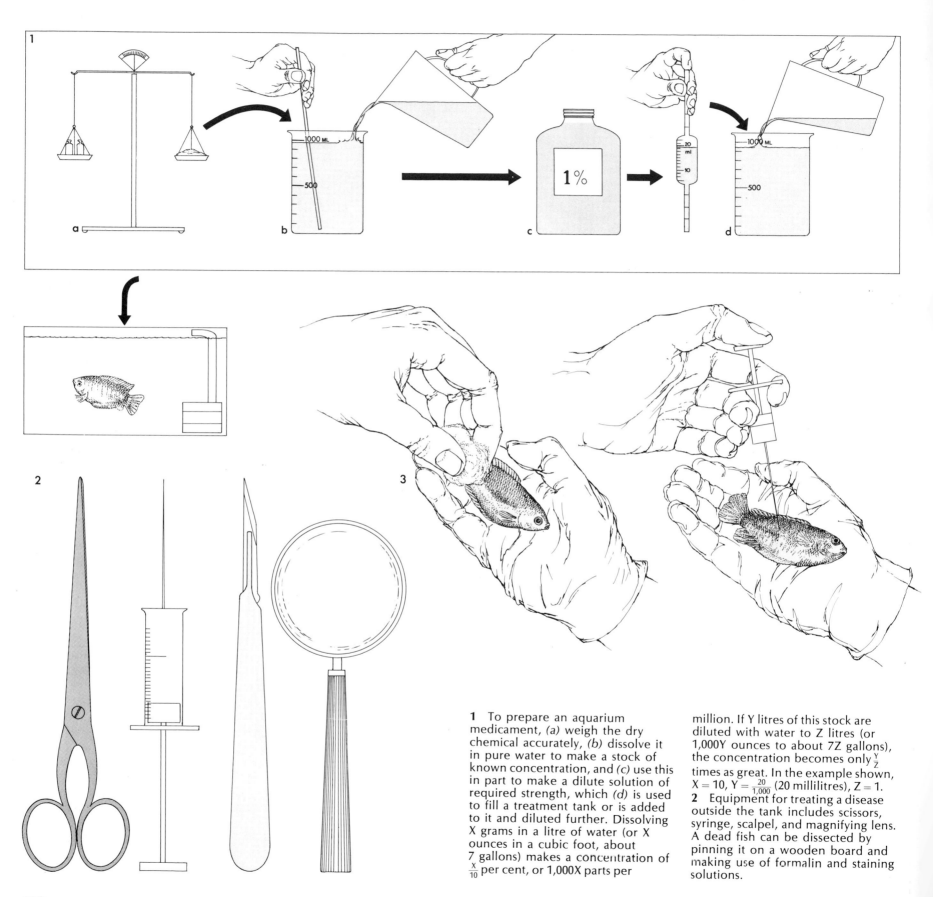

1 To prepare an aquarium medicament, (a) weigh the dry chemical accurately, (b) dissolve it in pure water to make a stock of known concentration, and (c) use this in part to make a dilute solution of required strength, which (d) is used to fill a treatment tank or is added to it and diluted further. Dissolving X grams in a litre of water (or X ounces in a cubic foot, about 7 gallons) makes a concentration of $\frac{X}{10}$ per cent, or 1,000X parts per million. If Y litres of this stock are diluted with water to Z litres (or 1,000Y ounces to about 7Z gallons), the concentration becomes only $\frac{Y}{Z}$ times as great. In the example shown, X = 10, Y = $\frac{20}{1,000}$ (20 millilitres), Z = 1.
2 Equipment for treating a disease outside the tank includes scissors, syringe, scalpel, and magnifying lens. A dead fish can be dissected by pinning it on a wooden board and making use of formalin and staining solutions.

4

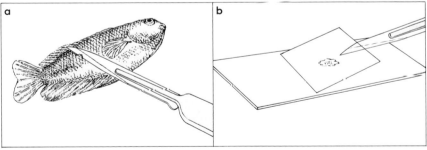

a

b

3 A medicament may be applied directly by a gentle swab or careful injection, holding the animal with rubber gloves, then returning it to a treatment tank for several days of observation. All instruments should be well sterilized before use. Medicaments dissolved in the tank water can be removed later by filtering and renewing the water.
4 Microscopic examination is the most reliable way of identifying diseases. (a) To obtain a small external sample, gently scrape the infected area with the back of a scalpel blade. (b) Put the scraping onto a glass slide, add a drop of water over it, slowly lower a transparent covering slip on top of it, and move the slide to the microscope. Increase the power of the microscope lens gradually until clear observation of the sampled organisms is possible. Special kits are also available for the analysis of bacteria.

Preparations of many medicines are available for the aquarist, but often are not given proper chemical names. Such treatments should, therefore, always follow the instructions of the manufacturer or an expert. Moreover, certain medicaments must not be used in combination, as this produces lethal conditions. Some compounds, including malachite green and acriflavine, should be administered in subdued light, as they are photosensitive and would otherwise have harmful effects. Various medicaments are influenced by the water quality—for example, acidity, temperature, and hardness—which must be considered when determining concentrations. Organic matter in the water will greatly reduce the useful dosage of many drugs, such as methylene blue, malachite green, potassium dichromate, and permanganate.

The life cycles of disease agents are also important. Many agents can complete their cycles in the aquarium, from eggs to free-swimming young to the parasitic adult, and thus are infectious. The adult is often difficult to treat as it lives within its host, and numerous species have eggs which are resistant to medications. But the free-swimming stage is usually vulnerable and often cannot live long without a suitable host. Other species, such as the digenean trematodes, require a secondary host in which to complete their life cycle. In these cases, all potential hosts may be removable. Alternatively, prolonged or repeated treatments are necessary to kill juveniles as eggs hatch.

Medicaments must be stored properly and safely. Some, such as formalin, are best kept in darkened glass bottles. All should be placed in air-tight, corrosion-proof containers which are clearly labelled with the contents, concentration, and date of preparation or purchase. Certain chemicals have a restricted lifetime, beyond which their properties—including toxicity—may change, so that old stock should not be used. It is, of course, essential to store medicaments away from children and other possible misusers.

Important medicaments

The following range of treatments should be able to cope with the great majority of aquarium diseases. Each medicament is specified by its form, principal uses, method of application, dosage, rate, and other factors. Dosage refers to the concentration of the chemical in the water being used to treat the sick organism. This is expressed in parts per hundred (percentage) or per million (abbreviated *ppm*). For example, dissolving 10 grams in a litre of water (or about 1.5 ounces in a gallon) gives a dosage of one per cent, and dissolving only $\frac{5}{1,000}$ as much in the same volume gives a dosage of fifty parts per million.

Formalin is a colourless liquid, used as a general prophylactic (applied by dip, at 80 ppm, for 1 hour daily during 3 days) or against external protozoa, flukes, and some crustacea except *Lernaea* (dip, 80 ppm, for 1 hour). It is available as a thirty-two per cent solution of formaldehyde and must be methanol-free, fresh, and stored in a dark bottle. When old, it is very toxic to fishes. A white deposit of paraformaldehyde indicates that the solution is too old for use.

Malachite green consists of metallic-green crystals, a convenient stock solution being at 0.1 per cent. It is used as a prophylactic for large organisms (dip, 2 ppm, 1 hour daily for 3 days), against protozoa and fungi (dip, 1 ppm, 30 minutes daily for 3 days) or bacteria and external fungi (dip, 10–50 ppm, 10–30 seconds daily for 3 days). A zinc-free medical grade must be used. It is photosensitive, absorbed by organic material, and too strong for toleration by some small fishes.

Diverse techniques are available for the collection of animals underwater. Above, a drop net is spread by divers at a moderate height over a relatively level area of the bottom, and released without frightening fishes away, so as to fall uniformly upon them. Below, a barrier seine net of fairly fine mesh is fully closed around a reef outcrop, and the occupants are hand-netted from the top to be kept in a polythene bag. Animals hiding in an outcrop can be subdued by injecting mild anaesthetic into their refuge from a large plastic pipette with a valve and tube, while a net is ready to catch them if they should emerge suddenly.

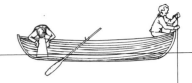

Methylene blue is a blue dye, with stock solution at 1 per cent. It is used as a prophylactic especially for small fishes (dip, 2–3 ppm, 1 hour daily for 3 days), against protozoa and some fungi (bath, 2 ppm, 5–10 days) and flukes (bath, 7 ppm, 3 days). A medical grade must be used. It is absorbed by organic material. Higher concentrations may damage plants.

Acriflavine consists of red-orange tablets or powder, with stock solution at 10 ppm. It is used against flagellate protozoa, bacteria, fungi, flukes, and some viruses (bath, 2–10 ppm, 12 hours every other day for one week, or as necessary). A neutral solution (pH value of 7) must be used. It is photosensitive, insoluble in salt water, and not recommended for treatment of eggs or young fishes. It may cause temporary sterility, and kill plants.

Copper sulphate ($CuSO_4$) consists of blue crystals or powder, with stock solution at 0.1 per cent. It is used against flagellate protozoa (bath, 0.1 ppm, for a total of 5 days, adding a second dose of 0.1 ppm on the third day). It is quite toxic, and the dose must be carefully measured. It should not be used to treat crustacea or other such invertebrates, or in very soft water. More stable chelated compounds are safer, but a higher dose is required.

Sodium chloride (NaCl, common salt) is used only for freshwater organisms, as a disinfectant of plants (dip, 1 per cent, 15–30 seconds) or against flagellate protozoa, crustaceans, leeches, and flukes (dip, 2–5 per cent, 10–15 minutes).

Phenoxethol is an oily liquid, with stock solution at 1 per cent. It is used against bacteria, fungi, and digenean trematodes (bath, 100 ppm, 5 days; or in food, 1 per cent). It is commonly available as "Liquitox".

Potassium dichromate consists of orange-red crystals or powder, with stock solution at 1 per cent. It is used as a general prophylactic (bath, 50 ppm, 5 days maximum) or against fungi and bacteria (bath, 50 ppm, 5 days maximum; or dip, 100 ppm, 30 minutes; or swab, 1 per cent). It is absorbed by organic material.

Potassium permanganate consists of purple crystals, with stock solution at 0.1 per cent. It is used against crustacea (dip, 10 ppm, 30 minutes; or swab, 0.1 per cent) or for disinfection of the tank, equipment, plants, and live food (bath, 3–5 ppm, 2–3 days). It is absorbed by organic material. In alkaline or neutral water, including sea water, the tank must be well aerated to discourage the formation of manganese dioxide, which may damage gills.

"Neguvon" is used against flagellate protozoa, crustacea, and flukes (dip, 2–3 per cent, 2–3 minutes).

Iodine, a dark brown solution, is used against fungi (swab, 10 per cent).

Nitrofurazone is an antibiotic and is used as a general prophylactic (bath, 15 ppm built up over 3 days, for 5–8 days). Other antibiotics are chlortetracycline or aureomycin, oxytetracycline or terramycin,

More limited but useful devices are
(**1**) a weighted net thrown into the water with a line for retrieval,
(**2**) a scoop net lowered with bait and raised rapidly when filled,
(**3**) a glass-bottomed viewing box or mask for the wading collector,
(**4**) a waterproof torch for a diver at night with a hand-net,
(**5**) a fine-mesh net for hauling food such as plankton from deep water.

kanamycin, and chloramphenicol or chloromycetin. They are used against sporozoa, many bacteria, and some viruses and fungi (in bath, swab, food, or injection, according to the manufacturer's instructions). All must be used with great care, and other medicaments should be substituted if possible. An insufficient dose will not kill the agent and may allow a resistant strain to become established and spread dangerously.

Collection in the wild

It is of great value and interest for the aquarist to collect specimens personally in the wild. Each animal or plant becomes more individual in character, when one has a direct knowledge of its natural origins, and therefore, a deeper understanding of its requirements. All aspects of familiarity with the natural habitat can increase the learning and pleasure which are derived from an aquarium. Observations made in the field, particularly by underwater methods, can be used to establish specimens in the best possible aquarium surroundings.

Field work

An expedition to collect specimens should be conducted according to careful principles. Its main stages are preparation, handling, and transportation. Such operations need patience and attention to detail. Only through experience will the collector learn how best to approach each situation, work while concealed, observe specimens, improvise equipment, and use it effectively.

Preparation

The first step is to obtain a clear idea of which species and particular types of organisms are required. Research in biology, botany, and zoology will indicate a suitable location and habitat, as well as definite kinds of site to be examined within the habitat. One should also determine the optimum collection time (of day, year, or tide), techniques of retrieval and transport, features of equipment, and reception facilities such as quarantine tanks. It is often useful to experiment with various procedures, and to test equipment, methods, and personnel, in a "dry run" before departure.

Safety in the field demands further measures: to carry appropriate first-aid and emergency materials, a tool kit, and spare parts; to check protective clothing such as gloves, boots, waterproof covers, life-jackets, and wet-suits; to learn the weather and water conditions; to notify a responsible person of the destination, times of departure and estimated return, and completion of a safe journey; and to beware of bites, spines, or other dangers when collecting certain animals.

Capture and handling

The objective is to collect a minimum number of specimens in perfect condition, which are exactly right for their intended purpose. Hasty or greedy collection will result in damage to the specimens and site. Before even trying to catch a specimen, the collector must be sure that it can be selected, observed, and retrieved as gently as possible, then transported and cared for properly.

To reduce the stress which animals suffer in being captured, it is essential to minimize the duration of pursuit and retrieval, the operating time of traps, the delays caused by transport, and so on. Harmless materials such as polythene sheeting are to be used, and abrasive netting avoided. Specimens should be handled as little as pos-

sible, since any contact may strip areas of epidermis from the body surface of an animal, and plants are easily bruised or crushed by rough treatment.

When handling fishes, thin rubber gloves are a good precaution, as they help to protect the animal's delicate skin. The fish must be held gently but firmly in a fold of very soft material (not rough netting), with minimal movement against the material or pressure on the fragile body. Also in need of protection is the handler—from the sharp and toxic spines of some fishes and echinoderms, the venomous excretions of some molluscs, the stings of jellyfishes and anemones, the sharp teeth or pincers of various fishes and crustaceans, and the strong jaws of other fishes or octopi. Animals may even carry parasites and further disease-causing agents which can infect humans.

Specimens should not be raised from deep water, in a trap or container, without allowing time for physiological adjustment to the reduced pressure. A fish is best brought up to intermediate depths for as long as possible—hours or days if necessary. If it shows signs of positive buoyancy or imbalance, it must be recompressed by lowering slightly. Measures may be required to prevent alarm when specimens are removed from their bottom shelter, for example by covering the container. With some species, it is less damaging to minimize the time spent in suspension, by hauling slowly but steadily to the surface.

A specimen must not be lifted out of water; this can be avoided by immersing a receptacle in the water. An aquatic animal's body structure is designed to support itself when buoyed up by water. Out of water, the body weight is too great and may cause severe rupturing, torn tissues, and bleeding, both internally and from the gills. Changes in the quality of water surrounding the specimen are also to be avoided, particularly by checking the aeration and temperature of water in receptacles.

Transportation

The holding container used during collection and transportation will give the captive specimens their first experience of aquarium life. It must be not only mobile enough to minimize stressful delays, but also large enough for the animals. Its weight tends to be the limiting factor: a cube of water, with each side 60 cm (2 ft) long, weighs over 200 kilograms (440 pounds), and five such cubes weigh more than a ton. The container should be dark inside, and smoothly lined.

If the container is not supervised by a responsible individual during transportation, it must be sealed. Double polythene bags should be half filled with water, and the air replaced—partly or wholly— by pure oxygen. The sealed bags must be put into strong, doubly corrugated boxes of cardboard or solid foam, labelled with contents and warnings. When a container is carried under the collector's own care, for example by boat or trailer, it need not be sealed. In this case, plastic buckets, bins, or foam boxes, of 20 to 50 litres (about 5 to 12 gallons), are suitable. Good water quality must be maintained. Aerators can be fitted, using a battery-driven pump or a compressed-air cylinder with a reducing-valve. If feasible, partial water changes should be made periodically. The water must not move violently during transportation.

Tranquillizing concentrations of anaesthetics, such as quinaldine or "MS–222", or prophylactic medication may be used during the journey. This has enabled many commercial shippers to reduce the incidence of damage and disease amongst arriving specimens.

Techniques and equipment

A suitable collection method or apparatus is one which selects only the specimens required, causes them minimal damage or stress, and is appropriate for the location, personnel, and transportation available. Various choices are described below, covering a wide range of species and situations. Each expedition will involve modifications and improvisations which exercise the collector's skill and ingenuity.

Simple methods

Plants and most invertebrates can be collected easily by hand. Gloves, a small trowel, or a blade if necessary, are the best implements for moving the animal, rooted plant, or small stones with attached algae into a container. Shallow waters of the sea-shore, small pool, swamp, lake, or stream margin can be explored thoroughly by wearing boots that are waterproof or may get wet. Barefoot collecting is unwise. A glass mask is useful, as it will be difficult to see clearly through a disturbed water surface by eye. Glass-bottomed buckets can also be used, even in murky water, to see what is growing on the bottom.

Catching fishes, and some invertebrates, on a hook and line can be convenient for some situations and species. Small or barbless hooks, attached to a short leader, may be employed to catch burrowing fishes such as gobies (family Gobiidae) and jawfishes (Opisthognathidae). Generally, fishes hooked on a line from the surface suffer great stress, struggle violently, are damaged, and require intensive care during quarantine. To increase its chances of survival, a hooked fish should be drawn to the surface very carefully, or preferably transferred to a container on the sea bed and raised slowly by a diver.

Underwater work

Swimming underwater is the best means of access to many collection sites. The aquarist–diver combines two fascinating activities which complement each other. Using scuba, snorkel, or hookah (hose to a surface air-pump) equipment, one can study organisms in their most intricate natural habitats and share some of their sensations. A diver, who must learn how to move and operate underwater, is able to handle fishing gear or direct a submerged catching activity with greater attention than can those on the surface. An experienced diver, in addition to hands, may use hooks, slurp guns, various nets, traps, and anaesthetics, which make collection highly selective.

An excellent tactic for divers is to collect at night-time with nets and torches. Many fishes can be illuminated in a torch beam and netted with relative ease, as they rest in crevices or on the bottom. Many hole-dwelling invertebrates move out to feed in the dark and are retrievable in this manner.

Anaesthetics

As well as being useful during transportation and examination, anaesthetics are often the only solution to the problem of catching elusive animals. This treatment works best in areas which are physically constricted, and when dilution by water movement is slight. Examples include intertidal pools, lake or river margin pools, and isolated coral heads or rocky outcrops. For underwater use by divers, a barrier net should first be placed around the outcrop with minimal disturbance. Slurp guns, polythene bags, hand nets, and rubber gloves are convenient for collecting the animals gently in a container.

Correct dosage of the anaesthetic is important and should barely stun the fish. In the case of isolated pools, the enclosed water should be changed, manually if necessary, once the collection has been made, to prevent overexposure of any uncollected animals to the anaesthetic. As their indirect effects may be considerable, anaesthetics should be used with restraint in all natural waters. Animals which are stunned but not collected will remain vulnerable to incoming predators long after the collector has departed.

Traps

Trapping is the best way of catching various invertebrates—octopus, cuttlefish, crab, and lobster—as well as being useful for fishes. In general, the animal enters a trap and cannot, or does not try to, find its way out again. Animals go into traps for diverse reasons. Many will seek a bait of food, or a shiny object. Others are attracted by the trap's structure itself, some liking dark enclosures, and others an open framework. Certain fishes will enter by accident and, if one of a group goes in, for example a jack or trevally (family Carangidae), the rest may circle the trap until they have all gone in. Species tend to be caught successively if the trap is left too long: scavengers go after the bait, predators are attracted by the distress of trapped scavengers, and larger predators are drawn in by the whole commotion. Traps have even been wrecked by dolphins after the fishes inside.

Numerous sorts and sizes of traps have been developed in different regions by fishermen seeking food animals. Some are permanent fixed structures, but most are transportable. Many of these can be adapted to catch aquarium specimens. Traps may also be purpose-built, using similar principles, but designed to catch small quantities of specimens of particular sizes and kinds. In practice, all delicate animals should be retrieved from the trap with minimum delay, to prevent damage of fins, skin, mouth, or eyes by the trap walls.

Barrier seine nets

Small lengths of net can be set and worked, in both fresh and marine waters, to catch fishes amongst vegetation, rock or coral outcrops, and rock cliffs or ledges, and on sand flats or stony rubble. Clear or blue monofilament netting, of 12–20 mm (0.5–0.8 in) mesh, should be made into suitable lengths, buoyed, and lead-weighted. A good length is 15 m (50 ft) by 2 m high (6 ft) for open areas, or 3 m (10 ft) by 1 m high (3 ft) for confined work.

In shallow water, the net can be handled by three people wading, one at each end and one in the middle to clear the lead line as it is dragged along the bottom. The net should be walked or rowed, in a semicircle towards the shore or another suitable obstacle, and slowly gathered until any encircled fishes are accessible.

In clear, deeper water, the seine can be set by divers, as an almost invisible barrier into which fishes may be lured or driven. The site should be chosen with respect to fish cover, obstacles, and currents. The divers unfold the length of the net by swimming separately above the bottom. Then, they move over the chosen site, lowering the ends and bottom of the net, and secure these into a suitable configuration. The divers move away, perhaps after baiting the area, before driving the fishes into the net. Some of the fishes become entangled, and others can be taken by hand net from a "hooked" end. Undamaged specimens are transferred carefully into appropriate containers.

Unfortunately, netting can damage fishes quite easily. During quarantine, netted fishes should be given prophylactic treatment, and signs of infection must be watched for.

A portable trap for fishes can be made of fine netting on a wire frame, up to 1–2 m (3–6 ft) long, with an entrance shaped like a funnel to lead fishes inside while hindering their escape. At right is shown a trap for small invertebrates. It is of transparent plastic, up to 30 cm (1 ft) on each side, with a funnel-shaped door and sloped floor at each end.

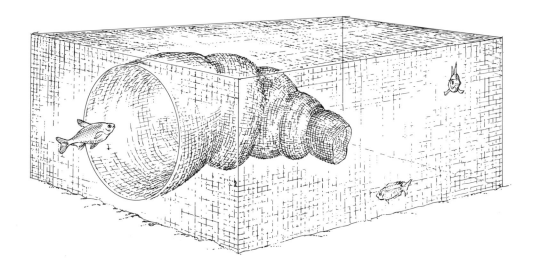

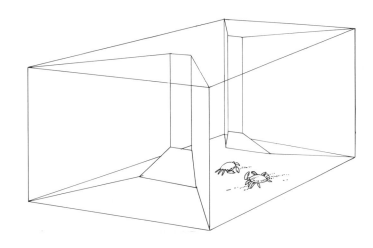

Other nets

Hand nets made from fine-mesh netting or clear polythene can, with dexterity and patience, be used to trap individual fishes or mobile crustaceans. Hand-netting is a good technique for species which dart away from the collector and seek refuge beneath a stone or within a clump of weeds. The net should be almost invisible as it is held very still, in a suitable position to catch the animal fleeing when the cover is penetrated.

A small seine, known as a purse net, can be stretched around a raft of floating plants or debris, by two or three people using a boat or floats. The bottom edge of the net is drawn together, forming a complete enclosure. The plants are lifted out and inspected for specimens, any fishes being transferred into containers.

Drop nets and throw nets are also valuable but require special skill and patience. A circle of fine netting, edged with small lead weights, can be thrown from the bank or a boat, or dropped by two or three divers, to entangle fishes against the bottom.

A dip net or scoop, large and lightweight, can be made by attaching fine netting to a wooden frame. It is designed to be lifted quickly out of the water, either vertically on a rope or else upon a levered pivot. The centre of the scoop, resting on the bottom, is baited to attract the fishes.

Trawls, dredges, push nets, and tow nets are sometimes employed. Various fishing gears have been designed to be pulled or pushed across a reasonably flat bottom or through the water. The speed of travel must be faster than the flight of the animals, and boat power is usually required. Damage to specimens, particularly at the "cod end" of a trawl when bottom debris is caught as well, makes these methods generally unsuitable for the aquarist, except as good sources of live or fresh food, ranging from plankton to prawns. With very short tows, although not many specimens are taken, a few will be in adequate condition to be carefully retrieved and quarantined for the aquarium.

The aquarist's code of conduct

The conservation of wild animals and plants is an important principle which all aquarists, suppliers, and collectors should observe. This may be expressed by the following imperatives. Consider at all times the future survival of the species in the wild, by learning about its biology, habitat, and conservation status both locally and globally. Do not collect any very rare species and do not buy them unless they have been bred and reared on a farm. Collect only single specimens, and return unwanted specimens to their own habitat. Use selective techniques and choose sites carefully, collecting without damage to the habitat or other organisms, and do not release alien species into natural water bodies. Do not collect for identification purposes if a photograph or sketch would suffice, and be particularly sure to collect only the smallest adequate fragments of plants. Do not take specimens from any protected or notably valuable or interesting natural site, least of all without the site owner's permission.

Commercial trade in aquatic life

The current extent of the trade in ornamental aquatic species, and of fishes in particular, is staggering. There may be over one hundred million aquaria in the world, and it is estimated that the retail trade may involve two billion specimens annually, worth over four to five billion dollars. These figures are alarming as well as impressive. Most specimens are captured from wild populations, and there is growing concern about the damage done to the latter and to natural habitats.

One major problem is the number of fishes likely to die during the course of a typical commercial operation of capture, export, and retail. To satisfy a market demanding a certain number of specimens, at least twice that number may have to be taken from the wild. Added to this is the damage to the natural habitat and community as a result of the operation. Some techniques are highly destructive, and many habitats are fragile. Most fishing methods are unselective, yielding specimens of several species together, whose popularity and commercial value vary greatly. The specimens of unwanted species are jettisoned and must largely die.

For example, on coral reefs, commercial collectors often remove entire pieces of living coral into a polythene bag or container, then break and remove the coral to retain the fishes which were sheltering within its structure. Another common practice on coral and rocky reefs is to dose an area of crevices and holes with a poison—such as formalin, chlorine, sodium cyanide, or Rotenone—in order to stun the animals and permit easy capture. The poison damages all forms of life along entire stretches of reef. Even "safe" anaesthetics such as quinaldine and MS–222 affect predation patterns and the natural community organization.

Because of the size of the market they serve, there is great danger to natural regions and wild populations from the hobbyist who follows trends. Aquarists, indeed, are far more numerous than many species of aquatic animals are. If just half of the world's aquarists were to decide

that each must have a piece of *Acropora* coral on display, at least six thousand hectares (over twenty square miles) of reef would need to be destroyed. Certain species enjoy extreme popularity, such as the neon tetra *(Paracheirodon innesi)*. It is so widely acclaimed that up to twenty per cent of all ornamental fishes imported into the United States are of this species, amounting to over one million neon tetras each month from South America. The impact of such exploitation upon wild stocks should not be underestimated.

Conservation

Although little ecological research has been done in the majority of countries from which live aquatic animals and plants are exported, it is clear from the extent and character of trade operations that their collecting of various species and their damage to certain habitats and wild populations are probably excessive.

Some species are very limited in distribution and, therefore, in total numbers. Many species of cichlids are confined to single African Rift Valley lakes, and some even to distinct areas of one lake. An example is *Tropheus moorei,* divided into several sub-species, each highly localized and with quite distinctive behaviour. One of these is now regarded as a separate species, *T. duboisi.* Specimens are greatly prized for the European aquarium market, but all are likely to come from a small area of the rocky littoral of Lake Tanganyika. What intensity of collection can be survived by such a population is unknown. The blind

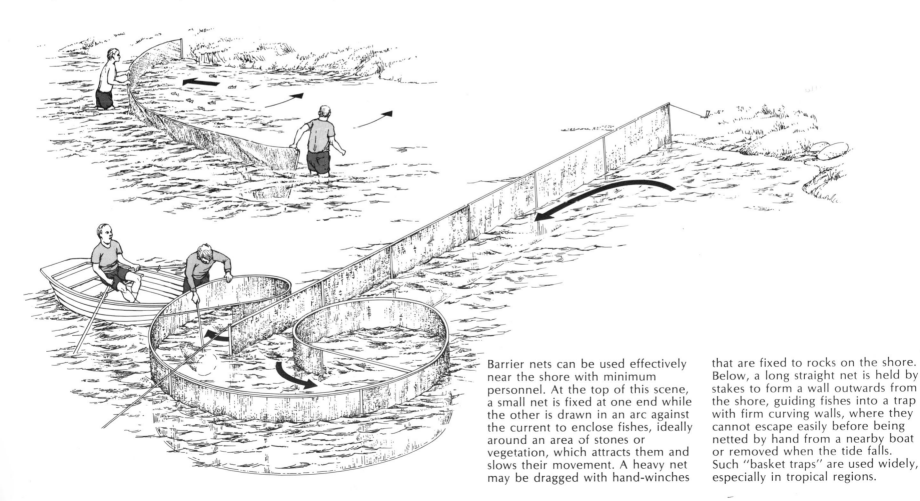

Barrier nets can be used effectively near the shore with minimum personnel. At the top of this scene, a small net is fixed at one end while the other is drawn in an arc against the current to enclose fishes, ideally around an area of stones or vegetation, which attracts them and slows their movement. A heavy net may be dragged with hand-winches that are fixed to rocks on the shore. Below, a long straight net is held by stakes to form a wall outwards from the shore, guiding fishes into a trap with firm curving walls, where they cannot escape easily before being netted by hand from a nearby boat or removed when the tide falls. Such "basket traps" are used widely, especially in tropical regions.

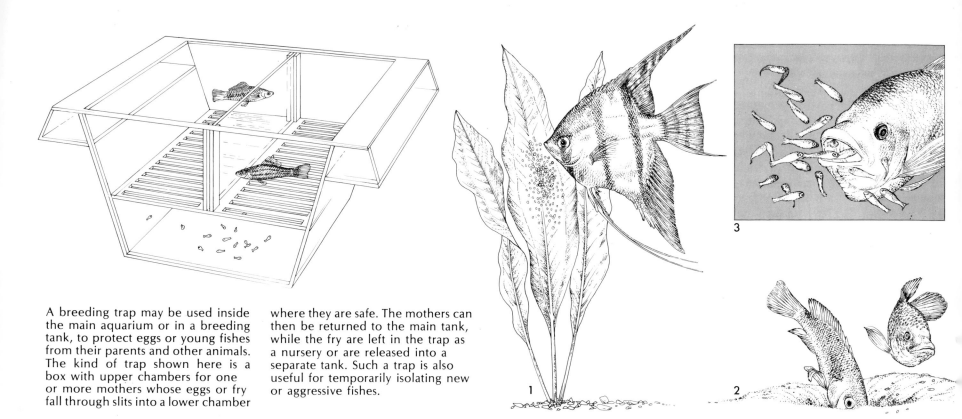

A breeding trap may be used inside the main aquarium or in a breeding tank, to protect eggs or young fishes from their parents and other animals. The kind of trap shown here is a box with upper chambers for one or more mothers whose eggs or fry fall through slits into a lower chamber where they are safe. The mothers can then be returned to the main tank, while the fry are left in the trap as a nursery or are released into a separate tank. Such a trap is also useful for temporarily isolating new or aggressive fishes.

cave fishes (family Amblyopsidae) provide similar instances, and it seems that too many have already been taken from several of their natural sites for the continued survival of species.

There are indications that numerous species of fishes are threatened with extinction as a direct result of demand by aquarists. For example, the status of *Arapaima gigas,* which is the largest fish living wholly in fresh water, has been described officially as "depleted" and "decimated" in large areas of the Amazon basin, especially in the River Negro. Reasons for this decline are given as excessive capture to serve the aquarium trade, by fishing and—when the parents are located and killed—taking the young. Prohibition of any aquarium trade in the young fishes is proposed.

In such cases, the species should be effectively boycotted by aquarists, retailers, importers, and exporters. They have a responsibility to the wild animals, upon which their enjoyment or profit is based, to reject the market so strongly that the incentive to collect disappears.

It is worth adding that the aquarist should not collect or buy specimens which cannot be expected to remain alive healthily for a reasonable length of time. For instance, a natural coral reef is among the most beautiful, productive, and diverse ecosystems on the earth. But most corals are difficult to keep alive in the aquarium. Under good conditions, a few hardy species may live for a year or two. But on average, the life expectancy of a piece of coral placed in a typical marine system is negligible.

Aquaculture

The demand for many popular ornamental fish species has been high enough for them to be raised commercially on farms. Aquaculture is now practised extensively, and particularly in Asia where about half of all exported freshwater fishes have been bred on specialized farms. In Europe and the United States as well, tropical species are reared for the aquarium market. Around a hundred species of freshwater fishes are bred commercially in captivity. But success with marine species is limited to about half a dozen, including the clownfish (species of *Amphiprion*), neon gobies (*Elacatinus oceanops*), the grey angelfish (*Pomacanthus arcuatus*), and the pygmy seahorse (*Hippocampus rosterae*).

Fish breeding

Every species of organism must reproduce in order to survive. Some lower animals can multiply by simply splitting into two or more, or by "budding off" small new individuals. Most higher animals are differentiated into male and female individuals, the males producing sperm to fertilize the females' eggs, which develop into the new generation.

Fishes reproduce sexually in this way. Most species have a coordinated release of eggs and sperm into the water, so that fertilization is external. In many species, the male and female are paired off, and courtship rituals before spawning have often evolved. Copulation takes place, most elaborately in species which have developed internal fertilization. After fertilization, there is great diversity in the extent and type of care shown by the parents for the eggs and young.

Numerous freshwater fish species have been induced successfully to breed in aquaria, and this has enabled their behaviour and requirements to be studied carefully. But only a few marine species have been bred, partly because a planktonic egg or fry phase is essential in many

Some of the ways in which fishes lay their eggs in nature are shown here.
1 An angelfish chooses the leaf of a large plant, cleans it carefully, and deposits adhesive eggs on it, then guards them against predators.
2 Cichlids excavate a shallow nest in the substrate, where the eggs are laid and fertilized, then are taken into the mouth of a parent to be hatched and also protected as fry (3).
4 The splashing tetra deposits eggs on a leaf just above the water surface.

5 Many species release sticky eggs while swimming amongst vegetation near the bottom, and leave them to hatch, as do the barbs shown.
6 Certain fishes prefer to spawn in a dark refuge where the eggs can also be guarded easily, as do these cichlids.
7 Eggs may be laid on the top of a flat stone and guarded, or allowed to fall amongst pebbles and hatch safely.
8 The stickleback builds a nest with algae on the bottom, and other fishes may use plants or debris to do so.

species and cannot be provided for in captivity. The general guideline for breeding fishes in aquaria is to learn as much as possible about how the species breeds in the wild, and to try to create the suitable conditions and events in the aquarium. Seasonal patterns, incentives to spawning, optimum surroundings, and the behaviour of the parents during courtship, mating, spawning, incubation, and nursery periods, are all important kinds of information.

Planning and preparation

The following basic procedure may be adapted to suit the needs of each particular species. A separate tank should be used, rather than expecting eggs and young to survive the activity of a normal community display aquarium. The tank must be large enough, and of suitable shape, to house the specimens to be bred. The physical environment should consist of substrates and cover which are adequate for the adults and juveniles to inhabit, and for the attachment of eggs. Stone surfaces, a sand or clean gravel base layer, or plants with fine or broad leaves or hanging roots may be required for different species.

Illumination may need to be subdued, and many egg-layers will choose shaded spots on which to spawn. The tank should be open only to light through the water surface, so it is essential to maintain the viewing area in darkness or to cover transparent tank walls. Temperature control will be necessary, and the tank should be well insulated from disturbance by knocks and noise. An attached or buried mass of eggs must be supplied with large quantities of oxygen, making efficient aeration and circulation of the water vital. Exceptions include

bubble-nest builders, whose efforts may be thwarted by excessive water movement.

The tank, fittings, and substrates should be cleaned thoroughly and sterilized prior to breeding operations. The water must be specified and prepared carefully. Eggs and sperm are particularly sensitive to water quality, and many freshwater egg-laying species must be provided with water of low hardness. The breeding tank should be filled with clean water of the correct salinity for the species and, once set up, the whole unit may be treated with ultraviolet irradiation for a day or so before the specimens are introduced.

An important consequence of maintaining fishes in the aquarium is that they are confined in a small space which does not connect with other volumes of water. In the wild, at some stage, offspring are naturally dispersed from the spawning site. This may occur as eggs drift up to the surface and away, or as young fry swim away. But in the aquarium, neither the parents nor juveniles are able to move away from the spawning site or from each other. This artificial situation can lead to abnormal behaviour, including aggressiveness between parents and the eating of young by parents. Thus, it may be necessary for the aquarist to separate the parents and offspring, in some cases by removing the newly hatched fry to a nursery tank, or by using a mesh screen through which only the fry may swim or the eggs may fall.

Simple enclosures can be made to retain the parents. Alternatively, small rounded stones or marbles may be placed on the clean bottom of the tank. The eggs will fall in between them, away from a potentially cannibalistic parent. Another method is to prepare an attractive spawning area like a basin or shelf, in very shallow water. The

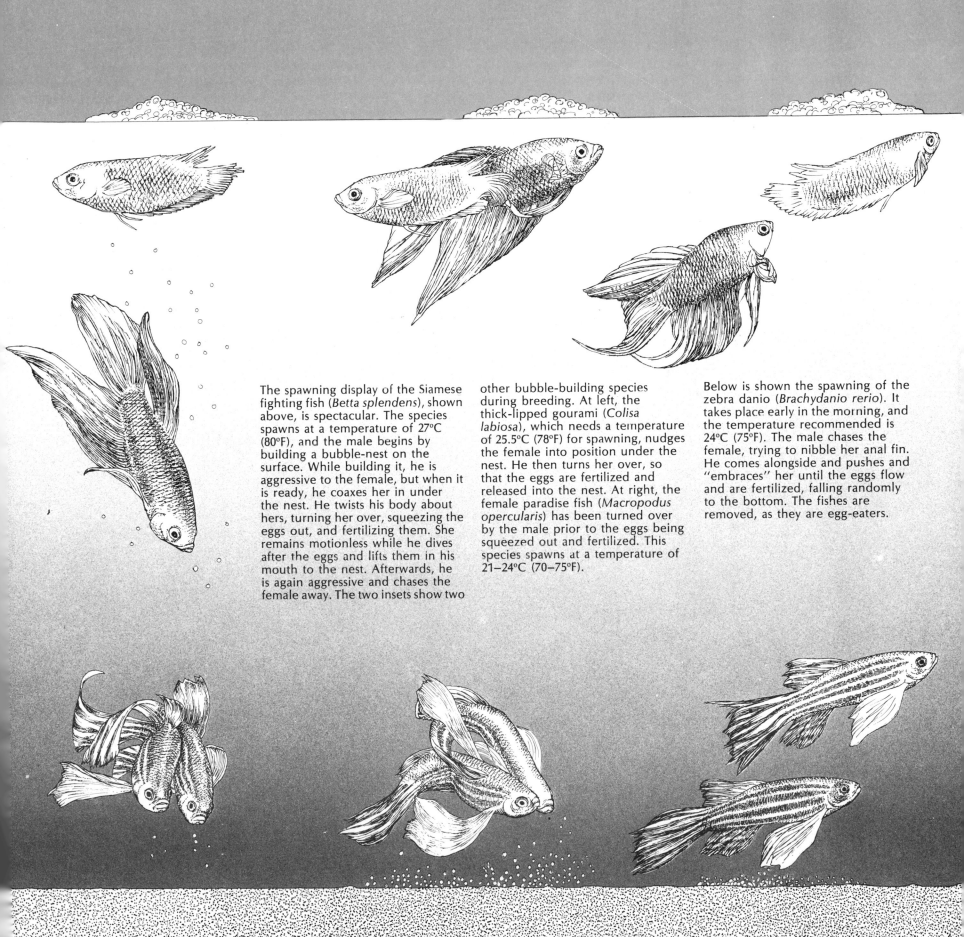

The spawning display of the Siamese fighting fish (*Betta splendens*), shown above, is spectacular. The species spawns at a temperature of 27°C (80°F), and the male begins by building a bubble-nest on the surface. While building it, he is aggressive to the female, but when it is ready, he coaxes her in under the nest. He twists his body about hers, turning her over, squeezing the eggs out, and fertilizing them. She remains motionless while he dives after the eggs and lifts them in his mouth to the nest. Afterwards, he is again aggressive and chases the female away. The two insets show two

other bubble-building species during breeding. At left, the thick-lipped gourami (*Colisa labiosa*), which needs a temperature of 25.5°C (78°F) for spawning, nudges the female into position under the nest. He then turns her over, so that the eggs are fertilized and released into the nest. At right, the female paradise fish (*Macropodus opercularis*) has been turned over by the male prior to the eggs being squeezed out and fertilized. This species spawns at a temperature of 21–24°C (70–75°F).

Below is shown the spawning of the zebra danio (*Brachydanio rerio*). It takes place early in the morning, and the temperature recommended is 24°C (75°F). The male chases the female, trying to nibble her anal fin. He comes alongside and pushes and "embraces" her until the eggs flow and are fertilized, falling randomly to the bottom. The fishes are removed, as they are egg-eaters.

mating pair will move onto the basin to spawn, but will not usually return to eat the eggs after leaving this area to swim in the deeper parts of the tank.

In the aquarium, the procedure varies between egg-layers, mouth-incubators, and live-bearers. With the first two types, the pair or group which are to be bred should be identified, and males separated from females. For a week or more, they should be fed on a selection of richer foods before being brought together again in the breeding tank and allowed to commence courtship and mating. If mouth-incubators spawn within the general community tank, it is preferable that the brooding parent with spawn is not disturbed by transference to a nursery tank, as the spawn may be rejected. A fine mesh partition across a corner of the tank might be used instead, to keep other animals, including the non-brooding parent, away from the family group. But with live-bearers there is no need to remove the fish from the community tank until the female's abdomen shows the first signs of pregnancy. Then, she should be transferred immediately and carefully to the breeding tank, and before giving birth, she is placed in a "breeding trap" to enable the young to escape being eaten.

When preparing for a breeding session, it is important to organize feeding for the anticipated brood. At some stage, when the young fry become independent of the parent or the yolk supply, suitable foods must be supplied, as has been indicated earlier in this chapter. Although fry should be given as much food as they can eat, several times per day, excess food is dangerous as it provides a substrate for surplus bacteria and—in the case of live foods such as *Cyclops nauplii*—the food may even grow to become a predator of the fry!

Season and sex
Fishes spawn and eggs hatch at definite times. The water temperature is the major stimulus. In temperate waters, most species spawn during the spring and summer as warmth increases. In tropical waters, the annual temperature range is far more restricted, and most species breed over a large part of the year. Light also has a great influence and, even in species which can reproduce all year round, there is increased sexual activity in the spring as light levels grow. In special situations, more uncertain factors may be essential incentives: many fishes respond to changing water quality as annual floods arrive, whilst others spawn as their seasonal pool dries up. Many inhabitants of the intertidal zone may be responsive to lunar and tidal cycles.

In numerous species of fishes, there are obvious external differences between males and females, which tend to become most apparent during the time of breeding. Most sexual characteristics are related to courtship and mating, whereas others relate to brood care. In species with internal fertilization, copulatory organs are developed. All elasmobranch males have a pair of grooved claspers. Male live-bearers (such as the family Poeciliidae) have external genitalia. Many female fishes possess long ovipositor organs for extruding the eggs and attaching them to the substrate.

Less essential differences between males and females include colouring, elongate fin rays, and "pearl organs" on the male body, which probably hold the fishes together during mating. There is often a distinction in size: larger females tend to be associated with the production of large broods, whilst males are the larger sex in species whose males guard the brood. Extreme examples are the species

which produce dwarf males. These, in the deep-sea anglerfishes (Ceratoidea), become permanently fused to the female and parasitic upon her. In some species of *Apogon*, the male has a larger mouth and pharynx, in which to incubate the eggs.

Types of reproduction
Most marine fishes produce floating eggs. Fertilization occurs outside the female body, and large numbers of tiny eggs are released to drift with the surface plankton. When the larvae hatch, each has an attached yolk sac. In the majority of species, the larvae are only a few millimetres (or hundredths of an inch) long when hatched, and in the first few months of life, they are quite vulnerable to predation and disease, so that mortality rates are high. In the mackerel, *Scomber scombrus,* it is estimated that the population of adults is maintained if only one egg out of every million survives to maturity. But the greatest variety of reproductive methods is seen primarily amongst freshwater species, as shown below.

Egg-layers with no care
Most freshwater fishes, including the majority of characins and cyprinids, and many species in coastal seas as well, belong to a group which produces adhesive or non-buoyant eggs, released on the bottom but not cared for by the parents. Cyprinids tend to release eggs with adhesive threads, which lie amongst bottom vegetation. The perch (*Perca fluviatilis*) of Europe and northern Asia yields strings of eggs which stick onto plants, submerged wood, and stones. The hatched larvae have small yolk sacs and swim up to gulp air at the surface; then they disperse.

Sand eels (family Ammodytidae) scatter eggs over an area of the coastal sea-bed, where the eggs attach to grains of sand. Flatfishes such as the flounder (species of *Pleuronectes*) migrate into shallow waters and lay large numbers—a million or more—of eggs which sink and stick to the bottom in clusters. The young larvae also remain near the bottom, so that fewer are swept away from the nursery grounds by currents. Suckerfishes such as *Lepadogaster lepadogaster* attach rows of fairly large yolk-filled eggs to the undersides of stones and amongst kelp holdfasts along the shore bottom.

Although most cartilaginous fishes are live-bearers, the hundred or more species of the skate in the genus *Raja* are oviparous, as are some sharks, including dogfishes. Very large, yolky eggs are laid—those of the whale shark *Rhincodon* are about 30 cm (1 ft) long—within a horny covering which is secreted as the egg passes down the oviduct. This egg case is usually rectangular, with a projection at each corner which coils round or adheres to a piece of seaweed or stone on the sea bed. Incubation takes from four to fifteen months usually, depending upon the species and water temperature. The case splits, letting water in, and eventually the young fish swims out. The empty case may become one of the familiar "mermaid's purses" cast up onto the shore.

Egg-buriers
Some fishes bury their eggs in the bottom sediment. In swift-flowing fresh waters, this group includes the grayling (species of *Thymallus*), barbel (*Barbus*), and some of the North American darters (*Etheostoma*), as well as trout and salmon (*Salmo*). In seasonal pools and streams in the tropics, the small top-minnows, species of

Aphyosemion and *Cynolebias* (family Cyprinodontidae), and others bury eggs in the mud before the water dries up. The eggs are able to survive the drought in the damp mud, and they hatch when rain or flood fills the pool once more.

Amongst inshore marine species, the grunion (*Leuresthes tenuis*) has well-known and remarkable breeding habits. Spawning occurs on the shore at night during the high water of spring tides. The female, with the male curled round, burrows into the sand at the very top of the beach and lays the eggs, which are fertilized. The eggs hatch within a week, but the young fishes remain under the sand until the next spring tides, about a fortnight after spawning, wash them out to sea.

Egg-layers with care

In many species, particularly in fresh water, the eggs are placed carefully on the substrate, then guarded and looked after by a parent, usually the male. Besides defending the mass of eggs against being eaten, the guardian may fan water over the eggs with his fins, which tends to aerate them and remove silt, and he may also take away unhealthy eggs. This type of spawning and brood care is common amongst shallow marine fishes, such as blennies (family Blenniidae), gobies (Gobiidae), damselfishes (Pomacentridae), and triggerfishes (Balistidae).

Many species of gobies, in both freshwater and coastal habitats, attach their eggs inside the empty shells of bivalves or on the undersides of flat stones, often excavating and carefully preparing a burrow. Other species attach eggs to plant leaves or seaweed fronds, whilst species which normally live in burrows—often together with shrimps—fasten their eggs to the walls of the tunnel. In most cases, the male guards the spawn until the young fry hatch. The bullhead (*Cottus gobio*), an inhabitant of cool clear freshwater streams, is a typical example of this group. The male digs a shallow nest amongst stones into which the fishes spawn. Then the male guards the site and periodically fans the spawn until the young bullheads hatch.

Cichlids and many characoids demonstrate very interesting and elaborate reproductive behaviour of this type. In species of *Aequidens, Etroplus, Cichla, Hemichromis,* and *Cichlasoma,* the parents lay and fertilize the eggs carefully and neatly on a stone or rock surface, then guard and fan them continually until they hatch. The egg site is chosen and cleaned attentively before spawning and, at the same time, one or several shallow holes are excavated in gravel or sand nearby, by fanning and mouth-carrying. Upon hatching, the young are transferred by mouth from the attachment site to the prepared hole where they are guarded. Occasionally, they may be moved from one hole to another. Soon, they can swim, and the parents round up any which stray away, or may lead the school about in search of food, until the brood scatters and the parents lose interest.

Species of *Pterophyllum,* and *Symphysodon discus,* deposit eggs on carefully chosen plant leaves or stems, or on steep stone surfaces, then tend and fan them until hatching occurs. The young are moved from plant to stone by mouth, being blown to the new surface and sticking on it. This continues until the young fry can swim, and then they follow the parent, keeping close to the head and eyes so that the parents may notice stragglers and keep the brood together. The young feed, until several weeks old, on a nutritious mucus which is produced by the parents' skin.

Peculiar spawning behaviour is shown by the splashing tetra, a South American characin (*Copeina arnoldi*). The spawn is attached to and fertilized on a firm stone or leaf surface above the water surface, by the male and female leaping side by side and sticking for several seconds to the spot pre-selected by the male. Up to a dozen eggs are laid at a time, and the leap may be made half a dozen times. The male then keeps the mass of eggs moist by splashing water over them with his tail and body every twenty minutes or so, throughout the incubation period of several days. Upon hatching, the fry wriggle down into the water. Another fish with special spawning habits is the leaffish, *Monocirrhus polyacanthus,* which attaches its eggs by adhesive threads to the underside of a leaf, where the male guards them.

Mouth-incubators

Certain freshwater fishes, including nearly all species of *Haplochromis, Tilapia, Pseudotropheus,* and other cichlids, and a few anabantids such as *Betta brederi,* as well as marine fishes including the cardinals (family Apogonidae) and some catfishes (Ariidae), use their mouth and pharynx as an incubation chamber. This habit is less developed in other species, such as those of *Geophagus* and *Pelmatochromis,* which only take their young fry into their mouths when danger threatens.

In mouth-brooding species, the eggs are collected into the mouth of the female (for example in cichlids) or the male (as in *Betta, Apogon,* and Ariidae) parent. They are fertilized either in the short period between being released and being taken into the mouth, or else within the mouth, when sperm as well as eggs are sucked in. Throughout the incubation period, the brooding parent rests quietly, moving the eggs around the mouth. As the larvae hatch, they move out of the mouth and swarm over the head of the parent. The school of fry follows the parent around and will flee back into its mouth if alarmed, until they can swim away independently.

In the Apogonidae, the eggs are shed in a single clump attached to each other by thin tendrils and are immediately taken into the mouth of the male. There they are held, with water being passed over them, until hatching. Some twenty thousand eggs, of diameter 0.5 mm (0.02 in), may be incubated at a time.

Nest-builders

Besides the pits or burrows made by many cichlids, for example as nurseries, many freshwater fishes construct some form of nest for their spawn. Male sticklebacks (family Gasterosteidae) illustrate the making of nests from plant or algae fragments, glued together with a secretion from the kidney. In spring, this fish starts to claim and defend an area of the shallow bottom, within which he builds a nest, often by first removing mouthfuls of sand or gravel and then sticking together pieces of algae and other plant material. The male develops bright colouration throughout this phase, and now tries to lure females into the nest. The female pushes into the nest tunnel, lays her eggs, and leaves, whereupon the male enters and fertilizes the eggs. He may entice two or three females to spawn in the nest, which he will then guard and fan with pectoral fins for a week or so. As they hatch, the father keeps the young fry together in the nest by herding and picking up wanderers in his mouth and blowing them back, until they are strong enough to swim away.

The North American freshwater basses and sunfishes (family Centrarchidae) excavate a nesting hollow amongst stones. Several species of cyprinid minnows, of genera *Hybopsis, Semotilus,* and others, construct nests of stones, which consist of a mound of carefully chosen and carried stones piled up over an excavated pit.

Various species in still fresh waters, where the bottom is often of fine mud and the water is low in dissolved oxygen, form a mass of tiny bubbles in which to suspend the spawn mass. In this group are the Siamese fighting fish *(Betta splendens),* gouramis (species of *Colisa* and *Trichopis*) and other anabantids, and some armoured catfishes (species of *Callichthys*). The bubble nest is made by the male, gulping air at the surface and forcing out a stream of bubbles, each coated with a sticky mucus from the mouth, through the gill opening. The nest may be 7 or 8 cm (3 in) in diameter and is anchored amongst plants near the water surface, or floated freely under the surface. When the nest is complete, a female is sought and the pair spawn beneath it. The fertilized eggs are caught by the male and blown into the bubble mass. The male guards the nest, blows back any fallen eggs or fry, and makes repairs with more bubbles, until the brood is able to swim away.

Egg-carriers

Diverse species have evolved other means of protecting their eggs and young fry. In catfishes of the family Bunocephalidae, the mother lies upon the fertilized eggs and her folds of skin grow around to envelop them. In pipefishes, the males carry the eggs around, either stuck to the underside of the tail or, in species of *Syngnathus,* within a special brood fold. The young are released when fully formed, and the brood fold shrinks back to normal size.

Male seahorses, also in the family Syngnathidae, have a special pouch under the tail into which the eggs are released by the female and incubated, and from which fully formed juveniles emerge. The pouch lining secretes a nutrient "milk" and has many blood vessels conveying oxygen to the developing eggs.

Live-bearers

Fishes which bear live young rather than laying eggs may be divided into ovoviviparous and viviparous species. In the former, eggs are internally fertilized and released into the ovary cavity, where the embryo completes its development, nourished by a yolk sac or, in some species, by secretions from the ovary lining. The guppy, *Poecilia reticulata,* is a well-known example. In various scorpionfishes (species of *Sebastes*), the eggs are retained within the ovary until about the time of hatching, when they are laid.

In the more advanced viviparous species, the eggs are kept within the follicles of the ovary, which are supplied with a mass of blood capillaries. A very close placental connection between the embryo and follicle is maintained by the interlocking of small finger-like or bulbous outgrowths. The young are born in a developed state, usually as miniature versions of the parent.

Amongst the teleosts, there are not many live-bearers. Most belong to the Poeciliidae family: guppies, swordtails, platies, and mollies. But other examples are shown by freshwater halfbeaks (family Hemirhamphidae), four-eyed fishes (Anablepsidae), Mexican topminnows (Goodeidae), and Jenynsiidae, besides the scorpionfishes (Scorpaenidae).

Within the cartilaginous fish groups, most sharks and all rays—apart from the skates—are ovoviviparous. The embryos are released from the egg capsule within the oviduct, where they are nourished by their attached yolk sacs and by milk-like secretions from the mother. Some blue sharks, hammerheads, and smooth dogfishes (of the families Carcharhinidae and Sphyrnidae) are viviparous. The yolk sac forms a sort of placenta with the lining of the uterus. The young sharks and rays are born fully formed.

Bibliography

Angel, H. and Angel, M. *Ocean Life*. London, 1975.

Axelrod, Glen S. *Rift Lake Cichlids*. Neptune, N. J., 1979.

Axelrod, Herbert R. *Breeding Aquarium Fishes 1-6*. Jersey City, N. J., 1976.

Barret, J. *Life on the Sea Shore*. London, 1974.

Bryant, P. et al. *Backyard Fish Farming*. London, 1980.

Cihar, J. *A Colour Guide to Freshwater Fishes*. London, 1975.

Dal Vesco, Vanna, et al. *Aquarium Life*. London and Secaucus, N. J., 1975.

Dutta, R. *Tropical Fish*. London, 1975.

George, D. and George, J. *Marine Life*. London, 1979.

Goldstein, Robert. *Diseases of Aquarium Fishes*. Jersey City, N. J., 1971.

Gos, Michael W. *Brackish Aquariums*. Neptune, N. J., 1979.

Green, J. *The Biology of Estuarine Animals*. London, 1968.

Greenwood, et al. "Phyletic Studies of Teleostean Fishes with a Provisional Classification of Living Forms." *Bulletin of the American Museum of Natural History*, Vol. 131: Art. 4. New York, 1966.

Haslam, S. et al. *British Water Plants*. London, 1979.

Hoedeman, J. J. *Naturalists' Guide to Freshwater Aquarium Fish*. New York, 1974.

Hynes, H. B. N. *The Ecology of Running Water*. London, 1978.

Lowe-McConnell, R. H. *Fish Communities in Tropical Waters*. London, 1975.

Lythgoe, J. and Lythgoe, G. *Fishes of the Sea*. London, 1971.

Maitland, P. S. *Biology of Fresh Water*. London, 1978.

Marshall, N. B. *The Life of Fishes*. London, 1965.

Muus, B. J. and Dahlström, P. *The Sea Fishes of Britain and North-Western Europe*. London, 1974.

Nelson, Joseph S. *Fishes of the World*. New York, 1976.

Nikolsky. *The Ecology of Fishes*. Neptune, N. J., 1978.

Ray, Carleton and Ciampi, Elgin. *The Underwater Guide to Marine Life*. New York, 1956; London, 1958.

Reid, G. K. and Wood, R. D. *Ecology of Inland Waters*. New York, 1976.

Spotte, S. *Seawater Aquaria - the Captive Environment*. New York, 1979.

Stodola, Jiri. *Encyclopedia of Water Plants*. Neptune, N. J., 1967.

Van Duijn. *Diseases of Fishes*. London, 1973.

Whitton. *River Ecology*. Oxford, 1975.

Index